This illustration is reproduced in full color on the insert attached to the inside back cover of this volume

AMEN-RĀ, THE KING OF THE GODS, THE LORD OF HEAVEN.

THE GODS OF THE EGYPTIANS

OR STUDIES IN EGYPTIAN MYTHOLOGY

BY

E. A. WALLIS BUDGE

Late Keeper of the Egyptian and Assyrian
Antiquities in the British Museum

IN TWO VOLUMES

Volume II

DOVER PUBLICATIONS, INC.

NEW YORK

This Dover edition, first published in 1969, is an unabridged republication of the work originally published by The Open Court Publishing Company, Chicago, and Methuen & Company, London, in 1904.

In addition to the 131 text illustrations from the standard edition, this reprint includes black-and-white halftone reproductions of the 98 color plates from the limited edition. Six of these plates are also reproduced in full color on an insert attached to the inside back cover of Volume II of this edition.

Library of Congress Catalog Card Number: 72-91925

International Standard Book Number

ISBN-13: 978-0-486-22056-7
ISBN-10: 0-486-22056-7

Manufactured in the United States by LSC Communications
22056729 2020
www.doverpublications.com

CONTENTS

LIST OF PLATES

[The illustrations marked by an asterisk are reproduced in full color on the insert attached to the inside back cover of this volume.]

LIST OF ILLUSTRATIONS

THE GODS OF THE EGYPTIANS

CHAPTER I

ÀMEN AND ÀMEN-RĀ, 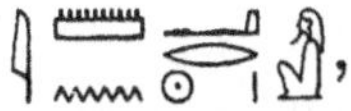, KING OF THE GODS, AND THE TRIAD OF THEBES

AMONG the gods who were known to the Egyptians in very early times were ÀMEN and his consort ÀMENT, 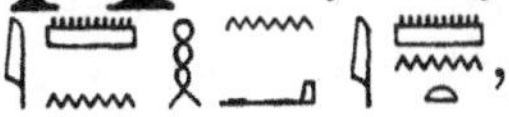, and their names are found in the Pyramid Texts, e.g., Unȧs, line 558, where they are mentioned immediately after the pair of gods NÀU and NEN, 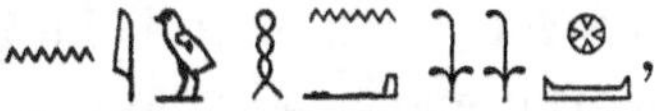, and in connexion with the twin Lion-gods Shu and Tefnut, who are described as the two gods who made their own bodies,[1] and with the goddess TEMT, the female counterpart of Tem. It is evident that even in the remote period of the Vth Dynasty Àmen and Àment were numbered among the primeval gods, if not as gods in chief certainly as subsidiary forms of some of them, and from the fact that they are mentioned immediately after the deities of primeval matter, Nȧu and Nen, who we may consider to be the equivalents of the watery abyss from which all things sprang, and immediately before Temt and Shu and Tefnut, it would seem that the writers or editors of the Pyramid Texts

1 

assigned great antiquity to their existence. Of the attributes ascribed to Åmen in the Ancient Empire nothing is known, but, if we accept the meaning "hidden" which is usually given to his name, we must conclude that he was the personification of the hidden and unknown creative power which was associated with the primeval abyss gods in the creation of the world and all that is in it. The word or root *åmen*, certainly means "what is hidden," "what is not seen," "what cannot be seen," and the like, and this fact is proved by scores of examples which may be collected from texts of all periods. In hymns to Åmen we often read that he is "hidden to his children," and "hidden to gods and men," and it has been stated that these expressions only refer to the "hiding," i.e., "setting" of the sun each evening, and that they are only to be understood in a physical sense, and to mean nothing more than the disappearance of the god Åmen from the sight of men at the close of day. Now, not only is the god himself said to be "hidden," but his name also is "hidden," and his form, or similitude, is said to be "unknown;" these statements show that "hidden" when applied to Åmen, the great god, has reference to something more than the "sun which has disappeared below the horizon," and that it indicates the god who cannot be seen with mortal eyes, and who is invisible, as well as inscrutable, to gods as well as men. In the times approaching the Ptolemaïc period the name Åmen appears to have been connected with the root *men*, "to abide, to be permanent;" and one of the attributes which were applied to him was that of *eternal*.

Åmen is represented in five forms:—1. As a man, when he is seen seated on a throne, and holding in one hand the sceptre, , and in the other the symbol of "life;" in this form he is one of the nine deities who compose the company of the gods of Åmen-Rā, the other eight being Åment, Nu, Nut, Ḥeḥui, Ḥeḥet, Kekui, Keket, and Hathor.[1] 2. As a man with the head of a frog, whilst his female counterpart Åment has the head of a uraeus. 3. As a man with the head of a uraeus, whilst his female counterpart has the head of a cat. 4. As an ape. 5. As a lion couchant upon a pedestal.

[1] See Lanzone, op. cit., pl. 12.

THE GODDESS APIT.

Of the early history of the worship of Åmen we know nothing, but as far as the evidence before us goes it appears not to have been very general, and in fact, the only centre of it of any importance was the city of Thebes. Under the XIIth Dynasty we find that a sanctuary and shrine were built in honour of Åmen at Thebes in the northern quarter of the city which was called ÅPT, , later, ; from this word, with the addition of the feminine article T, the Copts derived their name for the city Tape, **Ⲧⲁⲡⲉ**, and from it also comes the common name "Thebes." Over Åpt the quarter of the city there presided a goddess also called Åpt, , who was either the personification of it, or a mere local goddess to whom accident or design had given the same name as the quarter; it is, however, most probable that the goddess was the spirit or personification of the place. In the reliefs on which she is represented we see her in the form of a woman holding the sceptre, , and "life," , in her hands, and wearing upon her head the disk and horns, , which rest upon , the hieroglyphic which has for its phonetic value *Åpt*, and stands for the name of the goddess. The disk and the horns prove that the tutelary goddess of Thebes was a form of Hathor.

Up to the time of the XIIth Dynasty Åmen was a god of no more than local importance, but as soon as the princes of Thebes had conquered their rival claimants to the sovereignty of Egypt, and had succeeded in making their city a new capital of the country their god Åmen became a prominent god in Upper Egypt, and it was probably under that dynasty that the attempt was made to assign to him the proud position which was afterwards claimed for him of "king of the gods." His sanctuary at Karnak was at that time a comparatively small building, which consisted of a shrine, with a few small chambers grouped about it and a forecourt with a colonnade on two sides of it, and it remained, practically, in this form until the rise to power of the kings of the XVIIIth Dynasty. It is difficult to decide if the sanctuary of Åmen at Thebes was a new foundation in that city by the kings of the XIIth Dynasty, or whether the site had been previously occupied by a temple to the god; the probability is that the god possessed a temple in Åpt from the earliest times, and that all that they did was to rebuild Åmen's sanctuary. As soon as the Theban princes became kings of Egypt their priests at once began to declare that their god was not only another form of the great creative Sun-god who had been worshipped for centuries at Ånnu, or Heliopolis, in the North of Egypt, under the names of Rā, Temu, Kheperȧ, and Ḥeru-khuti, but that all the attributes which were ascribed to them were contained in him, and that he was greater than they. And as Thebes had become the capital instead

Horus and Ḥekau presenting Åmen-ḥetep III., when a babe, and his double, to Åmen-Rā, lord of the thrones of Egypt, king of the gods.

of Memphis, it followed as a matter of course that all the attributes of all the great gods of Memphis were contained in Åmen also. Thus by these means the priests of Åmen succeeded in making their god, both theologically and politically, the greatest of the gods in the country.

Owing to the unsettled state of Egypt under the XIIIth and XIVth Dynasties, and under the rule of the Hyksos, pretensions of this kind passed unchallenged, especially as they were supported by arms, and by the end of the XVIIth Dynasty Åmen had attained to an almost unrivalled position among the gods of the land. And when his royal devotees in this dynasty succeeded in expelling the Hyksos from the land, and their successors the kings of the XVIIIth Dynasty carried war and conquest into Palestine and founded Egyptian cities there, the power and glory of Åmen their god, who had enabled them to carry out this difficult work of successful invasion, became extraordinarily great. His priests began by asserting his equality with the other great gods of the old sanctuaries of Heliopolis, Memphis, Herakleopolis, and other ancient cities, and finally they satisfied, or, at all events, attempted to do so, all worshippers of every form of the Sun-god Rā by adding his name to that of Åmen, and thus forming a great god who included within himself all the attributes of the primeval god Åmen and of Rā. The highest conception of Åmen-Rā under the XIXth and XXth Dynasties was that of an invisible creative power which was the source of all life in heaven, and on the earth, and in the great deep, and in the Underworld, and which made itself manifest under the form of Rā. Nearly every attribute of deity with which we are made familiar by the hymns to Rā was ascribed to Åmen after his union with Rā; but the priests of Åmen were not content with claiming that their god was one of the greatest of the deities of Egypt, for they proceeded to declare that there was no other god like him, and that he was the greatest of them all.

The power and might ascribed to Åmen-Rā are well described in hymns which must be quoted in full. The first of these occurs in the Papyrus of Hu-nefer (Brit. Mus., No. 9,901, sheet i.), where it follows immediately after a hymn to Rā; this papyrus was written in the reign of Seti I., and it is interesting to observe that the two gods are addressed separately, and that the hymn to Rā precedes that to Åmen-Rā. The text reads:—"Homage to thee, "O Åmen-Rā, who dost rest upon Maāt; as thou passest over the "heavens every face seeth thee. Thou dost wax great as thy "majesty doth advance, and thy rays [shine] upon all faces. "Thou art unknown, and no tongue hath power to declare thy "similitude; only thou thyself [canst do this]. Thou art One, "even as is he that bringeth the *ṭenā* basket. Men praise thee in "thy name, and they swear by thee, for thou art lord over them. "Thou hearest with thine ears and thou seest with thine eyes.

" Millions of years have gone over the world, and I cannot tell the ' number of those through which thou hast passed. Thy heart " hath decreed a day of happiness in thy name of 'Traveller.' " Thou dost pass over and dost travel through untold spaces " [requiring] millions and hundreds of thousands of years [to pass " over]; thou passest through them in peace, and thou steerest " thy way across the watery abyss to the place which thou lovest; " this thou doest in one little moment of time, and then thou dost " sink down and dost make an end of the hours." How far the attributes ascribed to Åmen-Rā in this hymn represent those generally bestowed upon the god in the XIXth Dynasty is unknown, but the points chiefly dwelt upon are the unity, and the invisibility, and the long duration of the existence of the god; nothing is said about Åmen-Rā being self-begotten and self-born, or of his great creative powers, or of his defeat of the serpent-fiend Nåk, and it is quite clear that Hu-nefer drew a sharp distinction between the attributes of the two gods.

The following hymn,[1] which was probably written under the XXth or XXIst Dynasty, well illustrates the growth of the power both of Åmen-Rā and of his priests:—" Praise be to Åmen-Rā, the " Bull in Ånnu, the chief of all the gods, the beautiful god, the " beloved one, the giver of the life of all warmth to all beautiful " cattle.[2] Homage to thee, O Åmen-Rā, lord of the thrones of the " two lands, the governor of the Åpts (i.e., Thebes, north and south), " thou Bull of thy mother, who art chief in thy fields, whose steps are " long, who art lord of the land of the South, who art lord of the " Mātchau peoples, and prince of Punt, and king of heaven, and first-" born god of earth, and lord of things which exist, and stablisher of " creation, yea, stablisher of all creation. Thou art One among the " gods by reason of his seasons. Thou art the beautiful Bull of the " company of the gods, thou art the chief of all the gods, thou art " the lord of Maāt, and the father of the gods, and the creator of

[1] For the hieratic text see Mariette, *Les Papyrus Égyptiens du Musée de Boulaq*, pll. 11-13; and a French version of the hymn is given by Grébaut, *Hymne à Ammon-Ra*, Paris, 1875.

[2] The word used here for cattle is *menmen*, and a play is intended upon it and the name *Åmen*, who in his character of " bull of Ånnu " was the patron of cattle.

"men and women, and the maker of animals, and the lord of "things which exist, and the producer of the staff of life (i.e., "wheat and barley), and the maker of the herb of the field which "giveth life unto cattle. Thou art the beautiful Sekhem who wast "made (i.e., begotten) by Ptaḥ, and the beautiful Child who art "beloved. The gods acclaim thee, O thou who art the maker of "things which are below and of things which are above. Thou "illuminest the two lands, and thou sailest over the sky in peace, "O king of the South and North, Rā, whose word hath unfailing "effect, who art over the two lands, thou mighty one of two-fold "strength, thou lord of terror, thou Being above who makest the

Åmen-Rā, with his attributes.

"earth according to thine own designs. Thy devices are greater "and more numerous than those of any other god. The gods "rejoice in thy beauties, and they ascribe praise unto thee in the "great double house, and at thy risings in (or, from) the double house "of flame. The gods love the smell of thee when thou comest from "Punt (i.e., the spice land), thou eldest born of the dew, who "comest from the land of the Mātchau peoples, thou Beautiful "Face, who comest from the Divine Land (Neter-ta). The gods "tremble at thy feet when they recognize thy majesty as their "lord, thou lord who art feared, thou Being of whom awe is great, "thou Being whose souls are mighty, who hast possession of

" crowns, who dost make offerings to be abundant, and who dost " make divine food (*tchefau*).

" Adorations be to thee, O thou creator of the gods, who hast " stretched out the heavens and made solid the earth. Thou art " the untiring watcher, O Åmsu-Åmen (or Min-Åmen), the lord of " eternity, and maker of everlastingness, and to thee adorations " are paid as the Governor of the Åpts. Thou hast two horns " which endure, and thine aspects are beautiful, and thou art the " lord of the *ureret* crown (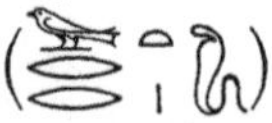), and thy double plumes are " lofty, thy tiara is one of beauty, and thy White Crown () " is lofty. The goddess Meḥen (), and the Uatcheti " goddesses (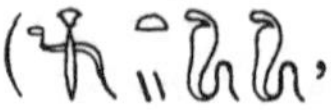, i.e., Nekhebet and Uatchet), are about " thy face, and the crowns of the South and North (), and the " Nemmes crown, and the helmet crown are thy adornments (?) in " thy temple. Thy face is beautiful and thou receivest the Atef " crown (), and thou art beloved of the South and the North; " thou receivest the crowns of the South and the North, and thou " receivest the *amesu* sceptre (), and thou art the lord of the " *makes* sceptre (), and of the whip (or flail, ).[1] Thou art " the beautiful Prince, who risest like the sun with the White " Crown, and thou art the lord of radiant light and the creator of " brilliant rays. The gods ascribe praises unto thee, and he who " loveth thee stretcheth out his two hands to thee. Thy flame maketh " thine enemies to fall, and thine Eye overthroweth the *Sebàu* fiends, " and it driveth its spear through the sky into the serpent-fiend " Nåk and maketh it to vomit that which it hath swallowed.

" Homage to thee, O Rā, thou lord of Maāt, whose shrine is " hidden, thou lord of the gods; thou art Kheperå in thy boat, " and when thou didst speak the word the gods sprang into being.

[1] In the text of Unås (l. 206 f.) we have, " O Unås, thou hast not departed " as one dead, but as one living thou hast gone to sit upon the throne of Osiris. " Thy sceptre *āb* () is in thy hand, and thou givest commands to the living, thy " sceptre *mekes* () and thy sceptre *neḥbet* () are in " thy hands, and thou givest commands to those whose places are hidden."

THE GOD AMSU.

"Thou art Temu, who didst create beings endowed with reason; "thou makest the colour of the skin of one race to be different "from that of another, but, however many may be the varieties of "mankind, it is thou that makest them all to live. Thou hearest "the prayer of him that is oppressed, thou art kind of heart unto "him that calleth upon thee, thou deliverest him that is afraid "from him that is violent of heart, and thou judgest between the "strong and the weak. Thou art the lord of intelligence, and "knowledge is that which proceedeth from thy mouth. The Nile "cometh at thy will, and thou art the greatly beloved lord of the "palm tree who makest mortals to live. Thou makest every work "to proceed, thou workest in the sky, and thou makest to come "into being the beauties of the daylight; the gods rejoice in thy "beauties, and their hearts live when they see thee. Hail, Rā, "who art adored in the Ȧpts, thou mighty one who risest in the "shrine: O Ȧni (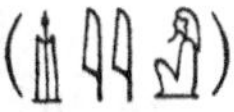), thou lord of the festival of the new "moon, who makest the six days' festival and the festival of the "last quarter of the moon. Hail, Prince, life, health, and strength, "thou lord of all the gods, whose appearances are in the horizon, "thou Governor of the ancestors of Ȧuḳert (i.e., the underworld), "thy name is hidden from thy children in thy name 'Ȧmen.'

"Hail to thee, O thou who art in peace, thou lord of joy of "heart, thou crowned form, thou lord of the *ureret* crown, whose "plumes are exalted, whose tiara is beautiful, whose White Crown "is lofty, the gods love to look upon thee; the crowns of the "South and North are established upon thy brow. Beloved art "thou as thou passest through the two lands, as thou sendest "forth rays from thy two beautiful eyes. The dead are rapturous "with delight when thou shinest. The cattle become languid "when thou shinest in full strength; beloved art thou when thou "art in the southern sky, and thou art esteemed lovely when thou "art in the northern sky. Thy beauties take possession of and "carry away all hearts, and love for thee maketh all arms to relax, "thy beautiful form maketh the hands to tremble, and all hearts "melt at the sight of thee.

"Hail, thou FORM who art ONE, thou creator of all things;

"hail, thou ONLY ONE, thou maker of things which exist. Men "came forth from thy two eyes, and the gods sprang into being "as the issue of thy mouth. Thou makest the green herbs whereby "cattle live, and the staff of life for the use of man. Thou makest "the fish to live in the rivers, and the feathered fowl in the sky; "thou givest the breath of life to that which is in the egg, thou "makest birds of every kind to live, and likewise the reptiles that "creep and fly; thou causest the rats to live in their holes, and "the birds that are on every green tree. Hail to thee, O thou "who hast made all these things, thou ONLY ONE; thy might "hath many forms. Thou watchest all men as they sleep, and "thou seekest the good of thy brute creation. Hail, Åmen, who "dost establish all things, and who art Åtmu and Harmachis, all "people adore thee, saying, 'Praise be to thee because of thy "'resting among us; homage to thee because thou hast created "'us.' All creatures say, 'Hail to thee'! and all lands praise "thee; from the height of the sky, to the breadth of the earth, "and to the depths of the sea thou art praised. The gods bow "down before thy majesty to exalt the Will of their Creator; they "rejoice when they meet their begetter, and say to thee, 'Come "'in peace, O father of the fathers of all the gods, who hast spread "'out the sky, and hast founded the earth, maker of things which "'are, creator of things which exist, thou Prince (life, health, and "'strength [to thee !]), thou Governor of the gods. We adore thy "'Will (or, souls) for thou hast made us; thou hast made us and "'hast given us birth.'

"Hail to thee, maker of all things, lord of Maāt, father of the "gods, maker of men, creator of animals, lord of grain, who "makest to live the cattle on the hills. Hail, Åmen, bull, "beautiful of face, beloved in the Åpts, mighty of rising in the "shrine, who art doubly crowned in Heliopolis; thou art the "judge of Horus and Set in the Great Hall. Thou art the head "of the company of the gods, ONLY ONE, who hast no second, "thou governor of the Åpts, Åni at the head of the company of the "gods, living in Maāt daily, thou Horus of the East of the double "horizon. Thou hast created the mountain, and the silver and "real lapis-lazuli at thy will. Incense and fresh *ānti* are prepared "for thy nostrils, O beautiful Face, who comest forth from the "land of the Mātchau, Åmen-Rā, lord of the thrones of the two "lands, at the head of the Åpts, Åni, the chief of thy shrine. "Thou king who art ONE among the gods, thy names are manifold, "and how many they are is unknown; thou shinest in the eastern "and western horizons, and overthrowest thy enemies at thy birth "daily. Thoth exalteth thy two eyes, and maketh thee to set in "splendour; the gods rejoice in thy beauties which those who are "in thy [following] exalt. Thou art the lord of the Sektet Boat "and of the Ātet Boat, which travel over the sky for thee in "peace. Thy sailors rejoice when they see Nåk overthrown, "and his limbs stabbed with the knife, and the fire devouring "him, and his filthy soul beaten out of his filthy body, and his "feet carried away. The gods rejoice, Rā is content, and Ånnu "(Heliopolis) is glad because the enemies of Åtmu are over- "thrown, and the heart of Nebt-Ānkh (i.e., Isis) is happy because "the enemies of her lord are overthrown. The gods of Kher-āḥa "rejoice, and those who dwell in the shrine are making obeisance "when they see thee mighty in thy strength. Thou art the "Sekhem (i.e., Power) of the gods, and Maāt of the Åpts in thy "name of 'Maker of Maāt.' Thou art the lord of *tchefau* food, "the Bull of offerings (?) in thy name, 'Åmen, Bull of his mother.' "Thou art the fashioner of mortals, the creator, the maker of all "things which are in thy name of Temu-Kheperå. Thou art the "Great Hawk which gladdeneth the body; the Beautiful Face "which gladdeneth the breast. Thou art the Form of [many] "forms, with a lofty crown; the Uatcheti goddesses (i.e., Nekhebet "and Uatchet) fly before his face. The hearts of the dead (?) go "out to meet him, and the denizens of heaven turn to him; his "appearances rejoice the two lands. Homage to thee, Åmen-Rā, "lord of the throne of the two lands; thy city loveth thy radiant "light."

The chief point of interest in connexion with this hymn is the proof it affords of the completeness with which Åmen had absorbed all the attributes of Rā and of every other ancient form of the Sun-god, and how in the course of about one hundred years he had risen from the position of a mere local god to that of the "king of the gods" of Egypt. In the XVIIIth and XIXth Dynasties the wealth of his priesthood must have been enormous, and the religious and social powers which they possessed made them, in many respects, as powerful as the reigning family. Thebes, the capital of Egypt and the centre of the worship of Åmen-Rā, was rightly called the "city of Åmen," 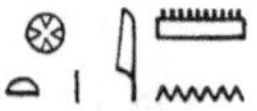 (the No-Amon of Nahum iii. 8), and there is reason to think that many of the great Egyptian raids in Syria and Nubia were made as much for the purpose of supplying funds for the maintenance of the temples, and services, and priests of Åmen-Rā as for the glory and prestige of Egypt. The slavish homage which the Thothmes kings, and the Åmen-ḥeteps, and the Ramessids paid to Åmen-Rā, and their lavish gifts to his sanctuaries suggest that it was his priests who were, in reality, the makers of war and peace. Under the XXth Dynasty their power was still very great, and the list of the gifts which Rameses III. made to their order illustrates their influence over this monarch. Towards the close of this dynasty we find that they had succeeded in obtaining authority from the feeble and incapable successors of Rameses III. to levy taxes on the people of Thebes, and to appropriate to the use of their order certain of the revenues of the city; this was only what was to be expected, for, since the treasury of the god was no longer supplied by expeditions into Syria, the priests found poverty staring them in the face. When the last Rameses was dead the high-priest of Åmen-Rā became king of Egypt almost as a matter of course, and he and his immediate successors formed the XXIst Dynasty, or the Dynasty of priest-kings of Egypt.

Their chief aim was to maintain the power of their god and of their own order, and for some years they succeeded in doing so; but they were priests and not warriors, and their want of funds became more and more pressing, for the simple reason that they had no means of enforcing the payment of tribute by the peoples and tribes who, even under the later of the kings bearing the name of Rameses, acknowledged the sovereignty of Egypt. Meanwhile the poverty of the inhabitants of Thebes increased rapidly, and they were not only unable to contribute to the maintenance of the acres of temple buildings and to the services of the god, but found it difficult to obtain a living. These facts are proved by many considerations, but chiefly by the robberies which are described or referred to in several papyri of the royal tombs in the Valley of the Tombs of the Kings at Thebes; and the discoveries of the royal mummies at Dêr al-Baḥarî shows that the Government of the period was unable either to protect the royal tombs or to suppress the gang of robbers who systematically pillaged them. The robberies were carried out with the connivance of several high officials, and it was to the interests of large numbers of the inhabitants of Thebes to make abortive the legal proceedings which were taken by the Government against them. Notwithstanding their growing poverty and waning influence the priests in no way abated the pretensions of their god or of themselves, and they continued to proclaim the glory and power of Åmen-Rā in spite of the increasing power of the Libyans in the Delta.

In a very remarkable document written for Nesi-Khensu, the daughter of one of the priest-kings of Åmen-Rā, the god is made to enter into an agreement to provide for the happiness and deification of the deceased in the Underworld, and the terms of this agreement are expressed with all the precision, and in the phraseology, of a legal document. This is interesting enough as illustrating the relations which the priests assumed to exist between themselves and their gods, but the introduction to the agreement is more important for our purpose here, because in it are enumerated all the chief attributes which were ascribed to Åmen-Rā under the XXIst Dynasty. The following is a rendering of this portion of the papyrus of Nesi-Khensu:—[1]

"This holy god, the lord of all the gods, Åmen-Rā, the lord of "the thrones of the two lands, the governors of Åpt; the holy soul "who came into being in the beginning; the great god who liveth "by (*or* upon) Maāt; the first divine matter which gave birth "unto subsequent divine matter![2] the being through whom every

[1] A hieroglyphic transcript of the hieratic text of this remarkable document, together with a French translation, has been published by Maspero in *Les Momies Royales de Déir-el-baharî*, p. 594 f.

[2] Or, "the primeval *paut* which gave birth unto the [other] two *pautti*."

"[other] god hath existence; the One One who hath made every-"thing which hath come into existence since primeval times when "the world was created; the being whose births are hidden, whose "evolutions are manifold, and whose growths are unknown; the "holy Form, beloved, terrible, and mighty in his risings; the lord "of wealth, the power, Kheperå who createth every evolution of "his existence, except whom at the beginning none other existed; "who at the dawn in the primeval time was Åtennu, the prince of "rays and beams of light; who having made himself [to be seen, "caused] all men to live; who saileth over the celestial regions "and faileth not, for at dawn on the morrow his ordinances are "made permanent; who though an old man shineth in the form of "one that is young, and having brought (*or* led) the uttermost "parts of eternity goeth round about the celestial regions and "journeyeth through the Ṭuat to illumine the two lands which he "hath created; the God who acted as God, who moulded himself, "who made the heavens and the earth by his will (or heart); the "greatest of the great, the mightiest of the mighty, the prince who "is mightier than the gods, the young Bull with sharp horns, the "protector of the two lands in his mighty name of 'The everlast-"'ing one who cometh and hath his might, who bringeth the "'remotest limit of eternity,' the god-prince who hath been prince "from the time that he came into being, the conqueror of the two "lands by reason of his might, the terrible one of the double "divine face, the divine aged one, the divine form who dwelleth in "the forms of all the gods, the Lion-god with awesome eye, the "sovereign who casteth forth the two Eyes, the lord of flame "[which goeth] against his enemies; the god Nu, the prince who "advanceth at his hour to vivify that which cometh forth upon his "potter's wheel, the disk of the Moon-god who openeth a way "both in heaven and upon earth for the beautiful form; the "beneficent (*or* operative) god, who is untiring, and who is "vigorous of heart both in rising and in setting, from whose "divine eyes come forth men and women; at whose utterance the "gods come into being, and food is created, and *tchefau* food is "made, and all things which are come into being; the traverser of "eternity, the old man who maketh himself young [again], with

" myriads of pairs of eyes and numberless pairs of ears, whose " light is the guide of the god of millions of years; the lord of " life, who giveth unto whom he pleaseth the circuit of the earth " along with the abode of his divine face, who setteth out upon his " journey and suffereth no mishap by the way, whose work none " can destroy; the lord of delight, whose name is sweet and " beloved, at dawn mankind make supplications unto him the " Mighty one of victory, the Mighty one of twofold strength, the " Possessor of fear, the young Bull who maketh an end of the " hostile ones, the Mighty one who doeth battle with his foes, " through whose divine plans the earth came into being; the " Soul who giveth light from his two Utchats (Eyes); the god " Baiti who created the divine transformations; the holy one who " is unknown; the king who maketh kings to rule, and who " girdeth up the earth in its courses, and to whose souls the gods " and the goddesses pay homage by reason of the might of his " terror; since he hath gone before that which followeth endureth; " the creator of the world by his secret counsels; the god Kheperå " who is unknown and who is more hidden than the [other] gods, " whose vicar is the divine Disk; the unknown one who hideth " himself from that which cometh forth from him; he is the flame " which sendeth forth rays of light with mighty splendour, but " though he can be seen in form and observation can be made of " him at his appearance yet he cannot be understood, and at dawn " mankind make supplication unto him; his risings are of crystal " among the company of the gods, and he is the beloved object of " every god; the god Nu cometh forward with the north wind in " this god who is hidden; who maketh decrees for millions of " double millions of years, whose ordinances are fixed and are not " destroyed, whose utterances are gracious, and whose statutes fail " not in his appointed time; who giveth duration of life and " doubleth the years of those unto whom he hath a favour; who " graciously protecteth him whom he hath set in his heart; who " hath formed eternity and everlastingness, the king of the South " and of the North, Åmen-Rā, the king of the gods, the lord of " heaven and of earth, and of the deep, and of the two mountains " in whose form the earth began to exist, he the mighty one, who "is more distinguished than all the gods of the first and foremost "company."

The definiteness of the assertions of this composition suggest that it formed the creed of the worshippers of Åmen-Rā, for every one of them appears to have been made with the express purpose of contradicting the pretensions urged by the priests of other gods, e.g., Åten and Osiris; and an examination of the sentences will show that Åmen is made to be the source of life of all things, both animate and inanimate, and that he is identified with the great unknown God who made the universe. It is, however, important to note that he is not in any way identified with Osiris in this text, a fact which seems to indicate that the national god of the Resurrection in Egypt was ignored by the priests of Åmen who composed the contents of Nesi-Khensu's papyrus. From what has been said above as to the importance of Åmen-Rā it will be evident that a large number of shrines of this god must have existed throughout the country, but in nearly all of them he was an intruder, and his priests must have lived chiefly upon the endowments which the pious Egyptians had provided for gods other than he.

We may now consider the various forms[1] in which Åmen-Rā is depicted on monuments and papyri. His commonest form is that of a strong-bearded man who wears upon his head lofty double plumes, the various sections of which are coloured alternately red and green, or red and blue; round his neck he wears a deep collar or necklace, and his close-fitting tunic is supported by elaborately worked shoulder-straps. His arms and wrists are provided with armlets and bracelets, in his right hand is the symbol of life, and in his left the sceptre . Hanging from his tunic is the tail of some animal, the custom of wearing which by gods and kings was common in Egypt in the earliest times. In this form his title is "Åmen-Rā, lord of the thrones of the two lands," . Instead of the sign of life, 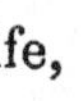, he sometimes holds the *khepesh* war knife, , in his right hand.[2]

[1] For a number of them see Lanzone, op. cit., pll. 18 ff.

[2] Lanzone, op. cit., pl. 21.

At times he is given the head of a hawk which is surmounted by the solar disk encircled by a serpent, [hieroglyph]; as "Åmen-Rā-Temu in Thebes" he has the head of a man surmounted by the solar disk encircled by a serpent; before him is the *ānkh*, ☥, which is provided with human legs and arms, offering lotus flowers to the god.[1] Thus he becomes the god both of Heliopolis and Thebes." In many scenes we find Åmen-Rā with the head of a ram, when he usually wears the solar disk, plumes, and uraeus; at times, however, he wears the disk and uraeus, or the disk only. In this form he is called "Åmen-Rā, lord of the thrones of the two lands, the "dweller in Thebes, the great god who appeareth in the horizon,"

Ḥeru-sa-åtep, king of Ethiopia, adoring Åmen-Rā.

or "Åmen-Rā, lord of the thrones of the two lands, governor of "Ta-Kenset (Nubia)." Another form of Åmen-Rā is that in which he is represented with the body of the ithyphallic god Åmsu, or Min, or Khem, i.e., as the personification of the power of generation. In this form he wears either the customary disk and plumes, or the united crowns of the South and North, and has one hand and arm raised to support [hieroglyph], which he holds above his shoulder; he is called "Åmen-Rā, the bull of his mother," [hieroglyphs], and possesses all the attributes of Fa-ā, i.e., the "god of the lifted hand," [hieroglyphs].

[1] Lanzone, op. cit., pl. 19.

In one of the examples reproduced by Lanzone[1] Åmen-Rā in his ithyphallic form stands by the side of a pylon-shaped building, on the top of which are two trees, one on each side of a large lotus flower; the lotus flower represents the rising sun, which was supposed to issue daily from between two persea trees. In another form Åmen-Rā has the head of a crocodile, and he wears the crown which is composed of the solar disk, plumes, and horns, and is called the "disposer of the life of Rā and of the years of Temu." Finally, the god was sometimes represented in the form of a goose; the animal sacred to him in many parts of Egypt, and all over Nubia, was the ram. In very late dynastic times, especially in the Ptolemaïc period, it became customary to make figures of Åmen-Rā in bronze in which every important attribute of the god was represented. In these he has the bearded head of a man, the body of a beetle with the wings of a hawk, the legs of a man with the toes and claws of a lion, and is provided with four hands and arms, and four wings, the last named being extended. One hand, which is stretched along the wing, grasps the symbols 𓌀, 𓋹, 𓊽, and two knives; another is raised to support 𓍋, after the manner of the "god of the lifted hand;" a third holds the symbol of generation and fertility; and the fourth is lifted to his head. The face of the god is, in reality, that of the solar disk, from which proceed the heads and necks of eight rams. Resting on the disk is a pair of ram's horns, with a disk on each, and stretching upwards are the two characteristic plumes of the god Åmen. From the tip of each of these projects a lion-headed uraeus which ejects moisture from its mouth. This form of the god was a production probably of the period immediately following the XXVIth Dynasty, but some modifications of it are not so old. The idea which underlies the figure is that of representing the *paut* or company of the gods, of which Åmen was the chief, and of showing pictorially how every one of the oldest gods of Egypt was contained in him.

In the Saïte Recension of the *Book of the Dead* we find several passages relating to Åmen, or Åmen-Rā, which appear to

[1] Op. cit., pl. 20, No. 1.

belong to the same period, and as they illustrate the growth of a set of new ideas about the god Àmen, some of them being probably of Nubian origin, they are reproduced here. The first is found in the Rubric to Chapter clxii. which contains the texts to be recited over the amulet of the cow, and was composed with the view of keeping heat in the body of the deceased in the Underworld. The first address is made to the god PAR, , which is clearly a form of Àmen-Rā, for he is called "lord of the phallus," , "lofty of plumes," "lord of transformations, whose skins (i.e., complexions) are manifold," , the "god of many names," "the mighty runner of mighty strides," etc. The second address is to the Cow AHAT, , i.e., the goddess Meḥ-urt or Net, who made a picture of herself and placed it under the head of Rā when he was setting one evening, and is the petition which is to be said when a similar amulet is placed under the head of the deceased, and runs, "O Àmen, O Àmen, who art in "heaven, turn thy face upon the dead body of thy son, and make "him sound and strong in the Underworld."

In Chapter clxiii. we have the second passage as follows:— "Hail, Àmen, thou divine Bull Scarab (), "thou lord of the two *Utchats*, thy name is ḤES-TCHEFETCH "(), the Osiris (i.e., the deceased) is the "emanation of thy two *Utchats*, one of which is called SHARE-"SHAREKHET (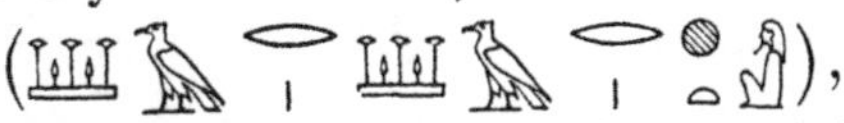), and the other "SHAPUNETERÀRIKA (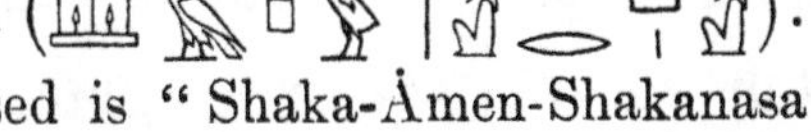)." The magical name of the deceased is "Shaka-Àmen-Shakanasa er hatu Tem seḥetch-nef-taui,"[1] and on his behalf the following prayer is made:—"Grant that he may be of the land of Maāt, let him not "be left in his condition of solitude, for he belongeth to this land

[1] 
.

"wherein he will no more appear, and 'Ān' (?) (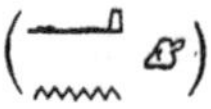) is his "name. O let him be a perfect spirit, or (as others say) a strong "spirit, and let him be the soul of the mighty body which is in "Sau (Saïs), the city of Net (Neith)."

The third passage is Chapter clxv., which is really a petition to Åmen-Rā by the deceased wherein the most powerful of the magical names of the god are enumerated. The vignette of the chapter contains the figure of an ithyphallic god with the body of a beetle; on his head are the characteristic plumes of Åmen, and his right arm is raised like that of Åmsu, or Min, the god of the reproductive powers of nature. The text reads, "Hail, thou "BEKHENNU (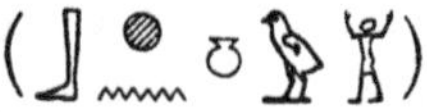), Bekhennu! Hail, Prince, Prince! "Hail Åmen, Hail Åmen! Hail PAR, Hail IUKASA ( ")! Hail God, Prince of the gods of the eastern "parts of heaven, ÅMEN-NATHEKERETHI-ÅMEN ( "). Hail, thou whose skin is hidden, whose "form is secret, thou lord of the two horns [who wast born of] "Nut, thy name is Na-åri-k (, or Ka-åri-k, "), and Kasaika (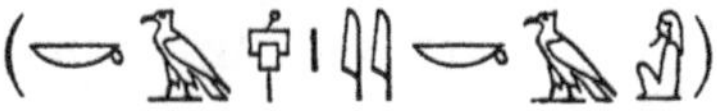), "is thy name. Thy name is Arethi-kasathi-ka (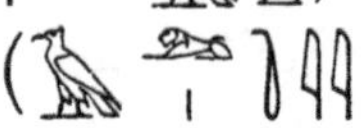 "), and thy name is Åmen-naiu-ån- "ka-entek-share (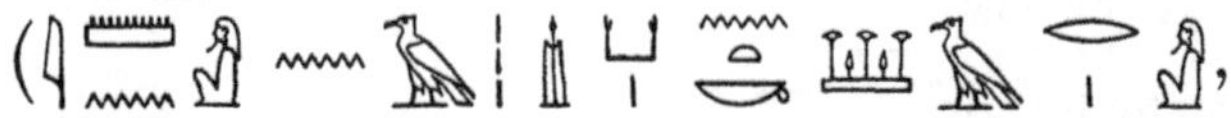, "or Thekshare - Åmen - Rerethi,  "). Hail, Åmen, let me make supplication unto thee, "for I know thy name, and [the mention of] thy transformations "is in my mouth, and thy skin is before mine eyes. Come, I pray "thee, and place thou thine heir and thine image, myself, in the "everlasting underworld. Grant thou that all my members may "repose in Neter-khertet (the underworld), or (as others say) "in Åkertet (the underworld); let my whole body become like "unto that of a god, let me escape from the evil chamber and let "me not be imprisoned therein; for I worship thy name. Thou "hast made for me a skin, and thou hast understood [my] speech, "and thou knowest it exceedingly well. Hidden "is thy name, O Letasashaka, "and I have made for thee a skin. Thy name is Ba-ire-qai, thy name is Mārqathå, thy name is Rerei, thy name is Nasaqebubu, thy name is Thånasa-Thanaså, thy name is Sharshathåkathå.

"O Åmen, O Åmen, O God, O God, O Åmen, I adore thy "name, grant thou to me that I may understand thee; grant "thou that I may have peace in the Ṭuat (underworld), and that "I may possess all my members therein." And the divine Soul which is in Nut saith, "I will make my divine strength to protect "thee, and I will perform everything which thou hast said." This interesting text was ordered to be recited over a figure of the "god of the lifted hand," i.e., of Åmen in his character of the god of generation and reproduction, painted blue, and the knowledge of it was to be kept from the god SUḲAṬI, in the Ṭuat; if the directions given in the rubric were properly carried out it would enable the deceased to drink water in the underworld from the deepest and purest part of the celestial stream, and he would become "like the stars in the heavens above."

A perusal of the above composition shows that we are dealing with a class of ideas concerning Åmen, or Åmen-Rā, which, though clearly based on ancient Egyptian beliefs, are peculiar to the small group of Chapters which are found at the end of the Saïte Recension of the *Book of the Dead.* The forms of the magical names of Åmen are not Egyptian, and they appear to indicate, as the late Dr. Birch said, a Nubian origin. The fact that the Chapters with the above prayers in them are found in a papyrus containing so complete a copy of the Saïte Recension proves that they were held to be of considerable importance in the Ptolemaïc period, and they probably represented beliefs which were widespread at that time. Long before that, however, Åmen-Rā was identified with Horus in all his forms, and Rā in all his forms, and Osiris in all his forms, and the fathers and mothers of these gods were declared to be his; he was also made to be the male counterpart of all the very ancient goddesses of the South and the North, and the paternity of their offspring was attributed to him.

From what has been said above it is evident that the worship of Åmen-Rā spread through all the country both to the north and south of Thebes, and the monuments prove that it made its way into all the dominions of Egypt in Syria, and in Nubia, and in the Oases. In Upper Egypt its centres were Thebes, Hermonthis, Coptos, Panopolis, Cusae, Hermopolis Magna, and Herakleopolis Magna; in Lower Egypt they were Memphis, Saïs, Xoïs, Metelis, Heliopolis, Babylon, Mendes, Thmuis, Diospolis, Butus, and the Island of Khemmis; in the Libyan desert the Oases of Kenemet, 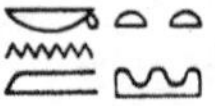 (i.e., the Oasis of the South, or Al-Khârgeh), Tchestcheset,  (i.e., Oasis Minor, or Dâkhel), Ta-åḥet, 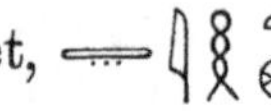 (i.e., Farâfra), and the great Oasis of Jupiter Ammon; in Nubia, Wâdî Sabû'a, Abû Simbel, Napata, and Meroë; and in Syria at several places which were called Diospolis.

The worship of Åmen-Rā was introduced into Nubia by its Egyptian conquerors early in the XIIth Dynasty, and the inhabitants of that country embraced it with remarkable fervour; the hold which it had gained upon them was much strengthened when an Egyptian viceroy, who bore the title of "royal son of Cush," was appointed to rule over the land, and no efforts were spared to make Napata a second Thebes. The Nubians were from the poverty of their country unable to imitate the massive temples of Karnak and Luxor, and the festivals which they celebrated in honour of the Nubian Åmen-Rā, and the processions which they made in his honour, lacked the splendour and magnificence of the Theban capital; still, there is no doubt that, considering the means which they had at their disposal, they erected temples for the worship of Åmen-Rā of very considerable size and solidity. The hold which the priesthood of Åmen-Rā of Thebes had upon the Nubians was very great, for in the troublous times which followed after the collapse of their power as priest-kings of Egypt, the remnant of the great brotherhood made its way to Napata, and settling down there made plans and schemes for the restoration of their rule in Egypt; fortunately for Egypt their designs were never realized. In Syria also the cult of Åmen-Rā was introduced by the Egyptians under the XVIIIth Dynasty, a fact which is proved by the testimony of the Tell el-'Amarna tablets. Thus in a letter from the inhabitants of the city of Tunep,[1] , to the king of Egypt (i.e., Åmen-ḥetep III. or his son Åmen-ḥetep IV.) the writers remind him that the gods worshipped in the city of Tunep are the same as those of Egypt, and that the form of the worship is the same. From an inscription[2] of Thothmes III. at Karnak we know that in the 29th year of his reign this king offered up sacrifices to his gods at Tunep, and it is probable that the worship of Åmen-Rā in Northern Syria dates from this time. On the other hand Akizzi, the governor of Ḳaṭna, in writing to inform Åmen-ḥetep III. that the king of the Khatti had seized and carried off the image of the Sun-god, begs that the king of Egypt will send him sufficient gold to ransom the image, and he does so chiefly on the grounds that in ancient days the kings of Egypt adopted the worship of the Sun-god, presumably from the Syrians, and that they called themselves after the name of the god. To emphasize his appeal Akizzi addresses Åmen-ḥetep III. as the "son of the Sun-god," a fact which proves that he was acquainted with the meaning of the title "sa Rā," i.e., "son of Rā," , which every Egyptian king bore from the time of the Vth Dynasty onwards. This evidence supports an old tradition to the effect that the Heliopolitan form of the worship of the Sun-god was derived from Heliopolis in Syria.

In connexion with Åmen-Rā must be mentioned an important form of the Sun-god which was called MENTHU, ,

[1] See *The Tell el-'Amarna Tablets in the British Museum*, pp. lxv., lxxi.

[2] Mariette, *Karnak*, pl. 13, l. 2.

or MENTHU-RĀ, [hieroglyphs]; though he was commonly described as "lord of Thebes," the chief seat of his worship was at Hermonthis, the Ȧnnu-Rest, [hieroglyphs], i.e., "Heliopolis of the South," of the hieroglyphic texts. Menthu was probably an old local god whose cult was sufficiently important to make it

Menthu giving "life" to Ptolemy Alexander.

necessary for the priests of Ȧmen to incorporate him with the great god of Thebes, and he appears to have been a personification of the destructive heat of the sun. The chief centres of his worship were Ȧnnu of the South, Thebes, Ȧnnu of the North, Tcherṭet, [hieroglyphs] (Edfû), Dendera, and perhaps the temples of

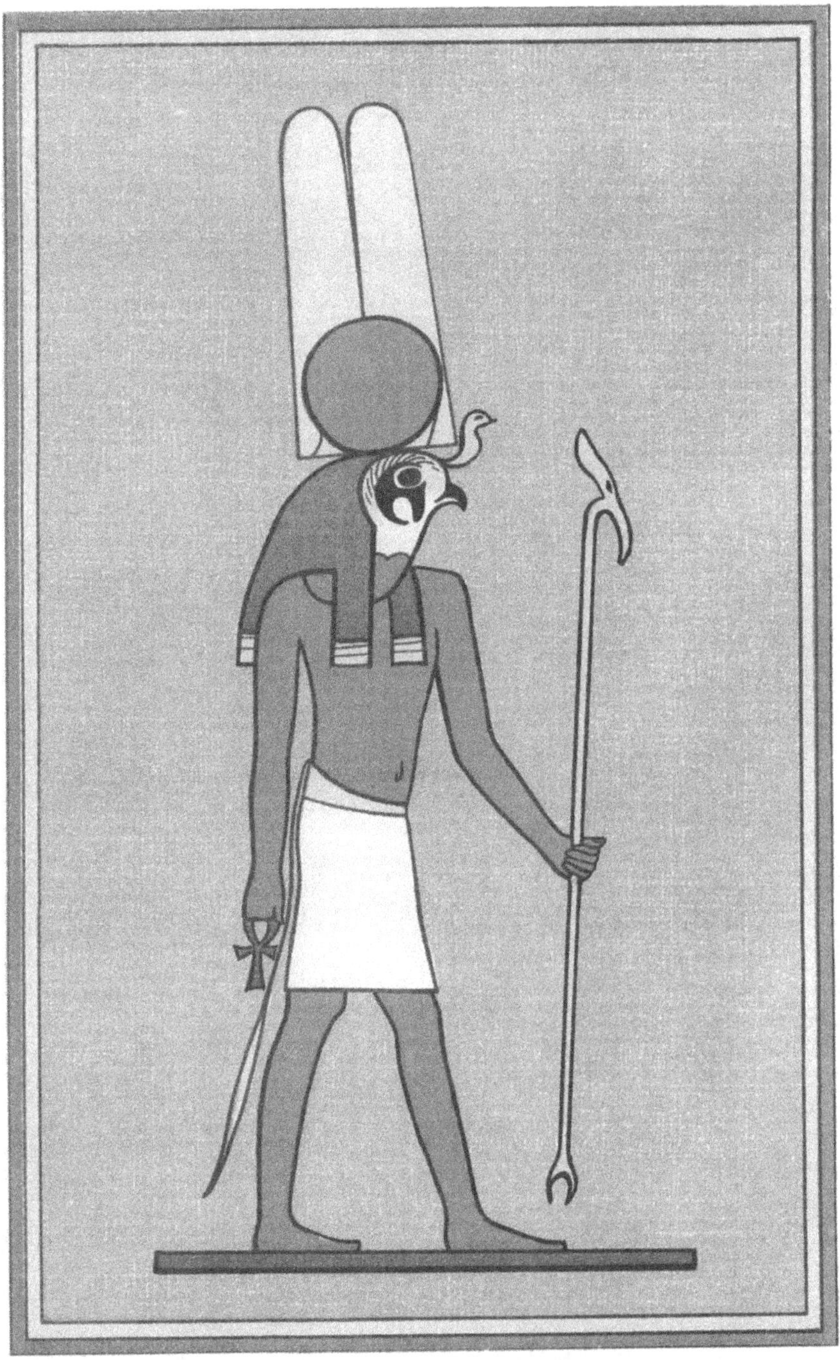

MENTHU, LORD OF THEBES.

the First Cataract, and his commonest titles are, "MENTHU-RĀ, lord "of Thebes, King of the gods, he who is on his throne in Åptet, "MERTI, mighty one of two-fold strength, lord of Thebes of the "North, Sma-taui, Governor of Beḥuṭet, lord of Ånnu of the South, "prince of Ånnu of the North,"[1] and "lord of Manu," i.e., the Libyan mountain.[2] Menthu is mentioned in the Pyramid Texts (Mer-en-Rā, line 784), together with a number of ancient gods, in such a way that we may be certain that his worship was widespread, even in the VIth Dynasty. Thus Kheperȧ , and Nu, , and Tem, and UASH, , the son of Seb, and Sekhem, the son of Osiris, , are entreated to hearken to the words which the dead king is about to address to them. Nekhebet of the Temple of Sar, , in Heliopolis is said to protect him, he is identified with the star Åpsh, , and the gods who traverse the land of the Theḥennu, , and who live on the "indestructible heavens," , are besought to allow him to be with them.

Five obscure gods are next mentioned, i.e., TCHENṬ, , KHER, , SHENTHET, 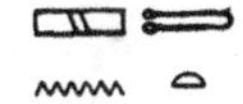, KHENU, 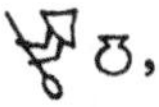, and BENUTCH, , and then it is said that "Seb hearkeneth to him, Tem "provideth him with his form, Thoth heareth for him that which "is in the books of the gods, Horus openeth out a path for him, "Set protecteth him, and Mer-en-Rā riseth in the eastern part of "heaven even as doth Rā. He hath gone forth from Pe with the "spirits of Pe, he is even as is Horus and is fortified by the Great

1 
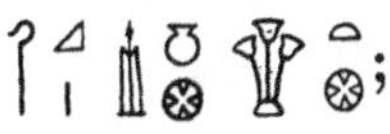; see Lanzone, op. cit., p. 294.

2 .

"and the Little Companies of the gods. He riseth in the condition of a king, he entereth into heaven like Åp-uat, he hath "received the White Crown and the Green Crown (), "his club is with him, his weapon (or sceptre) *ams* (), "is in his grasp, his mother is Isis, his nurse is Nephthys, and the "cow SEKHAT-ḤERU () giveth him milk. Net "is behind him, Serqet is on his two hands. . . . Let him pass, "and let his flesh pass, let him pass, and let his apparel pass, "for he hath gone forth as MENTH (), he hath gone down "like BA (), and he hath hunted like BA-ĀSHEM-F" (). Of the origin and early history of Menthu nothing is known, but his worship must have been very ancient if we are to judge by the passage quoted above from the text of king Mer-en-Rā, for, although mentioned with the two obscure gods Ba and Ba-āshem-f, it is quite clear that he was a great god and that the deceased hoped to resemble him in the Underworld. Menthu is twice mentioned in the Theban Recension of the *Book of the Dead*, but curiously enough, only as one of a number of gods. Thus, in Chapter cxl. 6, together with Rā, Tem, Uatchet, Shu, Seb, Osiris, Suti, Horus, Bāḥ, Rā-er-neḥeḥ, Teḥuti, Nāåm, Tchetta, Nut, Isis, Nephthys, Hathor, Nekht, Mert (?), Maāt, Ånpu, and Ta-mes-tchetta, he is said to be the "soul and body of Rā," and in Chapter clxxi. his name occurs among the names of Tem, Shu, Tefnut, Seb, Nut, Osiris, Isis, Set, Nephthys, Ḥeru-khuti, Hathor, Kheperå, Åmen, etc., who are entreated to bestow a garment of purity upon the deceased. Menthu is usually depicted in the form of a man with the head of a hawk, whereon he wears a crown formed of the solar disk with the uraeus and two high plumes; as such he is styled "lord of Thebes."

In a figure reproduced by Lanzone [1] he has two hawks' heads, each of which is provided with the solar disk, two uraei, and two plumes; in his right hand Menthu grasps the scimitar, , which

[1] Op. cit., pl. 119, No. 3.

indicates that he was a god of war. Another proof of his warlike attributes is a scene[1] in which he is depicted, with a long spear having a bronze or iron head, in the act of spearing a foe, whose hands and feet are tied together. In the city of Tchert, , Menthu was worshipped under the form of a man with the head of a bull, but instead of the solar disk he wears on his head the lunar crescent and disk, sometimes with and sometimes without plumes. The warlike character of this local form of Menthu is indicated by the bow and arrows, and club, and knife which he holds in his hands, and we are justified in assuming that he was a personification of the fierce, destroying heat of the sun which warred against the enemies of the Sun-god, and smote them to the death with his burning rays which were like fiery spears and darts. In the narrative of the battle of Kadesh we are told that Rameses II. "rose up as Rā riseth, and took the weapons () "of father Menthu," and that when he saw the foe before him "he raged at them like Menthu, lord of Thebes, and took his "weapons in his hand," and that having become like "Bār () in his hour," he leaped into his chariot and drove headlong into the battle, wherein he, of course, gained a great victory. Elsewhere Menthu is often styled the "mighty bull," and it is possible that originally this god was nothing but a personification of the strength and might of the raging bull when fighting a foe, and that his worship in one form or another existed in predynastic times. It must, in any case, be very ancient, because when joined to Rā his name comes first in the compound name and we have "Menthu-Rā" instead of Rā-Menthu. The pictures of the god reproduced by Lanzone[2] prove that the god possessed other phases which are not at present well understood. Thus he is represented standing upright, with the head of a hawk, and he holds in the right hand what appears to be an ear of corn and in the left a vase, as if he were in the act of making offerings. In another scene the god, hawk-headed and wearing the solar disk encircled by a uraeus, is seated on a throne and is represented

[1] Op. cit., pl. 120, No. 4. [2] *Ibid.*, pl. 120.

in the act of embracing a young Horus god who wears on his head the solar disk with plumes, and a tight-fitting cap with a uraeus in front of it, and who stands on the edge of the throne by the side of the god.

The principal female counterpart of Åmen-Rā, the king of the gods, in the New Empire was MUT, , whose name means "Mother," and in all her attributes we see that she was regarded as the great "world-mother," who conceived and brought forth whatsoever exists. The pictures of the goddess usually represent her in the form of a woman wearing on her head the united crowns of the South and the North, and holding in her hands the papyrus sceptre and the emblem of life. Elsewhere we see her in female form standing upright, with her arms, to which large wings are attached, stretched out full length at right angles to her body; at her feet is the feather of Maāt. She wears the united crowns, as before stated, but from each shoulder there projects the head of a vulture; one vulture wears the crown of the North, , and the other two plumes, ,[1] though sometimes each vulture head has upon it two plumes, which are probably those of Shu or Åmen-Rā. In other pictures the goddess has the heads of a woman or man, a vulture, and a lioness, and she is provided with a phallus, and a pair of wings, and the claws of a lion or lioness. In the vignette of the clxivth Chapter of the *Book of the Dead* she is associated with two dwarfs, each of whom has two faces, one of a hawk and one of a man, and each of whom has an arm lifted to support the symbol of the god Åmsu or Min, and wears upon his head a disk and plumes. In the text which accompanies the vignette, though the three-headed goddess is distinctly called "Mut" in the Rubric, she is addressed as "SEKHET-BAST-RĀ," , a fact which accounts for the presence of the phallus and the male head on a woman's body, and proves that Mut was believed to possess both the male and female attributes of reproduction.

We have already seen that the originally obscure god Åmen was, chiefly through the force of political circumstances, made to

[1] Lanzone, op. cit., pl. 136.

THE GODDESS MUT, THE LADY OF THEBES.

TA-URT (THOUERIS), THE ASSOCIATE OF HATHOR.

usurp the attributes and powers of the older gods of Egypt, and we can see by such figures of the goddess as those described above that Mut was, in like fashion, identified with the older goddesses of the land with whom, originally, she had nothing in common. Thus the head of the lioness which projects from one shoulder indicates that she was identified with Sekhet or Bast, and the vulture heads prove that her cult was grafted on to that of Nekhebet, and the double crowns show that she united in herself all the attributes of all the goddesses of the South and North.

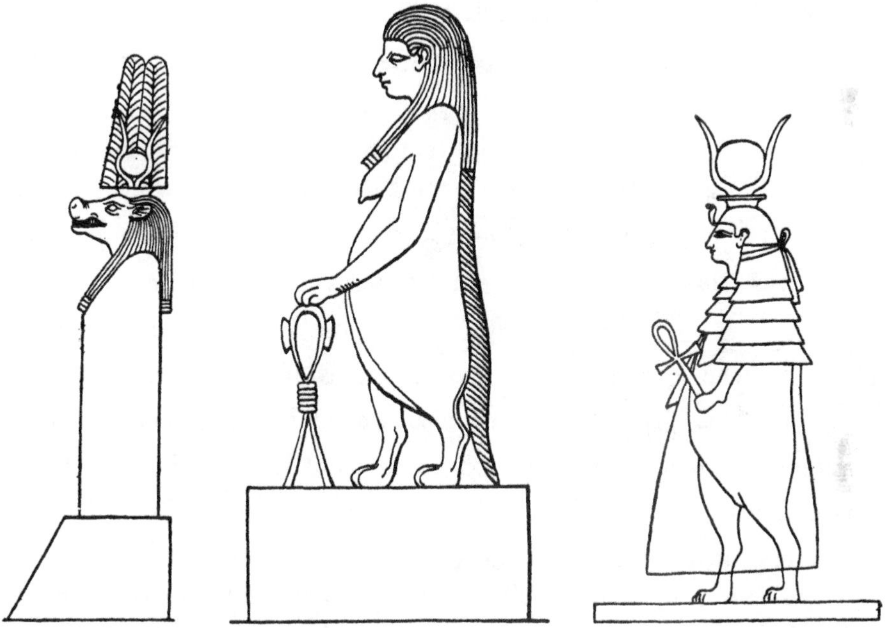

Ȧpet.

Thus we find her name united with the names of other goddesses, e.g., Mut-Temt, Mut-Uatchet-Bast, Mut-Sekhet-Bast-Menḥit, and among her aspects she included those of Isis, and Iusāaset. Locally she usurped the position of Ȧment, , the old female counterpart of Ȧmen and of Ȧpet, , the personification of the ancient settlement Ȧpt, from which is derived the name "Thebes" (Ta-ȧpt); she was also identified with the goddess of Ȧmentet, i.e., Hathor in one of her forms as lady of the

Underworld; and with the primeval goddess ÅMENT, who formed one of the four goddesses of the company of the gods of Hermopolis, which was adopted in its entirety by the priests of Åmen for their gods; and with the predynastic goddess TA-URT, , or ÅPI, , (or, ÅPT, ); and, in short, with every goddess who could in any way be regarded as a "mother-goddess." The centre of the worship of Mut was the quarter of Thebes which was called Åsher, or Åshrel, or Ashrelt,[1] and which probably derived its name from the large sacred lake which existed there; the temple of the goddess, , Ḥet-Mut, with its sanctuary, , was situated a little to the south of the great temple of Åmen-Rā. From the inscriptions which have been found on the ruins of her temple we find that she was styled "Mut, the great lady of Åshert, the lady of heaven, the queen of the gods," 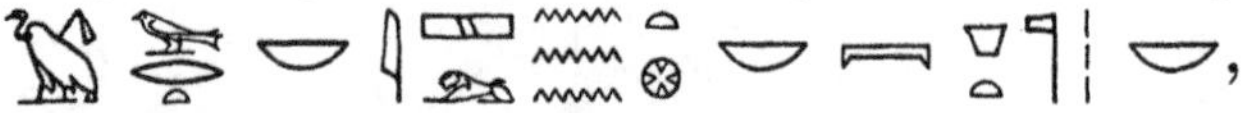, and that she was thought to have existed with Nu in primeval time, 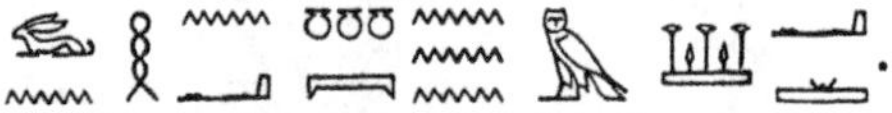. She was, moreover, called "Mut, who giveth birth, but was herself not born of any," 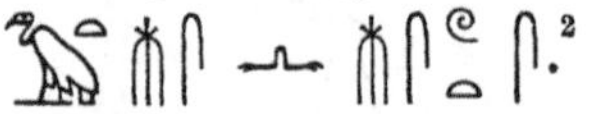.[2] Here also we find her associated with several goddesses,[3] and referred to as the "lady of the life of the two lands," , and "lady of the house of Ptaḥ, lady of heaven, queen of the two lands," etc.

The great temple of Mut at Thebes was built by Åmen-ḥetep III., about B.C. 1450, and was approached from the temple of Åmen-Rā by an avenue of sphinxes; the southern half of the

[1] The forms of the name given by Brugsch (*Dict. Géog.*, p. 73) are 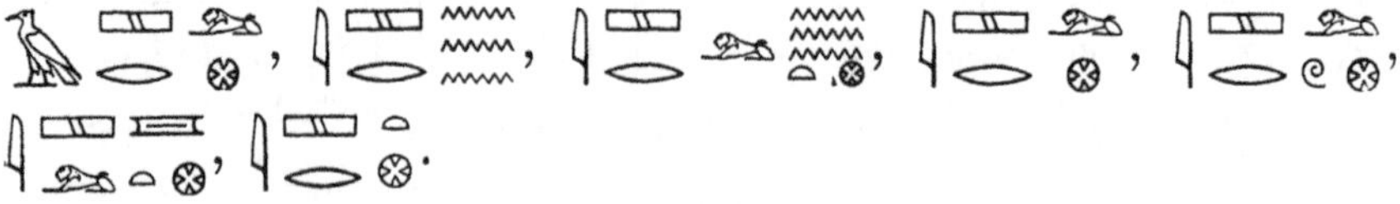.

[2] Champollion, *Notices*, ii., p. 207.

[3] .

building overlooked a semi-circular lake on which the sacred procession of boats took place, and at intervals, both inside and outside the outer wall of the temple enclosure were placed statues of the goddess Mut, in the form of Sekhet, in black basalt. Another famous sanctuary of Mut was situated in the city of Pa-khen-Ȧment, , the Παχναμουνίς of Ptolemy (iv. 5, § 50), and the capital of the nome, , Sma-Beḥuṭet, the Diospolites of Lower Egypt. This city was also called "Thebes of the North," , or the "City of the North," , to distinguish it from Thebes, the great city of Ȧmen which is always referred to as the "City," *par excellence*. From the Egyptian word *nut*, "city," is derived the Biblical form "No," and the "No Amon" of Nahum iii. 8, which "was situate among "the rivers, *that had* the waters round about it, whose rampart "*was* the sea, *and* her wall *was* from the sea," can hardly be any other than the city of Ȧmen and Mut in the Delta. Among other shrines of Mut must be mentioned Bekhen, , a town in the Delta, which was probably situated in the sixth nome of Lower Egypt, the Khas, , of the Egyptians, and the Gynaecopolites of the Greeks. Dr. Brugsch pointed out that the deities worshipped at Bekhen were "the Bull Osiris," Ȧmen-Rā, Mut, and Khensu, and he considered[1] it probable that the city lay near the capital of the nome which was called Khasut, , by the Egyptians and Χοΐς by the Greeks. Another shrine of Nut was situated at Ān, , by which we are probably to understand the region in which Ἡρώωνπόλις, or Heroopolis, lay. The district of Ān, according to Dr. Brugsch, formed the neutral border between the South and the North, and a text quoted by him concerning it, says, "When Horus and Set were dividing "the country they took up their places one on one side of the "boundary and the other on the other, and they agreed that the

[1] *Dict. Géog.*, p. 202.

"country of Ān should form the frontier of the country on one "side of it, and that it should be the frontier of the other also." [1]

From what has been said above it appears that Mut was originally the female counterpart of Nu, and that she was one of the very few goddesses of whom it is declared that she was "never born," i.e., that she was self-produced. Her association with Nu suggests that she must be identified with or partake of some of the characteristics of a remarkable goddess who is mentioned in the Pyramid Texts (Unȧs, line 181) under the name of MUT, , a variant spelling of which is MĀUIT,[2] . Her name occurs in a passage in which a prayer is made on behalf of Unȧs that "he may see," and following is the petition, "O Rā, be good to him on this day since yester-"day" (*sic*); [3] after this come the words, "Unȧs hath had union "with the goddess Mut,[4] Unȧs hath drawn unto himself the flame "of Isis, Unȧs hath united himself to the lotus," etc.[5] The only mention of Mut in the Theban Recension of the *Book of the Dead* is found in a hymn to Osiris,[6] which forms the clxxxiiird Chapter; the deceased is made to say to the god, "Thou risest up like an "exalted being upon thy standard, and thy beauties exalt the "face of man and make long his footstep[s]. I have given unto "thee the sovereignty of thy father Seb, and the goddess Mut, thy

1 , *Dict. Géog.*, p. 118.

2 *Recueil de Travaux*, tom. iii., p. 197, note 1.

3 .

4 If , MUT, and , MĀUIT, and , MUIT, are the same goddess as , it would seem that her name was read as Mut, under the Early Empire.

5 .

6 *Papyrus of Hunefer*, Brit. Mus., No. 9,901, sheet 3.

"mother, who gave birth to the gods, brought thee forth as the "first-born of five gods, and created thy beauties and fashioned "thy members." The papyrus which contains this passage was written during the reign of Seti I., about B.C. 1370, and it is evident that at that period Mut was identified with Nut, and that she was made to be the female counterpart of Seb.

The third member of the great triad of Thebes was KHENSU, , who was declared to be the son of Åmen-Rā and Mut, and who was worshipped with great honour at Thebes. According to Dr. Brugsch,[1] the name "Khensu" is derived from the root *khens*, 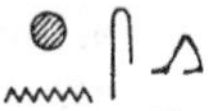, "to travel, to move about, to run," and the like, and Signor Lanzone[2] renders the name by "il fugatore, il persecutore"; for both groups of meanings there is authority in the texts, but the translations proposed by the former scholar represent the commonest meaning of the word. Khensu was, in fact, the "traveller," and as he was a form of Thoth and was identified by the Thebans with the Moon-god the epithet was appropriate. As far back as the time of Unås the motion of Thoth as the Moon-god in the sky was indicated by the word *khens*, for in line 194 we read, "Unås goeth round about heaven like Rā, and travelleth "through heaven like Thoth."[3] In the passage of the text of the same king (line 510) which describes how he hunted, and killed, and ate the gods, mention is made of the god "KHENSU the slaughterer," , who "cut their throats for "the king, and drew out their intestines for him," and he is described as the "messenger whom he sent out to meet them."[4] Khensu the slaughterer and the messenger can, then, be no other than Khensu the Moon-god of later times, and thus we see that, under the Early Empire, Khensu occupied a very important position in the mythology of the period as the "messenger" of the great gods, and the "traveller" who journeyed through the sky

[1] *Religion*, p. 359. [2] Op. cit., p. 973.

[3] 

[4] 

under the form of the moon. We have already referred to the great antiquity of the section of the text of Unås in which the hunting of the gods by the king is described, and there is every reason to believe that the existence of Khensu was formulated in the minds of the Egyptians in very primitive times, and that his name is older than the dynastic period. We may note in passing that the other gods mentioned in the section are Aker, , Tem, and Seb, all of whom are well known from texts of the dynastic period, and Tcheser-ṭep-f, Ḥer-Thertu, and Sheshemu,[1] who assist in marking, and snaring, and cutting up the gods. Among certain ancient Oriental nations the worship of the Moon always preceded that of the Sun, and there is reason for thinking that several of the oldest gods of Egypt were forms of the Moon in her various phases. In the theological system which the priests of Heliopolis succeeded in imposing upon the country some of these were preserved either by identification with the gods of the new scheme or by adoption, and comparatively fixed attributes were assigned to them. At a still later period, when the cult of Åmen and Åmen-Rā was common throughout the country, a further selection from the old gods was made, and some gods had positions apportioned to them in the company of the gods of Åmen-Rā at Thebes. The priesthood of that city showed great astuteness in making Khensu, one of the most ancient forms of the Moon-god, to be the son of Åmen-Rā, and in identifying him with the sons of the great cosmic gods Horus and Rā.

The chief centre of the worship of Khensu in the latter part of the dynastic period was Thebes, where Rameses III. built the famous "House of Khensu in Thebes," , or "House of Khensu in Thebes, Nefer-ḥetep," 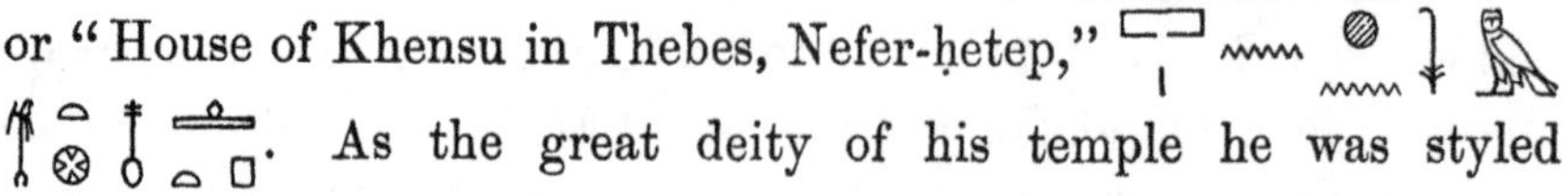. As the great deity of his temple he was styled "great god, lord of heaven," "Khensu in Thebes, (surnamed) "Nefer-ḥetep, Horus, lord of joy of heart in the Åpts," and the texts show that shrines were built in his honour at Bekhent, 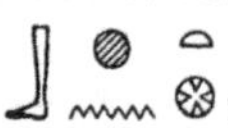,

[1] , 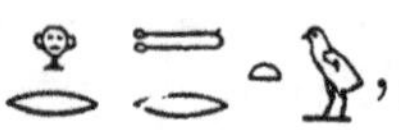, and .

KHENSU IN THEBES, NEFER-HETEP.

THE DUAL GOD KHENSU STANDING UPON CROCODILES.

in the Delta (?), at Shentu, , at Nubit,  (Ombos), at Beḥuṭet,  (Edfû), at Sma-Beḥuṭet, , and at Khemennu (Hermopolis). In the last-named place he was called "KHENSU-TEḤUTI, the twice great, the lord of Khemennu,"[1] a fact which proves that in the late dynastic times he was wholly identified with Thoth; as Khensu-Teḥuti he was also worshipped at Beḥuṭet, or Edfû. In Thebes his name was united with that of Rā and of Shu, and we find such forms as KHENSU-RĀ, , and KHENSU-SHU, . The great temple of Khensu at Thebes appears to have contained three shrines, which probably corresponded to three aspects of the god, and we thus have:—1. The Temple of Khensu. 2. The Temple of Khensu in Thebes, Nefer-ḥetep. 3. The Temple of Khensu, who worketh [his] plans in Thebes, .[2] The forms of the god KHENSU-PA-KHARṬ, , i.e., "Khensu the Babe," and KHENSU-ḤUNNU, , i.e., "Khensu the Child," were probably worshipped in the main portion of the temple, for they were purely forms of the Moon-god, and they bore the same relation to him that Ḥeru-pa-kharṭ (Harpocrates) and Ḥeru-Ḥunnu bore to Horus the Great or to Rā.

From a series of extracts quoted by Dr. Brugsch[3] from the inscriptions on the temple of Khensu at Thebes we find that he was the "lord of Maāt," like Ptaḥ, and the "moon by night"; as the new moon he is likened to a mighty, or fiery bull, and as the full moon he is said to resemble an emasculated bull. As Khensu-pa-kharṭ he caused to shine upon the earth the beautiful light of the crescent moon, and through his agency women conceived, cattle became fertile, the germ grew in the egg, and all nostrils and throats were filled with fresh air. He was the second great light in the heavens, and was the "first great [son] of Åmen, the "beautiful youth, who maketh himself young in Thebes in the

1 .

2 Brugsch, *Dict. Géog.*, p. 600. 3 *Religion*, p. 360 f.

"form of Rā, the son of the goddess Nubit, , a child in "the morning, an old man in the evening, a youth at the beginning "of the year, who cometh as a child after he had become infirm, "and who reneweth his births like the Disk."[1] From this passage it appears that Khensu-pa-khart was both the spring sun, and the spring moon, and also the moon at the beginning of each month, in fact, the symbol of the renewed light of the sun and moon, and the source of generation and reproduction. In these aspects he was readily identified with many forms of the young Sun-god, whether Horus or Rā, and with some of the gods of reproduction, e.g., Åmsu, or Min. As a Horus god he became the son of Osiris, the "Bull of Åmentet," and of one of the forms of Isis, and as the "Bull of his mother," , he was identified with ÅMSU-RĀ, , and was regarded as the brother of the Bull Osiris. As Dr. Brugsch pointed out,[2] the "two Bulls" mentioned in texts of the late period are Osiris and Khensu, and they represent the Sun and the Moon.

The forms in which Khensu is depicted on the monuments are of considerable interest, and may be thus described. Whether standing or seated on a throne he has usually the body of a man with the head of a hawk; sometimes, however, his head also is that of a man. He wears on his head the lunar disk in a crescent, , or the solar disk with a uraeus, or the solar disk with the plumes and a uraeus. As "Khensu of Beḥuṭet, the great god, lord of heaven," he is seen seated on a throne and holding in his hands and . As Khensu Nefer-ḥetep he appears on the stele of Pai, , in the form of a mummied man seated on a throne;[3] over his forehead is the uraeus of royalty and by the side of his head is the lock of youth. Behind his neck hangs the *menȧt* , and below his chin is the collar which is usually worn by Hathor; in his hands are , , , and . On the stele behind his back are two pairs of ears and two pairs of eyes,

[1] Brugsch, *Thesaurus*, p. 511. [2] *Religion*, p. 362.
[3] See Lanzone, op. cit., pl. 340.

, and the deceased is made to address the god as "lord of the gods, Khensu-Nefer-ḥetep-Teḥuti, lord of Ȧnnu "rest (i.e., Ȧnnu of the South), chief Mābi (), peace, "peace, O gracious one, who art at peace, and who lovest "peace." As "Khensu, the mighty, who cometh forth from Nu," 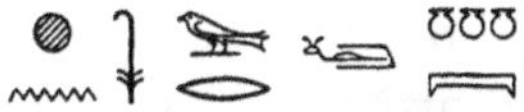, he is provided with two hawks' heads, one facing to the right and the other to the left, and four wings, and he stands with each foot upon the head of a crocodile; on his heads rest the lunar crescent and disk. In this form he represents both the sun at sunrise and the new moon, and the two crocodiles symbolize the two great powers of darkness over which he has triumphed. As "Khensu, the chronographer," 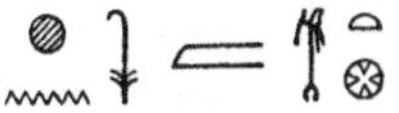 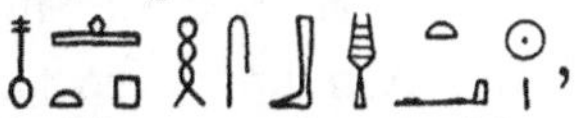, he wears the solar disk on his head and holds a stylus in his right hand, and as Khensu-Rā, , he wears the crown, .

The phase of Khensu which appears to have been of the greatest interest to the Egyptians was that which was deified under the name of Khensu Nefer-ḥetep. This god not only ruled the month, but he was also supposed to possess absolute power over the evil spirits which infested earth, air, sea, and sky, and which made themselves hostile to man and attacked his body under the forms of pains, sicknesses, and diseases, and produced decay, and madness, and death. He it was, moreover, who made plants to grow, and fruit to ripen, and animals to conceive, and to men and women he was the god of love. We have no means of knowing what views the Egyptians held concerning the influence of the moon on the minds of human beings on the seventh, fourteenth, and twenty-first day of its age, but it is probable that, like the Arabs, they assigned to it different and special powers on each of these days. In the reign of Rameses III. a large temple was built at Thebes in honour of the Moon-god, and according to a tradition which his priests in very much later times caused to be inscribed upon a stone stele, the fame of his Theban representative was so wide-spread that it reached to a remote country called Bekhten, which was situated at a distance of a journey of seventeen months from Egypt.[1] According to this tradition a king of Egypt, who was probably Rameses II., was in the country of Nehern, , i.e., a portion of Western Syria near the Euphrates, collecting tribute according to an annual custom, when the "prince of Bekhten" came with the other chiefs to salute his majesty and to bring a gift. The other chiefs brought gold, and lapis-lazuli, and turquoise, and precious woods, but the prince of Bekhten brought with his offerings his eldest daughter, who was exceedingly beautiful; the king accepted the maiden, and took her to Egypt, where he made her the chief royal wife and gave her the Egyptian name of Rā-neferu 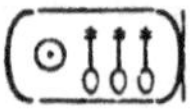, i.e., the "beauties of Rā," the Sun-god.

Some time after, that is to say, in the fifteenth year of the reign of the king of Egypt, the prince of Bekhten appeared in Thebes on the xxiind day of the second month of summer, and when he had been led into the presence he laid his offerings at the feet of the king, and did homage to him. As soon as he had the opportunity he explained the object of his visit to Egypt, and said that he had come on behalf of the young sister of Queen Rā-neferu, who was grievously sick, and he begged the king to send a physician to see his daughter Bent-Reshet, 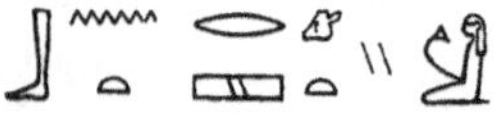, or Bent-enth-reshet, 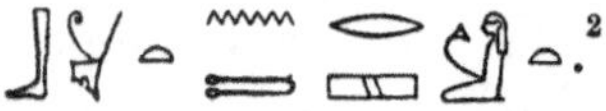.[2] Thereupon the king summoned into his presence all the learned men of his court, and called upon them to choose from among their number a skilled physician that he might go to Bekhten and heal the Queen's young sister; the royal scribe Teḥuti-em-ḥeb was recommended for this purpose, and the king at once sent him off with the envoy from Bekhten to that country. In due course he arrived there and found that the princess of Bekhten was under the influence of

[1] See Rosellini, *Monumenti Storici*, tom. ii., tav. 48; de Rougé, *Journal Asiatique*, 5e série, tom. viii., pp. 201-248; x., pp. 112-168; xi., pp. 509-572; xii., pp. 221-270; and my *Egyptian Reading Book*, pp. xxvii. ff. and 40 ff.

[2] The meaning of this name appears to be "daughter of joy," or "daughter of pleasure," *reshet* being a well-known word for pleasure, joy, and the like; the first part of the name *bent* must represent the Semitic word *bath*, בַּת, "daughter," from בֶּנֶת = בַּנְת.

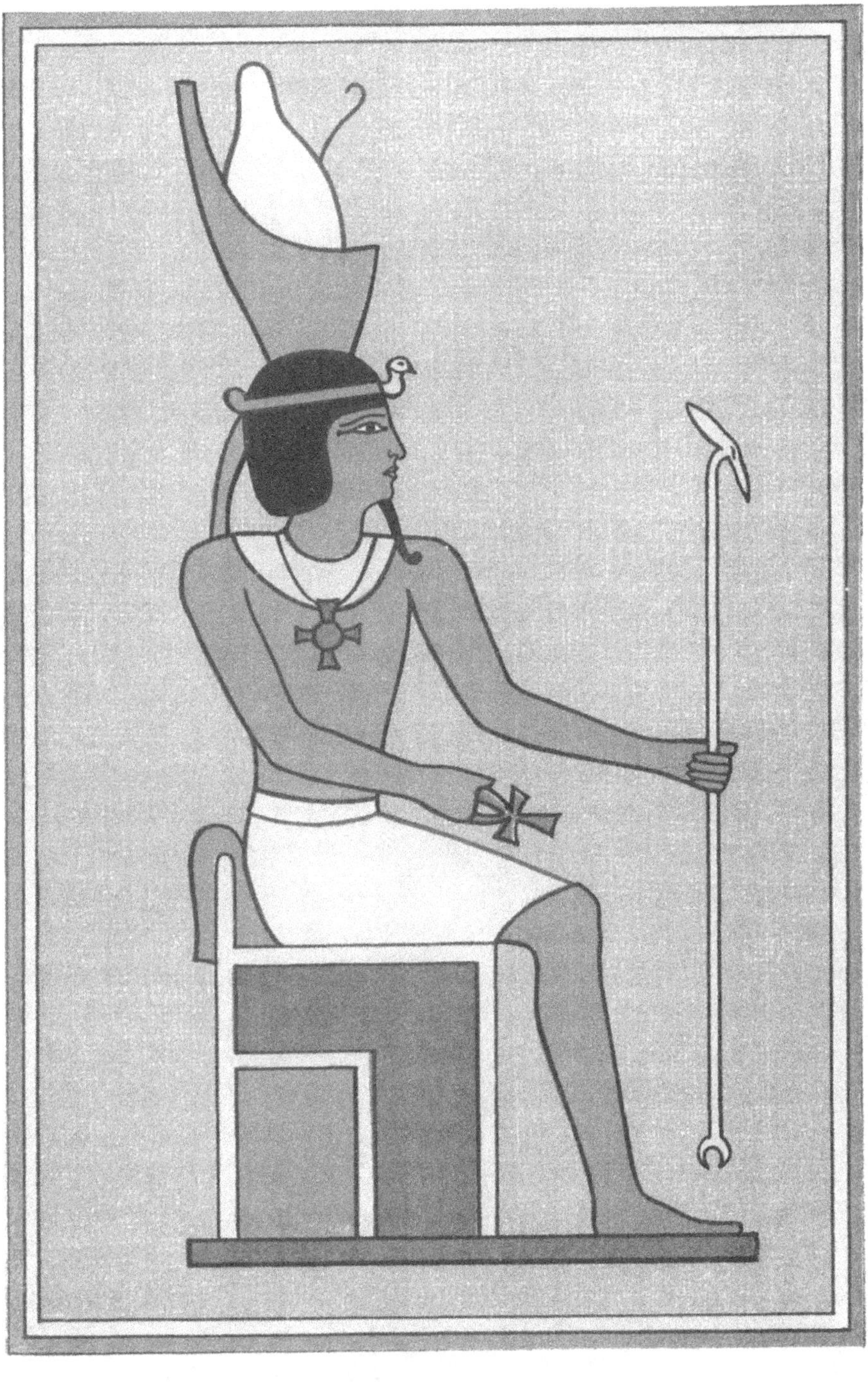

NEFER-ḤETEP.

some evil spirit, which he was powerless either to exorcise or to contend with in any way successfully. When the king of Bekhten saw that his daughter was in no way benefited by the Egyptian scribe, he despatched his envoy a second time to Egypt with the petition that the king would send a god to heal his daughter, and the envoy arrived in Thebes at the time when the king was celebrating the festival of Åmen.

As soon as the king had heard what was wanted he went into the temple of Khensu Nefer-ḥetep, and said to the god, "O my "fair Lord, I have come once again into thy presence [to entreat] "thee on behalf of the daughter of the Prince of Bekhten"; and he entreated him to allow the god Khensu to go to Bekhten, and said, "Grant that thy magical (or, saving) power may go with "him, and let me send his divine Majesty into Bekhten to deliver "the daughter of the Prince of that land from the power of the "demon." The king of Egypt, of course, made his request to a statue of the god Khensu Nefer-ḥetep, and the text of the stele affords reason for believing that the statue was provided with a moveable head, for after each of the petitions of the king we have the words *hen ur sep sen* , which mean that the god "nodded firmly twice" as a sign of his assent to the king's wishes. The head of the statue was worked by some mechanical contrivance which was in the hands of the priests, and there is little doubt that not only the head, but also the arms and hands of statues of the gods were made to move by means of cords or levers that were under the control of the high priest or priest in charge. When the god was unwilling to grant the request of the suppliant the head or limbs of his statue remained motionless. In the present case the king first asked Khensu-Nefer-ḥetep to send Khensu to Bekhten, and when the god had nodded his assent, he further asked him to bestow upon Khensu his *sa* , i.e., his magical, or divine, or saving power.

From this passage we learn that a god was able to transfer his power to work wonders from himself to a statue, and the text tells us that Khensu Nefer-ḥetep bestowed upon the statue of Khensu which was to go to Bekhten a fourfold portion of his power and spirit, . How this was done is not stated, but it is tolerably certain that the statue of Khensu was brought near that of Khensu Nefer-ḥetep, and that the hands of the latter were made to move and to rest upon the head or shoulders of the former four times. That statues of gods were made to move their arms and hands on special occasions is well known, and in proof may be quoted the instance given in the Stele of the Nubian prince Nȧstasenen. Before this prince was crowned king, we are told, he was one of those who were chosen by the priests of Ȧmen, the great god of Napata, to appear in the Temple of the Holy Mountain in order that their god might tell them which was to be king of those of the royal family who were claimants of the throne of Nubia. On a certain day all the young princes assembled in the chamber wherein was the statue of the god, and as they passed before it the arms and hands of Ȧmen-Rā extended themselves and took hold of the prince whom the god had chosen to be his representative upon the throne of Nubia, and he was forthwith acclaimed by the priests and generals of the soldiers, and in due course his coronation took place. It would be idle to assume that statues of gods with moveable heads and limbs were employed in this way in Nubia only, and we may be quite certain that the Nubian priests of Ȧmen-Rā merely followed the customs connected with the election of kings which were current in Egypt. The better informed among the people must have known that the limbs of the statue were moved by mechanism worked by the priests, but the ignorant, who believed that the doubles of the gods animated their statues, would assume that it was they who moved the head and limbs of the statues and gave them a voice to speak.[1]

Returning to the narrative of the Stele we find that the king of Egypt despatched Khensu to Bekhten, where the god arrived after a journey of seventeen months. As soon as he had been welcomed to the country by the Prince of Bekhten and his generals and nobles the god went to the place where the princess

[1] Compare also Maspero, *Annuaire*, 1897, Paris, 1896, pp. 15 ff.; and *Le Double et les Statues Prophétiques*, p. 88.

was, and he found that Bent-reshet was possessed of an evil spirit; but as soon as he had made use of his magical power the demon left her and she was healed straightway. Then that demon spoke to Khensu, and acknowledged his power, and having tendered to him his unqualified submission he offered to return to his own place; but he begged Khensu to ask the Prince of Bekhten to make a feast at which they both might be present, and he did so, and the god, and the demon, and the Prince spent a very happy day together. When the feast was concluded the demon returned to his own land, which he loved, according to his promise. As soon as the Prince recognized the power of Khensu he planned to keep him in Bekhten, and the god actually tarried there for three years, four months, and five days, but at length he departed from his shrine and returned to Egypt in the form of a hawk of gold. When the king saw what had happened, he spoke to the priest, and declared to him his determination to send back to Egypt the chariot of Khensu, and when he had loaded him with gifts and offerings of every kind the Egyptians set out from Bekhten and made the journey back to Thebes in safety. On his return Khensu took all the gifts which had been given to him by the Prince of Bekhten, and carried them to the temple of Khensu Nefer-ḥetep, where he laid them at the feet of the god. Such is the story which the priests of Khensu under the New Empire were wont to relate concerning their god "who could perform mighty "deeds and miracles, and vanquish the demons of darkness."[1]

[1] 

CHAPTER II

ḤĀP, , OR ḤĀPI, , THE GOD OF THE NILE

IT has already been said above that the god Osiris was probably in predynastic times a river-god, or a water-god, and that in course of time he became identified with Ḥāp, or Ḥāpi, the god of the Nile; when such an identification took place we have no means of knowing, but that such was undoubtedly the case is apparent from large numbers of passages in texts of all periods. The meaning of the name of the Nile-god has not yet been satisfactorily explained, and the derivation proposed[1] for it by the priests in the late dynastic period in no way helps us; it is certain that Ḥep, later Ḥāp, is a very ancient name for the Nile and Nile-god, and it is probably the name which was given to the river by the predynastic inhabitants of Egypt. One of the oldest mentions of Ḥep is found in the text of Unås[2] (line 187), where it is said, "Keep watch, O messengers of Qa ( ), keep watch, "O ye who have lain down, wake up, O ye who are in Kenset, "O ye aged ones, thou Great Terror (, Seṭaa-"ur), who comest forth from Ḥep, thou Åp-uat ( ), who "comest forth from the Åsert Tree ( ), the mouth of Unås "is pure." It is important to note that Ḥep is mentioned in connexion with Kenset, ; now Kenset here means the first nome of Egypt, in which were included the First Cataract

[1] *Ḥā-pu*, i.e., "this is the body"; see Brugsch, *Religion*, p. 638.
[2] See Tetà, l. 65.

Ḥāpi, God of the Nile of the South. Ḥāpi, God of the Nile of the North.

and its Islands Elephantine, Sâhel, Philae, Senmut, etc., and thus it would seem as if the Nile-god Ḥep, and Åp-uat, "the opener of the ways," were even in the Vth Dynasty connected with the places in which in later times the Nile was thought to rise. In the lines which follow the extract given above there is an allusion to the food which Unȧs is to eat in the Underworld, and to the Sekhet-Åaru, or Elysian Fields, where he is to live, and it is clear that the Nile-god and Åp-uat were exhorted to send forth the waters of the river from Kenset in order that they might produce grain for the needs of the king. In another passage (Unȧs, line 431) the destroying power of Ḥep is referred to, and it is said that the houses of those who would steal away the king's food shall be given to the thieves (?), and their habitations to GREAT ḤEP, .

Ḥep, or Ḥāpi, is always depicted in the form of a man, but his breasts are those of a woman, and they are intended to indicate the powers of fertility and of nourishment possessed by the god. As the Egyptians divided their country into two parts, the South and the North, so they divided the river, and thus there came into being the god of the Nile of the South and the god of the Nile of the North. An attempt has been made to show that the Nile of the South was that portion of the river which flowed from the Sûdân to Philae, but this is not the case, for the Egyptians believed that the Nile rose in the First Cataract, in the QERTI, 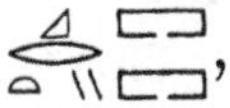, or "Double Cavern," and the Nile of the South was to them that portion of the river which extended from Elephantine to a place some little distance north of the modern Asyût. The god of the South Nile has upon his head a cluster of lotus plants, , whilst he of the North Nile has a cluster of papyrus plants, ; the former is called ḤĀP-RESET, 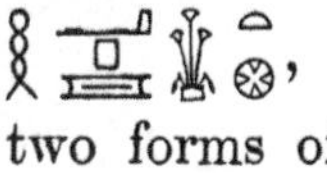, and the latter ḤĀP-MEḤT, 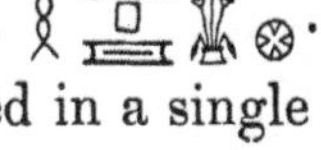. When the two forms of Ḥep or Ḥāpi are indicated in a single figure, the god holds in his hands the two plants, papyrus and lotus, or two vases, from which he was believed to pour out the two Niles. By a pretty device, in which the two Nile-gods are seen tying in a knot the stems of the lotus and papyrus round , the emblem of union, the Egyptians symbolized the union of the South and North, and a slight modification of the design, , was cut upon the sides of the thrones of kings, from very early times, to indicate that the thrones of the South and North had been united, and that the rule of the sovereigns who sat upon such thrones extended over Upper and Lower Egypt. When once Ḥāpi had been recognized as one of the greatest of the Egyptian gods he became rapidly identified with all the great primeval, creative gods, and finally he was declared to be, not only the maker of the universe, but the creator of everything from which both it and all things therein sprang. At a very early period he absorbed the attributes of Nu, , the primeval watery mass from which Rā, the Sun-god, emerged on the first day of the creation; and as a natural result he was held to be the father of all beings and things, which were believed to be the results of his handiwork and his offspring. When we consider the great importance which the Nile possessed for Egypt and her inhabitants it is easy to understand how the Nile-god Ḥāpi held a unique position among the gods of the country, and how he came to be regarded as a being as great as, if not greater than Rā himself. The light and heat of Rā brought life to all men, and animals, and to every created thing, but without the waters of Ḥāpi every living being would perish.

There was, moreover, something very mysterious about Ḥāpi, which made him to be regarded as of a different nature from Rā, for whilst the movement of the Sun-god was apparent to all men, and his places of rising and setting were known to all men, the source of the waters of the Nile-god was unknown. The Egyptians, it is true, at one period of their history, believed that the Nile rose out of the ground between two mountains[1] which lay between the Island of Elephantine and the Island of Philae, but they had no exact idea where and how the Inundation took place,

[1] Herodotus calls these mountains Κρῶφι and Μῶφι, which have, by some, been derived from Qer-Ḥāpi, , and Mu-Ḥāpi, 
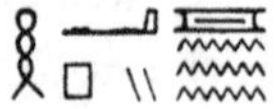

and the rise and fall of the river were undoubtedly a genuine mystery to them. The profound reverence and adoration which they paid to the Nile are well expressed in the following extract from a hymn to the Nile, as found in a papyrus of the XVIIIth or XIXth Dynasty, it reads:—"Homage to thee, O Ḥāpi, thou "appearest in this land, and thou comest in peace to make Egypt "to live. Thou art the Hidden One, and the guide of the dark-"ness on the day when it is thy pleasure to lead the same. Thou "art the Waterer (or Fructifier) of the fields which Rā hath "created, thou givest life unto all animals, thou makest all the "land to drink unceasingly as thou descendest on thy way from "heaven. Thou art the friend of bread and of Tchabu (, "i.e., the god of drink), thou makest to increase and be strong "Neprá (, i.e., the god of corn), thou makest pros-"perous every workshop, O Ptaḥ, thou lord of fish; when the "Inundation riseth, the water-fowl do not alight upon the fields "that are sown with wheat. Thou art the creator of barley, and "thou makest the temples to endure, for millions of years repose "of thy fingers hath been an abomination to thee. Thou art the "lord of the poor and needy. If thou wert overthrown in the "heavens the gods would fall upon their faces, and men would "perish. He causeth the whole earth to be opened by the cattle, "and princes and peasants lie down and rest. . . . . Thy form is "that of Khnemu. When thou shinest upon the earth[1] shouts of "joy ascend, for all people are joyful, and every mighty man "receiveth food, and every tooth is provided with food. Thou art "the bringer of food, thou art the mighty one of meat and drink, "thou art the creator of all good things, the lord of divine meat "(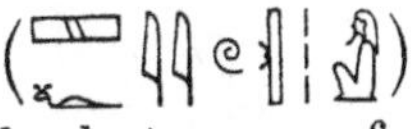), pleasant and choice. . . . Thou makest the "herb to grow for the cattle, and thou takest heed unto what is "sacrificed unto every god. The choicest incense is that which "followeth thee, thou art the lord of the two lands. Thou fillest "the storehouses, thou heapest high with corn the granaries, and "thou takest heed to the affairs of the poor and needy. Thou

[1] The form of Khnemu here referred to is Khnemu-Rā.

"makest the herb and green things to grow that the desires "of all may be satisfied, and thou art not reduced thereby. Thou "makest thy strength to be a shield for man."

The following passage is of particular interest, for it proves that the writer of the hymn felt how hopeless it was to attempt to describe such a mighty and mysterious god as the Nile. "He "cannot be sculptured in stone, he is not seen in the images on "which are set the crowns of the South and the North and the "uraei, neither works nor offerings can be made to him. He "cannot be brought forth from his secret abodes, for the place "wherein he is cannot be known. He is not to be found in "inscribed shrines, there is no habitation which is large enough "to contain him, and thou canst not make images of him in thy "heart. . . . . His name in the Ṭuat is unknown, the God doth "not make manifest his forms, and idle are imaginings concerning "them."[1] From this passage it is clear that the Egyptians paid peculiar honour to Ḥāpi, and that he was indeed regarded as the "Father of the gods," 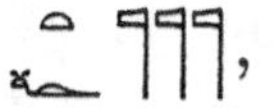, and "the creator of things which exist," 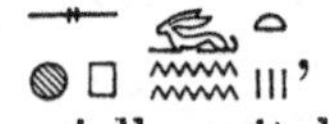, and that the epithet of "Vivifier," , was especially suitable to him. It must be noted too that in one aspect Ḥāpi was identified with Osiris, and this being so Isis became his female counterpart, and it is probable that, when offerings were made to Osiris, i.e., Osiris-Apis, or Serapis, in late dynastic times, when every sanctuary of this double god was called

1 
The hieratic text is published by Birch, *Select Papyri*, pll. xx. ff.; see also Maspero, *Hymne au Nil*, Paris, 1868; and my *First Steps in Egyptian*, p. 204.

a "Serapeum," Ḥāpi was held to be included among the forms of the god. From a number of passages found chiefly in comparatively late texts we learn that the festival of the annual rise of the Nile was celebrated throughout Egypt with very great solemnity, and statues of the Nile-god were carried about through the towns and villages that men might honour him and pray to him. When the inundation was abundant the rejoicings which took place after the performance of the religious ceremonies connected with it were carried out on a scale of great magnificence, and all classes kept holiday. The ancient Egyptian festival has its equivalent among the Muḥammadans in that which is celebrated by them about June 17, and is called *Lêlet al-Nuḳta*, i.e., Night of the Drop, because it is believed that on that night a miraculous drop falls from heaven into the Nile and makes it to rise.

It has been said above that Osiris was identified with Ḥāpi, and this being so, Isis was regarded as the female counterpart of Ḥāpi, but there is little doubt that in very early dynastic times other goddesses were assigned to him as wives or sisters. Thus of Ḥāpi of the South the female counterpart was undoubtedly Nekhebet, but then this goddess was only a form of Isis in dynastic times, whatever she may have been in the predynastic period. In the north of Egypt the ancient goddess Uatch-urà, , appears to have been the equivalent of Nekhebet in the South. But Ḥāpi was also identified with Nu, the great primeval water abyss from which all things sprang, and as such his female counterpart was Nut, or one of her many forms. The oldest form of this goddess appears to be Mut, , or Muit, , or Māuit, , who is mentioned in the text of Unàs (line 181). The text generally shows that the deceased king is identified with Ḥāpi the Nile-god, and he thus became master of the Nile-goddesses of the South and North, for it is said, "O Rā, be thou good to Unàs this "day as yesterday. Unàs has been united to the goddess Mut, "and he hath breathed the breath of Isis, and he hath been joined "to the goddess Nekhebet, and he hath been the husband of the

"Beautiful One," 

. The mention of Mut, Isis, and Nekhebet in this connexion proves that all these three goddesses were intimately related, and it is clear that even when the text of Unȧs was written the ancient goddesses Mut and Nekhebet were identified with Isis. We should expect Uatchet to appear in connexion with Nekhebet, but this goddess must have been absorbed in Isis long before the copies of the Pyramid Texts which we have were written.

CHAPTER III

THE TRIAD OF ĀBU (ELEPHANTINE), KHNEMU, , SATET, 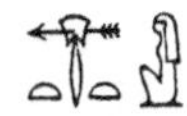, AND ĀNQET, 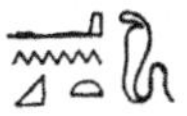

KHNEMU, the first member of the great triad of Ābu, or Elephantine, is one of the oldest gods of Egypt, and we find him mentioned in the text of Unȧs in such a way as to show that even at the remote period of the reign of that king his cult was very old. The views which the Egyptians held concerning this god changed somewhat in the course of their long history, but the texts show that Khnemu always held an exalted position among the ancient gods of their country, and we know from Gnostic gems and papyri that he was a god of great importance in the eyes of certain semi-Christian sects for some two or three centuries after the birth of Christ. It is probable that Khnemu was one of the gods of the predynastic Egyptians who lived immediately before the archaic period, for his symbol was the flat-horned ram, and that animal appears to have been introduced into Egypt from the East; he disappears from the monuments before the period of the XIIth Dynasty. In the text of Unȧs the name of Khnemu is found in a section which contains twenty-five short paragraphs, the greater number of which must certainly date from a period far older than the reign of this king, for the forms of the words and the language are very archaic, and few of the names of the serpents which are addressed in them occur in later texts. Khnemu is represented on the monuments in the form of a ram-headed man who usually holds in his hands the sceptre , and the emblem of life, . He wears the White Crown, to which are sometimes attached plumes, uraei, a disk, etc.; in one example quoted by Lanzone[1] he has the head of a hawk, which indicates that he possessed a solar aspect. As a water-god he is seen with outstretched hands over which flows water, and he is sometimes seen with a jug, , above his horns, which indicates his name. The name of Khnemu is connected with the root *khnem*, , "to join, to unite," and with *khnem*, , "to build"; astronomically the name refers to the "conjunction" of the sun and moon at stated seasons of the year,[2] and we know from the texts of all periods that Khnemu was the "builder" of gods and men. He it was who, according to the statements which were made by his priests at Elephantine, the chief seat of his worship, made the first egg from which sprang the sun, and he made the gods, and fashioned the first man upon a potter's wheel, and he continued to "build up" their bodies and maintain their life.

The portion of Egypt in which the worship of Khnemu was supreme extended from Thebes to Philae, but the principal sanctuaries of the god were at the two ends of the First Cataract, i.e., on Elephantine on the north and on Philae and the adjoining islands on the south. He was the god *par excellence* of the First Cataract, throughout which, with his female counterpart Satet and the local Nubian goddess Ānqet, he was worshipped from the earliest dynasties; the goddess Satet was identified as a form of the star Sepṭ, , of Elephantine and of Menḥet, lady of Latopolis. An examination of the texts makes it clear that Khnemu was originally a water or river-god, and that in very early times he was regarded as the god of the Nile and of the annual Nile-flood, and as such he bore the name of QEBḤ, , and appeared as the ram-headed god, . In the passages quoted by Signor Lanzone[3] and Dr. Brugsch[4] he is called the "builder of "men and the maker of the gods and the Father who was in the "beginning," ; "maker of "things which are, creator of things which shall be, the source

[1] Op. cit., pl. 336, No. 4.
[2] Brugsch, *Religion*, p. 290.
[3] *Dizionario*, p. 957.
[4] *Religion*, p. 291.

THE GOD KHNEMU FASHIONING A MAN UPON A POTTER'S TABLE, BEHIND HIM STANDS THOTH MARKING HIS SPAN OF LIFE.

"of things which exist, Father of fathers, and Mother of mothers," ; "Father of "the fathers of the gods and goddesses, lord of created things from "himself, maker of heaven, and earth, and the Ṭuat, and water, "and mountains;" , and "raiser up of heaven upon its four pillars and "supporter of the same in the firmament," .

Khnemu united within himself the attributes of the four great gods Rā, Shu, Qeb or Seb, and Osiris, and in this aspect he is represented in pictures with four rams' heads upon a human body; according to Dr. Brugsch these symbolize fire, air, earth, and water. When depicted with four heads Khnemu was the type of the great primeval creative force, and was called SHEFT-ḤĀT, . The first ram's head was the head of Rā, and symbolized Khnemu of Elephantine; the second was the head of Shu, and symbolized Khnemu of Latopolis; the third was the head of Seb, and symbolized Khnemu of Ḥet-urt; and the fourth was the head of Osiris, and symbolized Khnemu as lord of Hypselis. As SHEFT-ḤĀT Khnemu was the lord of Hermopolis Magna and of Thmuis, and possessed all the attributes which have been enumerated above. From another text we learn that the four rams also symbolized the life of Rā, the life of Shu, the life of Seb, and the life of Osiris, and that the ram of Rā gave him sovereignty over the South and North, and identified him with the Ram of Mendes, Ba-neb-Ṭeṭṭu, .

The principal shrines of KHNEMU-RĀ were situated at Sunnu, , the modern Syene, on the Island of Ābu, ,[1] the modern Elephantine, and on the Island of Senmut, , the modern Biggeh, which marked the frontier of Ta-kens, , or Nubia. He appears in these as the lord of all the

[1] Or . The Island was also called , "Qebḥet."

South of Egypt, and is associated with Isis, the great goddess of the South, and in fact is to the South of Egypt exactly what Ptaḥ-Tanen, who was associated with Nephthys, was to the Delta and the North of Egypt. To him was ascribed every attribute of Rā, and thus he is described as the god who existed before anything else was, who made himself, and who was the creative power which made and which sustains all things. When the cult of Khnemu-Rā became general in the south his priests increased the importance of their god by identifying him with Nu, 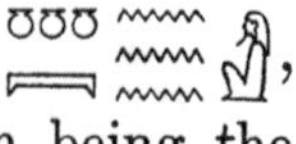, the great primeval god of the watery abyss, and from being the local river-god of the Nile in the First Cataract he became the god Ḥāp-ur, , or the Nile of heaven; in the latter aspect he was said to dwell in the Island of Senmut.

The views which were held about Khnemu-Rā as god of the earthly Nile are best illustrated by the famous inscription which was discovered on a rock on the Island of Sâhal in 1890 by the late Mr. Charles Wilbour. According to it, in the xviiith year of king Tcheser , who has been identified with the third king of the IIIrd Dynasty, the whole of the region of the South, and the Island of Elephantine, and the district of Nubia were ruled by the high official Māṭer, 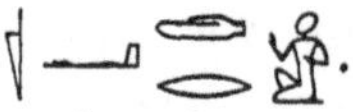. The king sent a despatch to Māṭer informing him that he was in great grief by reason of the reports which were brought to him into the palace as he sat upon his throne, and because for seven years there had been no satisfactory inundation of the Nile. As the result of this grain of every kind was very scarce, vegetables and garden produce of every kind could not be found, and in fact the people had very little food to eat, and they were in such need that men were robbing their neighbours. Men wished to walk out, but could not do so for want of strength; children were crying for food, young men collapsed through lack of food, and the spirits of the aged were crushed to the earth, and they laid themselves down on the ground to die. In this terrible trouble king Tcheser remembered the god I-em-ḥetep, , the son of Ptaḥ of the South Wall, who, it would seem, had once delivered Egypt from a similar calamity, but as his help was no longer forthcoming Tcheser asked his governor Māṭer to tell him where the Nile rose, and what god or goddess was its tutelary deity. In answer to this despatch Māṭer made his way immediately to the king, and gave him information on the matters about which he had asked questions. He told him that the Nile flood came forth from the Island of Elephantine whereon stood the first city that ever existed; out of it rose the Sun when he went forth to bestow life upon man, and therefore it is also called "Doubly Sweet Life," . The spot on the island out of which the river rose was the double cavern (?) Qerti, 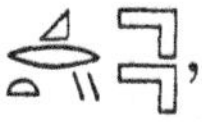, which was likened to two breasts, 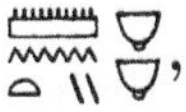, from which all good things poured forth; this double cavern was, in fact, the "couch of the Nile," 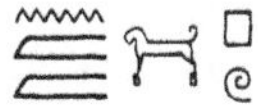 , and from it the Nile-god watched until the season of inundation drew nigh, and then he rushed forth like a vigorous young man, and filled the whole country.[1] At Elephantine he rose to a height of twenty-eight cubits, but at Diospolis Parva in the Delta he only rose seven cubits. The guardian of this flood was Khnemu, and it was he who kept the doors that held it in, and who drew back the bolts at the proper time. Māṭer next went on to describe the temple of Khnemu at Elephantine, and told his royal master that the other gods in it were Sepṭ (Sothis), Ānuqet, Ḥāpi, Shu, Seb, Nut, Osiris, Horus, Isis, and Nephthys, and after this he enumerated the various products that were found in the neighbourhood, and from which offerings ought to be made to Khnemu. When the king heard these words he offered up sacrifices to the god, and in due course went into his temple to make supplication before him; finally Khnemu appeared before him, and said, "I am Khnemu the Creator. My hands rest upon "thee to protect thy person, and to make sound thy body. I "gave thee thine heart. . . . I am he who created himself. I am "the primeval watery abyss, and I am Nile who riseth at his will

[1] His inundation is thus described 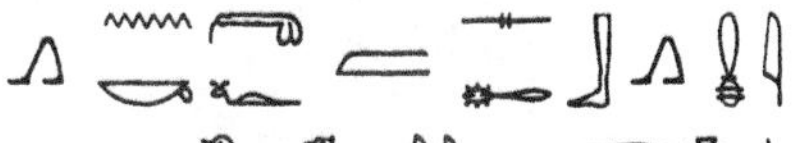
.

"to give health for me to those who toil. I am the guide and "director of all men, the Almighty, the father of the gods, "Shu, the mighty possessor of the earth." Finally the god promised that the Nile should rise every year, as in olden time, and described the good which should come upon the land when he had made an end of the famine. When Khnemu ceased to speak king Tcheser remembered that the god had complained that no one took the trouble to repair his shrine, even though stone lay near in abundance, and he immediately issued a decree in which it was ordered that certain lands on each side of the Nile near Elephantine should be set apart for the endowment of the temple of Khnemu, and that a certain tax should be levied upon every product of the neighbourhood, and devoted to the maintenance of the priesthood of the god; the original text of the decree was written upon wood, and as this was not lasting, the king ordered that a copy of it should be cut upon a stone stele which should be set in a prominent place.[1] It is nowhere said that the god kept his promise to Tcheser, but we may assume that he did. The form of the narrative of the Seven Years' Famine summarized above is not older than the Ptolemaïc period, but the subject matter belongs to a much older time, and very probably represents a tradition which dates from the Early Empire.

We have seen that the spirit, or soul, of Khnemu pervaded all things, and that the god whose symbol was a ram was the creator of men and gods, and in connexion with this must be noted the fact that, together with Ptaḥ, he built up the edifice of the material universe according to the plans which he had made under the guidance and direction of Thoth. As the architect of the universe he possessed seven forms which are often alluded to in texts; they are sometimes represented in pictures, and their names are as follows:—

, KHNEMU NEḤEP, "Khnemu the Creator."

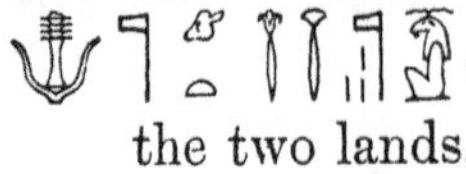, KHNEMU KHENTI-TAUI, "Khnemu, governor of the two lands."

[1] For the hieroglyphic text see Brugsch, *Die biblischen sieben Jahre der Hungersnoth*, Leipzig, 1891.

THE GODDESS SATI.

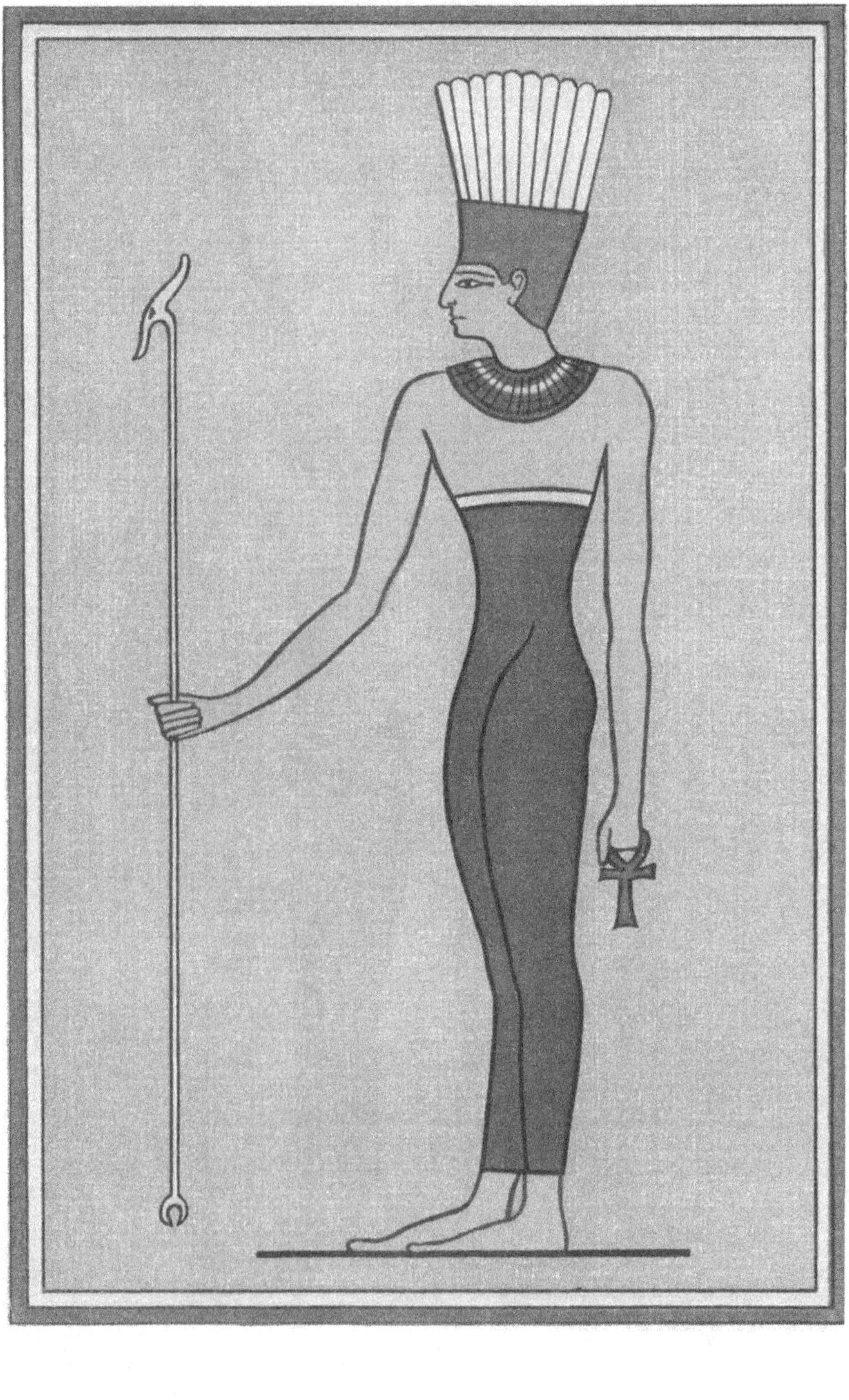

THE GODDESS ANQET.

, KHNEMU SEKHET ÅSHSEP-F, "Khnemu, weaver of his light."

, KHNEMU KHENTI PER-ĀNKH, "Khnemu, Governor of the House of Life."

, KHNEMU NEB-TA-ĀNKHTET, "Khnemu, lord of the Land of Life."

, KHNEMU KHENTI NETCHEMTCHEM ĀNKHET, "Khnemu, Governor of the House of Sweet Life."

, KHNEMU NEB, "Khnemu, Lord."

SATI, , or SATET, ,[1] or, , was the principal female counterpart of Khnemu, and was worshipped with him at Elephantine, where she was a sister goddess of Ānqet. Her name appears to be connected with the root *sat*, , "to shoot, to eject, to pour out, to throw," and the like, and *sat* is also used in connexion with the scattering abroad and sowing of seed, and with the sprinkling of water; thus at any rate at one period she must have been regarded as the goddess of the inundation, who poured out and spread over the land the life-giving waters of the Nile, and as the goddess of fertility. She sometimes carries in her hands a bow and arrows, a fact which suggests that in her earliest form she was a goddess of the chase; according to Dr. Brugsch, she was identified by the Greeks with their goddess Hera.[2] In many pictures of the goddess we see her wearing the crown of the South and a pair of horns, which prove that she was a form of ÅST-SEPṬ, , or ISIS-SOTHIS. At the time when the temple of Dendera was built she was identified with the local goddess Isis-Hathor of Dendera, with ÅMENT, , of Thebes, and MENĀT, , of Heliopolis, and RENPIT of

[1] This goddess must not be confounded with the SATET, , who is represented in the form of a woman, and bears upon her head the *Utchat* , and was a local Alexandrian form of Isis; see Lanzone, *Dizionario*, p. 1124.

[2] *Religion*, p. 299.

Memphis, the goddess of the year, etc. In the text of Pepi I. Sati is mentioned (line 297) under the form Sethȧt, 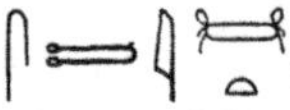, and we see from the context that in that early period the goddess possessed a temple at Elephantine. The dweller in Ṭep, , is said to have aided the king, who "has censed himself and "performed his ceremonies of purification with a vessel of wine, "which hath come from the vine of the god.[1] . . . Seb stretcheth "out his hand to Pepi and guideth him through the gates "of heaven, a god in his beautiful place, a god in his place, ", and behold Sethȧt washeth "him with the water which is in her four vases in Ābu" (Elephantine). The mention of Ṭep shows that there was some connexion between the goddess of the city of Per-Uatchet and the goddess of Elephantine long before the period of the VIth Dynasty. In the preface to the cxxvth Chapter of the *Book of the Dead* the deceased enumerates the various sacred places which he has visited, and says, "I have been in the waters of the stream, and I "have made offerings of incense. I have guided myself to the "Shenṭet Tree of the [divine] children, and I have been in Ābu "(Elephantine) in the Temple of Satet," . This is the only mention of Sati, or Satet, in the Theban Recension of the *Book of the Dead*, but it is of great importance as showing that the temple of the goddess at Ābu was regarded as one of the principal holy places in Egypt. It has already been said that Sati was connected by the Egyptians with the star Sepṭ, , wherein dwelt the soul of Isis, and from this point of view Sati was a form of Isis, and became in consequence a female counterpart of Osiris; this fact will account for the mention of Sati in the *Book of the Dead*. The centre of the worship of Sati appears to have been the Island of Sâhal, ساحل, which lies about two miles to the south of Elephantine, in the First Cataract.

1 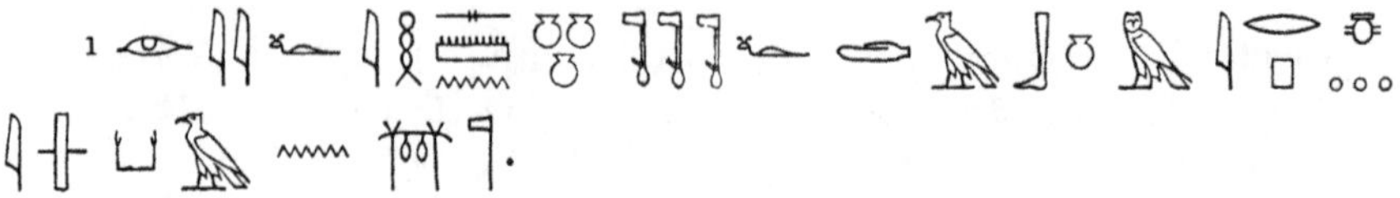

ĀNQET, , was the third member of the triad of Elephantine, which consisted of Khnemu, Sati, and Ānqet, and she seems to have possessed many of the attributes of her sister-goddess Sati. In pictures Ānqet is represented in the form of a woman who holds in her hands the sceptre , and the emblem of "life," ; she wears on her head a crown of feathers which are arranged in such a way as to suggest a savage origin. She appears to have been originally a goddess of some island in the First Cataract, but in early dynastic times she was associated with Khnemu and Sati, and her worship was common throughout Northern Nubia; later the centre of her worship was at Sâhal, and she was regarded as a goddess of that island, and was called "lady of Satet," , NEBT SATET. Her temple there seems to have been named "Åmen-heri-åb," , but it is clear from the appearance of Åmen's name in its title that it cannot be older than the XVIIIth Dynasty. At Philae another temple was built in her honour, and it bore the name of "Pa-mer," , and it seems that from this island southwards she was identified with Nephthys. In very early times Osiris, Isis, and Nephthys were associated in a triad, and as Osiris was a form of Khnemu, and Khnemu a form of Osiris, and Isis and Sati were sister goddesses, it followed as a matter of course that Ānqet should be identified with Nephthys. According to Dr. Brugsch,[1] the name "Ānqet" is derived from the root *ānq*, , "to surround, to embrace," and the like, and has reference to the goddess as the personification of the waters of the Nile which embrace, and nourish, and fructify the fields. Among the pictures of Ānqet reproduced by Signor Lanzone[2] is one in which the goddess is seen seated in a shrine with a table of offerings before her; the shrine is placed in a boat, at each end of which is an aegis of a goddess, who wears on her head a disk and horns, , and is probably Isis; the boat floats on a stream from which runs a small arm. The goddess is styled "Ānqet, lady of Satet (i.e.,

[1] *Religion*, p. 302. [2] *Dizionario*, pl. xliv. ff.

"the Island of Sâhal), lady of heaven, mistress of all the gods," . In another picture she is seen suckling a young king whose neck she embraces with her left arm, and in a text which accompanies another representation she is described as the "giver of life, and of all power, and of all "health, and of all joy of heart," .

We have now to consider two very important forms of KHNEMU, that is to say, 1. Khnemu who, under the form of ḤER-SHEF, was worshipped at Herakleopolis Magna, and 2. Khnemu who, under the form of Osiris, was worshipped at Mendes.

1. Khnemu as ḤER-SHEF, , or ḤER-SHEFT, , was worshipped at Suten-ḥenen, or Ḥenen-su, , or Ḥet-Ḥenen-su, , under the form of a horned, ram-headed man, and wore the White Crown with plumes, a disk, and uraei attached. The Greeks transcribed the name Ḥer-shef by Ἀρσαφης, and as Plutarch says that it means "strength, bravery," it is clear that in his time the latter portion of it, *shef* or *sheft*, was derived from *shef*, or *sheft*, , , "strength, power, bravery," and the like. On the other hand two variant forms of the name of the god are:—ḤER-SHE-F, , i.e., "He who is on his lake," and ḤERI-SHĀ-F, , i.e., "He who is on his sand." The first form would connect the god with Lake Moeris, and the second refers to him as an aspect or phase of Osiris, who bears this title in Chapter cxli., line 109, and Chapter cxlii., line 24, of the *Book of the Dead*. In Chapter xlii., line 14, the god ĀA-SHEFIT, , is mentioned, and it is probable that he also is to be identified with Osiris. Ḥenen-su, the centre of the worship of Khnemu under the form of Ḥer-shefi, is often referred to in the *Book of the Dead*, and a number of important mythological events are said to have taken place there. Thus it was here that Rā rose for the first time when the heavens and the earth were created (xvii. 7-9), and it was this rising which formed the first great act

ḤERU-SHEFIT, THE LORD OF SUTEN-ḤENEN

THE GODDESS ANIT.

of creation, because as soon as Rā rose he separated the earth from the sky. Osiris was here crowned lord of the universe, and here his son Horus assumed the throne of his father left vacant by the death of Osiris. When Rā ordered the goddess Sekhet to go forth and destroy mankind because they had mocked him and had spoken lightly of his age, she started on her journey from Ḥenen-su. To this place also returned Set after his defeat by Horus, who had wounded him severely, and Osiris was believed to have taken a spade and covered over with earth the blood [1] which dropped from him and his fiends, and to have buried the bodies of those whom Horus had slain. It is this act which is alluded to by the deceased when he says (Chapter i., line 30), "I have grasped the spade on "the day of digging the earth in Suten-ḥenen (or Ḥenen-su)." Elsewhere (xvii. 49) we have an allusion to the "day of the union of the two earths," , *smat taui*, which is explained by the stronger expression, "the completing of the two earths," 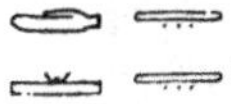, *temṭ taui*. The text which follows says that it refers to "the mingling of earth with earth in the coffin of Osiris, "who is the Soul that dwelleth in Ḥenen-su, and the giver of "meat and drink, and the destroyer of wrong, and the guide of "the everlasting paths, i.e., Rā himself." An entirely different matter in connexion with the two earths is mentioned in line 129, where there is an allusion to "Shu, the strengthener of the two "lands in Ḥenen-su," 
, and there is little doubt that the words refer to the part which Shu played at the Creation, when he held up with his arms and hands the sky which Rā had made to separate it from the earth.

At Ḥenen-su lived the Great Bennu, 
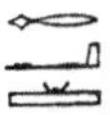 (Chapter cxxv. 18), and in the neighbourhood dwelt the awful "Crusher of Bones," 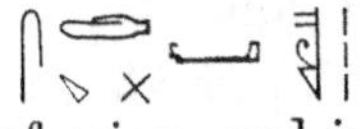, Seṭ-qesu, who is mentioned in the Negative Confession, and in this place the souls of the beatified found a place of rest in the realm of Osiris in this

[1] Naville, *Heracleopolis*, p. 8.

place (cxxxvii.A, 25). Near Ḥenen-su were the two great mythological lakes called ḤEḤ, , and UATCH-URÀ, ; the variant forms of the first of these are:—SEMU-ḤEḤ, , and UTET-ḤEḤ, . The sanctuary of Osiris at Ḥenen-su was called Nareref, , or "Ȧn-ruṭ-f," , i.e., "the place where nothing groweth," and it was entered by a door on the south side called RE-STAU, (Chapter xvii. 52); in some portion of the sanctuary was the Ȧat-en-shet, , or "region of fire," and near it was the torture chamber named "Sheni," . This chamber was guarded by a god with the face of a greyhound and the eyebrows of a man, and he sat watching at the "Elbow," , of the "Lake of Fire" for the dead who passed that way, and as he remained himself unseen he was able to seize upon them and tear out their hearts and devour them. The texts show that there was great difference of opinion about the name of this monster, which is given as MĀṬES, , and BEBA, , and ḤERI-SEP-F, .

These facts, which are derived chiefly from the xviith Chapter of the *Book of the Dead*, prove that Ḥenen-su, or Herakleopolis, possessed a system of theology of its own, and that this system must be very ancient, but whether it is older than that of Heliopolis it is impossible, at present, to say definitely. What is certain, however, is that the great local god Ḥer-shef was sufficiently important to be regarded as a form of the great ram-god Khnemu. It must be noted also that Ḥer-shef was a solar god, and that as such many of the titles of Rā were bestowed upon him; it is said that he lit up the world with his beams, that his right eye was the sun and his left eye the moon, that his soul was the light, and that the north wind which gave life to all came forth from his nostrils. He is said, moreover, like Rā, to be "One."[1] In a figure of the god reproduced by Lanzone[2] he has

[1] *Religion*, p. 304. [2] *Dizionario*, p. 552.

four heads; one is the head of a bull, one that of a ram, and two are the heads of hawks. Above these are the characteristic horns of Khnemu which are surmounted by two plumes and four knives. These four heads represent the four gods who formed Khnemu of Ḥenen-su, i.e., Rā, Shu, Seb, and Osiris, and thus he might be identified with Rā-Tem of Heliopolis, or Ȧmen-Rā of Thebes, and either of these compound gods might be worshipped as one of his forms.

The female counterpart of Ḥer-shef possesses various names, and as she was identified with various goddesses this is not to be wondered at; her chief attributes were those of Hathor and Isis, and her local name was ĀṬET, , or MERSEKHNET, . Many of her attributes, however, were those of Net (Neith), , and Meḥ-urt, and ḤEQET, and ȦNIT, ; as the last named goddess she was the sister of KA-ḤETEP, i.e., Osiris. According to a text quoted by Dr. Brugsch,[1] Āṭet, the local goddess of Ḥenen-su, in the form of a cat slew Āpep, the great serpent of darkness. From this it is clear that she was a female counterpart of Rā, who, as we knew from the xviith Chapter of the *Book of the Dead*, took the form of a cat, and slew Āpep, the prince of darkness, who had taken the form of a monster serpent. The text says, "I am the CAT (MȦU,), which "fought (?) hard by the Persea Tree (Ȧsheṭ,), in Ȧnnu, on "the night when the foes of NEB-ER-TCHER[2] () were "destroyed." The explanation of this statement which follows the question, "Who then is this?" is "The male CAT is Rā himself, "and he is called 'Mȧu' by reason of the words of the god SA,[3] "who said about him, '[Who] is like (*mȧu*,), unto him?' "and thus his name became 'Mȧu' (i.e., Cat)." The fight here referred to is the first battle which the god of light waged against

1 *Dict. Géog.*, p. 399.

2 A form of Osiris, both as the lord of the universe, and as lord of his re-united body.

3 The god of Reason, or Intelligence.

the fiends of darkness at Ȧnnu, after which he rose in the form of the sun upon this world.

Finally, in connexion with the city Ḥenen-su we must note that there existed in the temple there a shrine which was dedicated to the goddess NEḤEB-KAU , who was worshipped there in the form of a huge serpent. She was one of the Forty-two Assessors of the Hall of Maāti (Negative Confession, line 40), and in the Papyrus of Nu (cxlix. 5) the deceased says that she has "stablished his head for him;" elsewhere she seems to be mentioned as a form of Nut, and to be the female counterpart of the serpent god NĀU.[1] She was a goddess who provided for the dead meat and drink, not the material offerings of earth, but the divine *tchefaut* food, , or , or *tcheftchef*, , which may be compared to the nectar and ambrosia on which the gods of Olympus lived, and which grew in the portion of the Sekhet-Ȧaru, or Elysian Fields, called TCHEFET, . What this food was cannot be said, but the word *tchef* or *tcheftchef* is connected with *tcheftchef*, 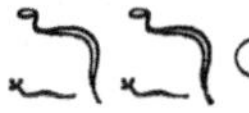, "to shed light," and *tchefetch* , the "pupil of the eye" of Rā, i.e., the "Eye of Horus," , which is mentioned so often in the Pyramid Texts, and it must then either be a celestial food made of light, or some product of the mythological Olive Tree, , Baqet, which grew in Ȧnnu (Unȧs, line 170). In any case Neḥeb-kau was a very ancient goddess who was connected with the Elysian Fields of the Egyptians, and she is often depicted in the form of a serpent with human legs and arms, and sometimes with wings also, and she carries in her hands one or two vases containing food for the deceased. In the text of Unȧs (line 599) she is referred to in the following passage:—"Homage to thee, O Horus, in the domains of Horus! Homage "to thee, O Set, in the domains of Set! Homage to thee, thou

1 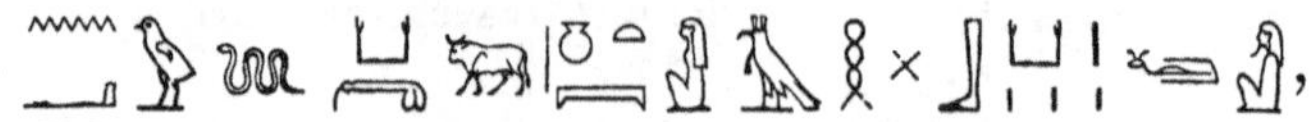, Chap. cxlix. Ȧat x., l. 6.

"god Åar ( ), in Sekhet-Åarer ( ). Homage to thee, Netetthåb ( ), "daughter of these four gods who are in the Great House. Even "when the command of Unås goeth not forth, uncover yourselves "in order that Unås may see you as Horus seeth Isis, as Neḥebu-"kau ( ) seeth Serqet, as Sebek seeth Net "(Neith), and as Set seeth Netetthåb."

Among the greatest of the festivals at Ḥenen-su were those in honour of Neḥeb-kau which, according to Dr. Brugsch,[1] were celebrated on the first of Tybi, that is to say, nine days after the "Festival of Ploughing the Earth," Khebs-ta, , when men began to plough the land after the subsidence of the waters of the Inundation. Under the heading "Osiris" reference is made to the performance of the ceremony of "ploughing the earth," which gave the name to the festival, but it may be noted in passing that it appears to have had a double signification, i.e., it commemorated the burial of Osiris, and it symbolized the ploughing of the land throughout the country preparatory to sowing the seed for the next year's crop. Other festivals were those of Bast, which were celebrated in the spring of the Egyptian year, and those of the "hanging out of the heavens," , i.e., the supposed reconstituting of the heavens each year in the spring. Finally, in connexion with Ḥenen-su may be mentioned the God Ḥeneb,[2] , for whom in the Saïte period the official Ḥeru planted two vineyards; of the attributes of this god we know nothing, but it is probable that he was supposed to preside over grain and other products of the land. In several passages of the *Book of the Dead* we have the word *ḥenbet* , "corn-lands, provisions," and the like, and in Chapter clxxx. line 29, a god called Ḥenbi, , is mentioned, and he appears to be identical with the Ḥeneb of the stele of Ḥeru.

[1] *Religion*, p. 305.

[2] Brugsch, *Dict. Géog.*, pp. 852, 1364.

Coming now to the second great form of Khnemu, viz., that under which he was worshipped at Mendes, we find that at a very early date he was identified with the great god of that city, and was known as BA-NEB-ṬEṬṬU, , i.e., the Ram, lord of Ṭeṭṭu. Now as the word for "soul" in Egyptian was *Ba*, and as a name of the ram was also *Ba*, the title Ba-neb-Ṭeṭṭu was sometimes held to mean the "Soul, the lord Ṭeṭṭu," and this was the name at Mendes of the local form of Khnemu, whose symbol there, as elsewhere, was a ram. Ba-neb-Ṭeṭṭu, whose name was corrupted by the Greeks into Μένδης, and Tamai al-Amdîd[1] by the Arabs, was said to be the "living soul of Rā, the holy Sekhem "who dwelleth within Ḥāt-meḥit, 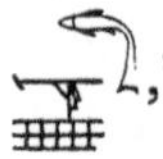," and the "life of Rā," 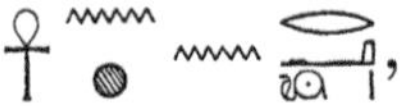, and he was worshipped throughout the sixteenth nome from the earliest times. He was regarded as the virile principle in gods and men, and is styled, "King of the South and "North, the Ram, the virile male, the holy phallus, which stirreth "up the passions of love, the Ram of rams, whose gifts are brought "forth by the earth after it hath been flooded by the Nile, the "Soul, the life of Rā, who is united with Shu and Tefnut, the One "god, who is mighty in strength, who riseth in the heavens with "four heads, who lighteth up the heavens and the earth (like Rā), "who appeareth in the form of the Nile like (Osiris), who vivifieth "the earth (like Seb), and who formeth the breath of life for all "men, the chief of the gods, the lord of heaven and the king of "the gods."[2] Ba-neb-Ṭeṭṭu was originally a local form of Rā, but he subsequently was made to include within himself not only the Soul of Rā, but the Souls of Osiris, and Seb, and Shu. These four Souls are reproduced by Signor Lanzone,[3] and appear in the form of four rams, the horns of each being surmounted by a uraeus; they are described as "The Soul of Seb, lord of Ḥet-

[1] تمى الامديد. As a matter of fact the first portion of this name represents Θμουίς, the Greek name of one portion of the ancient city of Ṭeṭṭu, and the second —"al-Amdîd"—is a corruption of Ba-neb-Ṭeṭṭu, which became Ba-neb-Ṭeṭ, then Ba-n-Ṭeṭ, and finally Man-Ṭeṭ, Mendes.

[2] See Brugsch, *Religion*, p. 309.

[3] *Dizionario*, pl. 68.

The God Ba-neb-Ṭāṭāu, ṭhe Ram God of Mendes.

"teft; the Soul of Osiris, lord of Ta-sent; the Soul of "Shu, lord of Ȧnit; and the Soul of Rā, dweller in . . . . ." In allusion to these Souls the Ram of Mendes is sometimes described as the Ram with "Four faces (or, heads) on one neck,"
[1]

The female counterpart of Ba-neb-Ṭeṭṭu was ḤĀT-MEḤIT, , and her son by the god was Ḥeru-pa-kharṭ, the dweller within Ṭeṭṭu, . This goddess is always represented as a woman, who bears on her head the fish, , which is the symbol of the nome, . She is described as the dweller in Ȧtemet, 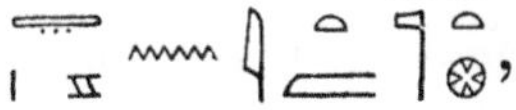, and she was in some way connected with Punt, but the centre of her worship in Egypt was the city of Mendes, of which she is called the "Mother;" she was, of course, a form both of Isis and Hathor, and as such was called "the Eye of Rā, the lady of heaven, and the mistress of the gods." In late dynastic times, when Ba-neb-Ṭeṭṭu was especially regarded as the Soul of Osiris, and when the other aspects of the god were not considered of so much importance, Ḥāt-Meḥit was wholly identified with Isis, and her son "Harpocrates, the dweller in Mendes," became to all intents and purposes "Horus, the son of Isis," by Osiris. Thus we see that the local god of Mendes, who was originally a form of Rā, the Sun-god by day, was merged into Osiris, the Sun-god by night; the priests, however, were careful to preserve the peculiar characteristics of their god, i.e., virility and the power to create, and to recreate, and they did so by declaring that the phallus and the lower part of the backbone, , of Osiris were preserved in the temple of the city which bore the name of Per-khet, 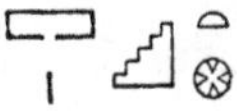, i.e., the "House of the staircase." The Ram of Mendes was then a form of "Osiris as the Generator," , as he is called

[1] Piehl in *Recueil*, tom. ii., p. 30; de Rougé, *Géog. Ancienne*, p. 114.

in Chapters cxli. and cxlii. of the *Book of the Dead*, and the popularity of his cult in the Delta was probably due to the elaborate phallic ceremonies which were celebrated at Mendes and in the neighbourhood annually.

Before the close of the Ptolemaic period, however, some calamity seems to have fallen upon Mendes, and her sanctuary was forsaken and her god forgotten; on the other hand, the portion of the city which was known by the name Thmuis, Θμουις, survived, and was sufficiently important in Christian times to possess a bishop of its own. The Copts called the place **ⲑⲙⲟⲩⲉⲱⲥ**, or **ϯⲃⲁⲕⲓ ⲑⲙⲟⲩⲓ**, and a Bishop of Thmoui was present both at the Council of Nice and the Council of Ephesus.[1]

Finally, we have to note that Khnemu as a form of Shu, i.e., as a personification of the wind, and atmosphere, and the supporter of heaven, and the light of the Sun and Moon, was worshipped at several places in Upper Egypt and in Heliopolis under the form of a ram; the centre of his worship at this last-named place was Ḥet-Benben, or the "House of the Obelisk." At Latopolis he absorbed the attributes of Tem, and he was identified with Nu, the maker of the universe and creator of the gods; similarly, he was regarded as a form of Ptaḥ and of Ptaḥ-Tanen, and his female counterparts were Menḥit, Sekhet, and Tefnut. In a hymn which is inscribed on the walls of the temple of Esna he is called, "The "prop of heaven who hath spread out the same with his hands," and the sky is said to rest upon his head whilst the earth beareth up his feet. He is the creator of heaven and earth and of all that therein is, and the maker of whatsoever is; he formed the company of the gods, and he made man upon his potter's wheel. He is the One god, the source from which sprang the regions on high, the primeval architect, the maker of the stars, the creator of the gods, who was never born, and the begetter or maker of his own being, whom no man can understand or comprehend. Many other passages in the inscriptions at Esna ascribe to him naturally all the powers and attributes[2] of Ptaḥ. Among several interesting

[1] Amélineau, *La Géographie de l'Égypte*, p. 501.

[2] For the enumeration of several of them see Brugsch, *Religion*, p. 504.

addresses to the god may be mentioned that wherein it is said, "Thou hast raised up heaven to be a dwelling-place for thy soul, "and thou didst make the great deep that it might serve as a "hiding-place for thy body." Finally, it may be noted that as Khnemu-Shu absorbed the attributes of Nu, Rā, Ptaḥ, Thoth, etc., so also several great goddesses, besides those already mentioned, were identified with his female counterparts, e.g., Nut, Net (Neith), Nebuut, etc.

CHAPTER IV

ÅTEN, , THE GOD AND DISK OF THE SUN

IN connexion with the Sun-gods of Egypt and with their various forms which were worshipped in that country must be considered the meagre facts which we possess concerning ÅTEN, who appears to have represented both the god or spirit of the sun, and the solar disk itself. The origin of this god is wholly obscure, and nearly all that is known about him under the Middle Empire is that he was some small provincial form of the Sun-god which was worshipped in one of the little towns in the neighbourhood of Heliopolis, and it is possible that a temple was built in his honour in Heliopolis itself. It is idle to attempt to describe the attributes which were originally ascribed to him under the Middle or Early Empire, because the texts which were written before the XVIIIth Dynasty give us no information on the subject. Under the XVIIIth Dynasty, and especially during the reigns of Åmen-ḥetep III. and his son Åmen-ḥetep IV., he was made to usurp all the titles and attributes of the ancient solar gods of Egypt, Rā, Rā-Ḥeru-khuti, Horus, etc., but it does not follow that they originally belonged to him. In the Theban Recension of the *Book of the Dead*, which is based upon the Heliopolitan, we find ÅTEN mentioned by the deceased thus:—"Thou, O Rā, "shinest from the horizon of heaven, and Åten is adored when he "resteth (or setteth) upon this mountain to give life to the two "lands."[1] Hunefer says to Rā, "Hail, Åten, thou lord of beams "of light, [when] thou shinest all faces (i.e., everybody) live;"

[1] See my *Chapters of Coming Forth by Day* (Translation), p. 7; for the passages which follow see the *Vocabulary*, s.v. *åten*, p. 48.

Nekht says to Rā, "O thou beautiful being, thou dost renew "thyself and make thyself young again under the form of Åten;" Ani says to Rā, "Thou turnest thy face towards the Underworld, "and thou makest the earth to shine like fine copper. The dead "rise up to see thee, they breathe the air and they look upon thy "face when Åten shineth in the horizon;" ". . . . I have come "before thee that I may be with thee to behold thy Åten daily;" "O thou who art in thine Egg, who shinest from thy Åten," etc.

These passages show that Åten, at the time when the hymns from which they are taken were composed, was regarded as the material body of the sun wherein dwelt the god Rā, and that he represented merely the solar disk and was the visible emblem of the great Sun-god. In later times, owing to protection afforded to him by Åmen-ḥetep III., the great warrior and hunter of the XVIIIth Dynasty, other views were promulgated concerning Åten, and he became the cause of one of the greatest religious and social revolutions which ever convulsed Egypt. After the expulsion of the Hyksos, Åmen, the local god of Thebes, as the god of the victorious princes of that city, became the head of the company of the gods of Egypt, and the early kings of the XVIIIth Dynasty endowed his shrine with possessions, and gave gifts to his priesthood with a lavish hand. In spite of this, however, some of these kings maintained an affection for the forms of the Sun-god which were worshipped at Heliopolis, and Thothmes IV., it will be remembered, dug out the Sphinx from the sand which had buried him and his temple, and restored the worship of Rā-Harmachis, and he was not the only monarch who viewed with dismay the great and growing power of the priests of Åmen-Rā, the "king of the gods" at Thebes.

Åmen-ḥetep III., the son of Thothmes IV., held the same views as his father in this respect, and he was, apparently, urged to give effect to them by his wife Thi, 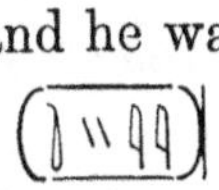, the daughter of Iuåa, , and Thuåu, , who was a foreigner and who was in no way connected with the royal house of Egypt. Having married this lady, he gave her as dowry the frontier city of Tchāru, , and her natural ability, coupled with the favour of her husband, made her chief of all the royal wives, and a great power in the affairs of the government of the country. It has been thought by some that she was a native of the country near Heliopolis, and it is possible that she herself was a votary of Åten, but be that as it may, she appears to have supported the king in his determination to encourage the worship of this god. At an early period in his reign he built a temple in honour of Åten at Memphis, and later he built one at Thebes, quite close to the great sanctuary of Åmen-Rā, the priests of whom were, of course, powerless to resist the will of such an active and able king. Soon after

The beams of Åten illumining the names of Khu-en-Åten and his family.

his marriage with Thi, Åmen-ḥetep III. dug, in his wife's city of Tchāru, a lake, which was about 6000 feet long by 1000 feet broad,[1] and on the day of the festival when the water was allowed to flow into it, he sailed over it in a boat called "Åten-neferu," , i.e., the "Beauties of Åten;" the name of the boat is a clear proof of his devotion to the god Åten. Åmen-ḥetep IV., the son of Åmen-ḥetep III. by the foreign lady Thi, not only held the religious views of his father, but held them very strongly, and his

[1] 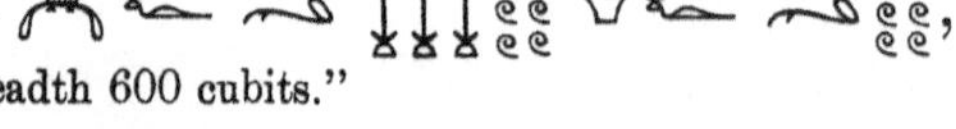, i.e., "its length 3600 cubits, its breadth 600 cubits."

life shows that he must have been from his youth up an adherent of the worship of Àten; it is supposed, and with much probability, that the intensity of his love for Àten and his hatred for Àmen-Rā were due to his mother's influence.

Àmen-ḥetep IV. succeeded his father without difficulty, even though his mother was not a member of the royal family of Egypt, and for the first few years of his reign he followed the example of the earlier kings of his dynasty, and lived at Thebes, where he no doubt ruled according to his mother's wishes; he offered up sacrifices to Àmen-Rā at the appointed seasons, and was, outwardly at least, a loyal servant of this god, whose name formed a part of his name as "son of the Sun." We may note in passing, that he had adopted on his accession to the throne the title "High-"priest of Rā-Ḥeru-khuti, the exalted one in the horizon, in his "name of Shu who is in Àten,"  , which is a clear proof that he was not only a worshipper of Rā-Harmachis, another of the forms of the Sun-god of Heliopolis, but also that he endorsed the views and held the opinions of the old College of Priests at Heliopolis, which made Shu to be the creator of the gods, and which assigned the disk (Àten) to him for a dwelling-place. Àmen-ḥetep's titles as lord of the shrines of the cities of Nekhebet and Uatchet,[1] and as the Horus of gold[2] also prove his devotion to a Sun-god of the South whose attributes were the same as the Sun-god of Heliopolis. During the early years of his reign at Thebes he built a massive Benben, 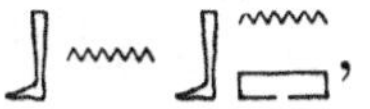, in honour of Rā-Harmachis at Thebes, and it is probable that he took the opportunity of restoring or enlarging the temple of Àten which had been built by his father; at the same time we find that he worshipped both Àmen and Àten, the former in his official position as king, and the latter in his private capacity. It was, however,

1 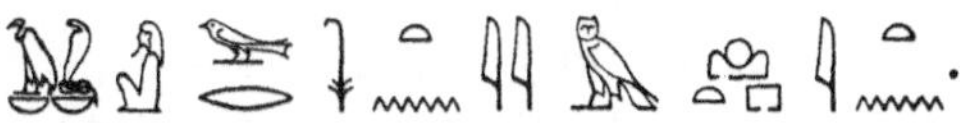.

2 .

impossible for the priests of Åmen-Rā to tolerate the presence of the new god Åten and his worship in Thebes, and the relations between the king and that powerful body soon became strained. On the one hand the king asserted the superiority of Åten over every god, and on the other the priests declared that Åmen-Rā was the king of the gods. As, however, Åmen-Rā was the centre of the social life of Thebes, and his priests and their relatives included in their number the best and greatest families of the capital city, it came to pass that the king found himself and the worship of Åten wholly unsupported by the great mass of its population, whose sympathies were with the old religion of Thebes, and by those who gained their living in connexion with the worship of Åmen-Rā. The king soon realized that residence in Thebes was becoming impossible, and in the fifth year of his reign he began to build a new capital on the east bank of the Nile, near a place which is marked to-day by the Arab villages of Haggi Ḳandîl and Tell el-'Amarna; he planned that it should include a great temple to Åten, a palace for the king, and houses for all those who were attached to the worship of Åten and were prepared to follow their king there.

Whilst the new capital was building the dispute between the king and the priests of Åmen-Rā became more severe, and matters were much aggravated by Åmen-ḥetep IV. when he promulgated the edict for obliterating the name of Åmen and his figure from every monument in Egypt. At length the king left Thebes and took up his abode in his new capital, which he called "Khut-Åten," 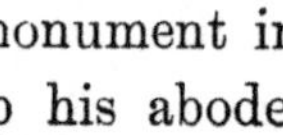, i.e., "Horizon of Åten," and as a sign of the entire severance of his connexion with the traditions of his house in respect of Åmen-Rā he discarded his name "Åmen-ḥetep" and called himself Khut-en-Åten 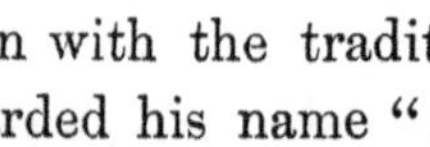, i.e., "Glory of Åten," or, "Spirit of Åten." At the same time he changed his Horus name of "Exalted One of the double plumes" to "Mighty Bull, beloved of Åten" (or, lover of Åten), and he adopted as lord of the shrines of Nekhebet and Uatchet the title of "Mighty one of sovereignty in Khut-Åten," and as the Horus of gold he styled himself, "Exalter of the name of Åten." The temple of Åten at

Khut-Àten was, like that at Heliopolis, called Ḥet Benben, , a name which probably means "House of the Obelisk;" it was begun on a very large scale, but was never finished. It contained many altars whereon incense was burnt and offerings were laid, but no sacrifices of any kind were offered up on them. The high-priest of Àten assumed the title of the high-priest of Rā at Heliopolis, Ur-maàu, , and in many respects the new worship was carried on at Khut-Àten by means of many of the old forms and ceremonies of the Heliopolitan priesthood; on stated occasions the king himself officiated. The worship of Àten as understood by Àmen-ḥetep IV. was, however, a very different thing from the ancient worship of Àten, for whereas that was tolerant the new worship was not. It is clear from the reliefs which have been found in the city of Khut-Àten that Àten was regarded as the giver of life, and the source of all life on this earth, and that his symbols were the heat and light of the sun which vivified and nourished all creation. Àten was also the one physical body of the Sun, and the creed of Àten ascribed to the god a monotheistic character or oneness, of which it denied the existence in any other god. This being so, the new religion could neither absorb nor be absorbed by any other; similarly, Àten could neither absorb nor be absorbed by the other gods of Egypt, because he had nothing in common with them. Attempts have been made to prove that the Àten worship resembled that of the monotheistic worship of the Hebrews, and to show that Àten is only another form of the name

Àmen-ḥetep IV. and his Wife adoring Àten.

Âdôn, i.e., the Phoenician god אָדֹן, whom the Greeks knew as Ἄδωνις; but as far as can be seen now the worship of Àten was something like a glorified materialism, which had to be expounded by priests, who performed ceremonies similar to those which belonged to the old Heliopolitan sun-worship, without any connexion whatsoever with the worship of Yahweh, and a being of the character of Âdôn, the local god of Byblos, had no place in it anywhere. In so far as it rejected all other gods, the Àten religion was monotheistic, but to judge by the texts which describe the power and works of Àten, it contained no doctrines on the unity or oneness of Àten similar to those which are found in the

Àmen-ḥetep IV. seated on his throne beneath the Disk.

hymns to Rā, and none of the beautiful ideas about the future life, with which we are familiar from the hymns and other compositions in the *Book of the Dead*.

The chief source of our knowledge of the attributes ascribed to Àten is obtained from the hymns to this god which Àmen-ḥetep IV. caused to be inscribed on his monuments, and from one of them which has twice been published in recent years[1] we

[1] First by Bouriant in *Mémoires de la Mission*, tom. i., pp. 2 ff., and later, with numerous corrections of Bouriant's text and a running commentary by Mr. Breasted, in *De Hymnis in Solem sub rege Amenophide IV. conceptis*, Berlin (no date).

obtain the following extracts. The hymn is prefaced by these words:—

"1. A hymn of praise to Ḥeru-khuti (Harmachis), who "springeth up joyfully in the horizon in his name of 'Shu who is "in the Disk,' and who liveth for ever and for ever, Åten the "Living One, the Great One, he who is [celebrated] in the thirty "year festival, the lord of the orbit (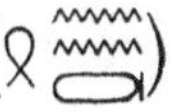) of the sun, the lord "of the sun, the lord of heaven, the lord of earth, the lord of the "House of Åten in the city of Khut-Åten, 2. by the king of the "South and of the North, who liveth by Maāt, the Lord of the Two "Lands, (Nefer-kheperu-Rā-uā-en-Rā),[1] the son of the Sun, who "liveth by Maāt, the lord of crowns, (Khu-en-Åten),[2] who is great "in the duration of his life, 3. and by his great royal wife, his darling, "the Lady of the Two Lands, (Nefert-iti, Nefer-neferu-Åten),[3] "the living one, the strong one for ever." The hymn proper begins after the words, "He (i.e., the king) saith, 4. 'Thy rising is "'beautiful in the horizon of heaven, 5. O thou Åten, who hadst "'thine existence in primeval time. 6. When thou risest in the "'eastern horizon thou fillest every land with thy beauties, 7. thou "'art beautiful to see, and art great, and art like crystal, and art "'high above the earth. 8. Thy beams of light embrace the lands, "'even every land which thou hast made. 9. Thou art as Rā, "'and thou bringest [thyself] unto each of them, 10. and thou "'bindest them with thy love. 11. Thou art remote, but thy beams "'are upon the earth. 12. So long as thou art in the heavens day "'shall follow in thy footsteps. 13. When thou settest in the "'western horizon the earth is in darkness, and is like a being that "'is dead. 14. They lie down and sleep in their habitations, "'15. their heads are covered up, and their nostrils are stopped, "'and no man can see his neighbour, 16. and all their goods and

[1] These titles mean something like, "Beauty of the creations of Rā, the only one of Rā."

[2] I.e., "Glory of Åten."

[3] The proper name is Nefert-iti, and her title means "Beauty of the beauties of Åten."

" 'possessions may be carried away from under their heads without
" 'their knowing it. 17. Every lion cometh forth from his den,
" '18. and serpents of every kind bite; 19. the night becometh
" 'blacker and blacker, 20. and the earth is silent because he who
" 'hath made them hath sunk to rest in his horizon.

"21. When thou risest in the horizon the earth lightens, and
"when thy beams shine forth it is day. 22. Darkness taketh to
"flight as soon as thy light bursteth out, and the Two Lands keep
"festival daily. 23. Then [men] wake up and stand upon their
"feet because thou hast raised them up, 24. they wash themselves,
"and they array themselves in their apparel, 25. and they lift up
"to thee their hands with hymns of praise because thou hast risen.
"26. [Over] all the earth they perform their work. 27. All beasts
"and cattle repose in their pastures, 28. and the trees and the
"green herb put forth their leaves and flowers. 29. The birds
"fly out of their nests, and their wings praise thy Ka as they fly
"forth. 30. The sheep and goats of every kind skip about on
"their legs, 31. and feathered fowl and the birds of the air also
"live [because] thou hast risen for them. 32. The boats float
"down and sail up the river likewise, 33. for thy path is opened
"when thou risest. 34. The fish in the stream leap up towards
"thy face, 35. and thy beams shine through the waters of the
"great sea.

"36. Thou makest male seed to enter into women, and thou
"causest the liquid seed to become a human being. 37. Thou
"makest the man child to live in the body of his mother.
"38. Thou makest him to keep silent so that he cry not, 39. and
"thou art a nurse to him in the womb. 40. Thou givest breath
"that it may vivify every part of his being. 41. When he goeth
"forth from the belly, on the day wherein he is born, 42. thou
"openest his mouth that he may speak, 43. and thou providest
"for him whatsoever is necessary. 44. When the chick is in the
"the egg, and is making a sound within the shell, 45. thou givest
"it air inside it so that it may keep alive. 46. Thou bringest it
"to perfection so that it may split the eggshell, 47. and it cometh
"forth from the egg to proclaim that it is a perfect chick,
"48. and as soon as it hath come forth therefrom it runneth

" about on its feet. 49. How many are the things which thou " hast created !

" 50. There were . . . . . in the face of the One God, and his " . . . . . had rest. 51. Thou didst create the earth at thy will " when thou didst exist by thyself, 52. and men and women, and " beasts and cattle, and flocks of animals of every kind, 53. and " every thing which is upon the earth and which goeth about on " its feet, 54. and everything which is in the air above and which " flieth about with wings, 55. and the land of Syria and Nubia,

Åmen-ḥetep IV. and his Wife and Daughter.

" and Egypt. 56. Thou settest every man in his place, 57. and " thou makest for them whatsoever they need. 58. Thou pro- " videst for every man that which he should have in his storehouse, " and thou computest the measure of his life. 59. They speak in " tongues which are different [from each other], 60. and their " dispositions (or characteristics) are according to their skins. " 61. Thou who canst discern hast made the difference between " the dwellers in the desert to be discerned.

" 62. Thou hast made Ḥāpi (i.e., the Nile) in the Ṭuat, 63. and

" thou bringest him on according to thy will to make rational " beings to live, 64. inasmuch as thou hast made them for thyself, " 65. O thou who art the lord of all of them, and who dost remain " with them. 66. Thou art the lord of every (?) land, and thou " shinest upon them, 67. thou art Àten of the day, and art " revered in every foreign land (?), 68. and thou makest their " lives. 69. Thou makest Ḥāpi in heaven to come down to them, " 70. and he maketh his rushing waters to flow over the hills like " the great green sea. 71. and they spread themselves abroad " and water the fields of the people in their villages. 72. Thy " plans (or, counsels) are doubly beneficent. 73. Thou art the " Lord of eternity, and thou thyself art the Nile in heaven, and " all foreign peoples and all the beasts on all the hills 74. go about " on their feet [through thee]. 75. Ḥāpi (i.e., the Nile) cometh " from the Ṭuat to Egypt, 76. and thou givest sustenance to its " people and to every garden, and 77. [when] thou hast risen they " live for thee.

" 78. Thou hast made the seasons of the year so that they " may cause the things which thou hast made to bring forth, " 79. the winter season bringeth them cold, and the summer " season fiery heat. 80. Thou hast created the heavens which are " far extending that thou mayest rise therein and mayest be able " to look upon all which thou didst create when thou didst exist " by thyself, 81. and thou dost rise in thy creations as the living " Àten, 82. and thou dost rise, and dost shine, and dost depart on " thy path, and dost return. 83. Thou didst create [the forms] " of created things in thyself when thou didst exist alone. 84. " Cities, towns, villages and hamlets, roads and river[s], 85. from " these every eye looketh upon thee, 86. for thou art the Àten of " the day and art above the earth. 87. Thou journeyest through " that which existeth in thine Eye. 88. . . . . 89. " Thou art in my heart, 90. and none knoweth thee except thy " son (Nefer-kheperu-Rā-uā-en-Rā), 91. and thou makest him to " be wise and understanding through thy counsels and through " thy strength. 92. The earth is in thy hand, inasmuch as thou " hast made them (i.e., those in it). 93. When thou risest man-

"kind live; and when thou settest they die. 94. As long as thou "art in the sky they live in thee, 95. and the eyes of all are upon "thy beauties until thou settest, 96. and they set aside their "work of every kind when thou settest in the west. 97. Thou "risest and thou makest to grow . . . . for the king. "98. . . . . from the time when thou didst lay the foundations "of the earth, 99. and thou didst raise them up for thy son who "proceeded from thy members." [Here follow two lines wherein the names and titles of the king are repeated.]

The above version of the hymn to Åten will serve to illustrate the views held by the king and his followers about this god, and may be compared with the hymns to Rā, which are quoted in the section on the forms of the Sun-god, when it will be seen that many of the most important characteristics of hymns to sun-gods are wanting. There is no mention of enemies or of the fiends, Āpep, Sebåu, and Nåk, who were overcome by Rā when he rose in the eastern horizon; no reference is made to Kheperå, or to the services which Thoth and Maāt were believed to render to him daily; and the frequent allusions to the Māṭet and Sektet Boats in which Rā was thought to make his journey over the sky are wholly omitted. The old myths which had grown up about Rā are ignored, and the priests of Åten proclaimed with no uncertain voice the unity of their god in terms which provoked the priests of Åmen to wrath. Åten had existed for ever, they said, he was beautiful, glorious, and self-existent, he had created the sun and his path, and heaven, and earth, and every living being and thing therein, and he maintained the life in man and beast, and fed all creatures according to his plans, and he determined the duration of their life. Everything came from Åten, and everything depended upon him; he was, moreover, everlasting. From the absence of any mention of the "gods" or of the well-known great gods of Egypt it is evident that they wished to give a monotheistic character to the worship of Åten, and it was, manifestly, this characteristic of it which made the king and his god detested at Thebes; it accounts for the fact that Åmen-ḥetep IV. felt it to be necessary to build a new capital for himself and his god, and supplies us with the reason why he did not settle in one of the ancient religious centres of his kingdom. We should expect that, as he styled himself the high-priest of Ḥeru-khuti (i.e., Harmachis), he would have taken up his abode in Memphis or Heliopolis, where this god was greatly honoured, but as he did not, we are driven to conclude that there was in the worship of Åten and in the doctrines of his priests something which could neither brook nor tolerate the presence of another god, still less of other gods, and that that something must have been of the nature of monotheism.

Now although the hymn quoted above gives us an idea of the views held by Åmen-ḥetep IV. and his adherents concerning Åten, it is impossible to gather from it any very precise imformation about the details of the belief or doctrine of Åten, but it is clear that in practice the religion was of a sensuous character, and eminently materialistic. Incense was burnt freely several times in the day, and the hymns sung to Åten were accompanied by the sounds of the music of harps and other instruments, and the people vied with each other in bringing gifts of fruit, and flowers, and garden produce to lay on the altars which were never drenched with the blood of animals offered up for sacrifice. The worship of Åten was of a joyous character, and the surroundings among which it was carried on were bright and cheerful. The mural decorations in the temple were different from those of the older temples of Egypt, for they were less severe and less conventional, and they were painted in lively colours; in fact, the artists employed by Åmen-ḥetep IV. threw off many of the old trammels of their profession, and indulged themselves in new designs, new forms, new colours, and new treatment of the subjects which they wished to represent. We may see from the remains of their wall decorations that the artists of the city of Khut-Åten made one great step in advance, that is to say, they introduced shading into their painting, and it is greatly to be regretted that it was retraced later; it was only during the reign of Åmen-ḥetep IV. that the Egyptian artist ever showed that he understood the effects of light and shade in his work. The texts and inscriptions which were placed upon the walls relate to the glory and majesty and beneficence of Åten, and everywhere are seen representations of the visible emblem of the god. The form in which he is depicted is that of the solar disk, from which proceed rays, the ends of which terminate in hands wherein are the emblems of life, ☥, and sovereignty, 𓌀; in the bas-reliefs and frescoes we see these human-handed rays shining upon the king, and his queen and family, and upon the cartouches containing the names of himself and of his queen Nefert-ith. The simple interpretation of such scenes is that the sun is the source of all life and of everything which supports it upon earth, but it is probable that the so-called Ȧten heresy was in some way founded upon the views which the Ȧtenites held about this method of representing their god. Be this as it may, Ȧmen-ḥetep IV. loved to be depicted with the human-handed rays falling upon him, and whatever his doctrines of Ȧten were he preached them with all the enthusiasm of an Oriental fanatic, and on special occasions he himself officiated as high-priest of the cult. The wisdom of his policy is open to doubt, but there is no reason for regarding him as anything but an earnest and honest propagandist of a new creed.

Now, as the king changed his religion and his name, so he also caused his own form and figure when represented in bas-reliefs to be changed. In the earlier monuments of his reign he is depicted as possessing the typical features of his father and of others of his ancestors, but at Tell el-'Amarna his physical characteristics are entirely different. Here he is portrayed with a very high, narrow, and receding forehead, a large, sharp, aquiline nose, a thin, weak mouth, and a large projecting chin, and his head is set upon a long and extremely slender neck; his chest is rounded, his stomach inflated, his thighs are large and broad, and in many respects his figure resembles that of a woman. It is impossible that such representations of the king would be permitted to appear in bas-reliefs in his city unless he approved of them, and it is clear that he did approve, and that his officials understood that he approved of this treatment of his person at the hands of sculptors and artists, for some of the high officials were themselves represented in the same manner. Still, some of the drawings of the king must be regarded as caricatures, but whether intentional or otherwise cannot be said.

For a few years Åmen-ḥetep IV. led a life of great happiness and enjoyment in his new capital, and his whole time seems to have been passed in adorning it with handsome buildings, fine sculptures, and large gardens filled with trees and plants of every kind; he appears to have bestowed gifts with a lavish hand upon his favourites, who it must be admitted, were his officials who seconded his wishes and gave effect to them. Life at Khut-Åten was joyous, and there is no evidence that men troubled themselves with thoughts about death or the kingdom of Osiris; if they did, they made no mention of them in their hymns and inscriptions.

On the other hand Åmen-ḥetep IV. did not, or could not, abolish the characteristic funeral customs and beliefs of his country, and the tombs of the adherents of Åten bear witness to the fact. The king caused a tomb to be hewn out of the rock in the mountains near the town, on its eastern side, and it contained, when discovered in 1892 by the natives, the things which are usually found in tombs of men of high rank. The sarcophagus was broken in pieces, but scattered about the mummy-chamber and along the corridor which led to it were numbers of objects and fragments of objects made of the beautiful purple and blue glazed faïence which is so characteristic of the reign of Åmen-ḥetep IV. The body of the king must have been mummified, and on it must have been laid the same classes of amulets that are found on the royal mummies at Thebes. Portions of several granite *ushabtiu* figures were also found, a fact which shows that those who buried the king assumed he would enjoy a somewhat material life in Sekhet-ḥetepet and Sekhet-Åarru in the kingdom of Osiris. That Åmen-ḥetep IV. thought little about his death and burial is proved by the state of his tomb, which shows that he made no attempt to prepare it for the reception of his body when the need should arise. This is the more strange because he had caused his eldest daughter Åten-merit, 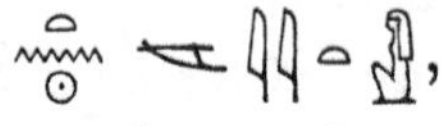, to be buried in it, and he must have known from sad experience what great preparations had to be made, and what complicated ceremonies had to be performed when a royal personage was laid to rest. The tombs of the adherents of Àten are very disappointing in many ways, though they possess an interest peculiar to themselves. From the scenes painted on their walls it is possible to obtain an idea of the class of buildings which existed in the city of Khut-Àten, and of the arrangements of its streets and gardens, and of the free manner in which the various members of the royal family moved about among the people. The king's tomb was never finished, and the remains of the greater number of the paintings on its walls show that they were executed not for him but for his eldest daughter, who has already been mentioned; the chief subject chosen for illustration is the worship of Àten, and both the scenes and the texts accompanying them represented that the god was adored by every nation in the world.

It is, unfortunately, not known how old the king was when he died, but he must have been a comparatively young man, and his reign could not have been so long as twenty years. In the ten or twelve years of it which he lived at Khut-Àten he devoted himself entirely to the building of his new capital and the development of the cult of Àten, and meanwhile the general condition of Egypt was going from bad to worse, the governors of Egyptian possessions in Syria and Palestine were quarrelling among themselves, strong and resolute rebels had risen up in many parts of these countries, and over and above all this the infuriated priesthood of Àmen-Rā were watching for an opportunity to restore the national god to his proper place, and to set upon the throne a king who would forward the interests of their brotherhood. This opportunity came with the death of Àmen-ḥetep IV., when Tut-ānkh-Àmen, a son of Àmen-ḥetep III. by a concubine, ascended the throne; he married a daughter of Àmen-ḥetep IV., who was called Ānkh-s-en-pa-Àten, but she changed her name into Ānkh-s-en-Àmen, and both the new king and queen were worshippers of the great god of Thebes. Tut-ānkh-Àmen at once began to restore the name and figure of Àmen which his father-in-law had cut out from the monuments, and began to build at Thebes; very soon after his accession he came to terms with the priests of Àmen, and in due course removed his court to the old capital. On the death of Ṭut-ānkh-Åmen, a "superintendent of the whole stud of Pharaoh" of the name of Åi ascended the throne by virtue of his marriage with Thi, who was in some way related to the family of Åmen-ḥetep IV.; before Åi became king he was a follower of Åten, and built himself a tomb at Khut-Åten, which was ornamented after the manner of those of the adherents of this god, but as soon as he had taken up his abode at Thebes and begun to reign over Egypt he built another tomb in the Valley of the Tombs of the Kings at Thebes.

The decoration of the sarcophagus which he placed in the latter tomb makes it quite certain that when he made it he had rejected the cult of Åten, and that he was, at all events outwardly, a loyal follower of the god Åmen-Rā. On the death of Åi several pretenders to the throne rose up in Egypt, and a period of anarchy followed. Of the details of the history of this period nothing is known, and the only certain fact about it is that the power of the XVIIIth Dynasty was broken, and that its downfall was certain. During the reigns of Tut-ānkh-Åmen and Åi the prosperity of the city Khut-Åten declined rapidly, and as soon as the period of anarchy which followed their reigns began its population left it, little by little, and its downfall was assured; the artists and workmen of all kinds who had obtained work there under Åmen-ḥetep found their occupation gone, and they departed to Thebes and the other cities whence they had come. Under the reign of Ḥeru-em-ḥeb the decay of the city advanced and it became generally deserted, and very soon after men came from far and near to carry off, for building purposes, the beautiful white limestone blocks which were in the temple and houses. Ḥeru-em-ḥeb was the nominee of the priests of Åmen-Rā, and he used all his power and influence to stamp out every trace of the worship of Åten, and succeeded. Thus Åmen-Rā conquered Åten, Thebes once more became the capital of Egypt, the priests of Åmen regained their ascendancy, and in less than twenty-five years after the death of Åmen-ḥetep IV. his city was deserted, the sanctuary of his god was desecrated, his followers were scattered, and his enemies were in undisputed possession of the country.

CHAPTER V

THE GREAT COMPANY OF THE GODS OF HELIOPOLIS

A PERUSAL of the Pyramid Texts reveals the fact that the priests of Heliopolis believed in the existence of three companies of gods, and that to each company they assigned at least nine gods; in certain cases a company contained eleven, twelve, or more gods. In the text of Unȧs (line 222 ff.) we find a series of addresses to Rā-Tem, wherein are mentioned Set and Nephthys, 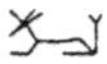, , Osiris, Isis, and Ḥer-ḥepes, , 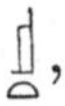, 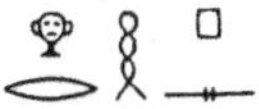, Thoth, Anubis, and Usert, , , , and Horus, which seems to show that one company of gods, of which the dual god Rā-Tem was the head, consisted of Set, Nephthys, Ḥer-ḥepes, Osiris, Isis, Thoth, Anubis, Usert, and Horus, i.e., in all ten gods. In the next section but one of the same king's text (line 240 f.) the Great Company of the gods of Heliopolis are declared to be:—1. Tem, . 2. Shu, 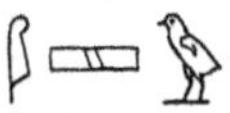. 3. Tefnut, . 4. Seb, . 5. Nut, . 6. Isis, . 7. Set, 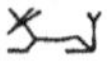. 8. Nephthys, . 9. Thoth, . 10. Horus, . Here again we have ten gods assigned to the divine company, but curiously enough the name of Osiris, one of the most important of the gods, is omitted. Following these ten names comes an address to the "Great Company of the Gods," 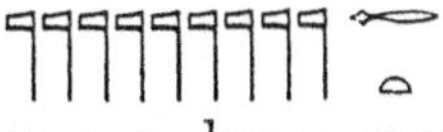, which clearly refers to the gods whose names we have mentioned. In the text of Pepi II. (line 665), the gods who are declared to form "the Great Company of the gods who are in Annu" are:—1. Tem. 2. Shu. 3. Tefnut. 4. Seb. 5. Nut. 6. Osiris. 7. Isis. 8. Set, , and 9.

NEPHTHYS, , and they are called the "offspring of Tem, who "made wide his heart when he gave them birth in your name of "'Nine.'"[1] A few lines lower down the king makes a petition to the "Great Company of the gods who are in Ȧnnu," and he includes in it the names of TEM, SHU, TEFNUT, SEB, NUT, OSIRIS, OSIRIS-KHENT-ȦMENTI, SET of Ombos, ḤERU of Edfu,[2] RĀ, KHENT-MAATI,[3] and UATCHET; thus the Great Company of the gods of Heliopolis may contain either nine or twelve gods. In several passages in the Pyramid Texts two groups or companies of gods, eighteen in number, are mentioned; thus in the text of Mer-en-Rā, line 453, allusion is made to the "very great "eighteen gods who are at the head of the Souls of Ȧnnu," but these, clearly, include the Great Company and the Little Company, who are addressed on behalf of the deceased in the text of Unȧs, lines 251, 252.

The triple Company to which allusion is sometimes made, 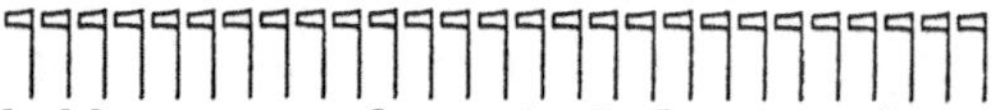 (Tetȧ, line 307), was probably supposed to include the Great Company of the gods of heaven, the Little Company of the gods of earth, and the Company of the gods of the Underworld, but from many passages it is evident that the Great and Little Companies represented to the Egyptian, for all practical purposes, the whole of the gods whom he attempted to worship. The priests of the provincial cities and towns adopted by degrees the more important of the views of the Heliopolitan priesthood concerning the Egyptian cosmogony and theogony, and as they were able to identify their local gods with Temu, or Rā-Tem, the head of the Heliopolitan Company of gods, and with the members of his company to whom their attributes were most akin, no serious opposition appears to have been offered by them to the tenets of the great religious centre of Heliopolis. The priests of this city were prudent enough to include as forms of the gods of their divine companies the great ancient gods and goddesses of the South and the North, as well as a number of

1

2

3

lesser gods whose worship was quite local, and in this way they succeeded in causing their doctrines to be accepted throughout the length and breadth of Egypt, and there is no doubt that the great theological system of Thebes under the Middle and New Empires was based entirely upon that of Heliopolis. We have now to describe the attributes of the gods of the Great Company, which for convenience may be assumed to consist of the following:—Tem, Shu, Tefnut, Seb, Nut, Osiris, Isis, Set, and Nephthys.

1. Tem , or .

Tem was a form of the Sun-god, and was the great local god of Ȧnnu, and the head of the company of gods of that place. His name is connected with the root *tem*, , or *temem*, , "to be complete," "to make an end of," and he was regarded as the form of the Sun-god which brought the day to an end, i.e., as the evening or night sun. He is always depicted in the human form. The attributes of the god have been already described in the section which treats of the forms of the Sun-god Rā.

2. Shu, 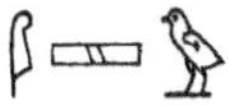, or , or , or .

3. Tefnut, 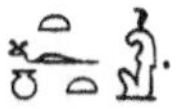.

Shu and his female counterpart Tefnut may be considered together, because they are usually mentioned together, at all events in the texts of the later periods. The name Shu appears to be derived from the root *shu*, , "dry, parched, withered, empty," and the like, and the name Tefnut must be connected with the root *tef*, , or *teftef*, 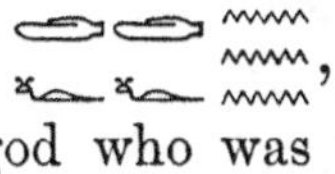, "to spit, be moist," and the like; thus Shu was a god who was connected with the heat and dryness of sunlight and with the dry atmosphere which exists between the earth and the sky, and Tefnut was a personification of the moisture of the sky, and made herself manifest in various forms. The oldest legend about the origin of the gods is contained in the text of Pepi I., wherein it is said (line 465) that once upon a time Tem went to the city of Ȧnnu and that he there produced from his own body by the irregular means of masturbation his two children Shu and Tefnut. In this crude form the myth is probably of Libyan origin, and it suggests that its inventors were in a semi-savage, or perhaps wholly savage, state when it was first promulgated. In later times, as we have already seen, the Egyptians appear to have rejected certain of the details of the myth, or to have felt some difficulty in believing that Shu and Tefnut were begotten and conceived and brought forth by Tem, and they therefore assumed that his shadow, , *khaibit*, acted the part of wife to him; another view was that the goddess Iusaāset was his wife.[1]

The old ideas about the origin of the twin gods, however, maintained their position in the minds of the Egyptians, and we find them categorically expressed in some of the hymns addressed to Ȧmen-Rā, who under the New Empire was identified with Tem, just as at an earlier period Rā was identified with the same god. In two hymns quoted by Brugsch[2] we have the following:—"O Ȧmen-Rā, the gods have gone forth from thee. What flowed "forth from thee became Shu, and that which was emitted by thee "became Tefnut; thou didst create the nine gods at the beginning "of all things, and thou wast the Lion-god of the Twin Lion-gods," [3]. The Twin Lion-gods are, of course, Shu and Tefnut, who are mentioned in the *Book of the Dead* in several passages.[4] In the second hymn to Ȧmen-Rā it is said,

[1] In the passage referred to the opening words are, "Tem came to take pleasure in himself,"  *iu sa*, and M. Maspero thinks that the name of the goddess Iusaāset, , may be derived from them. See *La Mythologie Égyptienne*, p. 247.

[2] *Religion*, p. 422.

[3] Brugsch, *Reise*, pl. 26, l. 26.

[4] The forms are 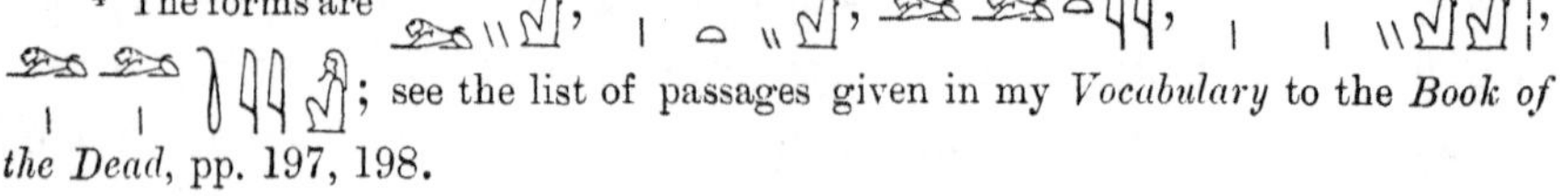; see the list of passages given in my *Vocabulary* to the *Book of the Dead*, pp. 197, 198.

The God SHU.

The Goddess TEFNUT.

"Thou art the One God, who didst form thyself into two gods, "thou art the creator of the Egg, and thou didst produce thy "Twin-Gods." In connexion with the production of Shu and Tefnut Dr. Brugsch refers to the well-known origin of the gods of Taste and Feeling, Ḥu, , and Sa, , who are said to have sprung into being from the drops of blood which fell from the phallus of Rā, and to have taken up their places among the gods who were in the train of Rā, and who were with Temu every day.[1] (*Book of the Dead*, xvii. 62).

Shu is represented in the form of a man who wears upon his head one feather, , or two, , or four, ; the phonetic value of the sign is *shu*, and the use of it as the symbol of the god's name seems to indicate some desire on the part of the Egyptians to connect the word *shu*, or *shāu*, "feather," with *shu*, "light, empty space, dryness," etc. As the god of the space which exists between the earth and the sky, Shu was represented under the form of a god who held up the sky with his two hands, one supporting it at the place of sunrise, and the other at the place of sunset, and several porcelain figures exist in which he is seen kneeling upon one knee, in the act of lifting up with his two hands the sky with the solar disk in it. When Shu wears no feather he bears upon his head the figure of the hind-quarter of a lion , *peḥ*; in mythological scenes we find him both seated and standing, and he usually holds in one hand the sceptre , and in the other . In a picture given by Lanzone[2] he grasps in his left hand a scorpion, a serpent, and a hawk-headed sceptre. The goddess Tefnut is represented in the form of a woman, who wears upon her head the solar disk encircled by a serpent, and holds in her hands the sceptre , and ; she, however, often appears with the head of a lioness, which is surmounted by a uraeus, and she is sometimes depicted in the form of a lioness.

1 

2 Op. cit., pl. 386.

An examination of the texts shows that Shu was a god of light, or light personified, who made himself manifest in the beams of the sun by day, and in the light of the moon by night, and his home was the disk (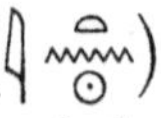) of the sun. Viewed in this connexion it is easy to understand the scene in which the god appears rising up from behind the earth with the solar disk upon his head, and his hands supporting that upon which it rests. In a text at Edfû published by Bergmann,[1] the creator of Shu is called TAUITH, 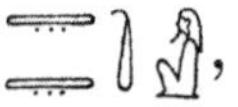, and to him the king who caused the words to be inscribed is made to say, "Thou hast emitted (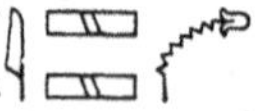 *àshesh*) SHU, and "he hath come forth from thy mouth. . . . He hath become a "god, and he hath brought for thee every good thing; he hath "toiled for thee, and he hath emitted for thee in his name of Shu, "the royal double. He hath laboured for thee in these things, "and he beareth up for thee heaven upon his head in his name "of SHU, and TAUITH giveth the strength of the body of heaven "in his name of PTAḤ. He beareth up (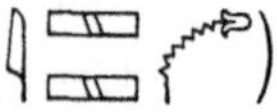) for thee "heaven with his hands in his name of SHU, the body of the "sky."[2] It must be noted that the same word *àshesh*, 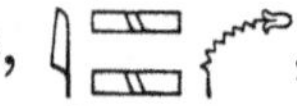, is used to express both the idea of "pouring out" and of "supporting," and it is difficult to reconcile these totally different meanings unless we remember that it is that which Tem, or Rā-Tem, has poured out which supports the heavens wherein shines the Sun-god. That which Tem, or Rā-Tem, has poured out is the light, and light was declared to be the prop of the sky.

[1] *Hieroglyphische Inschriften*, Vienna, 1879, pl. 42, ll. 1-4, 10, 11.

[2] 

From a number of passages examined by Dr. Brugsch[1] we find that Shu was a personification of the rays which came forth from the eyes of Rā, and that he was the soul of the god Khnemu, the great god of Elephantine and of the First Cataract; he also represented the burning, fiery heat of the sun at noon, and the sun in the height of summer.

In another aspect his abode was the region between the earth and the sky, and he was a personification of the wind of the North; Dr. Brugsch went so far as to identify him with the "spiritual Pneuma in a higher sense," and thought that he might be regarded as the vital principle of all living beings. He was certainly, like his father Tem, thought to be the cool wind of the North, and the dead were grateful to him for his breezes. Shu was, in fact, the god of the space which is filled with the atmosphere, even as Rā was the god of heaven, and Seb the god of the earth, and Osiris the god of the Underworld. From the *Book of the Dead* (xvii. 16) we learn that Shu and Tefnut were supposed to possess but one soul between them, but that the two halves of it were identified with the soul of Osiris and the soul of Rā, which together formed the great double soul which dwelt in Ṭaṭṭu. The gate of Tchesert in the Underworld was called the "gate of the pillars of Shu" (xvii. 56), and Shu and Tefnut laid the foundations of the house in which the deceased was supposed to dwell. From the xviiith Chapter of the *Book of the Dead* we find that the princes of Heliopolis were Tem, Shu, Tefnut, Osiris, and Thoth, and that Rā, Osiris, Shu, and Bebi were the prinċes of the portion of the Underworld which was known by the name of Ȧnruṭ-f. We may note in passing that BEBI, , or BÁBÁ, , or , or BABA, 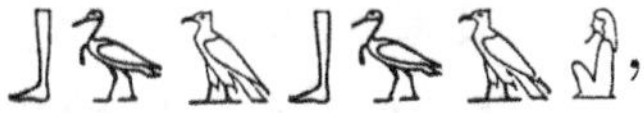, or BABAI, , was the first-born son of Osiris.

According to Dr. Brugsch, Baba was personified in the form of some Typhonic mythological animal, and was the god who presided over the phallus; the blood which fell from his nose grew up into plants which subsequently changed into cedars. Dr. Pleyte has

[1] *Religion*, p. 432.

rightly identified Bebi or Baba with the Βέβων or Βεβῶνα of Plutarch (*De Iside*, § 62) and with the Βάβυς of Hellanicus.[1] Bebôn was a name of Typhon, i.e., Set, and that he was represented by an animal is proved by the hieroglyphic form of his name, which is determined by the skin of an animal, . In Chapter xxiii. the deceased prays that his "mouth may be unclosed by Shu with the iron knife wherewith he opened the mouth of the gods." From Chapters xxxiii. and xxxv. we learn that Shu was believed to possess power over serpents, and he it was who made the deceased to stand up by the Ladder which would take him to heaven (xcviii. 4). That souls needed a ladder whereby to mount from earth to heaven was a very ancient belief in Egypt. The four pillars which held up the sky at the four cardinal points were called the "pillars of Shu" (cix. 5, cx. 13), and Shu was the breath of the god Rā (cxxx. 4). The deceased was nourished with the food of Shu, i.e., he lived upon light; and in the Roman period Shu was merged in Rā, the god of light. The part played in Egyptian mythology by Tefnut is not easily defined, and but little is known about her. In the text of Unȧs (line 453) she is mentioned together with the two Maāt goddesses, , and with Shu, but curiously enough, she seems to appear as the female counterpart of a god called Tefen, . The passage reads, "Tefen and Tefnet have weighed Unȧs, and the "Maāt goddesses have hearkened, and Shu hath borne witness," etc. In the Theban Recension of the *Book of the Dead* she is mentioned a few times in connexion with Shu (Chapters xvii., cxxx., etc.), and she is one of the group of gods who form the divine company and the "body and soul of Rā" (cxl. 7), but she performs no service for the deceased beyond providing him with breath. She was originally a goddess of gentle rain and soft wind, but at a comparatively late period of Egyptian history she was identified with Neḥemāuit at Hermopolis, with Menḥit at Latopolis, with Sekhet in Memphis, and with Apsit in Nubia.

Unlike most of the gods of Egypt, Shu and Tefnut do not appear

[1] *Aeg. Zeitschrift*, 1865, p. 55.

to have have had set apart for them any special city or district, but at the same time titles were given to certain cities which presupposed some connexion between them and these gods. Thus Dendera was called Per-Shu, , i.e., "House of Shu," and Apollinopolis Magna was called Hinu-en-Shu-nefer, 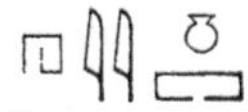 , and Edfû was the "Seat of Shu," , and Memphis bore the name of "Palace of Shu," .[1] Similarly, one portion of Dendera was known as the "House of Tefnut," or the "Åat of Tefnut," , 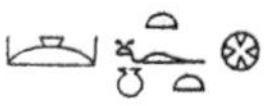, or . Whether there were statues of Shu and Tefnut in these cities cannot be said, but it is very probable that they were worshipped in their sanctuaries under the forms of lions, and in this connexion it is worthy of note that Aelian records (*De Nat. Animal.* xii. § 7) that the people of Heliopolis worshipped lions in the temple of Helios.

It has already been mentioned that Shu was the sky-bearer *par excellence*, and we may note in passing the interesting myth which the Egyptians possessed about him in this capacity, and the explanation which they gave of his occupying this position. According to the text which is found in the tomb of Seti I. in the Valley of the Tombs of the Kings at Thebes, in very remote times, when Rā ruled over gods and men and had his throne established in the city of Suten-ḥenen, or Ḥenen-su, mankind began to utter seditious words against him, and the great god determined to destroy them. He summoned Hathor, Shu, Tefnut, Seb, and Nut into his presence, and having told them what men, who had proceeded from his eye, had been saying about him, he asked them for their advice, and promised that he would not slay the rebels until he had heard what the "first-born god" and the "ancestor gods" had to say on the matter. In answer to this the first-born god Nu, , advised him to let his daughter Hathor, "the eye of Rā," go forth and slay men; Rā accepted the advice straightway, and Hathor went forth and slew all mankind,

[1] Brugsch, *Dict. Géog.*, p. 776.

and when she returned Rā was well pleased with her. Soon after this he became wearied with the earth, and the goddess Nut having been turned into a cow he mounted upon her back and remained there, but before long the cow began to shake and to tremble because she was very high above the earth, and when she complained to Rā about it he commanded Shu to be a support to her, and to hold her up in the sky. In the picture of the cow which accompanies the text we see her body resting upon the head and the two raised hands and arms of the god. When Shu had taken up his place beneath the cow and was bearing up her body, the heavens above and the earth beneath came into being, and the four legs of the cow became the four props of heaven at the four cardinal points; and thus it came to pass that the god Seb and his female counterpart Nut began their existence.

SEB, 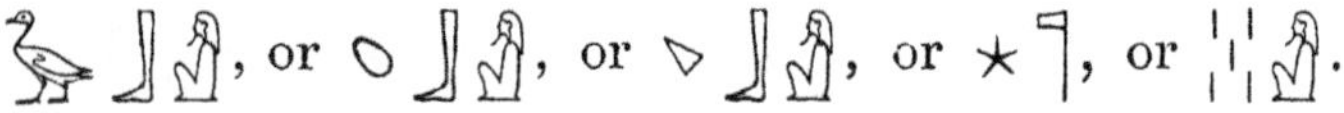

SEB was the son of Shu and Tefnut, and was the brother and husband of Nut, and the father of Osiris and Isis, Set and Nephthys, and some say of one of the Horus gods; according to the late Dr. Brugsch his name should be read Geb or Ḳeb, or Gebb, or Ḳebb, and in very early times this undoubtedly seems to have been the correct form of the god's name. He is usually represented in the form of a man who bears upon his head either the white crown , or the crown of the North, to which is added the *Atef* crown, , or a goose, , of the peculiar species called *seb*. This bird was sacred to him because he was believed to have made his way through the air in its form. Seb was the god of the earth, and the earth formed his body and was called the "house of Seb," just as the air was called the "house of Shu," and the heaven the "house of Rā," and the Underworld the "house of Osiris." As the god of the surface of the earth from which spring up trees, and plants, and herbs, and grain he played a very prominent part in the mythology of the Underworld, and as the god of the earth beneath the surface of the ground he had authority over the tombs wherein the dead were laid. In hymns

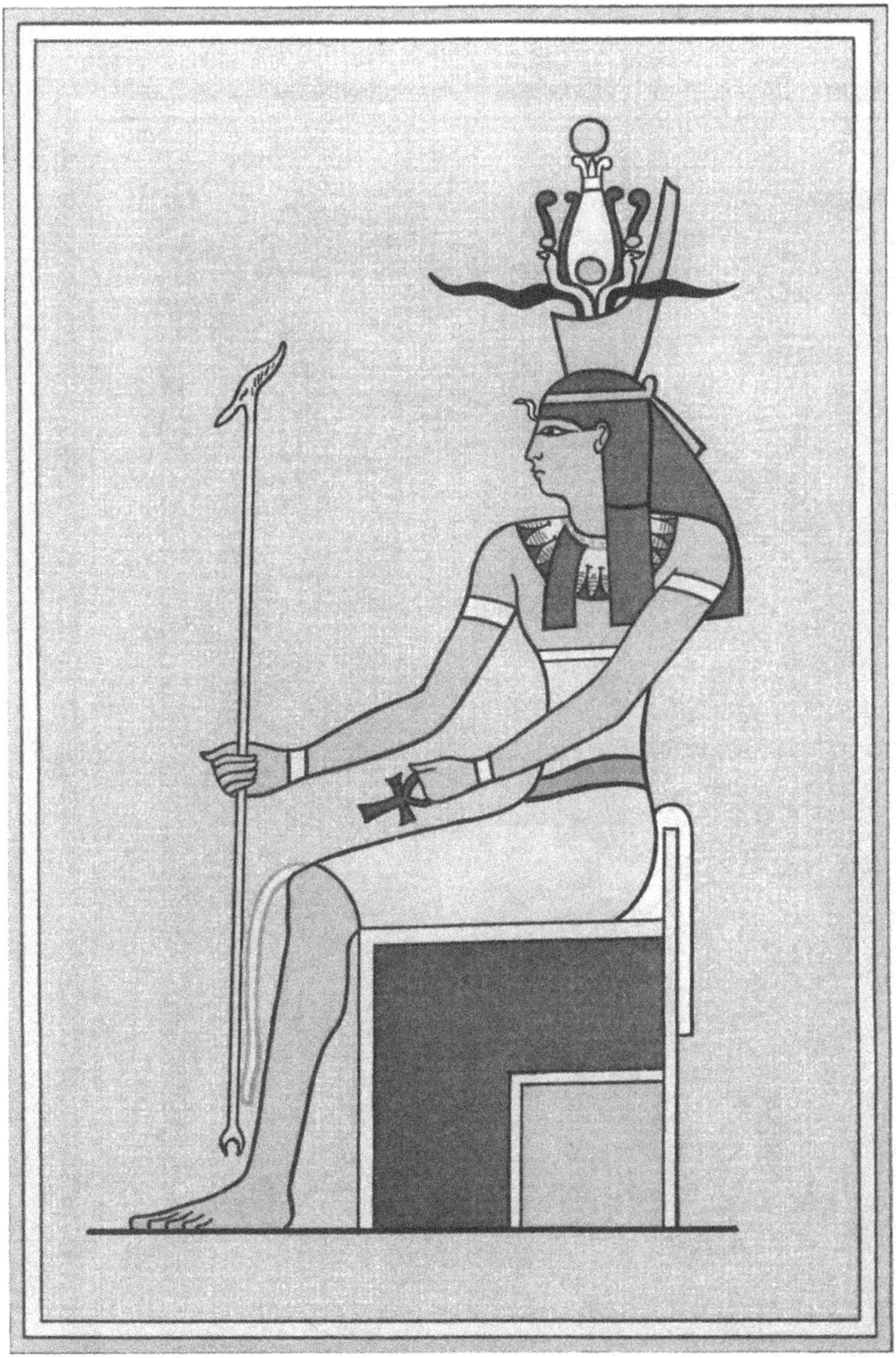

SEB, THE ERPĀ OF THE GODS.

The God SEB supporting NUT on Heaven.

and other compositions he is often styled the *erpāt*, 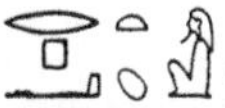, i.e., the hereditary, tribal chief of the gods, and he plays a very important part in the *Book of the Dead*. Thus he is one of the company of the gods who watch the weighing of the heart of the deceased in the Judgment Hall of Osiris, and on his brow rested the secret gates which were close by the Balance of Rā, and which were guarded by the god himself (xii. 2).

The soul of Seb was called SMAM-UR, , (xvii. 116). The righteous who were provided with the necessary words of power were enabled to make their escape from the earth wherein their bodies were laid, but the wicked were held fast by Seb (xix. 14); Sekhet and Ȧnpu were great helpers of the deceased, but it was Seb whom he asked to open wide his two jaws for him, whom he begged to open his eyes, and loose his legs which were bandaged (xxvi. 1). And of him the deceased said, "My "father is Seb, and my mother is Nut" (xxxi. 5). Like Shu the god Seb was appealed to by the deceased for help against serpents (xxxiii. 2), and he was never tired of boasting that his cakes were "on the earth with the god Seb" (liii. 4), and that the gods had declared that he was "to live upon the bread of Seb" (lxviii. 9). In a burst of joy, Nu, the overseer of the house of the overseer of the seal, is made to say, "The doors of heaven are opened for me, the "doors of earth are opened for me, the bars and bolts of Seb are "opened for me" (lxviii. 2), and "I exchange speech with Seb "(lxxviii. 12), I am decreed to be the divine heir of Seb, the "lord of the earth, and to be the protector therein. The "god Seb refresheth me, and he maketh his risings to be mine" (lxxx. 11, 12).

The religious texts show that there was no special city or district set apart for the god Seb, but a portion of the temple estates in Apollinopolis Magna was called the "Ȧat of Seb," 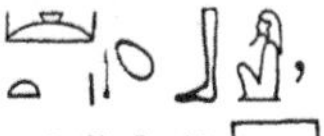, and a name of Dendera was "the home of the children of Seb," 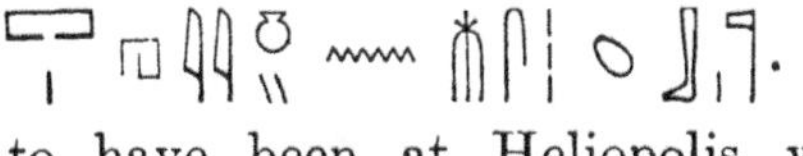. The chief seat of the god appears to have been at Heliopolis, where he and his female counterpart Nut produced the great Egg whereout sprang the Sun-god under the form of a phoenix.[1] Because of his connexion with this Egg Seb is sometimes called the "Great Cackler," ḲENḲEN-UR, . Thus the deceased says, "Hail, thou god Tem, "grant unto me the sweet breath which dwelleth in thy nostrils. "I embrace that great throne which is in the city of Hermopolis, "and I keep watch over the Egg of the Great Cackler (or, "according to another reading, I am the Egg which is in the "Great Cackler, and I watch and guard that mighty thing which "hath come into being wherewith the god Seb hath opened the "earth), I germinate as it germinateth; I live as it liveth; and "[my] breath is [its] breath" (*Book of the Dead*, Chapters liv., "lvi., lix.).

The name of the phoenix in Egyptian is "Bennu," , and this bird played a very prominent part in Egyptian mythology, but the texts do not bear out the extraordinary assertions which have been made about it by classical writers. According to the story which Herodotus heard at Heliopolis (ii. 73), the bird visited that place once every five hundred years, on its father's death; when it was five hundred, or fourteen hundred and sixty-one years old, it burnt itself to death. It was supposed to resemble an eagle, and to have red and gold feathers, and to come from Arabia; before its death it built a nest to which it gave the power of producing a new phoenix, though some thought that a worm crept out of its body before it died, and that from it the heat of the sun developed a new phoenix. Others thought that it died after a life of seven thousand and six years, and another view was that the new phoenix rose from the burnt and decomposing remains of his old body, and that he took these to Heliopolis where he burnt them.[2] All these fabulous stories are the result of misunderstandings of the Egyptian myth which declared that the renewed morning sun rose in the form of a Bennu, and of the belief which declared that this bird was the soul of Rā and also the living symbol of Osiris, and that it came forth from the very heart of the

[1] Brugsch, *Religion*, p. 577.

[2] See Lucian, *De Mort. Pers.*, xxvii.; Philostratus, *Vit. Apollon.*, iii. 49; Tzetzes, *Chiliar*, v. 397; Pliny, *Hist. Nat.*, x. 2; Pomponius Mela, iii. 8.

god. The sanctuary of the Bennu was the sanctuary of Rā and Osiris, and was called Ḥet Benben, , i.e., the "House of the Obelisk," and remembering this it is easy to understand the passages in the *Book of the Dead*, "I go in like the "Hawk, and I come forth like the Bennu, the Morning Star (i.e., "the planet Venus) of Rā" (xiii. 2); "I am the Bennu which is in "Heliopolis" (xvii. 27), and the scholion on this passage expressly informs us that the Bennu is Osiris. Elsewhere the deceased says, "I am the Bennu, the soul of Rā, and the guide of the gods "in the Ṭuat; (xxix.c 1); let it be so done unto me that I may "enter in like a hawk, and that I may come forth like Bennu, "the Morning Star" (cxxii. 6). On a hypocephalus quoted by Prof. Wiedemann,[1] the deceased is made to say, "I am in the form "of the Bennu, which cometh forth from Ḥet-Benbenet in Ȧnnu," and from many passages we learn that the Bennu, the Soul of Rā, which appeared each morning under the form of the rising sun, was supposed to shine upon the world from the top of the famous Persea tree wherein he renewed himself. We may note that a Chapter of the *Book of the Dead* (lxxxii.) was written with the special object of enabling the deceased to transform himself into a Bennu bird if he felt disposed to do so; in it he identifies himself with the god Kheperȧ, and with Horus, the vanquisher of Set, and with Khensu.

It has already been said that Seb was the god of the earth, and the Heliopolitans declared that he represented the very ground upon which their city stood, meaning that Heliopolis was the birthplace of the company of the gods, and in fact that the work of creation began there. In several papyri we find pictures of the first act of creation which took place as soon as the Sun-god, by whatsoever name he may be called, appeared in the sky, and sent forth his rays from the heights of heaven upon the earth, and in these Seb always occupies a very prominent position. He is seen lying upon the ground with one hand stretched out upon it, and the other extended towards heaven, which position seems to be referred to in the text of Pepi I., lines 338, 339, wherein we read,

[1] *Aeg. Zeit.*, 1878, p. 93.

"Seb throws out his [one] hand to heaven and his [one] hand "towards the earth," . By his side stands the god Shu, who supports on his upraised hands the heavens which are depicted in the form of a woman, whose body is bespangled with stars; this woman is the goddess Nut, who is supposed to have been lifted up from the embrace of Seb by Shu when he insinuated himself between their bodies and so formed the earth and the sky. This was the act of Shu which brought into being his heir Seb, and his consort Nut, and it was the heirship of this god which the kings of Egypt boasted they had received when they sat upon their thrones.

Seb was the hereditary tribal chief of the gods, and his throne represented the sovereignty both of heaven and of earth; as a creative god he was identified with Tem, and so, as Dr. Brugsch pointed out, became the "father of his father." As an elementary god he represented the earth, as Rā did fire, and Shu air, and Osiris water. In some respects the attributes of Nut were assigned to him, for he is sometimes called the lord of the watery abyss, and the dweller in the watery mass of the sky, and the lord of the Underworld. He is also described as one of the porters of heaven's gate, who draws back the bolts, and opens the door in order that the light of Rā may stream upon the world, and when he set himself in motion his movements produced thunder in heaven and quaking upon earth. He was akin in some way to the two Akeru gods, , who were represented as a lion with a head at each end of its body; this body was a personification of the passage in the earth through which the sun passed during the hours of night from the place where he set in the evening to that where he rose the next morning. The mouths of the lions formed

Seb and Nut.

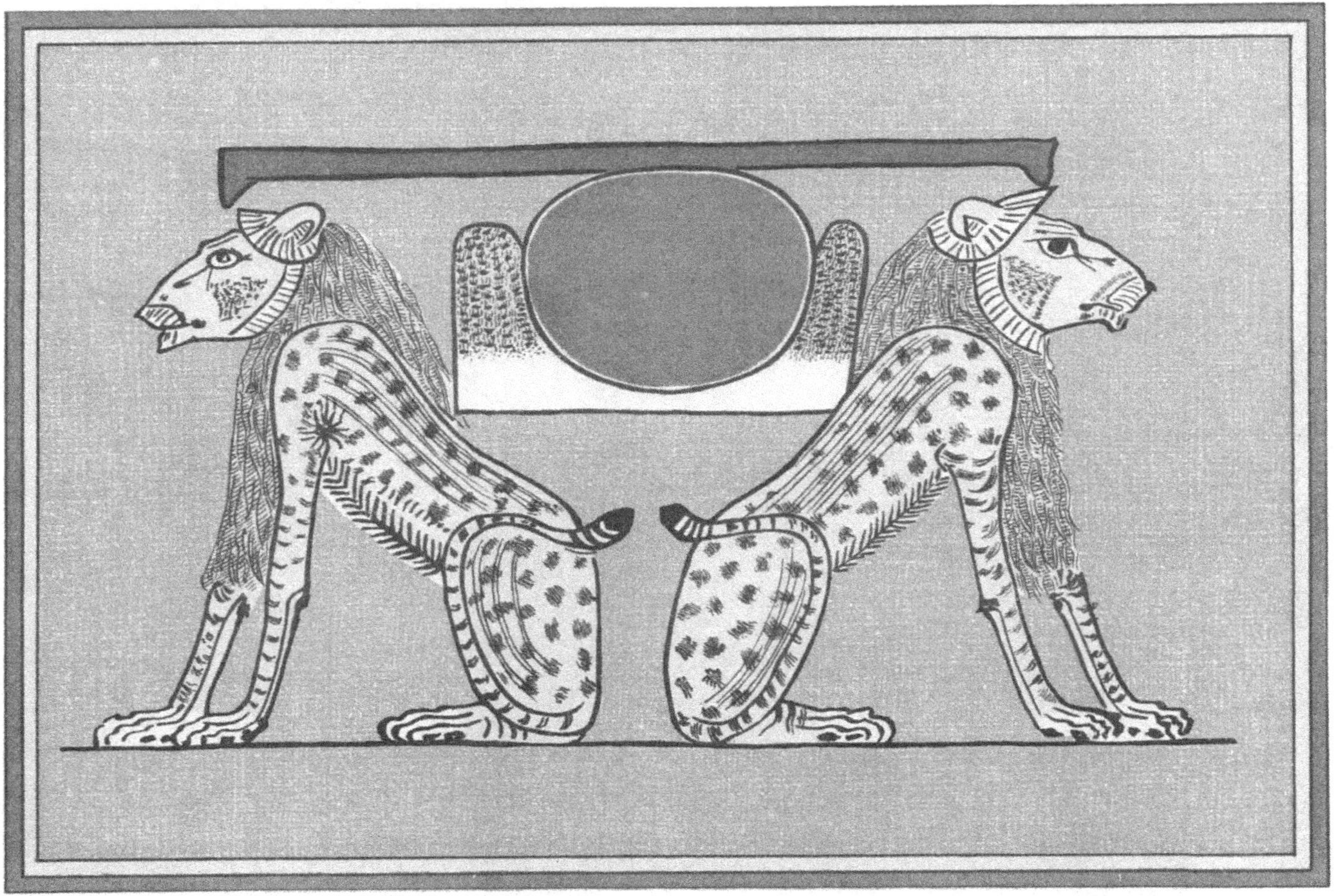

The Lion Gods of Yesterday and To-day.

the entrance into and the exit from this passage, and as the head of one lion symbolized the evening and the west, and the other symbolized the morning and the east, in later days each lion's head was provided with a separate body, and the one was called Sef, , i.e., "Yesterday," and the other was called Ṭuau, , i.e., "To-day" (*Book of the Dead*, xvii., lines 14, 15). Though he was god of the earth Seb also acted as a guide to the deceased in heaven, and he provided him with meat and drink; numerous passages in the *Book of the Dead* refer to the gifts which he bestowed upon Osiris his son, and the deceased prayed fervently that he would bestow upon him the same protection and help which he had bestowed upon Osiris.

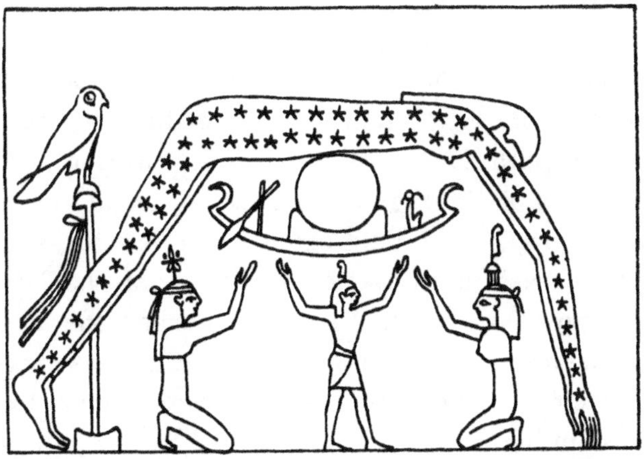

Shu supporting the boat of the Sun-god beneath the sky-goddess Nut.

In two passages in the *Book of the Dead* (Chapter xxxi. 3 of the Saïte Recension; and Chapter lxix. 7, Theban Recension) we appear to have an allusion to a myth concerning Seb which is otherwise unknown. In the former the deceased says, "I, even I, "am Osiris, who shut in his father Seb together with his mother "Nut on the day of the great slaughter. My father is Seb and my "mother is Nut"; and in the latter he says, "I, even I, am Osiris, "who shut in his father together with his mother on the day of "making the great slaughter," and the text adds, "now, the father "is Seb, and the mother is Nut." The word used for "slaughter" is *shāt*, , and there is no doubt whatsoever about its meaning, and according to Dr. Brugsch[1] we are to understand an act of self-mutilation on the part of Rā, the father of Osiris, similar to that which is referred to in the *Book of the Dead*, Chapter xvii., line 61. According to this passage the gods Ȧmmiu, , sprang from the drops of blood[2] which fell from Rā after the process of mutilation, and Dr. Brugsch compared the action of Osiris in shutting in, , his father Seb with the punishment which Kronos inflicted upon his father Uranus because he threw the Cyclopes into Tartarus, and the Ȧmmiu gods had an origin somewhat similar to that of the Erinnyes.

Nut, , or , or , or .

The goddess Nut was the daughter of Shu and Tefnut, and the wife of Seb, the Earth-god, and the mother of Osiris and Isis, and Set and Nephthys; she was the personification of the heavens and the sky, and of the region wherein the clouds formed, and in fact of every portion of the region in which the sun rose, and travelled from east to west. As a goddess of the late historical period in Egypt Nut seems to have absorbed the attributes of a number of goddesses who possessed attributes somewhat similar to those of herself, and the identities of several old nature goddesses were merged in her. In the Pyramid Texts (e.g., Unȧs, line 452) Nut appears as the regular female counterpart of Seb, who is described as the "Bull of Nut," , i.e., he was either the father, or husband, or son of the goddess; her name is sometimes written without , the determinative for sky, e.g., in Pepi I., line 242, where it is said, "Nut hath brought forth her daughter Venus," . Properly

[1] *Religion*, p. 581.

[2] 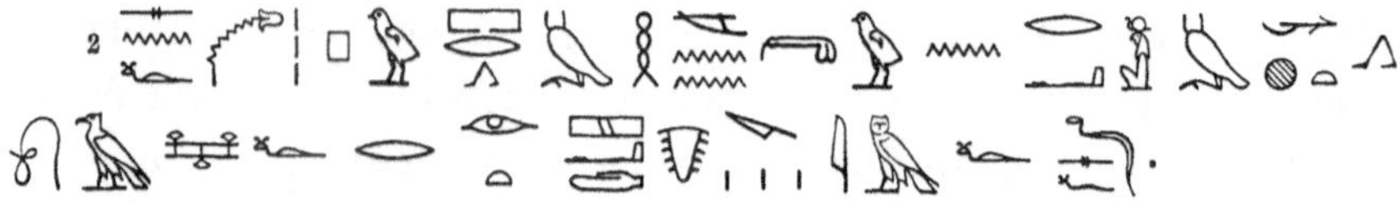

speaking, Nut, , is the personification of the Day-sky, i.e., of the sky which rests upon the two mountains of BAKHAU and Manu, that is, the Mountain of Sunrise and the Mountain of Sunset, but the Pyramid Texts prove that the Egyptians conceived the existence of a personification of the Night-sky, and it seems as if

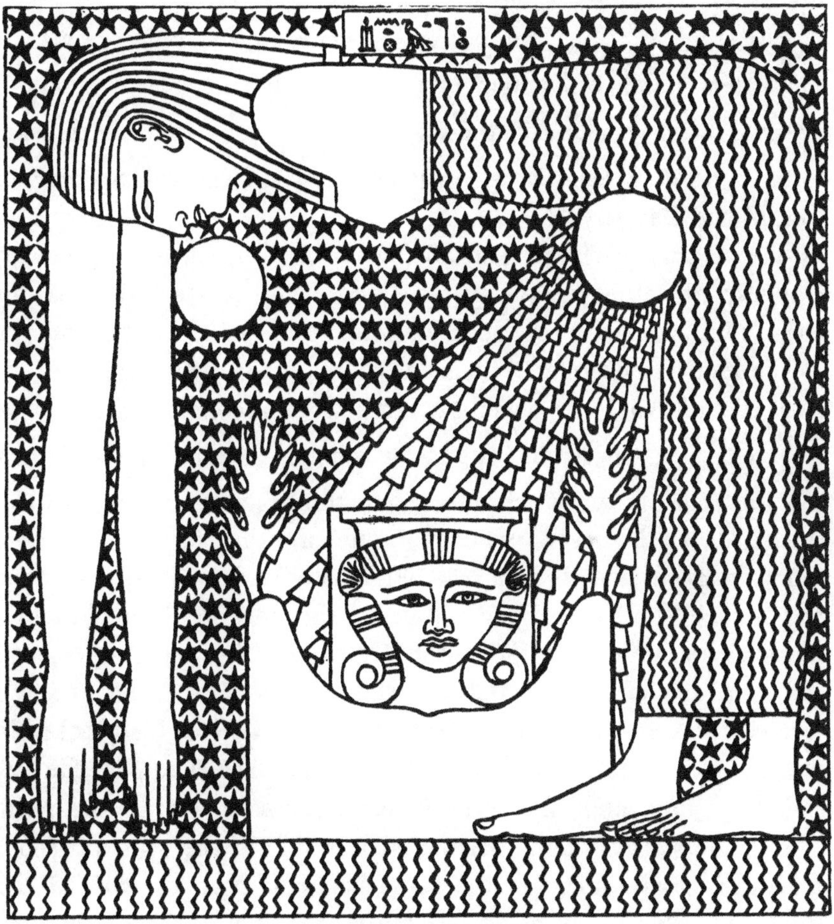

Nut giving birth to the Sun, the rays of which fall on Hathor in the horizon.

this goddess and her male counterpart were entirely different beings from Seb and Nut, and had different names. In the text of Unȧs (line 557) we find mentioned the two gods NȦU and NȦUT, , who are, however, regarded as one god and are addressed accordingly. Thus it is said, "Thy cake is to "thee, NÁU and NÁUT, even as one who uniteth the gods and who "maketh the gods to refresh themselves beneath their shadow." In this passage it is certainly right to assume that Nȧut represents the Night-sky because of the determinative of the name , which is the sky, or heaven, inverted. In another passage (Tetȧ, line 218) we read of the "star NEKHEKH of Nȧut" (or Nut), , i.e., the "star Nekhekh in the Night-sky"; on the other hand too much stress must not be laid upon the determinative, because in the word , which seems to mean the "firmament strewn with stars,"[1] the determinative is that of the Day-sky.

At a very early period, however, the difference between the Day-sky and the Night-sky was forgotten, at least in speaking, and it is chiefly from good funeral texts that we learn that a distinction between them was made in writing. In the Papyrus of Ani[2] are several examples of the name Nut written , or 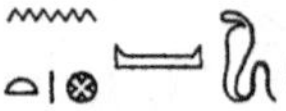, and the latter form is several times found in the Papyrus of Nu, which dates from the first half of the period of the XVIIIth Dynasty; whenever one or other of these forms is found in good papyri it is the Night-sky which is referred to in the text. We have already seen in the paragraphs on the god Nu that he had a female counterpart called Nut, who represented the great watery abyss out of which all things came, and who formed the celestial Nile whereon the Sun sailed in his boats; this watery path was divided into two parts, that whereon the Sun sailed by day, and that over which he passed during the night. The goddess Nut, whom the texts describe as the wife of Seb, is for all practical purposes the same being as Nut, the wife of Nu; this fact is proved by her titles, which are, "Nut, the mighty one, "the great lady, the daughter of Rā"; "Nut, the lady of heaven, "the mistress of the gods"; "Nut, the great lady, who gave birth "to the gods"; "Nut, who gave birth to the gods, the lady of

[1] Maspero, *Recueil*, tom. v., p. 25.
[2] See my *Vocabulary* to the *Book of the Dead*, p. 159.

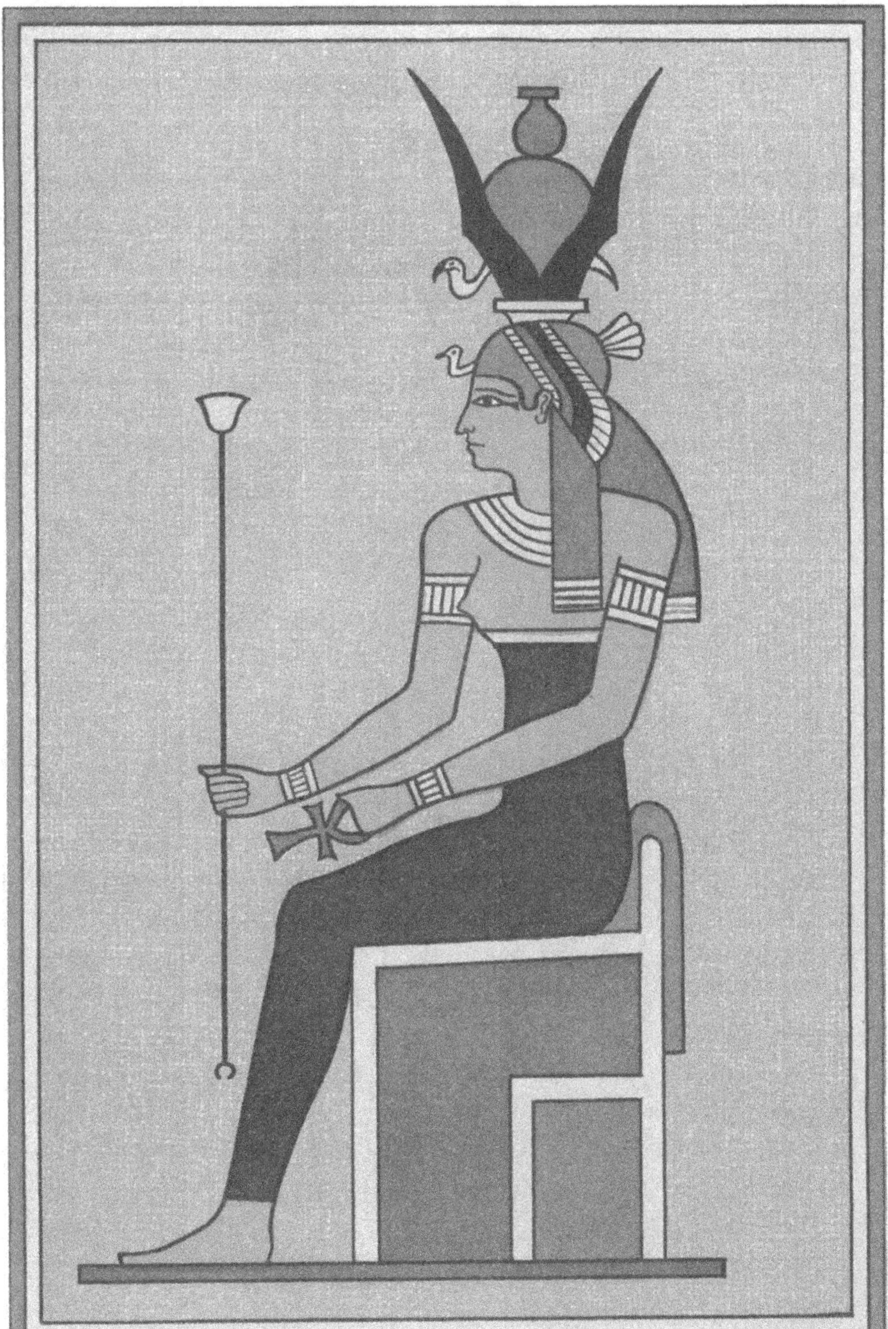

NUT, THE MOTHER OF THE GODS.

The Goddess NUT holding a Tablet on which stands HARPOCRATES.

"heaven, the mistress of the Two Lands."[1] The shrines of the goddess were not very numerous, but there was a Per-Nut, , in Memphis, and a Ḥet-Nut, , in the Delta, and three portions of the temple territory in Dendera were called respectively Ȧnt-en-Nut, Per-mest-en-Nut, and Per-netch-Nut-mā-Shu, , , and .[2] The goddess is usually represented in the form of a woman who bears upon her head a vase of water, , which has the phonetic value *Nu*, and which indicates both her name and her nature;[3] she sometimes wears on her head the horns and disk of the goddess Hathor, and holds in her hands a papyrus sceptre and the symbol of "life." She once appears in the form of the amulet of the buckle, , from the top of which projects her head, and she is provided with human arms, hands, and feet; sometimes she appears in the form which is usually identified as that of Hathor, that is as a woman standing in a sycamore tree and pouring out water from a vase, , for the souls of the dead who come to her. The "sycamore tree of Nut," , is mentioned in Chapter lix. of the *Book of the Dead*, and in the vignette we see the goddess standing in it.

On a mummy-case at Turin the goddess appears in the form of a woman standing on the

[1] 

[2] Brugsch, *Dict. Géog.*, p. 366.

[3] For a good collection of figures of the goddess see Lanzone, *op. cit.*, pl. 150 ff.

emblem of gold, . Above her head is the solar disk with uraei, and she is accompanied by the symbols of Nekhebet, Uatchet, and Hathor as goddess of the West; by her feet stand two snake-headed goddesses of the sky, each of whom wears the feather  on her head. The goddess herself wears the vulture crown with uraei, and above are the uraei of the South and North and the hawk of Horus wearing the white crown. Below her is the sycamore tree, her emblem, and in it sits the great Cat of Rā who is cutting off the head of Āpep, the god of darkness and evil. In the form in which she appears in this picture Nut has absorbed the attributes of all the great goddesses, and she is the type of the great mother of the gods and of the world.

On coffins and in many papyri we find her depicted in the form of a woman whose body is bent round in such a way as to form a semi-circle; in this attitude she represents the sky or heaven, and her legs and arms represent the four pillars on which the sky was supposed to rest and mark the position of the cardinal points. She is supported in her position by Shu, the son of Rā, who is supposed to have lifted her up from the embrace of Seb, and this last-named god is seen lying on the ground, with one hand raised to heaven and the other touching the earth. On each side of Shu is a hawk; the one represents the rising and the other the setting sun. According to one myth Nut gave birth to her son the Sun-god daily, and passing over her body he arrived at her mouth, into which he disappeared, and passing through her body he was re-born the following morning. Another myth declared that the sun sailed up the legs and over the back of the goddess in the Āṭet, or Māṭet Boat until noon, when he entered the Sektet boat and continued his journey until sunset. In the accompanying

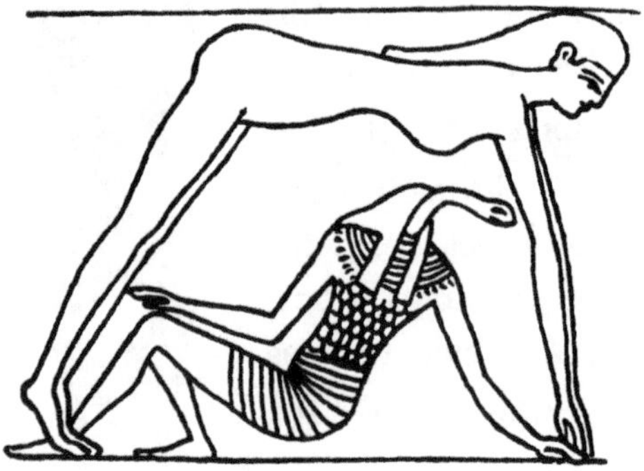

Seb and Nut.

picture we see Rā in his boat with Shu and Tefnut (?) sailing up through the watery abyss behind the legs of Nut, in the Āṭet Boat, and sailing down the arms of the goddess in the Sektet Boat into the Ṭuat or Underworld; the whole of the body and limbs of the goddess are bespangled with stars. In another remarkable picture we see a second body of a woman, which is also bent round in such a way as to form a semi-circle, within that of Nut, and within this second body is the body of a man which is bent round in such a way as to form an almost complete circle. Some explain this scene by saying that the outer body of a woman is the heaven over which Rā travels, and that the inner body is the heaven over which the Moon makes her way at night, whilst the male body within them is the almost circular valley of the Ṭuat; others, however, say that the two women are merely personifications of the Day and Night skies, and this view is, no doubt, the correct one. The raising up of Nut from the embrace of Seb represented, as we have before said, the first act of creation, and the great creative power which brought it about having separated the earth from the waters which were above it, and set the sun between the earth and the sky, was now able to make the gods, and human beings, animals, etc. The Egyptians were very fond of representations of this scene, and they had many variants of it, as may be seen from the collection of reproductions given by Lanzone.[1] In some of these we find Shu holding up the Boat of Rā under the body of Nut, in others we see the two boats of Rā placed side by side on her back, the god in one boat being Kheperȧ, and the god in the other being Osiris. Shu is sometimes accompanied by Thoth, and sometimes by Khnemu; in one instance Seb has a serpent's head, and in another the goose, which is his symbol, is seen standing near his feet with its beak open in the act of cackling. The Egyptian artists were not always consistent in some of their details of the scene, for at one time the region wherein is the head of Nut is described as the east, [hieroglyph], and at another as the west, [hieroglyph]; at one time Seb lies with his head to the east, and at another to the west. Finally, the goddess once

[1] Op. cit., pll. 150 ff.

appears holding up in her hands a tablet, on which stands a youthful male figure who is probably intended to represent Harpocrates, or one of the many Horus gods; in this example she is regarded as the Sky-mother who has produced her son, the Sun-god. According to another myth Nut was transformed into a huge cow, the legs of which were held in position by the Four Children of Horus, whilst her body was supported by Shu, as the body of Nut when in the form of a woman was borne up by this god.

From a large number of passages found in texts of all periods we learn that, from first to last, Nut was always regarded as a friend and protector of the dead, and the deceased appealed to her for food, and help, and protection just as a son appeals to his mother. In the text of Tetạ (line 175), it is said to the deceased, "Nut hath set thee as a god to Set in thy name of 'god,' and thy "mother Nut hath spread herself out over thee in her name of "'Coverer of the sky,'" ; and in line 268 we have, "Nephthys hath united again for thee "thy members in her name of Sesheta, , the lady "of the buildings through which thou hast passed, and thy mother "Nut in her name of Qersut, , hath granted that she "shall embrace thee in her name Qersu, 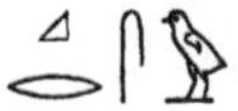, and that she "shall introduce thee in her name of 'Door.'" In the text of Pepi I. (line 256) it is said, "Pepi hath come forth from Pe with "the spirits of Pe, and he is arrayed in the apparel of Horus, and "in the dress of Thoth, and Isis is before him and Nephthys is "behind him; Åp-uat hath opened unto him a way, and Shu "lifteth him up, and the souls of Ånnu make him ascend the "steps and set him before Nut who stretcheth out her hand to "him." In the *Book of the Dead* are several allusions to Nut and to the meat and drink which she provides for the deceased, and a chapter (lix.) is found which was specially composed to enable him to "snuff the air, and to have dominion over the waters in the

This illustration is reproduced in full color on the insert attached to the inside back cover of this volume.

THE GODDESS MUT POURING OUT WATER FROM THE SYCAMORE TREE OVER THE DECEASED AND HIS SOUL.

"Underworld." The text reads:—"Hail, thou sycamore of the "goddess Nut! Grant thou to me of the water and of the air "which dwell in thee. I embrace the throne which is in Unnu "(Hermopolis), and I watch and guard the egg of the Great "Cackler.[1] It groweth, I grow; it liveth, I live; it snuffeth the "air, I snuff the air." To make sure that the recital of these words should have the proper result they were accompanied by a vignette, in which the goddess is seen standing in a tree, out of which she reaches to the deceased with one hand a table covered with bread and other articles of food; with the other she sprinkles water upon him from a libation vase as he kneels at the foot of a tree.

The sycamore of Nut was situated at Heliopolis, and is often mentioned in mythological texts. According to the *Book of the Dead* (cix. 4) there were *two* turquoise-coloured sycamores at Heliopolis, and the Sun-god passed out between them each morning when he began his journey across the sky, and "strode forward "over the supports of Shu (i.e., the four pillars, , which bore "up the sky) towards the gate of the East through which Rā "rose." The sycamore of Nut was probably one of these, but in any case Āpep, the personification of darkness and evil, was slain at its foot by the Great Cat Rā, and the branches of this tree became a place of refuge for weary souls during the fiery heats of noonday in the summer time. Here they were refreshed with that food whereon the goddess herself lived, and here they participated in the life of the divine beings who were her offspring and associates. Since the mythological tree of Nut stood at Heliopolis and was a sycamore it may well have served as the archetype of the sycamore tree under which tradition asserts that the Virgin Mary sat and rested during her flight to Egypt, and there seems to be little doubt that many of the details about her wanderings in the Delta, which are recorded in the Apocryphal Gospels and in writings of a similar class, are borrowed from the old mythology of Egypt. Associated with the sycamore of Nut

[1] I.e., the Egg out of which sprang the Sun, which was produced by Seb and Nut.

were the plants among which the Great Cackler Seb laid the Egg of the Sun, and these may well be identified with the famous balsam trees, from which was expressed the oil which was so highly prized by the Christians of Egypt and Abyssinia, and which was used by them in their ceremony of baptism; these trees were always watered with water drawn from the famous 'Ain Shems (a name really meaning the "Eye of the Sun"), i.e., the well of water which is fed by a spring in the immediate neighbourhood, and is commonly called the "Fountain of the Sun." We may note in passing another legend, which was popular among the Copts, to the effect that the Virgin Mary once hid herself and her Son from their enemies in the trunk of the sycamore at Heliopolis, and that it is based upon an ancient Egyptian myth recorded by Plutarch which declared that Isis hid the body of Osiris in a tree trunk.

In the later times of Egyptian history the priests of Dendera asserted that the home of Nut was in their city, and in an inscription on their temple[1] they recorded that it was the birthplace, , of Isis, and that it contained the birth-chamber, 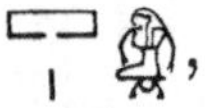, wherein Nut brought forth the goddess in the form of a dark-skinned child, whom she called "Khnemet-ānkhet, the lady of love," , on the fourth of the five epagomenal days. When Nut saw her child, she exclaimed, "Ȧs 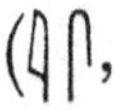, i.e., behold), I have become thy mother," and this was the origin of the name Ȧst, or Isis. In Thebes Nut was identified with Isis, the god-mother, , the lady of Dendera, the dweller in Ȧnt, the goddess Nubt, , who was born in Per-Nubt, and gave birth to her brother Osiris in Thebes, and to her son Horus (the Elder) in Qesqeset, 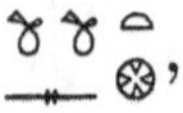, and to her sister Nephthys in Ḥet-Seshesh, 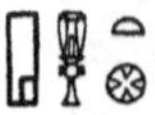;[2] and in the same city she was regarded as a

[1] Brugsch, *Astronomische und Astrologische Inschriften Altaegyptischer Denkmäler*, Leipzig, 1883, p. 101.

[2] Brugsch, *Dict. Géog.*, p. 865.

form of the goddess ÅPET, , or ÅPI, , i.e., the hippopotamus goddess TA-URT, , and also of the local city goddess ÅPET, , and so she became a form of Hathor. The identification of Nut with ÅPI the hippopotamus goddess is very ancient, for in the text of Unȧs (line 487 ff.) we read, "Come Shu, come Shu, come Shu, for "Unȧs is born on the thighs of Isis, and he hath sunk down "on the thighs of Nephthys, having been brought forth. O "Temu, thou father of Unȧs, grant that Unȧs himself may be "set among the number of the gods who are perfect, and "have understanding, and are indestructible;[1] O ÅPI, mother "of Unȧs,[2] give thou thy breast to this Unȧs in order that he "may convey it to his mouth, and that he may suck milk there-"from." Another form of Nut was ḤEQET, , a goddess who was, strictly speaking, the female counterpart of Sebek-Rā of Kom Ombo.

As the children of Nut were not all brought forth in one place so they were not all born on the same day; her five children, i.e., Osiris, Horus, Set, Isis, and Nephthys, were born on the five epagomenal days of the year, or as they are called in Egyptian, "the five days over the year," .[3] On the first, , took place the birth of Osiris, , on the second, , was born Ḥeru-ur, , on the third, , was born Set, , on the fourth, , was born Isis, , and on the fifth, , was born Nephthys, . The first, third, and fifth of the epagomenal days were unlucky, , the second is not described as either lucky or unlucky, but the fourth is said to be a "beautiful festival of heaven and earth,"

[1]

[2]

[3] Or

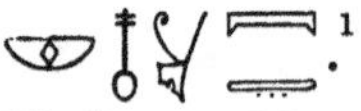[1] The part which Nut played in the Egyptian Underworld was a very prominent one, and from numerous passages in the *Book of the Dead* we can see that without her favour life would be impossible for those who have left this world, and have begun their journey through the Ṭuat. The care and protection which Nut exhibited towards her son Osiris caused her to be regarded as a tender and pitiful mother, and every pious Egyptian prayed that she might do for him even as she had done for Osiris, and hoped that through her he might shine in heaven like the star Sepṭ (, Sothis), when it shines in the sky just before sunrise.

The favour of Nut gave the deceased the power to rise in a renewed body, even as Rā rose from the Egg which was produced by Seb and Nut, and it enabled him to journey with the Sun-god each day from sunrise to sunset, and to pass through the dreary habitations of the Ṭuat in safety. So far back as the time of Men-kau-Rā (Mycerinus) the Egyptians delighted to inscribe on the cover of the coffins of their dead a portion of the following extract:—

peshesh-nes	*mut-k*	*Nut*	*ḥer-k*	*em*
Spreadeth herself	thy mother	Nut	over thee	in

ren-s	*en*	*shet-pet*	*erṭā-s*	*un-nek*	*em*
her name	of	coverer of heaven,	she maketh	thee to be	as

neter	*ȧn*	*khefti-k*	*em*	*ren-k*	*en*	*neter*
a god	without	thine enemy	in	thy name	of	god,

[1] Brugsch, *Thesaurus*, p. 481.

khnem-s thu mā khet neb ṭut em ren-s

she withdraweth thee from thing every evil in her name

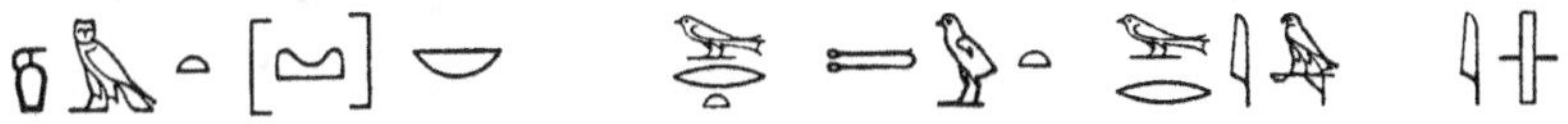

Khnemet ṭu neb urt thut Urȧ ȧm

of "Defender from every evil, great lady; and from Urȧ whom

[1]

mesu-s

she hath brought forth;"

and whenever it was possible they painted on them figures of the goddess, who was represented with her protecting wings stretched out over the deceased, and with the emblems of celestial water and air in her hands. They believed that the dead were safely under the protection of the goddess when a picture of her was painted on the cover of the coffin above them, and they rarely forgot to suggest her presence in one form or the other.

The following passages from the text of Pepi I. (line 100 ff.) illustrate other aspects of the goddess:—"Hail, Nut, in whose "head appear the Two Eyes (i.e., Sun and Moon), thou hast taken "possession of Horus and art his Urt-ḥekau (i.e., mighty one of "words of power), thou hast taken possession of Set and art his "Urt-ḥekau. Behold, O Nut, who didst decree that thou shouldst "be born in thy name of Pet-Ȧnnu (i.e., Sky of Heliopolis), decree "thou that this Pepi shall live, and that he may not perish. "O Nut, who hast risen as a queen that thou mayest take posses-"sion of the gods and of their doubles, and their flesh and their "divine food, and of everything whatsoever which they have, grant "thou that he may be without opposition, and that he may live, "and let thy life, O Nut, be the life of Pepi. Thy mother cometh "to thee and thou movest not. Nut cometh to thee and thou "movest not. The Great Protectress cometh to thee and thou

[1] See text of Tetȧ, ll. 175, 279; Pepi I., ll. 60, 103.

"movest not, but as soon as she hath bestowed her protection upon "thee thou dost move, for she hath given thee thy head, she hath "brought to thee thy bones, she hath collected thy flesh, she hath "brought thee thy heart in thy body, thou livest according to thy "precepts, thou speakest to those who are before thee, thou "protectest thy children from grief, thou purifiest thyself with the "purifications of all the gods, and they come to thee with their "doubles."

CHAPTER VI

OSIRIS, , ÀS-ÀR, OR , , , , [1]

FROM the hieroglyphic texts of all periods of the dynastic history of Egypt we learn that the god of the dead, *par excellence*, was the god, whom the Egyptians called by a name which may be tentatively transcribed ÀS-ÀR, or US-ÀR, who is commonly known to us as "Osiris." The oldest and simplest form of the name is , that is to say, it is written by means of two hieroglyphics, the first of which represents a "throne" and the other an "eye," but the exact meaning attached to the combination of the two pictures by those who first used them to express the name of the god, and the signification of the name in the minds of those who invented it cannot be said. In the late dynastic period the first syllable of the name appears to have been pronounced *Àus* or *Us*, and by punning it was made to have the meaning of the word *usr*, "strength, might, power," and the like, and there is little doubt that the Egyptians at that time supposed the name of the god to mean something like the "strength of the Eye," i.e., the strength of the Sun-god Rā. This meaning may very well have suited their conception of the god Osiris, but it cannot be accepted as the correct signification of the name. For similar reasons the suggestion that the name ÀS-ÀR is connected with the Egyptian word for "prince," or "chief," *ser*, cannot be entertained. It is probable that the second hieroglyphic in the name ÀS-ÀR is to

[1] Other forms are , USR-RĀ, , USER, , UASRI, and 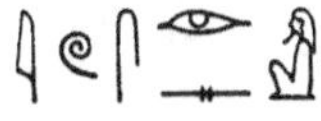, AUSĀRES.

be understood as referring to the great Eye of heaven, i.e., Rā, but the connexion of the first with it is not clear, and as we have no means of knowing what attributes were assigned to the god by his earliest worshippers the difficulty is hardly likely to be cleared up. The throne or seat, 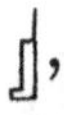, is the first sign in the name of Ȧs-t, , who is the female counterpart of Osiris, and it is very probable that originally the same conception underlay both names. It is useless to argue[1] that, because the dynastic Egyptians at a late period of their history substituted the disk of Rā, , for the eye, , in the name Ȧs-ȧr, and because they addressed to the god hymns in which they identified him as the source of light and as Rā, therefore Ȧs-ȧr was originally a solar god, especially when we remember the childish plays upon words which the priests resorted to whenever they attempted to find etymologies for the names of their gods.

In comparatively late times Osiris was called Un-nefer, 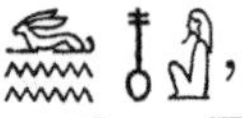, in religious and mythological texts, and the priests (like modern Egyptologists) tried to explain the name. The writer of a hymn quoted by Dr. Brugsch derived the word from *un*, , "to open, to appear, to make manifest," and *neferu*, , "good things," and when he wrote, "Thy beauty (or goodness) "maketh itself manifest in thy person to rouse the gods to life in "thy name Un-nefer," it is clear that he was only making a play of words on the name "Un-nefer"; and again when he wrote, "Thou comest as the strength (*usr*) of Rā in thy name of Ȧs-ȧr," his object was rather to play with words on the name Ȧs-ȧr than to afford a trustworthy derivation of the name of Osiris. We may note in passing that modern derivations and explanations of the name Un-nefer are equally unsatisfactory.[2] The truth of the matter seems to be that the ancient Egyptians knew just as little

[1] See Brugsch, *Religion*, p. 81.

[2] According to one writer the name means "beautiful hare," and according to another the "Good Being"; in one case *un* is connected with the verb *un*, "to be," and in the other with the god Un, , or Unti, , who is mentioned in the *Book of the Dead*, Chapters xv. (Litany), 1; cxxxvi.a 7.

OSIRIS – UNNEFER.

about the original meaning of the name Ȧs-ȧr as we do, and that they had no better means of obtaining information about it than we have.

Passing now to the consideration of the original characteristics and attributes of Osiris we find that the oldest religious texts known to us refer to him as the great god of the dead, and throughout them it is tacitly assumed that the reader will understand that he once possessed human form and lived upon earth, and that by means of some unusual power or powers he was able to bestow upon himself after his death a new life which he lived in a new body in a region over which he ruled as king, and into which he was believed to be willing to admit all such as had lived a good and correct life upon earth, and had been buried with appropriate ceremonies under the protection of certain amulets, and with the proper recital of certain "divine words" and words of power. The worship of Osiris is, however, very much older than these views, which, it is clear, could only belong to a people who had advanced to a comparatively high state of civilization and of mental development.

The oldest authorities for the religious views of the ancient Egyptians are the "Pyramid Texts," which are known to us from copies made in the IVth, Vth and VIth Dynasties, that is to say, in the period of their highest development; even at this remote time the priests of Ȧnnu had composed a system of theology which was supported by the authority of the king and his high officials, and there is no doubt that it was based upon older systems of religious thought and belief. What these may have been it is useless to speculate, and all that is certain about the Heliopolitan system is that, whilst proclaiming the supremacy of their local god Tem or Rā-Tem, its priests took care to include in it as many of the ancient provincial gods as possible, and to adopt wherever they were able to do so the ancient beliefs and traditions concerning them. Among such gods Osiris held a very prominent place, in fact he was in respect of the dead and of the Underworld what Rā, or Rā-Tem was to the living and to this world, and in some passages he is referred to simply as "god," 𓊹, without the addition of any name. No other god of the Egyptians was ever mentioned or alluded to in this manner, and no other god at any time in Egypt ever occupied exactly the same exalted position in their minds, or was thought to possess his peculiar attributes.

Up to the present no evidence has been deduced from the hieroglyphic texts which enables us to say specifically when Osiris began to be worshipped, or in what town or city his cult was first established, but the general information which we possess on this subject indicates that this god was adored as the great god of the dead by the dynastic Egyptians from first to last, and that the earliest dynastic centres of his worship were situated at Abydos in the South and at Ṭeṭṭu (Mendes) in the North; in proof of these statements the following considerations are submitted. In a Rubric to one of the versions of the lxivth Chapter of the Theban Recension of the *Book of the Dead* it is said that the Chapter was "found" during the reign of SEMTI,[1] that is to say, the Chapter was revised, or edited, or re-written, or received some kind of literary treatment, during the reign of the fifth king of the Ist Dynasty. If we look at the version of the Chapter to which this Rubric is appended we find this sentence:—"I am Yesterday, "and I am To-day; and I have the power to be born a second time. "I the hidden Soul create the gods, and I give sepulchral meals to "the divine beings in Åmenti and in heaven." Osiris is mentioned by name in connexion with "his city," and Tem, Kheperȧ, Shu, the Urti goddesses, i.e., Isis and Nephthys, the goddess Åuḳert, the Chief of Re-stau, Ḥeḥi, the Bennu, and the 4,601,200 spirits, who are twelve cubits high, are referred to, and we see that the whole of the religious and mythological systems of the Egyptians as made known to us by texts of later periods were in a well-developed state even in the Ist Dynasty.

Confirmation of this fact is afforded by a small wooden plaque, in the British Museum, which was made for a "royal chancellor" called Ḥemaka, 𓎛𓌳𓂓, who flourished in the reign of SEMTI, the king in whose reign the lxivth Chapter of the *Book of the Dead* was "found." On the right-hand side of the plaque is a scene in which the king is represented in the act of dancing before a deity,

[1] His name was formerly read ḤESEPTI.

who wears the crown of the South and is seated within a shrine set upon the top of some steps; from various texts and scenes inscribed upon papyri and coffins, etc., of the New Empire we know that Osiris was called the "god on the top of the steps," and that he was depicted as a being seated in a shrine set on the top of a flight of steps, and there is no doubt that the god before whom Semti danced was Osiris. Immediately below the scene on the plaque described above is a representation of a ceremonial boat, and if we compare it with certain vignettes in the *Book of the Dead* and elsewhere we cannot fail to identify it as the well-known Ḥennu Boat of the god Seker (Socharis). Now, in the Rubric of the Chapter already referred to, we are told that the Chapter was found "in the foundations of the shrine of Ḥennu," and thus the Chapter and the god Ḥennu, i.e., the god of the Ḥennu Boat, were in existence in the Ist Dynasty, and they were in some way specially connected with king Semti—if we are to believe an Egyptian tradition which was current under the XVIIIth Dynasty, about B.C. 1600. Moreover, if the gods whom the Egyptians under the IVth and Vth Dynasties declared to belong to the company of Osiris existed under the Ist Dynasty, Osiris also must have existed, and the mention of the Underworld by the name of Åmenti, or Åmentet, presupposes the existence of its god and king, one of whose chief titles was Khenti-Åmenti. It is important to note also that on the plaque of Ḥemaka Osiris wears the White Crown, or Crown of the South, a fact which suggests that at the time when it was made he was regarded as a god of the South, and to note that although in later times his cult was general throughout Egypt he was always represented with the White Crown on his head, and that it was one of his most characteristic attributes.

The plaque of Ḥemaka proves that a centre of the Osiris cult existed at Abydos under the Ist Dynasty, but we are not justified in assuming that the god was first worshipped there, and when we remember the frequent allusions in the Pyramid Texts to Pe and Ṭep, the two divisions of the city of Per-Uatchet in the Delta, it is difficult not to think that even under the Ist Dynasty shrines had been built in honour of Osiris at several places in Egypt. Dynastic tradition asserted that the head of Osiris was buried at

Abydos, and for this reason that city became of the first importance
to worshippers of the god, but we know that the local god of the
nome was ÀN-ḤER, and that his cult was thrust out by that of
Osiris, who was adored under the title of " Osiris Khent-Àmenti ; "
there must then have been a time when Osiris was brought to
Abydos, and it is probable that he was introduced into that city
from the North, for the following reasons. In the Pyramid Texts,
which are the oldest exponents of the religious system which made
Osiris the supreme god of the dead, we have frequent allusions to
the food and drink which the deceased enjoys, and to the apparel
wherein he is arrayed in the Underworld. We find that he wears
white linen garments and sandals, that he sits by a lake in the
Field of Peace with the gods, and partakes with them of the tree of
life, ⊙ ⌒ ⌇⌇⌇ ⚲ ⌇⌇⌇ , and that he eats figs and grapes, and drinks
oil and wine, and that he lives on the " bread of eternity," and
the " beer of everlastingness," ⌒ ⊖ ⌇⌇⌇ 🡒 ⚭ ◿ ⚬ ⌒ 𓃗 ⚭⚭ .[1]
His bread was made of the wheat which Horus ate, and the four
children of Horus, Mesthà, Ḥàpi, Ṭuamutef, and Qebḥsennuf
" appeased the hunger of his belly, and the thirst of his lips." He
abhorred the hunger which he could not satisfy, and he loathed
the thirst which he could not slake, and one of the greatest delights
of his existence was the knowledge that he was " delivered from
the power of those who would steal away his food."

Another source of great joy was the power which he possessed
of washing himself clean, and he and his double are represented as
sitting down to eat bread together, each having washed himself
clean ; yet another source of enjoyment was his journeying by
water in a boat which was rowed by the mariners of the Sun-god
Rā. All these and similar statements point clearly to the fact that
the reward which Osiris bestowed after death upon his follower
was a life which he led in a region where corn, and wine, and oil,
and water were abundant, and where circumstances permitted him
to wear white linen robes and white sandals, and where he was not
required to do work of any kind, and where he was able to perform

---

[1] See the Chapter " *Doctrine of Eternal Life* " in my *Papyrus of Ani*, London,
1894, pp. lxxv.-lxxvii.

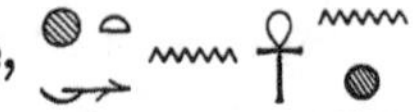

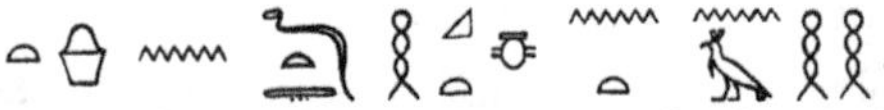

his ablutions at will, and to repose whensoever it pleased him to do so. He possessed his own estate, or homestead, where he abode with his parents, and presumably with a wife, or wives, and family, and his heavenly life was to all intents and purposes nothing but a duplicate of his life upon earth. In several passages in the Pyramid Texts we also have allusions to a life in which his enjoyments and delights were of a more spiritual character, but it is evident that these represent the beliefs and doctrines of the priests of Rā, who declared that the blessed fed upon light, and were arrayed in light and became beings of light, and that the place wherein they lived was the boat of the Sun-god Rā, wherein they passed over heaven, and wherefrom their souls flew down to earth to visit the scenes of their former life. Thus, as far back as the period of the Vth Dynasty texts belonging to two distinct cults, i.e., the cult of Osiris and the cult of Rā, existed side by side, and no attempt appears to have been made to suppress either that of Osiris or that of Rā; in other words, the priests of Heliopolis had the good sense to allow the beliefs which were connected with the cult of Osiris to find expression in the great Recension of religious texts which they promulgated about B.C. 3500. The cult of Osiris was very ancient, and was universal, and they saw that the cult of Rā would not take its place in the minds of the Egyptians for a very considerable time, if ever.

From what has been said above it is quite clear that the followers of Osiris believed in a material heaven, and we have now to consider where that heaven was situated. In a passage in the text of Unȧs (line 191 ff.) the Angels of Thoth, , and the Ancient Ones, , and the Great Terrifier, , who cometh forth from the Nile, 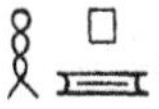, Ḥāp, and ȦP-UAT, 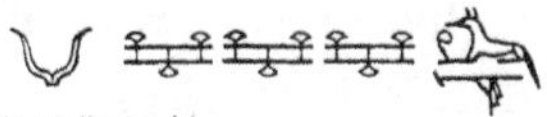, who cometh forth from the tree ȦSERT, 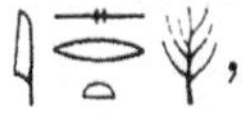, are called upon to witness that the mouth of the king is pure, because he eats and drinks nothing except that upon which the gods live. The text says, "Ye have taken Unȧs "with you, and he eateth what ye eat, he drinketh that which ye "drink, he liveth as ye live, he dwelleth as ye dwell, he is powerful "as ye are powerful, and he saileth about as ye sail about"; thus the heaven where Unȧs lived after death was in some place where there were waters whereon he could sail in a boat. The text continues, "Unȧs hath netted [fowl and fish] with the net in "Ȧaru, Unȧs hath possession over the waters in Sekhet-ḥetep, "and his offerings of meat and drink are among the gods. The "water of Unȧs is as wine, even as it is for Rā, and Unȧs goeth "about heaven like Rā, and he traverseth heaven like Thoth." From this extract we see that the region where the heaven of Unȧs was situated is called Ȧaru, , the name having as a determinative a sign which is intended to represent a mass of waving reeds; in another place (line 412) the region is called Sekhet-Ȧar, , and is identical with the Sekhet-Ȧarru, , and Sekhet-Ȧanru, , of the later Recensions of the *Book of the Dead*. From a number of other passages we find that Ȧaru or Sekhet-Ȧaru was divided into a number of districts, the chief of which was called Sekhet-ḥetepet, , i.e., "Field of Offerings," or Sekhet-ḥetep, , i.e., "Field of Peace," and was presided over by the god Sekhti-ḥetep, . To the south of this region lay Sekhet-Saneḥemu, , i.e., "Field of the Grasshoppers,"[1] and in it were the Lakes of the Ṭuat, , and the Lakes of the Jackals, . In the waters of Ȧaru, or Sekhet-Ȧaru, Rā purified himself (Pepi I., line 234), and it was here that the deceased also purified himself before he began his heavenly life; here also dwelt the three classes of beings who are called Ȧkhemu-seku, Ȧkhemu-Beṭesh, and Ȧkhemu-Sesh-emȧu,[2] that is to say, three classes of celestial bodies

[1] See *Book of the Dead*, cxxv. Pt. iii., l. 19.

[2] 

THE SEKHET-HETE

[FROM THE PAPYRUS OF

ANI PLOUGHING AND REAPIN
O

ELYSIAN FIELDS.

. MUS. No. 10.470, SHEET 35).]

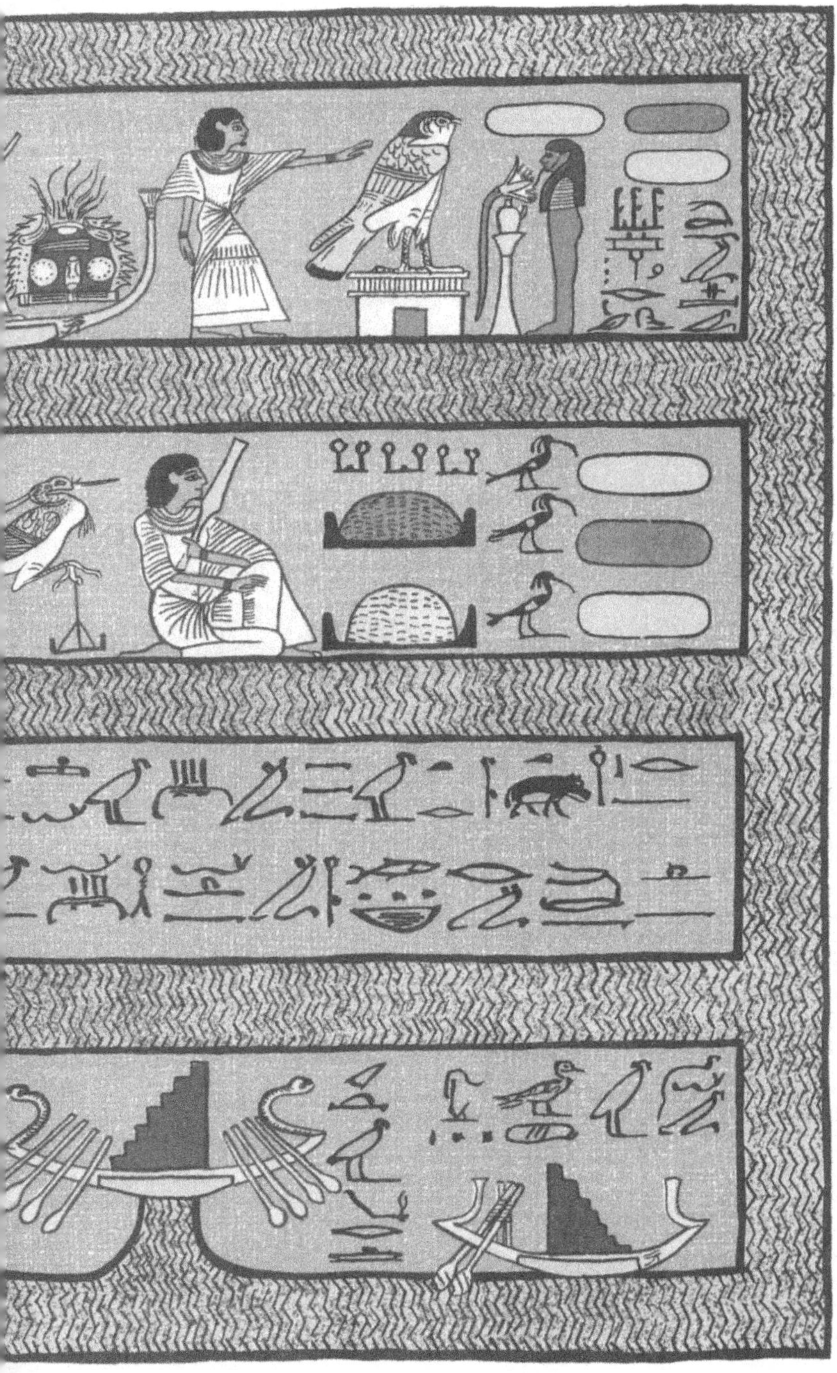

SHIPPING THE GODS IN THE ABODE
SSED.

or beings who were thought never to diminish, or melt away, or decay.

All the evidence as to the position of the region Åaru shows that originally it was thought to be in the sky, but, on the other hand, there are indications that it was entered from certain places in the Delta, and among such was the region which contained the double city, Pe-Ṭep and Ṭeṭṭu, or Ṭāṭāu. Thus in a passage in the text of Pepi I. (line 255) it is said, "Pepi hath gone forth from "Pe, and from being with the Souls of Pe, and as he is arrayed in "the apparel of Horus, and in the garment of Thoth, and as Isis is "before him and Nephthys is behind him, Åpuat openeth a way "for him, and Shu beareth him up, and the Souls of Ånnu make "him to mount the steps that they may present him to Nut "who stretcheth out her hands to him, even as they did for "Osiris when he arrived in the other world. O ḤRÅ-F-ḤA-F "(),[1] Pepi hath journeyed on to Sekhet-Åar, "(), he hath come forth from Uart, "(), and since he is the body which hath come forth "from God, and the uraeus which hath come forth from Rā, he "hath sailed on to Sekhet-Åar, having the four Spirits of Horus, "Ḥāp, Åmset, Ṭuamutef, and Qebḥsennuf, with him, two on each "side." This view of the position of Sekhet-Åaru is supported by several passages in the Theban Recension of the *Book of the Dead*, and the pictures of the district, with its lakes and canals which form the vignettes to the cxth Chapter, indicate that it was situated to the north of Egypt. The name Sekhet-Åaru appears to mean "Field of Reeds" or "Field of Plants," and the idea conveyed by it was that of some very fertile region where farming operations could be carried on with ease and success, and where it would be possible to possess a large, well-kept, and well-stocked homestead, situated at no great distance from the Nile, or from one of its main branches. In the text the deceased prays, "Let "me have the power to order my own fields in Ṭeṭṭu, and my own "growing crops in Ånnu. Let me live upon bread made of white

[1] I.e., "He whose face is behind him."

"grain, and let my beer be made from red grain, and may the "persons of my father and mother be given unto me as guardians "of my door, and for the ordering of my homestead. Let me be "sound and strong, and let me have much room wherein to move, "and let me be able to sit wheresoever I please" (Chapter lii.).

In the neighbourhood of Ṭeṭṭu, then, the original Sekhet-Åaru was thought to be located, and in Ṭeṭṭu the reconstruction of the dismembered body of Osiris took place, and it was here that the solemn ceremony of setting up his backbone was performed each year. The city of Ṭeṭṭu, , or Ṭāṭāu, , here referred to was the capital of the ninth nome of Lower Egypt called Per-Åsår-neb-Ṭeṭṭu, , by the Egyptians, and Busiris by the Greeks. In a portion of it called Neb-seḳert, , was preserved, according to one tradition, the backbone, , of Osiris; according to another his jaws were there preserved.[1]

From what has been said above it is clear that the cult of Osiris is certainly as old as the period of the Ist Dynasty, and that the oldest centre of his worship was situated in the Delta. Everything which the texts of all periods record concerning him goes to show that he was an indigenous god of North-east Africa, and that his home and origin were possibly Libyan. We have no means of finding out what were the earliest conceptions about Osiris, but it seems that he was originally a water spirit, or the god of some arm of the Nile, or portion of the main body of the Nile, and that he developed later into a great water-god; Dr. Brugsch[2] and M. Maspero[3] both regarded him as a water-god, and rightly consider that he represented the creative and nutritive powers of the Nile stream in general and of the Inundation in particular.

The natural opponent of Osiris was Set, who typified death and destruction, and who was the god *par excellence* of the desert; and in various forms and told in different ways we have the narrative of the contest between the powers of life and death, and

[1] See de Rougé, *Géog. Ancienne*, p. 59. [2] *Religion*, pp. 190, 197.
[3] *Histoire Ancienne*, tom. i., p. 172.

light and darkness, and decay and regeneration, which appears in the religious texts of every period. In fact, Set was the opponent in every way of Osiris who, in the words of Dr. Brugsch, typified the "unbroken rejuvenescence of immortal Nature according to "the Divine Will and according to eternal laws."[1] In the xviith Chapter of the *Book of the Dead* the deceased says, "I am "YESTERDAY (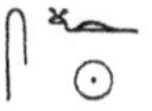 *sef*); I know TO-DAY ( *ṭuau*)," and in answer to the question which follows, "Who then is this?" it is said, "Yesterday is Osiris, and To-day is Rā, on the day when "he shall destroy the enemies of Neb-er-tcher, and when he shall "establish as prince and ruler his son Horus" (lines 15-18). This passage proves that although Osiris was the type of that which is gone, or dead, or the past, he possessed a power of regeneration which expressed itself in the young Horus. In his aspect of a water-god Osiris was the personification of the falling Nile, or the Nile in winter, and of the night sun, and of the winter sun, but he was, nevertheless, the cause of the fertility of Egypt, which was personified as Isis, and was the father of the young Horus, who in due course grew into an Osiris, and produced by means of Isis a young Horus to take his place, becoming thus the "father of his father."[2]

Among a people like the Egyptians it would not be very long before the annual rise, and inundation, and fall of the Nile would be compared to the chief periods in the lives of men, and before the renewed rise of the Nile in the following year would be compared to man's immortality, which in Egypt was taken for granted from the earliest times; and that this is exactly what happened the hieroglyphic texts supply abundant proof. Unfortunately, however, we find nowhere in Egyptian works a connected narrative of the life, acts and deeds, and sufferings and death, and resurrection of Osiris, the man-god, but we possess a tolerably accurate account of them in Plutarch's *De Iside et Osiride.*[3] The mythological history of Isis and Osiris by this

[1] "Die ununterbrochene Verjüngung der unsterblichen Natur nach gottlichem Willen und nach ewigen Gesetzen," *Religion*, p. 611.

[2] Brugsch, *Religion*, pp. 612, 613.

[3] Ed. Didot (*Scripta Moralia*, tom. iii., pp. 427–469), § xii. ff.

writer is so important that an English rendering of it by Mr. Squire is given at the end of this chapter, but it will be necessary here to summarize the main facts in it in order that they may be compared with the hieroglyphic texts which refer to the subject. According to these Osiris was the son of Rhea, the Egyptian Nut, the wife of Helios, the Egyptian Rā, by Kronos, the Egyptian Seb; when Helios found that his wife was with child by Seb he declared that she should not be delivered of her child in any month or in any year. By a stratagem Hermes, the Egyptian Thoth, played at tables with Selene, and won from her the seventieth part of each day of the year, i.e., in all five days, which he added to the year. On the first of these five days Osiris was born, and a voice was heard to proclaim that the lord of creation was born. In due course he became king of Egypt and taught men husbandry, and established a code of laws, and made men worship the gods; when Egypt had become peaceful and prosperous he set out to instruct the other nations of the world, and Isis ruled Egypt during his absence. On his return Typhon, the Egyptian Set, and his seventy-two comrades, made Osiris to lie down in a chest, which was immediately closed by them, and cast into the Nile, which carried it down to its Tanaitic mouths. When Isis heard what had befallen her husband she cut off a lock of her hair as a sign of grief, and then set out to find his dead body. At length she traced it to Byblos, whither it had been carried by the sea, and she found that the waves had gently laid it among the branches of a tamarisk tree, which had grown to a magnificent size, and had enclosed the chest within its trunk. The Byblos here referred to is not Byblos in Phoenicia, but the papyrus swamps of Egypt, which are called in Egyptian Ȧṭḥu,
, a name meaning "papyrus plants;" the Greeks rendered the Egyptian word for "papyrus" by *Βύβλος*, and some copyist of the Greek text misunderstood the signification of the word in this passage, and rendered it by the name of the city of Phoenicia.

The king of the country, admiring the tree, had it cut down and made a pillar for the roof of his house; it is this tree trunk which is referred to by the hieroglyphic sign 𓊽, *ṭeṭ*, and which is continually used in the texts with reference to Osiris. It has been said to represent a mason's table, but the four cross-bars have nothing to do with such a thing, for they are intended to indicate the four branches of a roof-tree of a house which were turned to the four cardinal points. When Isis heard that the tree had been cut down, she went to the palace of the king, and through the good offices of the royal maidens she was made nurse to one of the king's sons. Instead of nursing the child in the ordinary way, Isis gave him her finger to suck, and each night she put him into the fire to consume his mortal parts, changing herself the while into a swallow and bemoaning her fate. On one occasion the queen saw her son in the flames, and cried out, and thus deprived him of immortality. Then Isis told the queen her story, and begged for the pillar which supported the roof. This she cut open, and took out the chest and her husband's body, and departed with them to Egypt; having arrived there she hid the chest and set out in quest of her son Horus.

One night, however, Typhon was out hunting by the light of the moon, and he found the chest, and recognizing the body, tore it into fourteen pieces, which he scattered up and down throughout the land. When Isis heard of this she took a boat made of papyrus [1]—a plant abhorred by crocodiles —and sailing about she gathered together the fragments of Osiris's body. Wheresoever she found one, she buried it and built a tomb over it. Meanwhile Horus had grown up, and being encouraged in the use of arms by Osiris, who returned from the other world, he went out to do battle with Typhon the murderer of his father. The fight lasted some days, and Typhon was made captive, and was given over to the custody of Isis who, however, set him free. Horus in his rage tore from her head the royal diadem, but Thoth gave her a helmet in the shape of a cow's head. In two other battles fought between

[1] Moses was laid in an ark of bulrushes, and was therefore believed to be safe from the attacks of crocodiles.

Horus and Typhon Horus was the victor. The great battle between Horus and Typhon took place, we are told in the IVth Sallier Papyrus, on the 26th day of the month Thoth; they first of all fought in the form of two men, but they afterwards changed themselves into two bears, and they passed three days and three nights in this form.

From the above summary it is clear that in Plutarch's time the Egyptians believed that Osiris was the son of a god, that he lived a good life upon earth and ruled as a wise and just king, that he was slain by the malice of evil men, that his body was mutilated, and that his wife Isis collected his limbs which had been scattered throughout Egypt by Set, or Typhon, and that Osiris by some means obtained a new life in the next world, where he reigned as god and king. The hieroglyphic texts contain abundant testimony that the statements of Plutarch are substantially correct, and from first to last Osiris was to the Egyptians the god-man who suffered, and died, and rose again, and reigned eternally in heaven. They believed that they would inherit eternal life, just as he had done, provided that what was done for him by the gods was done for them, and they made use of amulets, and magical texts of all kind, and performed ceremonies connected with sympathetic magic in order that they might compel Osiris and the gods who had brought about his resurrection (i.e., Thoth, the "lord of divine words, the scribe of the gods," and Isis, who made use of the words with which Thoth supplied her, and Horus and his companion gods who performed the symbolic ceremonies which were effectual in producing the reconstitution of the body of Osiris and its revivification) to act on their behalf even as they had acted for the god. The species of the amulets used were constant, and they appear to have been sixteen in number, viz., four figures of the children of Horus each with his characteristic head, four lapis-lazuli Ṭeṭ pillars, two bulls, a figure of Horus, a figure of Thoth, two carnelian Ṭeṭ pillars, and two lapis-lazuli *utchats*, .

According to Plutarch the number of portions into which Set tore the body of Osiris was fourteen, but the hieroglyphic texts give at times fourteen and at others sixteen; the cities and sanctuaries wherein these were buried are :—1. Ȧment in Koptos. 2. Ȧa-āb in Elephantine. 3. Ȧn-ruṭ-f in Herakleopolis Magna. 4. Kusae. 5. Heliopolis. 6. Āt-Ȧment in Sma-beḥuṭet (Diospolis of Lower Egypt). 7. Letopolis. 8. Pa-Thuḥen in Saïs. 9. Meḥ-ta-f in Hermopolis of Lower Egypt. 10. Athribis. 11. Āq (Schedia). 12. Āb, in the Libyan Nome. 13. Ḥet-serȧ in the city of Netert. 14. Apis.[1] In the late period of Egyptian history, i.e., in Graeco-Roman times, the sanctuaries of Osiris were forty-two in number; in other words, each nome possessed its central shrine of Osiris, which was called a "Serapeum," or the place where Serapis was worshipped, but this happened because Osiris Khent Ȧmenti was identified with Serapis, who was not the god Osiris himself, but only a dead Ȧpis bull which had become an Osiris. It has already been said that in some lists the sanctuaries of Osiris are stated to be sixteen in number, but it is tolerably certain that the true number is fourteen, because in the inscriptions at Dendera which refer to the "mysteries" of Osiris, the statue of Seker-Osiris, which played such a prominent part in the ceremonies performed there, was made up of fourteen pieces,[2] although sixteen pieces are sometimes enumerated.[3] The sixteen members of the body of Osiris are :—his head, , the soles of his feet, , his bones, , his arms, , his heart, , his interior, , his tongue, , his eye, , his fist, , his fingers, , his back, , his ears, , his loins, , his body, ,

[1] See Brugsch, *Aeg. Zeitschrift*, 1881, p. 79 ff. Another list of the sixteen sanctuaries is given by M. Loret in *Recueil*, tom. v., p. 85, where they are enumerated in the following order:—Ṭeṭṭu, , Abydos, , Memphis, , Nubia, , Herakleopolis, , Kusae, , Ȧtef-khent, , Saïs, , Meḥtet, , Amu, , Sma-Beḥuṭet, , Re-āqiu, , Ḥen, , Netrȧt, , Bāḥet, , Ka-qem, , Dendera, .

[2] They are enumerated by Brugsch, *Aeg. Zeit.*, 1881, p. 90 ff.

[3] *Recueil*, tom. iii., p. 56; tom. iv., p. 23.

his head with the face of a ram, , and his hair, .[1]

All the evidence on the subject now available goes to prove, as the paragraphs above show, that the early Egyptians believed that Osiris was a man-god who was murdered and whose body was mutilated, and that the various members of his body were reconstituted; and we know from a very interesting text at Dendera[2] that during the month of Khoiak a number of festivals were celebrated at all the chief sanctuaries of Osiris in Egypt, and that elaborate ceremonies were performed in them in commemoration of every event which took place in the life, death, and resurrection of the god. In this text the uses of the various sanctuaries are described, and detailed instructions are given for the making of the funeral chest, and of the model of the god which was to be buried in the coffin, and of the incense, and of the amulets, and of the fourteen divine members, and of all the materials, etc., which were employed in the ceremonies. On the xiith day of Khoiak the Festival of the Ploughing of the Earth and the Festival of the TENÀ, , were celebrated; on the xivth day the great

[1] The hieroglyphic texts tell us that the head of Osiris was buried in the sanctuary of Ārq-ḥeḥ, , in Abydos; his left eye was buried in Ḥet-Maākheru, , in Lower Egypt; his eyebrows were buried in Ām, (Pelusium); his jaw-bones were buried at Fāket in Upper Egypt; certain portions of his head were buried at Ḥeb-ḳert, , in the Delta; his neck was buried in the Delta; an arm and his right leg were buried at Aterui qemā, ; his left leg was buried at Meḥet, ; a bone of his back (*os coccyx*) was buried at Heliopolis, and his thighs at Ḥet-ḥer-àteb, ; a foot was buried at Netert, , and his heart at Usekht-Maāti, ; his phallus was buried at Ḥet-Bennu, , and a portion of his backbone at Pa-paut-neteru, . Various other parts of his body were buried at different places, and in the case of a few members the honour of possessing them was claimed by more than one city.

[2] See Brugsch, *Recueil*, i., 15, 16; Dümichen, *Résultats*, iv. 1–27; Mariette, *Dendérah*, tom. iv., pll. 35–39.

Festival of Pert; on the xvith day the Festival of Osiris Khent Āmenti; on the xxivth day the model of the god of the preceding year was taken out from its place and buried suitably, and the new Osiris was embalmed in the sanctuary; on the last day of the month the Ṭeṭ, , was set up in Ṭeṭṭu, because on this day the divine members of Osiris, , were brought. The new Osiris remained without burial for seven days because of the tradition which declared that the god had remained for seven days in the womb of his mother Nut when she was with child.

In connexion with the ceremonies in the great sanctuaries, e.g., Dendera, thirty-four papyrus boats were employed, and these were lit up with 365 lights, or lamps, 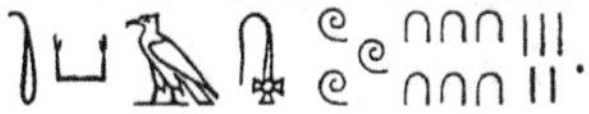. The gods of Mendes, with Anubis, occupied one boat, and Isis, Nephthys, Horus, and Thoth, each had a boat; the remaining twenty-nine boats were dedicated to the following gods:—MESTHÀ, ḤĀPI, ṬUAMUTEF, QEBḤ-SENNUF, SĀḤ-ḤEQ, , ĀRMĀUAI, , MAA-TEF-F, , ÀR-REN-F-TCHESEF, 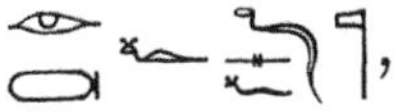, ÀM-ṬEṬ, 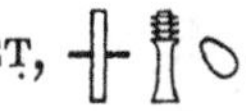, NEFER-ḤĀT, 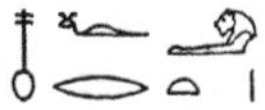, ÀST-SEN-ÀRI-TCHER, 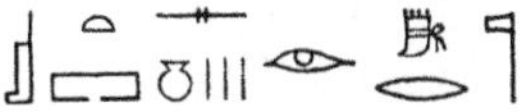, SEM, , ḤER-Ā-F,  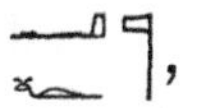, SENṬ, 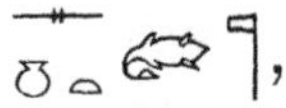, ÀRI-MAAT-F-TCHESEF, 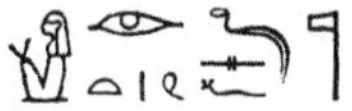, SEBAKHSEN, 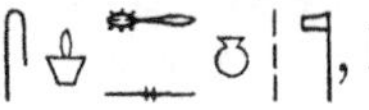, ḤEQES, 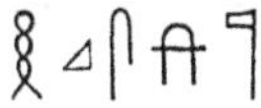, NETER-BAḤ, , QETET, , KHENTI-HEH-F, 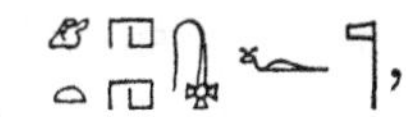, ĀQ-ḤER-ÀM-UNNUT-F, , NETCHEḤ-NETCHEḤ, 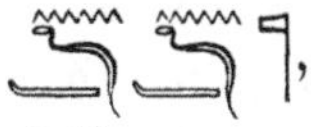, ÀSBU, , PER-EM-KHET-KHET, 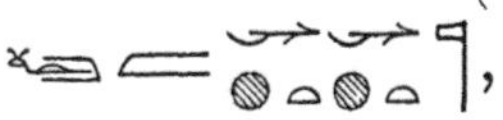, ERTĀ-NEF-NEBT, , ṬESHER-MAATI, , KHENT-ḤET-ÀNES, , MAA-EM-QERḤ,  ÀN-F-EM-HRU-SEKSEK, . The above facts prove that in the Ptolemaïc period the views which were held generally about Osiris were substantially the same as those which were in vogue in the times when the Pyramid Texts were composed, and it is clear that the cult of Osiris was widespread even in the Vth Dynasty, or about B.C. 3500.

From the Pyramid Texts we learn that the dead kings were already identified with Osiris, and that Osiris was identified with the dead Sun-god, but we have no means of knowing when he was merged in Seker, the god of the Memphite Underworld. The Heliopolitan priests declared that he was the son of Seb and Nut, but it is much to be regretted that they did not preserve for us the genealogy of the god according to the priests of the predynastic period. The festivals which were celebrated in the month of Khoiak were, no doubt, founded upon very ancient tradition, but the elaboration of detail given in the text at Dendera, to which reference has already been made, does not suggest a primitive antiquity, although it shows how deeply seated was the cult of Osiris in the hearts of the people. The numerous aspects under which the god was worshipped also show that some of the original conceptions of the attributes of the god were forgotten in comparatively early days, both by foreigners and Egyptians, and it is this fact which explains how he came to be identified with the Greek god Dionysos. The aspects of Osiris were nearly as numerous as those of Rā, hence we find him identified with the sun and moon, and with the great creative and regenerative powers of Nature, and he was at once the symbol of rejuvenescence, resurrection, and of life of every sort and kind which has the power of renewing itself.

We must now consider the various forms in which Osiris is represented on the monuments, and in papyri, etc. The common form of the god is that of a mummy, who wears a beard, and has the White Crown, , on his head, and a *menȧt*, , hanging from the back of his neck. In a scene reproduced by Lanzone[1] he appears in a group with the Hawk-god Seker, the Beetle-god Khepre, and the goddess SHENT, , and has two forms, i.e., Osiris, lord of Khut, and Khent Ȧmenti, , and . In another scene[2] he appears in the form of the Ṭeṭ

[1] *Dizionario*, plate 15. [2] *Ibid.*, pl. 17.

This illustration is reproduced in full color on the insert attached to the inside back cover of this volume.

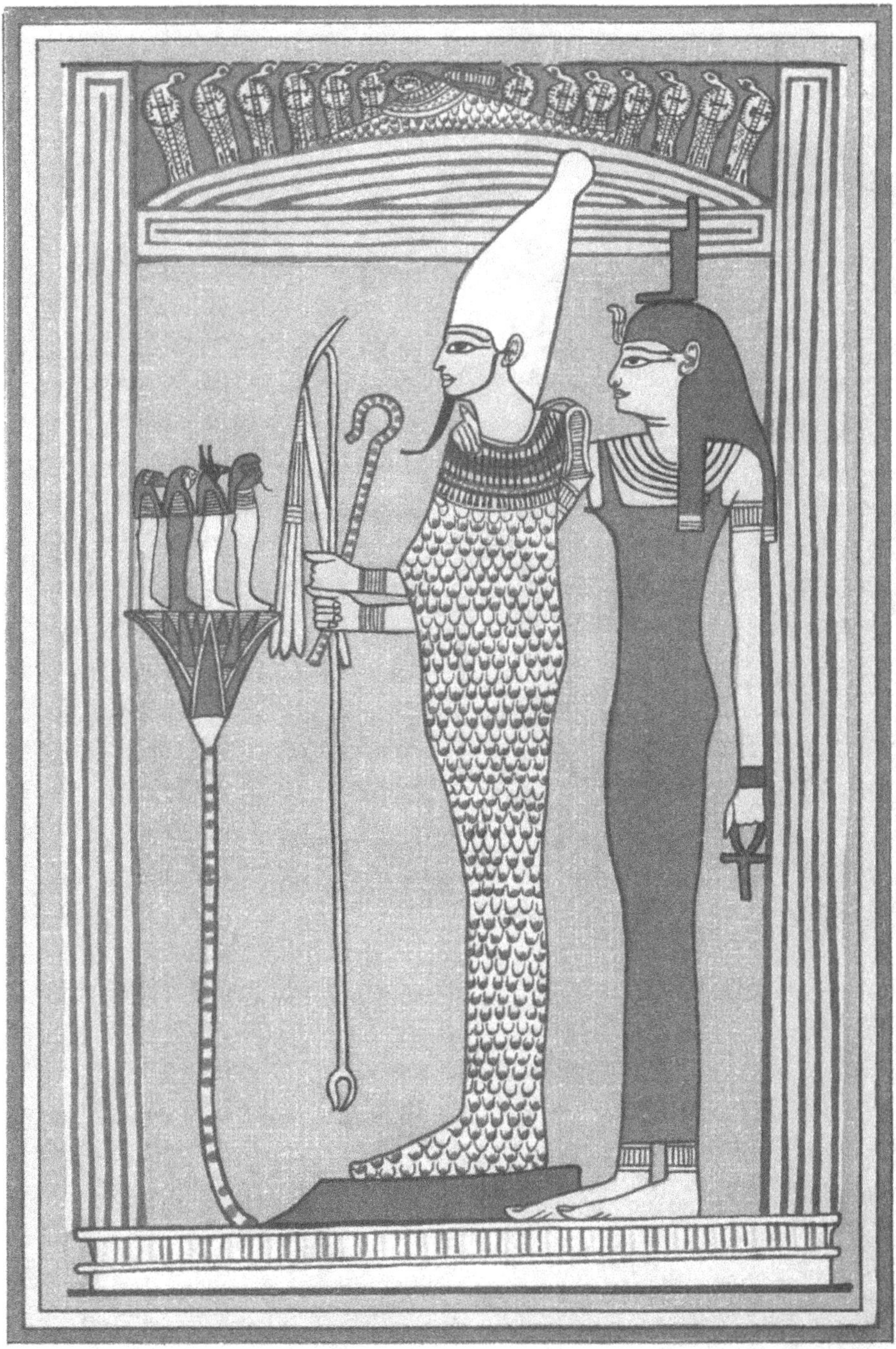

OSIRIS WEARING THE WHITE CROWN AND MENÀT AND HOLDING THE SCEPTRE, CROOK, AND FLAIL. BEFORE HIM ARE THE FOUR CHILDREN OF HORUS, AND BEHIND HIM IS HIS WIFE ISIS.

ANUBIS MINISTERING TO OSIRIS ON HIS BIER; AT THE HEAD KNEELS NEPHTHYS, AND AT THE FEET ISIS.

pillar, and is called "Osiris Ṭeṭ," and stands at the head of a bier, on which lies the god Seker in mummied form. On a stele at Turin[1] Osiris appears in mummied form, seated, and holding in his hands the sceptre , and the flail or whip ; on his head is the White Crown with plumes, to which the name *Atef* is usually given. His titles are "Osiris Khenti-Åmentet, Un-nefer, lord of Tatcheser, the great god, king of the living." Behind him are seated Ptaḥ-Sekri, 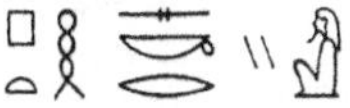, "lord of the hidden chest," Ånpu, "dweller in the city of embalmment," Horus, son of Isis, and Hathor. As a form of Khnemu-Rā he has the head of a ram, the horns of which are surmounted by a solar disk and by four knives.[2] A common symbol of the god is , i.e., the box which contained the head and hair of Osiris and which was preserved at Abydos, where these relics were buried. Elsewhere we see the body of the god bent round backwards in such a way as to form the region of the Ṭuat or Underworld (see vol. i., p. 229). Sometimes the god is seated on a throne, which is supported on the back of a monster serpent that rests on the top of the mythological flight of steps, , at Ḥenen-Su; he is accompanied by Maāt, Horus, son of Isis, Thoth, Ḥeka, , who holds a serpent in each hand, and the snake-headed goddess Ḥeptet, . The exact part which this last-named deity played in connexion with Osiris is unknown, but it is certain that it was of considerable importance, and that the goddess assisted in bringing about his resurrection. Ḥeptet has the body of a woman with the head of a bearded snake; on her head is a pair of horns which are surmounted by a solar disk, and Atef Crown, and uraei with disks and horns, . In each hand she holds a knife.[3]

On the walls of the temple of Dendera[4] is preserved a very interesting group of scenes connected with the story of the death and resurrection of the god, which may be briefly described thus:—

1. Osiris lying on his stomach on his bier, beneath which are his four crowns; he is called, "Osiris, beloved of his father, the

[1] Lanzone, op. cit., pl. 96. [2] *Ibid.*, pl. 143. [3] *Ibid.*, pl. 211.
[4] See Mariette, *Dendérah*, tom. iv., pl. 65 ff., Paris, 1873.

king of the gods, the lord of life, Osiris." In front of Osiris is Horus who presents to him a lotus flower.

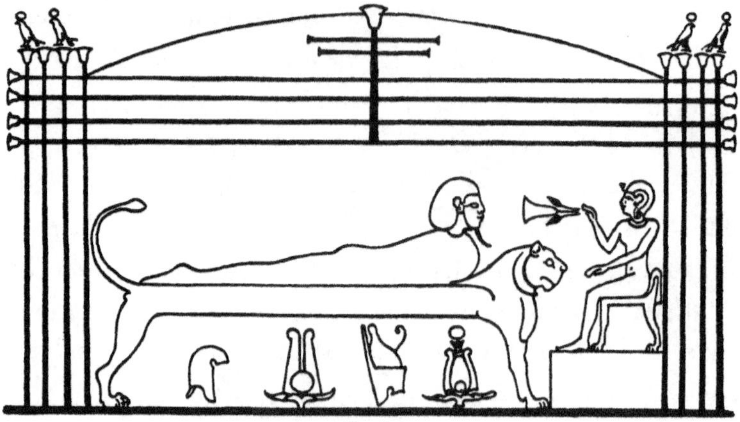

No. 1.

2. Osiris lying on his funeral bier; at the head stands

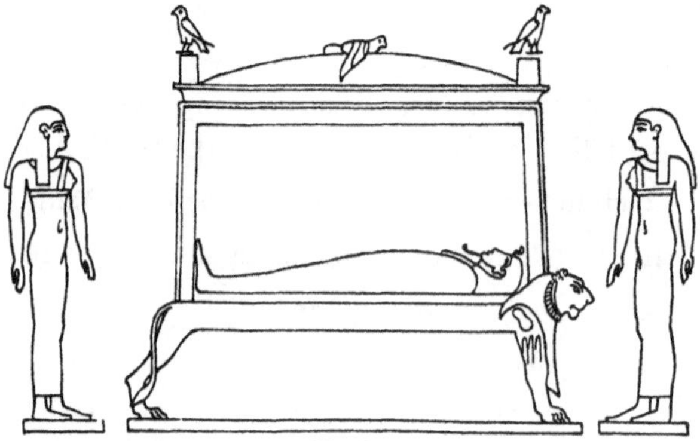

No. 2.

Nephthys, and at the foot Isis.

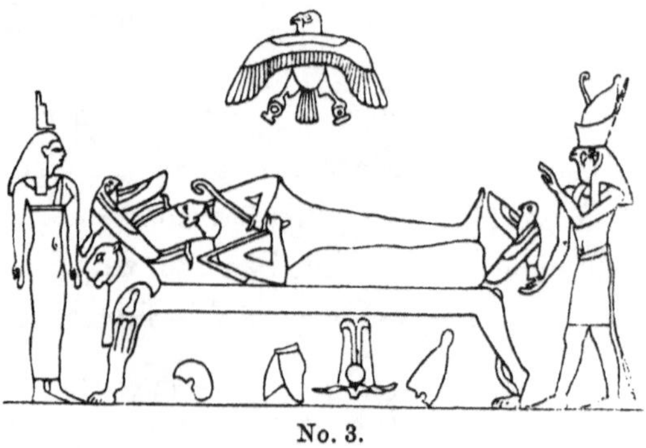

No. 3.

3. Osiris, ithyphallic, and wearing the Atef Crown, lying on his bier. On the head of the bier is a hawk with outstretched wings, and behind it stands Isis; on the foot is a similar hawk, and behind it stands Horus,

son of Isis. Above is the soul of Osiris. Below the bier are two crowns, a tunic, and a cap.

4. Osiris, naked and beardless, lying on his bier, at the head of which is a statue of Isis, and at the foot a statue of Nephthys.

5. Osiris, naked and beardless, lying on his bier, at the head of which stands Isis who is addressing the god; beneath the bier are figures of the four children of Horus, Mesthȧ, Ḥāpi, Ṭuamutef, and Qebḥsennuf, who, besides representing the gods of the four cardinal points, may here be considered as personifications of the four large, internal organs of the body.

6. Osiris, naked, lying upon his bier, over the foot of which is the vulture goddess Uatchet, and over the head the uraeus goddess Nekhebet.

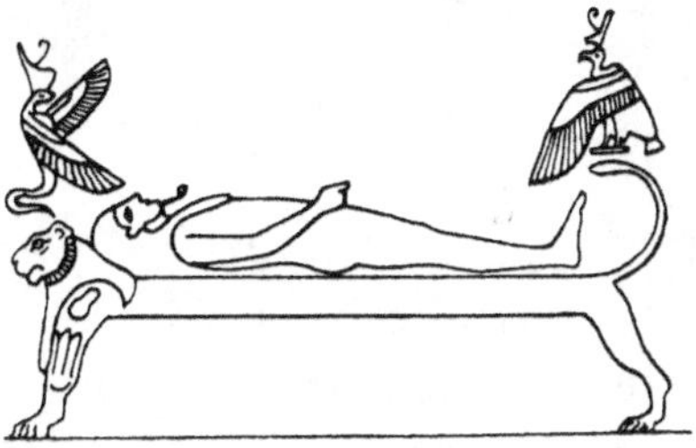

No. 6.

7. Osiris, in mummied form, lying on his bier beneath a funeral chest, over which a hawk stretches out its wings.

8. Osiris, , of Beḥuṭet (Edfû) lying on his bier, with

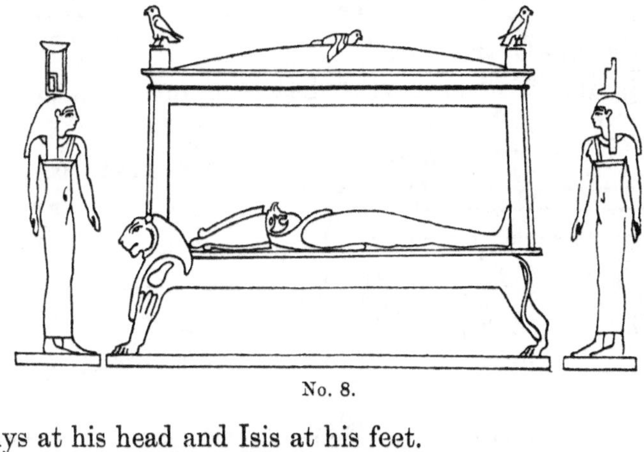

No. 8.

Nephthys at his head and Isis at his feet.

9. Osiris of Ta-khent lying on his bier, with a Hawk-goddess at the head and a Vulture-goddess at the foot.

10. Osiris of Ḥāp, , wearing the Atef Crown, lying face downwards on his bier, beneath which are a number of crowns and caps of the god.

11. Osiris lying on his bier in the Meskhen chamber with the four funeral vases beneath.

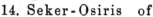

12. Osiris, ithyphallic, mummied, and beardless, lying on his bier; he is watched over by three hawks, and by Isis, who stands at the head, and by a frog-headed form of the god Horus. Beneath the bier are the ape-headed god Åurt, , and two snake-goddesses, one of which is called Ḥer-ṭept, , and an ibis-headed god.

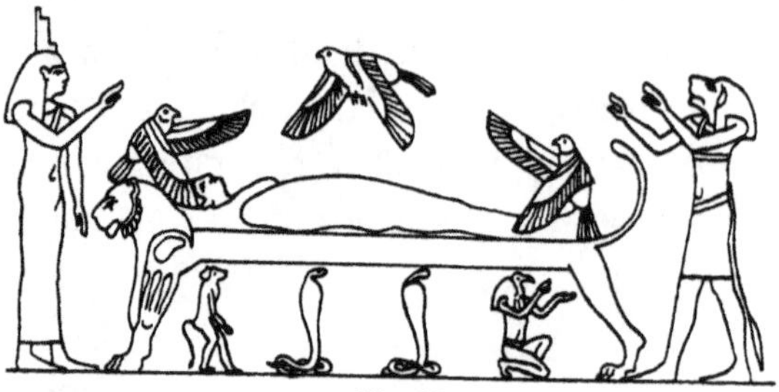

No. 12.

13. Seker-Osiris of Mendes, beardless, lying upon a bier, with Anubis in attendance, holding in his hands a vase of unguent, and an instrument used in embalming.

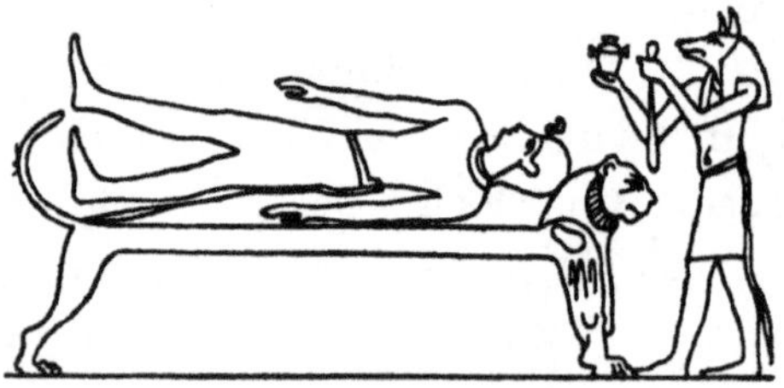

No. 13.

14. Seker-Osiris of Mendes, in the form of a hawk-headed mummy, lying upon his bier, beneath which grow three small trees.

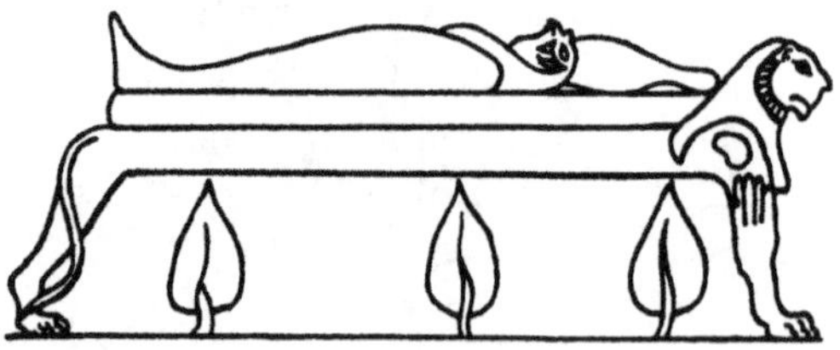

No. 14.

15. Seker-Osiris, naked, and bearded, and wearing the Atef Crown, lying upon his bier, beneath which grow three trees.

16. Ptaḥ-Seker-Åsår of Memphis, in mummied form and bearded, lying upon his bier, at the head of which, on a pedestal, stands a figure of Isis. The bier is placed within a funeral chest, the pillars of which are in the form of *Ṭeṭ*, . On the right is "Åsår Ṭeṭ, the holy one in Ṭeṭṭu, ," in the form of a Ṭeṭ pillar, which is provided with human hands and arms;

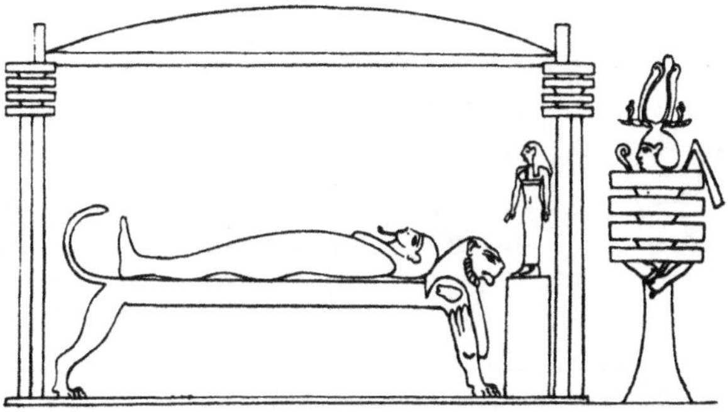

No. 16.

above it appear the head of Osiris and the sceptre and flail, or whip.

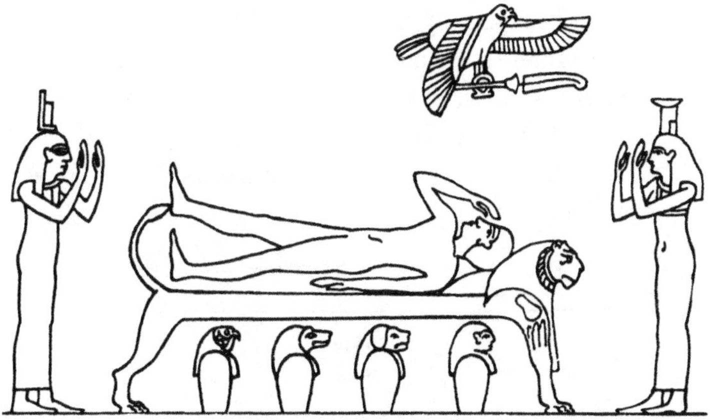

Osiris on his bier; beneath are the Canopic jars.

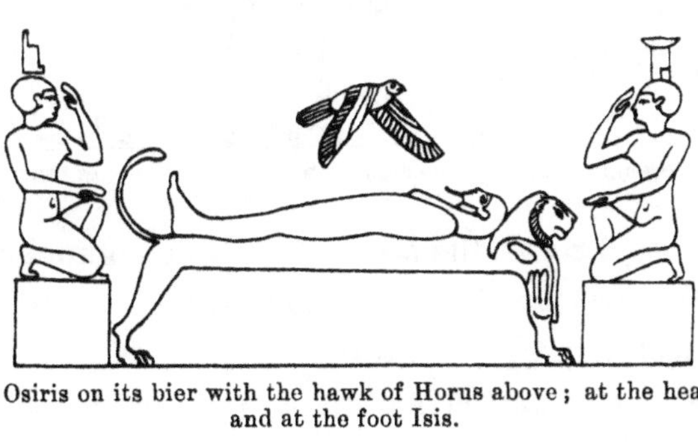

The mummy of Osiris on its bier with the hawk of Horus above; at the head is Nephthys, and at the foot Isis.

17. Osiris, beardless, and wearing the White Crown and plumes, in the act of raising himself from his bier at the command of Ḥeru-netch-tef-f.

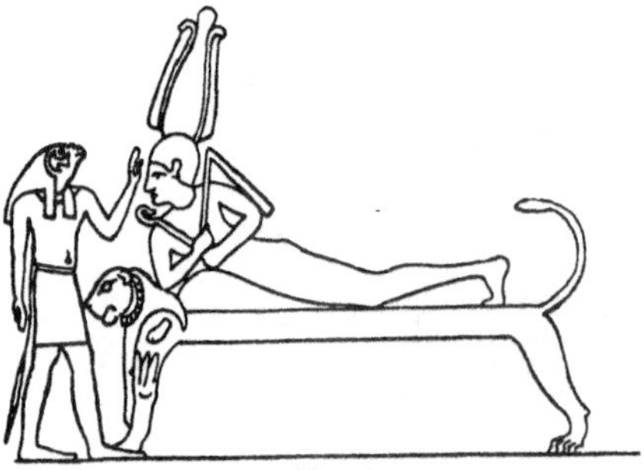

No. 17.

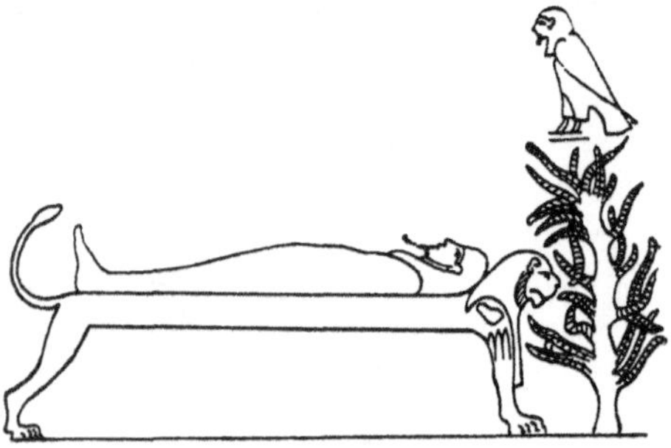

No. 18.

18. Osiris Un-nefer, in mummied form, lying on his bier, at the head of which grows the Persea tree, *Ȧsheṭ*; above the upper branches stands a soul in the form of a man-headed hawk.

19. Osiris, bearded, lying on his bier, which rests within an elaborately ornamented funeral chest; beneath the bier are a number of helmets, caps, etc., belonging to the god. Through one end of the chest Ḥeru-netch-tef-f thrusts his lance, and touches the face of Osiris with it, with the view, presumably, of effecting the "opening of the mouth."

Ceremonial scene connected with the resurrection of Osiris.

20. Osiris, ithyphallic and bearded, in mummied form, lying upon his bier; over his feet and his body hover two hawks. At the head kneels Hathor, "Mistress of Ȧmentet, who weepeth for "her brother," and at the foot is a frog, symbol of the goddess Ḥeqet; beneath the bier are an ibis-headed god holding the *Utchat*, two serpents, and the god Bes. It is interesting to note that the frog-headed goddess Ḥeqet, who was a form of

PTAḤ-SEKER-ÀUSÀR, THE TRIUNE GOD OF THE RESURRECTION.

King SETI I. Addressing OSIRIS Khent-Amentet.

Hathor, was connected by the Christians with the Christian Resurrection; in proof of this may be cited the lamp described by

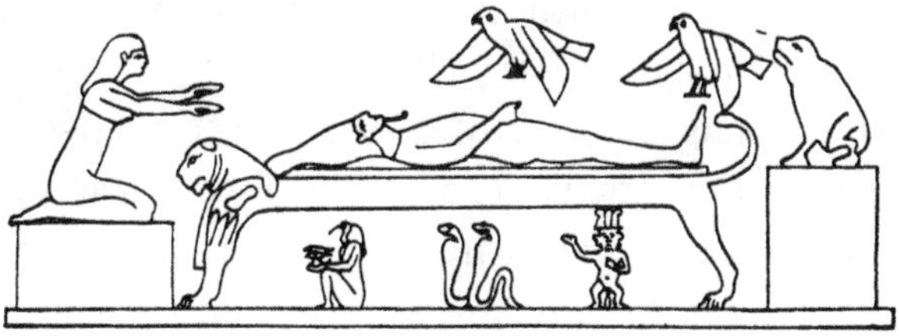

No. 20.

Signor Lanzone,[1] whereon, he tells us, is a figure of a frog, and the legend Ἐγω εἶμι Ἀναστάσις, "I am the resurrection."

21. Osiris, bearded, ithyphallic, in mummied form, and wearing the White Crown, lying on his bier, by the side of which stand Anubis, jackal-headed, and Ḥeqet, frog-headed. At the

Anubis addressing Osiris on his bier.

head stands Ḥeru-netch-tef-f in the form of a hawk, and Nephthys kneels; at the foot kneels Isis.

22. Osiris, bearded, wearing the White Crown with plumes,

No. 22.

[1] *Dizionario*, p. 853.

and holding in his hands the sceptre and flail, or whip, raising himself up on his knees from his bier, which is enclosed within the funeral chest. Beneath the bier are most of the crowns of the god. Beside it stands Isis.

23. Osiris rising up out of a basket (?), which rests upon a pedestal; behind him stands Isis with her wings stretched out on both sides of him, and before him is a bearded god who presents to him "life." On the right is a second scene in which the god is seen kneeling within the boat of the double Ṭeṭ, , wherein are

No. 23.

a papyrus plant and a lotus plant, the emblems of the South and North respectively. The boat rests upon a sledge, the supports of which are made in the form of inverted lotus flowers, which are well known types of the dawn and of renewed life. The title of the god here is "Osiris Seker, lord of the funeral chest [at] Abydos,"

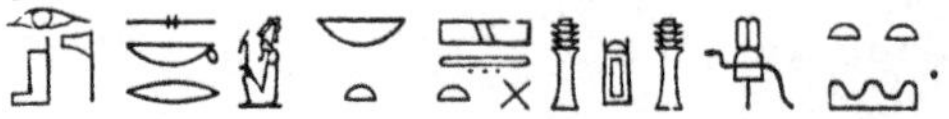

The two commonest titles of Osiris are "KHENT-ÅMENTI," , and "UN-NEFER," , or , and as such he holds in his hands one or two sceptres and the whip, or flail, , , , and wears the White Crown. Sometimes he appears as a man, with a large mouth and eyes and nose, and with a Ṭeṭ surmounted by a disk, plumes, horns, uraei, etc., issuing from his head.[1] He once appears in the form of Ptaḥ pouring out[2] water from a libation vase for a deceased person who kneels before him, and once he appears with the head of the Bennu.[3] In

[1] Lanzone, *Dizionario*, pl. 293. [2] *Ibid.*, pl. 294. [3] *Ibid.*, pl. 295.

some scenes Osiris appears as a god of vegetation, and in one instance the god is represented in mummied form, and wearing the Atef Crown, and from his body a row of plants is seen growing; in another he is represented by a small mound of earth, which is called "Osiris," , and from which four trees grow. Above the mound is a large serpent with the White Crown upon its head, and two small serpents growing out from its body; on the right are:— 1. A ram-headed god, holding a serpent, and 2. the serpent KHEBKHEB, ; on the left are a ram-headed god holding a serpent, and a feather. The Osiris ceremonies varied in different places, according as the god was identified with local gods, but in all great religious centres Osiris, under one name or another, possessed his own sanctuary. Thus, as Dr. Brugsch has pointed out,[1] in Northern Nubia Osiris was known as Khnemu, in Apollinopolis and Dendera as Ȧn, in Thebes as Khnemu-ut-em-ānkh, in Coptos as Ȧmsu-Ḥeru-ka-nekht, in Diospolis Parva as Sekhem, in Lycopolis as Sekhem-taui, in Antaeopolis as Maui, in Cusae as Urṭ-ȧb, in Memphis as Seker, in Cynopolis and Oxyrhynchus as Anubis, in Herakleopolis as Ka-ḥetep and Ḥeru-shefi, in the Libyan Nome as Khent-Ȧmenti, in Heroopolis as Ānkh and Tem, in Busiris as Ṭeṭ or Ṭeṭṭu, in Heliopolis as Ser-ȧa, and in other places in the Delta as Fenṭet-ānkh, Ḥeru-ȧp-shata. In the cxlist and cxliind Chapters of the *Book of the Dead* we have a complete list of the forms and shrines of Osiris, and as they are of great importance for forming a right idea of the universality of the cult of Osiris in Egypt, it will be found, in two versions, at the end of this section on the great gods of Heliopolis.

We have now traced the history of Osiris from the time when he was a river or water god, and of only quite local importance, up to the period when his worship reached from the north of the Delta to the Nubian Nome at Elephantine, and he had become in every sense of the word the national god of Egypt. We have now to consider Osiris in his character of god and judge of the dead, and as the symbol of the resurrection, and the best source upon which

[1] *Religion*, p. 618.

we can draw for information on this subject is the *Book of the Dead.* In this work Osiris is held to be the greatest of the gods, and it is he who is the judge of men after death, and he is the arbiter of their future destiny. He attained this exalted position because he was believed to have been once a human being who had died and had been dismembered; but his limbs had been reconstituted and he had become immortal. The most remarkable thing about him was that his body had never decayed like the bodies of ordinary men, and neither putrefaction nor worms ever acquired power over it, or caused it to diminish in the least degree. It is true that it was embalmed by Horus, and Anubis, and Isis, who carried out with the greatest care and exactitude all the prescriptions which had been ordered by Thoth, and who performed their work so thoroughly well that the material body which Osiris possessed on this earth served as the body for the god in the world beyond the grave, though only after it had undergone some mysterious change, which was brought about by the words of power which these gods said and by the ceremonies which they performed. A very ancient tradition declared that the god Thoth himself had acted the part of priest for Osiris, and although the Egyptians believed that it was his words which brought the dead god back to life, they were never able wholly to free themselves from the idea that the series of magical ceremonies which they performed in connexion with the embalmment and burial of the dead produced most beneficial results for their deceased friends.

The compositions which form the chapters of the *Book of the Dead* are declared to have been written by Thoth, and they were assumed to be identical with those which this god pronounced on behalf of Osiris; the ceremonies which were performed by the priests at the recital of such compositions were held to be identical with those which Horus and Anubis performed for the "lord of life," and if the words were said by duly appointed and properly qualified priests, in a suitable tone of voice, whilst the ministrants and libationers performed the sacred ceremonies according to the Rubrics, it was held to be impossible for Osiris to refuse to grant the deceased eternal life, and to admit him into his kingdom. It may be argued that the words and the ceremonies were the all-important factors of the resurrection of man and of his eternal life, but this was not the case, for the Egyptians only regarded them as means to be used with care and diligence; it was Osiris, the god-man himself, who had risen from the dead and was living in a body perfect in all its members, who was the cause of the resurrection. Osiris could give life after death because he had attained to it, and he could give eternal life to the souls of men in their transformed bodies because he had made himself incorruptible and immortal. Moreover, he was himself "Eternity and Everlastingness," and it was he who "made men and women to be born again," ; the new birth was the birth into the new life of the world which is beyond the grave and is everlasting. Osiris could give life because he was life, he could make man to rise from the dead because he was the resurrection; but the priesthood taught in all periods of Egyptian history that it was necessary to endeavour to obtain the favour of the god by means of magical and religious words and ceremonies. From the earliest times the belief in the immortality of Osiris existed, and the existence of the dead after death was bound up with that of the god. Thus in the text of Unȧs (line 240) it is said of the king to Tem, "O Tem, this is thy son Osiris. Thou hast given "him his sustenance and he liveth; he liveth and Unȧs liveth; he "dieth not, and this Unȧs dieth not; he is not destroyed, and this "Unȧs shall not be destroyed; if he begetteth not this Unȧs shall "not beget; if he begetteth this Unȧs shall beget." In a text nearly two thousand years later the deceased Ani is made to ask Tem, the head of the company of the gods of Heliopolis, "How "long have I to live?" and he replies, "Thou shalt exist for "millions of millions of years, a period of millions of years";[1] now Tem was identified with Rā, and Rā, at the time when this text was written, was held to be the father of Osiris, and to all intents and purposes the question of the scribe Ani was addressed to Osiris.

It has already been said that the great source of information

[1] 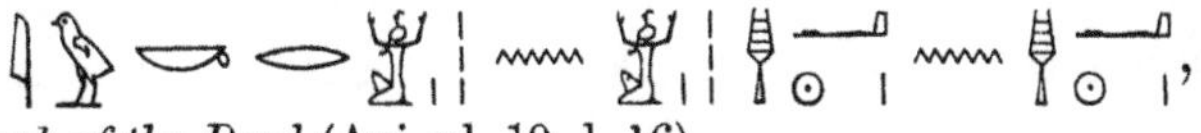, Chapter clxxv. of the *Book of the Dead* (Ani, pl. 19, l. 16).

about Osiris and his cult is contained in the *Book of the Dead*, which may be termed the Gospel of Osiris, wherein the god is made to point out to man the necessity for leading a pure and good life upon earth, and to instruct him in the words and deeds which will enable him to attain eternal life, and we must now briefly describe the relations which were believed to exist between this god of truth and life and the deceased. In the fold-out plate, which contains the famous "Judgment Scene" of the *Book of the Dead*, as contained in the Papyrus of Ani in the British Museum, we have a representation of Osiris in his capacity as the Judge of the dead, and a description of it will explain the views of the ancient Egyptians on the judgment of the souls of the dead. From certain passages and allusions in the Pyramid Texts it is clear that the ancient Egyptians believed that the souls of the dead, and perhaps also their bodies, were judged, and the place of their judgment seems to have been situated in the sky; no details of the manner in which it was performed are given, but it seems as if the judgment consisted in the "weighing of words," , *utchā meṭu*, that is to say, the weighing of actions, for the word *meṭu* means "deed, action," as much as "word" (like the Hebrew *dâbhâr*, דָבָר). The "weighing of words" (or actions) was carried out by means of a pair of scales, Mākhaȧt, , which were presided over by Thoth, who from very remote days was known as ȦP-REḤUI, , i.e., "Judge of the two combatant gods," that is to say, "Judge of Horus and Set," and as ȦP-SENUI, , "Judge of the Two Brothers." Thoth, however, only watched the Balance when "words" were being tried in it on behalf of Osiris—at least this was the view in later times.

The Egyptians, having once conceived the existence of a Balance in the Underworld, proceeded to represent it pictorially, and as a result we have in the vignette of the Judgment Scene a pair of scales similar to those with which they were acquainted in daily life. They were too logical to think that words, or even actions, could be weighed in a material balance, and they therefore

THE GODDESS MESKHENET.

represented the weighing of the material heart, from which they declared all thoughts and actions proceeded, and sometimes the whole body of the man who is to be judged was placed by the artist in one pan of the Scales. They had, moreover, in very early times arrived at the conception of "right, truth, law, and "rectitude," all of which they expressed by the word *maāt*, 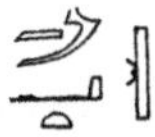, and it was against the emblem of *Maāt*, the feather, , that they weighed either the heart or the whole body. Why the feather was chosen as the symbol of *maāt* instead of the usual object, , it is impossible to say, and this fact suggests that all the views which the Egyptians held about the weighing of the heart have not yet been understood. As the Judgment Scene stands it represents a mixture of different views and opinions which belong to different periods, but it seems impossible to doubt that at some remote time they believed in the actual weighing of a portion of the physical body of a man as a part of the ceremony of judgment. The judgment of each individual seems to have taken place soon after death, and annihilation or everlasting life and bliss to have been decreed at once for the souls of the dead; there are no sufficient grounds for assuming that the Egyptians believed either in a general resurrection or in protracted punishment. How far they thought that the prayers of the living for the dead were efficacious in arresting or modifying the decree of doom cannot be said, but very considerable importance was attached by them to funeral prayers and ceremonies in all ages, and there is no doubt that they were the outcome of the firm belief that they would result in the salvation and well-being of the souls of the dead. The Judgment Scene as given in the Papyrus of Ani may be thus described :—

The scribe Ani and his wife Thuthu enter the Hall of Maāti, wherein the heart, symbolic of the conscience, is to be weighed in the Balance against the feather, emblematic of Right and Truth. In the upper register are the gods who sit in judgment, and who form the great company of the gods of Heliopolis, to whom are added Hathor, Ḥu, and Sa. On the standard of the Balance sits the dog-headed ape, the companion of Thoth, the scribe of the gods; and the god Anubis, jackal-headed, examines the pointer to make certain that the beam is exactly horizontal, and that the tongue of the Balance is in its proper place. On the left of the Balance are :—1. SHAI, , the god of luck, or destiny; 2. the MESKHEN, , or rectangular object with a human head which rests upon a pylon, and is commonly thought to be connected with the place of birth; 3. MESKHENET, , the goddess of the funeral chamber, and RENENET, , the goddess of nursing; 4. the soul of Ani in the form of a human-headed hawk standing upon a pylon. The lines of hieroglyphics which appear above the figures of Ani and his wife contain a version of Chapter XXX.B of the *Book of the Dead*, in which the deceased addresses his heart, and prays that the sovereign chiefs may not oppose his judgment, and that it may not be separated from him in the presence of the keeper of the Balance. The sovereign chiefs here referred to are Mesthȧ, Ḥāpi, Ṭuamutef, and Qebḥsennuf, the children of Horus. After the heart has been weighed, Thoth, being satisfied with the result, addresses the gods, saying, "The heart of Osiris Ani hath indeed been weighed, and "his soul hath borne witness concerning him (or it); it hath been "found true by trial in the Great Balance. No evil hath been "found in him, he hath not wasted the offerings in the temples, "he hath not done harm by his deeds, and he hath uttered no "evil report whilst he was upon earth." In answer to these words the gods ratify the sentence of Thoth, and they declare that he is holy and righteous, and that he hath not sinned against them; therefore the monster ĀMEMET, , or the "Eater of the dead," who is seen standing behind Thoth, shall not prevail over him, and they further decree that he shall have a homestead in Sekhet-ḥetepu for ever, and that offerings shall be made to him, and that he shall have the power to appear before Osiris at will.

In the second part of the scene Horus, the son of Isis, leads Ani by the hand into the presence of Osiris, who is enthroned within a shrine in the form of a funeral chest. Osiris has upon his head the Atef crown, and he holds his usual emblems of authority,

, , ; from his neck hangs the *menàt*, , i.e., the amulet which was associated with joy and pleasure. The title of the god is "Osiris, lord of everlastingness." Behind him stand Isis and Nephthys; before him, standing on a lotus flower, are the four Children of Horus, i.e., the four gods of the cardinal points. The first, Mesthà, has the head of a man; the second, Ḥāpi, the head of an ape; the third, Ṭuamutef, the head of a jackal; and the fourth, Qebḥsennuf, the head of a hawk. In some papyri the lotus on which these gods stand is seen to have its roots in a lake, or stream, of water, which flows from under the throne of Osiris. Near the lotus hangs the skin of the pied bull which was sacrificed at the beginning of that portion of the funeral ceremony when two gazelles and a goose were also slain as sacrifices. The side of the throne of Osiris is painted to resemble that of a funeral chest. The roof of the shrine is supported on pillars with lotus capitals, and is surmounted by a figure of Horus Sepṭ or Horus Seker, and by rows of uraei. The pedestal on which the shrine rests is in the form of the hieroglyphic which is emblematic of Maāt, , i.e., "Right and Truth." Before the shrine is a table of offerings, by the side of which, on a reed mat, kneels Ani with his right hand raised in adoration; in the left hand he holds the kherp sceptre. He wears on his head a whitened wig, and the so-called "cone," the signification of which is unknown. In his speech Horus, the son of Isis, says, "I have come to thee, O Un-nefer, and I have "brought unto thee the Osiris Ani. His heart is righteous, and it "hath come forth innocent from the Balance; it hath not sinned "against any god or any goddess. Thoth hath weighed it accord-"ing to the decree pronounced unto him by the company of the "gods; and it is most true and righteous. Grant that cakes and "ale may be given unto him, and let him appear in the presence "of Osiris; and let him be like unto the followers of Horus for "ever and ever." The scribe Ani then makes his prayer to Osiris in the following words:—"Behold I am in thy presence, O lord of "Åmentet. There is no sin in my body. I have not spoken that "which is not true knowingly, nor have I done aught with a false "heart. Grant thou that I may be like unto those favoured ones "who are in thy following, and that I may be an Osiris greatly "favoured of the beautiful god, and beloved of the lord of the "world, [I] who am indeed a royal scribe, who loveth thee, "Ani MAĀ KHERU before the god Osiris." The reply of the god Osiris is not recorded, but we may assume that the petition of Ani was granted by him, and that he ratified the decision of the gods in respect of a habitation in the Sekhet-Åaru. Thus Ani was free to pass into all the various regions of the dominion of Osiris, and to enter into everlasting life and happiness.

In the description of the Judgment Scene given above, reference is made to the Eater of the Dead, and in connexion with him it must be observed that he was supposed to devour straightway the souls of all those who were condemned in the Judgment Hall of Osiris, and that from one point of view the punishment of the wicked consisted of annihilation. Above, too, it has been said that Ani became "MAĀ KHERU, 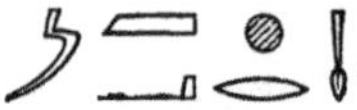, before Osiris," when once his heart had been weighed and had not been found wanting. Egyptologists have investigated the meaning of these words very carefully, but have not agreed as to their meaning; as a result MAĀ KHERU has been rendered "victorious, triumphant, "just, justified, truth-speaking, truthful, true of voice, mighty of "word or speech, etc." Their true meaning seems to be "he whose word is right and true," i.e., he whose word is held to be right and true by those to whom it is addressed, and therefore, whatsoever is ordered or commanded by the person who is declared in the Judgment Hall to be MAĀ KHERU is straightway performed by the beings or things who are commanded or ordered. Before a man who is MAĀ KHERU every door in the Underworld opened itself, and every hostile power, animate or inanimate, was made to remove itself from his path.

Passing now from the consideration of Osiris as the king and judge of the dead, we must briefly refer to the beautiful hymns to the god which are found in the *Book of the Dead* and elsewhere. First among these must be mentioned the very remarkable composition which is inscribed on a stele in the Bibliothèque Nationale, Paris, and which was first made known by Chabas. The text is in the form of a hymn addressed to Osiris, but it is of unique importance in that it contains a proof of the substantial accuracy of the account of the life and death of Osiris, and of the birth of Horus, given by Plutarch. After enumerating the various great shrines of Osiris in Egypt, and ascribing great praise to this god, and summarising his beneficent acts, an allusion is made to his death and to the search which Isis made for his body. This goddess, the sister and wife of Osiris, was a skilled worker of miracles, and she knew words of power and how to utter them in such a way that the greatest effect might result from them. In the form of a bird she sought her brother's body ceaselessly, and went round about over the face of the earth uttering cries and moans, and she did not desist from her quest until she found it. When she saw that he was dead she produced light with her feathers, and air by the beating of her wings, and then by means of the words of power which she had obtained from Thoth she roused Osiris from his state of helplessness and inactivity, and united herself to him, and became with child by him, and in due course brought forth her son Horus in a lonely place unknown to any. The hymn in which the passage occurs is so important that a rendering of it is here given; the hieroglyphic text, with interlinear transliteration and translation, will be found at the end of this section.

CHAPTER VII

HYMN TO OSIRIS

XVIIITH DYNASTY, ABOUT B.C. 1500

1. "HOMAGE to thee, O Osiris, the lord of eternity, the king of the gods, thou who hast many names, whose forms "of coming into being are holy, whose attributes are hidden in the "temples, whose Double is most august (or venerated). Thou art "the Chief of Ṭeṭṭu (or Busiris), the Great One who dwelleth 2. in "Sekhem (Letopolis), the lord to whom praises are offered in the "nome of Åthi,[1] the Chief of the divine food in Ånnu (On, or Helio-"polis), and the lord who is commemorated in the [Hall (or City) of] "two-fold Right and Truth. Thou art the Hidden Soul, the lord "of Qereret (Elephantine[2]), the holy one in the city of the White "Wall (Memphis), the Soul of Rā, and thou art of his own body. "Offerings and oblations are made to thy satisfaction in 3. Suten-"ḥenen (Herakleopolis), praise in abundance is bestowed upon "thee in Nārt,[3] and thy Soul hath been exalted as lord of the "Great House in Khemennu (Hermopolis). Thou art he who is "greatly feared in Shas-ḥetep, the lord of eternity, the Chief of "Åbṭu (Abydos), thy seat extendeth into the land of holiness "(Underworld), and thy name is firmly stablished in the mouth of "mankind. 4. Thou art the substance of [which were made] the "two lands (i.e., Egypt), thou art Tem, the divine food of the "doubles, thou art the chief of the company of the gods, thou art "the operative and beneficent Spirit among the spirits, thou drawest

[1] I.e., the ninth nome of Lower Egypt, also read *Anetch.*

[2] *Qereret* = Qerti, 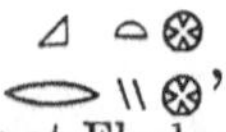, or , were the two caverns where the Nile was thought to rise at Elephantine.

[3] A sanctuary near Herakleopolis.

"thy waters from the abyss of heaven, thou bringest along the "north wind at eventide and air for thy nostrils to the satisfaction "of thy heart. 5. Thy heart germinateth, thou producest the light "for divine food, the height of heaven and the starry gods obey "thee, thou openest the great pylons [of heaven], and thou art he "unto whom praises are sung in the southern heaven, and to "whom adorations are performed in the northern heaven. The "stars which never set 6. are under the seat of thy face, and the "stars which never rest are thy habitations; and unto thee "offerings are made according to the decree of the god Seb.

"The company of the gods sing praises unto thee, and the "starry gods of the Underworld bow down with their faces to the "earth [before thee], the ends of the earth prostrate themselves "before thee, and the bounds of heaven make supplication unto "thee 7. when they see thee. Those who are among the holy "ones are in awe of thee, and the two lands in their length and "breadth ascribe praises unto thee when they meet thy majesty, "O thou glorious master, thou lord of masters, who art endowed "with divine rank and dignity, who art stablished in [thy] rule, "thou beautiful Sekhem of the company of the gods, who art "pleasant of face, 8. and art beloved by him that looketh upon "thee. Thou puttest thy fear in all the lands, and by reason of "love for thee all [men] proclaim thy name as being above that of "every name. All mankind make offerings unto thee, O thou lord "who art commemorated in heaven and in earth, and who art "greatly praised in the Uaḳ festival, and the two lands with one "consent 9. cry out unto thee with cries of joy, O thou great one, "thou chief of thy divine brethren, thou prince of the company of "the gods, thou stablisher of Maāt throughout the two lands, who "placest thy son upon the great throne of his father Seb, the "darling of his mother Nut.

"O thou great one of two-fold strength, thou hast cast down "Sebȧ, thou hast slain 10. thine enemy, and thou hast set thy "fear in thy foe. Thou bringest [together] remote boundaries, "thou art firm of heart, thy two feet are lifted up, thou art the "heir of Seb and of the sovereignty of the two lands, who hath "seen thy power and hath given command for thee to lead 11. the "two lands by thy hand until the end of time. Thou hast made "the earth in thy hand, and its waters, and its air, and its green "herb, and all its cattle, and all its birds, and all its fishes, and all "its reptiles, and [all] its four-footed beasts. The desert is thine "by right, O son of 12. Nut, and the two lands are content to "make him to rise up upon the throne of his father like Rā. "Thou risest in the horizon, thou givest light through the "darkness, thou makest light to spread abroad from thy plumes, "and thou floodest with light the two lands like the 13. Disk at "the beginning of sunrise. Thy crown pierceth heaven, thou art "a brother of the starry gods, and the guide of every god, and "thou dost work by decree and word, O thou favoured one of the "company of the gods, who art greatly beloved by the Lesser "Company of the gods.

"Thy sister protected thee, and she drove away thy foes, "14. and she warded off from thee evil hap, and uttered the "words of power with all the skill of her mouth; her tongue was "trained, and she committed no fault of utterance, and she made "[her] decree and [her] words to have effect, Isis, the mighty one, "the avenger of her brother. She sought thee without weariness, "15. she went round about through this land in sorrow, and she "set not to the ground her foot until she had found thee. She "made light with her feathers, she made air to come into being "with her wings, and she uttered cries of lamentation at the bier "of her brother. 16. She stirred up from his state of inactivity "him whose heart was still (i.e., Osiris), she drew from him his seed, "she made an heir, she suckled the babe in solitariness, and the "place wherein she reared him is unknown, and his hand is mighty "within the house 17. of Seb. The company of the gods rejoice "and are glad at the coming of Horus, the son of Osiris, whose "heart is stablished, and whose word taketh effect, the son of Isis "and the heir of Osiris. The assessors of Maāt gather together "unto him, and with them are assembled the company of the gods, "and Neb-er-tcher himself, and the lords of Maāt. 18. Verily "those who repulse faults rejoice in the house of Seb to bestow "the rank [of Osiris] upon its lord, to whom is by right all "sovereignty. The voice of Horus hath found the power of *maāt*.

"The rank of his father hath been given unto him, and he hath "come forth crowned 19. by the command of Seb. He hath "received the sceptre of the two lands, and the White Crown is "stablished upon his head. He judgeth the earth according to "his plans, and heaven and earth are open before his face. He "layeth his commands upon men, and spirits, and upon the *pāt* "and *ḥen-memet* beings, and Egypt, and the Ḥa-nebu, and all the "region 20. wherein the Disk revolveth are under his plans, as "well as the north wind, and the river flood, and the celestial "waters, and the staff of life, and every flower. [He is] Nepră, "and he giveth his green herbs; he is the lord of *tchefau* food, he "leadeth on abundance, and he giveth it unto all lands.

"21. There is joy everywhere, [all] hearts are glad, [all] "hearts are glad, every face is happy, and every one adoreth his "beauties. His love is doubly sweet unto us, and his active "beneficence embraceth all hearts, and the love for him is great in "every body, and they do what is right 22. for the son of Isis. "His enemy hath fallen before his wrath, and he that worketh "evil hath fallen at the sound of his voice; when the son of Isis, "the avenger of his father, the son of Isis, cometh against him, he "shooteth forth his anger in his season. Holy and beneficent is his "name, and the awe of him abideth in its place. 23. His laws are "stablished everywhere, the path is cleared, the roads are opened, "and the two lands are content; wickedness departeth, evil goeth "away, the earth is at peace under [the rule of] its lord, and Maāt "is stablished by 24. its lord, and setteth its back against iniquity. "The heart of Un-nefer, the son of Isis, is glad, for he hath "received the White Crown, and the rank of his father is his by "right in the house of Seb; he is Rā when he speaketh and Thoth "when he writeth. 25. The assessors [of Osiris] are content; let "what hath been decreed for thee by thy father Seb be performed "according to his word.

"May Osiris, Governor of Ȧmentet, lord of Abydos, give a "royal offering! May he give sepulchral meals of oxen, and fowl, "and bandages, and incense, and wax, and gifts of all kinds, and "the [power to] make transformations, and mastery over the Nile, "and [the power] to appear as a living soul, and to see the Disk "daily, and entrance into and exit from Re-stau; may [my] soul "not be repulsed in the Underworld, may it be among the favoured "ones before Un-nefer, may it receive cakes and appear before the

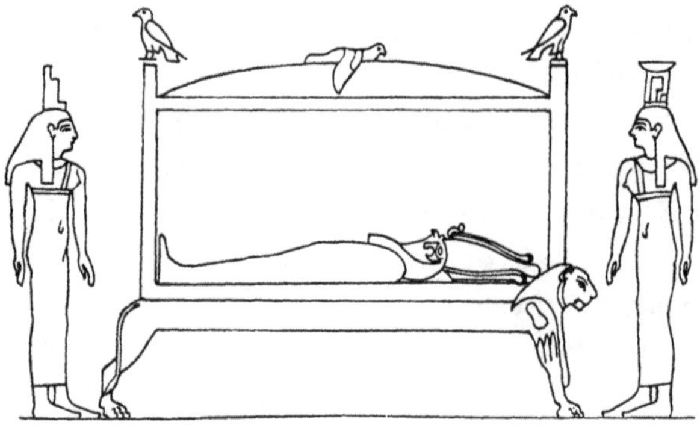

Osiris on his funeral bed.

"altar of the Great God, and snuff the sweet breath of the north "wind."

CHAPTER VIII

HYMNS TO OSIRIS, AND OSIRIS UN-NEFER, FROM THE BOOK OF THE DEAD

1. "GLORY[1] BE TO THEE, OSIRIS UN-NEFER, the great god who dwellest within Åbṭu (Abydos), thou king of eternity, "thou lord of everlastingness, who passest through millions of "years in the course of thine existence. Thou art the eldest son "of the womb of Nut, and thou wast engendered by Seb, the "Ancestor (*erpāt*); thou art the lord of the crowns of "the South and North, thou art the lord of the lofty white crown, "and as prince of gods and men thou hast received the crook, , and "the whip, , and the dignity of his divine fathers. Let thine "heart, O Osiris, who art in the Mountain of Åmentet, be content, "for thy son Horus is stablished upon thy throne. Thou art crowned lord of Ṭeṭṭu (Mendes), and ruler in Åbṭu (Abydos). "Through thee the world waxeth green in triumph before the "might of Neb-er-tcher. He leadeth in his train that which is, "and that which is not yet, in his name Ta-ḥer-sta-nef; he toweth "along the earth by Maāt in his name of 'Seker'; he is exceedingly "mighty and most terrible in his name 'Osiris'; he endureth for "ever and for ever in his name of 'Un-nefer.'

"Homage be to thee, O King of kings, Lord of lords, Ruler "of princes, who from the womb of Nut hast ruled the world and "the Underworld (Åḳert). Thy members are [like] "bright and shining copper, thy head is blue [like] lapis-lazuli,

[1] From the Papyrus of Ani, sheet 2.

"and the greenness of the turquoise is on both sides of thee, O thou "god Ȧn ( ) of millions of years, whose form and whose beauty "of face are all-pervading in Ta-tchesert (i.e., the Underworld)."

II. "PRAISE BE UNTO THEE,[1] OSIRIS, lord of eternity, UN-"NEFER-ḤERU-KHUTI ( ), whose forms are "manifold, and whose attributes are majestic, PTAḤ-SEKER-TEM "( ) in Ȧnnu (Heliopolis), the lord of the "Hidden House, the creator of Ḥet-ka-Ptaḥ (Memphis) and of "the gods [therein], thou guide of the Underworld, whom [the gods] "glorify when thou settest in the night sky of Nut ( ). Isis "embraceth thee with content, and she driveth away the fiends "from the mouth of thy paths. Thou turnest thy face upon "Ȧmentet, and thou makest the earth to shine as with refined "copper. Those who have lain down (i.e., the dead) rise up to "look upon thee, they breathe the air and they look upon thy face "when the disk riseth on the horizon; their hearts are at peace "inasmuch as they behold thee, O thou who art Eternity and "Everlastingness."

III. "1. HOMAGE[1] TO THEE, KHABESU (i.e., Starry deities "( ), in Ȧnnu (Heliopolis) and ḤEMEMET ( ) "in Kher-āḥa, thou god Unti, who art more glorious than the gods "who are hidden in Ȧnnu. 2. Homage to thee, O ȦN ( ) in "Ȧn-tes ( ), Great One, Ḥeru-khuti, thou stridest over "heaven with long strides, O Ḥeru-khuti. 3. Homage to thee, O "soul of eternity, thou god BAI ( ), who dwellest in "Ṭeṭṭu (Mendes), Un-nefer, son of Nut; thou art the lord of "Ȧḳert (i.e., the Underworld). 4. Homage to thee in thy dominion "in Ṭeṭṭu; the Ureret crown ( ) is stablished upon thy head; "thou art One and thou makest the strength which is thine own "protection, and thou dwellest in Ṭeṭṭu. 5. Homage to thee, O "lord of the Acacia Tree ( ), the Seker Boat is upon its

[1] From the Papyrus of Ani, sheet 19.

"sledge; thou drivest back the Fiend ( *Sebȧu*), the "worker of evil, and thou causest the Utchat (), to rest upon "its seat. 6. Homage to thee, thou who art mighty in thine hour, "thou great and mighty prince, who dwellest in Ȧn-rutˌ-f;[1] thou "art the lord of eternity and the creator of everlastingness, thou "art the lord of Suten-ḥenen (Herakleopolis Magna). 7. Homage "to thee, O thou who restest upon Maāt, thou art the lord of Ȧbṭu, "and thy limbs are joined unto Ta-tchesertet; what thou "abominatest is falsehood (or, deceit and guile). 8. Homage to "thee, O thou who art within thy boat, thou bringest along Ḥāpi "(Nile) from out of his source;[2] Shu shineth upon thy body, and "thou art he who dwelleth in Nekhen.[3] 9. Homage to thee, O "creator of the gods, king of the South and North, Osiris, "(), whose word is *maāt*, thou possessor of the two "lands in thy seasons of operative power; thou art the lord of the "Ȧṭebui (i.e., the two lands which lay one on each side of the "celestial Nile)." The above nine addresses form, in reality, a litany, and after each of them the deceased said to Osiris, "O "grant thou unto me a path whereon I may pass in peace, for I "am just and true; I have not spoken lies wittingly, nor have I "done aught with deceit."

IV. "HOMAGE[4] TO THEE, O OSIRIS UN-NEFER, whose word is "*maāt*, thou son of Nut, thou first-born son of Seb, thou mighty "one who comest forth from Nut, thou king in the city of Nifu-ur, "thou Governor of Ȧmentet, thou lord of Ȧbṭu, thou lord of souls, "thou mighty one of strength, thou lord of the *Atef* crown, , "in Suten-ḥenen, thou lord of the divine form in the city of "Nifu-ur, thou lord of the tomb, thou mighty one of souls in "Ṭaṭṭu, thou lord of [sepulchral] offerings, whose festivals are "many in Ṭaṭṭu. The god Horus exalteth his father in every "place, and he uniteth himself unto the goddess Isis and unto her

[1] A district of the Underworld.

[2] An allusion to the fact that Osiris was originally a Nile god.

[3] Nekhen was the sanctuary of the goddess Nekhebet of Nekhebet (Eileithyiapolis), whose male counterpart was Ȧn, a form of Osiris.

[4] *Book of the Dead*, Chap. cxxviii. (Saïte Recension).

"sister Nephthys; and the god Thoth reciteth for him the mighty "glorifyings which are within him, and which come forth from his "mouth, and the heart of Horus is stronger than that of all the "gods. Rise up, then, O Horus, thou son of Isis, and avenge thy "father Osiris. Hail, O Osiris, I have come unto thee; I am "Horus and I have avenged thee, and I feed this day upon the "sepulchral meals of oxen and feathered fowl, and upon all the "beautiful things offered unto Osiris. Rise up, then, O Osiris, for "I have struck down for thee all thine enemies, and I have taken "vengeance upon them for thee. I am Horus upon this beautiful "day of thy fair rising in thy Soul, which exalteth thee along with "itself on this day before thy divine sovereign princes. Hail, "O Osiris, thy double (*ka*) hath come unto thee and rests with "thee, and thou restest therein in thy name of Ka-Ḥetep. It "maketh thee glorious in thy name of Khu, and it maketh thee like "unto the Morning Star in thy name of Peḥu, and it openeth for "thee the ways in thy name of Åp-uat. Hail, O Osiris, I have "come unto thee, and I have set thine enemies under thee in "every place, and thy word is *maāt* in the presence of the gods "and of the divine sovereign chiefs. Hail, O Osiris, thou hast "received thy sceptre and the place whereon thou art to rest, and "thy steps are under thee. Thou bringest food to the gods, and "thou bringest sepulchral meals unto those who dwell in their "tombs. Thou hast given thy might unto the gods, and thou "hast created the Great God; thou hast thy existence with them "in their spiritual bodies, thou gatherest thyself unto all the gods, "and thou hearest the word of *maāt* on the day when offerings to "this god are ordered on the festivals of Uḳa."

V. "HOMAGE TO THEE,[1] O GOVERNOR OF ÅMENTET, UN-NEFER, "lord of Ta-tchesert, O thou who art diademed like Rā, verily I "come to see thee and to rejoice at thy beauties. His disk is thy "disk; his rays of light are thy rays of light; his *Ureret* crown is "thy *Ureret* crown; his majesty is thy majesty; his risings are "thy risings; his beauties are thy beauties; the terror which he "inspireth is the terror which thou inspirest; his odour is thy

[1] *Book of the Dead*, Chap. clxxxi.

"odour; his hall is thy hall; his seat is thy seat; his throne is thy "throne; his heir is thy heir; his ornaments are thy ornaments; "his decree is thy decree; his hidden place is thy hidden place; "his things are thy things; his knowledge is thy knowledge; the "attributes of greatness which are his are thine; the power which "protecteth him protecteth thee; he dieth not and thou diest not; "he is not overcome by his enemies and thou art not overcome by "thine enemies; no evil thing whatsoever hath happened unto "him, and no evil thing whatsoever shall happen unto thee for "ever and ever.

"Homage to thee, O Osiris, son of Nut, lord of the two horns, "whose *Atef* crown is exalted, may the *Ureret* crown be given "unto thee, along with sovereignty before the company of the "gods. May the god Temu make awe of thee to exist in the "hearts of men, and women, and gods, and spirits, and the dead. "May dominion be given unto thee in Ȧnnu; mayest thou be "mighty of transformations in Ṭaṭṭu (Mendes); mayest thou be "the lord greatly feared in the Ȧati; mayest thou be mighty "in victory in Re-stau; mayest thou be the lord who is com-"memorated with gladness in the Great House; mayest thou have "manifold risings like the sun in Ȧbṭu; may triumph be given "unto thee in the presence of the company of the gods; mayest "thou gain the victory over the mighty Powers; may the fear of "thee be made to go [throughout] the earth; and may the princes "stand up upon their stations before the sovereign of the gods of "the Ṭuat, before thee the mighty Sekhem of heaven, the Prince "of the living ones, the king of those who are in [his train], and "the Glorifier of thousands in Kher-āḥa. The denizens of heaven "rejoice in thee, O thou who art the lord of the chosen offerings in "the mansions above; a meat offering is made unto thee in the city "of Ḥet-ka-Ptaḥ (Memphis); and the 'things of the night' are "prepared for him in Sekhem (Letopolis). Behold, O mighty god, "thou great one of two-fold strength, thy son Horus avengeth thee. "He doeth away with every evil thing whatsoever that belongeth "to thee, he bindeth up in order for thee thy person, he gathereth "together for thee thy members, he collecteth for thee thy bones, "and he bringeth to thee whatsoever belongeth to thee. Thus "thou art raised up, O Osiris, and I have given unto thee thy "hand, and I make thee to stand up a living being for ever and "ever."

VI. "HOMAGE TO THEE,[1] O GOVERNOR OF THOSE WHO ARE IN "ÅMENTI, who makest mortals to be born again, who renewest thy "youth, thou comest who dwellest in thy season, and who art more "beautiful than . . . . . , thy son Horus hath avenged thee; the "rank and dignity of Tem have been conferred upon thee, O Un-"nefer. Thou art raised up, O Bull of Åmentet, thou art stablished "in the body of Nut, who uniteth herself unto thee, and who "cometh forth with thee. Thy heart is stablished upon that which "supporteth it, and thy breast is as it was formerly; thy nose is "firmly fixed with life and power, thou livest, and thou art "renewed, and thou makest thyself young like Rā each and every "day. Mighty, mighty is Osiris in victory, and he is firmly "stablished with life."

VII. "THY HEART REJOICETH,[2] O lord of the gods, thy heart "rejoiceth greatly; the Black Land and the Red Land are at "peace, and they serve thee humbly under thy sovereign power. "The temples are stablished upon their own lands, cities and "nomes possess firmly the goods which are inscribed in their names, "and we will make to thee the divine offerings which we are "bound to make, and offer sacrifices in thy name for ever. "Acclamations are made in thy name, libations are poured out to "thy double. Sepulchral meals [are brought unto thee] by the "*khus* who are in their following, and water is sprinkled upon "the offerings (?) upon both sides of the souls of the dead in "this land; every plan which hath been decreed for thee according "to the commands of Rā in the beginning hath been perfected. "Now, therefore, O son of Nut, thou art diademed as Neb-er-tcher "is diademed at his rising. Thou livest, thou art stablished, thou "renewest thy youth, thou art true and perfect; thy father Rā "maketh strong thy members, and the company of the gods make "acclamations unto thee. The goddess Isis is with thee, and she "never leaveth thee; [thou art] not overthrown by thine enemies.

1 *Book of the Dead*, Chap. clxxxii. (ll. 15-19).

2 *Ibid.*, Chap. clxxxiii. (ll. 17 ff.).

"The lords of all lands praise thy beauties even as they praise Rā "when he riseth at the beginning of each day. Thou risest up "like an exalted one upon thy standard, thy beauties exalt the "face and make long the stride. I have given unto thee the sove- "reignty of thy father Seb, and the goddess Mut, thy mother, who "gave birth to the gods, brought thee forth as the first-born of "five gods, and created thy beauties, and fashioned thy members. "Thou art stablished as king, the white crown is upon thy head, "and thou hast grasped in thy hands the crook and the whip; "whilst thou wert in the womb, and hadst not as yet come forth "therefrom upon the earth, thou wert crowned lord of the two "lands, and the *Atef* crown of Rā was upon thy brow. The gods "come unto thee bowing low to the ground, and they hold thee in "fear; they retreat and depart when they see thee possessing the "terror of Rā, and the victory of thy Majesty is in their hearts. "Life is with thee, and offerings of meat and drink follow thee, "and that which is thy due is offered up before thy face."

VIII. "Homage to thee,[1] O thou holy god, thou mighty and "beneficent being, thou Prince of eternity who dwellest in thy "abode in the Sektet Boat, thou whose risings are manifold in the "Ātet Boat, to thee are praises rendered in heaven and upon "earth. Peoples and nations exalt thee, and the majesty of thy "terror is in the hearts of men, and spirits, and the dead. Thy "Soul is in Ṭaṭṭu (Mendes) and the terror of thee is in Suten-ḥenen "(Herakleopolis); thou settest the visible emblems of thyself in "Ȧnnu and the greatness of thy transformations in the double "place of purification."

IX. "Homage to thee, O great God, thou Lord of Maāti, "I have come to thee, O my Lord, and I have brought myself "hither that I may behold thy beauties. I know thee, and I know "thy name, and I know the names of the Two and Forty gods who "exist with thee in the Hall of Maāti, who live as warders of "sinners and who feed upon their blood on the day when the lives "of men are taken into account in the presence of the god "Un-nefer; in truth thy name is 'Rekhti-merti-neb-Maāti.' In

[1] *Book of the Dead*, Chap. clxxxv.

"truth I have come to thee, and I have brought Maāt to thee, and "I have destroyed wickedness for thee. I have not done evil to "mankind. I have not oppressed the members of my family. "I have not wrought evil in the place of Maāt. I have had no "knowledge of worthless men. I have not wrought evil. I have "not made to be the first [consideration] of each day that excessive "labour should be performed for me. I have not brought forward "my name for honours. I have not ill-treated servants. I have "not thought scorn of God. I have not defrauded the oppressed "one of his goods. I have not done that which is an abomination "unto the gods. I have not caused harm to be done to the servant "by his chief. I have not caused pain. I have made no man to "suffer hunger. I have made no one to weep. I have done no "murder. I have not given the order for murder to be done for "me. I have not inflicted pain upon mankind. I have not "defrauded the temples of their oblations. I have not purloined "the cakes of the gods. I have not carried off the cakes offered to "the spirits. I have not committed fornication. I have not "entered the holy places of the god of my city in a polluted con- "dition. I have not diminished from the bushel. I have neither "added to nor filched away land. I have not encroached upon the "fields [of others]. I have not added to the weights of the scales "(i.e., cheated the seller). I have not misread the pointer of the "scales (i.e., cheated the buyer). I have not carried away the "milk from the mouths of children. I have not driven away the "cattle from their pastures. I have not snared the feathered fowl "of the preserves of the gods. I have not caught fish [with bait "made of] fish of their kind. I have not turned back the water at "the time [when it should flow]. I have not cut a cutting in a "canal of running water. I have not extinguished a fire when it "should burn. I have not violated the seasons of the chosen meat "offerings. I have not driven off the cattle from the property of "the gods. I have not repulsed God in his manifestations. I am "pure. I am pure. I am pure. I am pure. My purity is the "purity of that great Bennu which is in the city of Suten-ḥenen "(Herakleopolis Magna), for, behold, I am the nose of the god of "the winds who maketh all mankind to live on the day when the

"Eye of Rā is full in Ȧnnu at the end of the second month of the "season Pert[1] in the presence of the divine lord of the earth. "I have seen the Eye of Rā when it was full in Ȧnnu, therefore let "not evil befall me in this land and in this Hall of Maāti, because "I, even I, know the names of these gods who are therein and who "are the followers of the great god."

[1] I.e., the Season of Growing; the second month of Pert is the sixth month of the Egyptian year.

CHAPTER IX

HYMN TO OSIRIS[1]

XVIIITH DYNASTY, ABOUT B.C. 1500

1. 

ȧnetch ḥrȧ-k Ȧsȧr neb ḥeḥ suten neteru

Homage to thee, Osiris, lord of eternity, king of the gods,

āsh rennu tcheser kheperu sheta ȧru em

many of names, holy of creations, hidden of forms in

erperu shepses ka pu khent Ṭaṭṭu ur

the temples, whose *ka* is venerated, chief of Ṭaṭṭu, great one

khert 2. *em Sekhem neb hennu em*

contained in the temple of Sekhem, lord of praises in

Ȧthi khent tchef em Ȧnnu neb

the nome Ȧthi, chief of the sacred food in Heliopolis, the lord

[1] The stele on which the following text is inscribed is preserved in the Bibliothèque Nationale, Paris. Its importance was first recognized by Chabas (see *Revue Archéologique*, 1857, p. 65), and a complete copy of it will be found in Ledrain, *Monuments Égyptiens*, pll. xxii. ff.

sekhau	*em*	*Maāti*	*ba*	*sheta*	*neb*	*Qerert*
who is commemorated	in	Maāti,	soul	hidden,	lord	of Qerert,

tcheser	*em*	*Ȧneb-ḥetch*	*ba*	*Rā*	*tchet - f tchesef*
holy one,	in	White Wall,	the soul	of Rā,	of his very body,

ḥetep	*em*	3. *Suten-ḥenen*	*menkh*	*hennu*	*em*	*Nārt*
satisfied with offerings	in	Ḥenen-suten,	abundant	of praise	in	Nārt,

kheper setheset	*ba - f*		*neb*	*ḥet āa*	*em*	*Khemennu*
hath become exalted	his soul	[as]	lord	of the Great House	in	Khemennu,

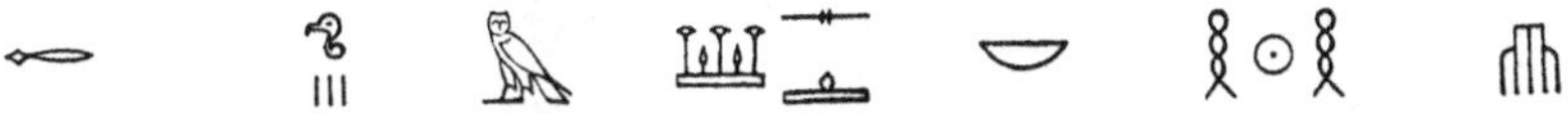

āa	*neru*	*em*	*Shas-ḥetep*	*neb*	*ḥeḥ*	*khent*
great one	of terror	in	Shas-ḥetep,	lord	of eternity,	chief

Ȧbṭu	*ḥer*	*ȧst - f*	*em*	*Ta-tcheser*	*ṭeṭṭeṭ*
of Abydos,	extendeth	his seat	in	the Land of holiness,	established

ren	*em*	*re*	*en*	*ret*	4. *pautti*	*en*
of name	in	the mouth	of	mankind,	the two-fold *paut*	of

taui	*Tem*	*tchef*	*kau*	*khent*	*paut*
the two lands,	Tem	the divine god	of the *kas*,	chief	of the *paut*

neteru khu menkh emmā khu khenp en nef
of the gods, spirit beneficent among the spirits, he draweth

Nu mu - f khent-nef meḥt meses
[from] Nu his waters, he bringeth along the wind of eventide

nef er fenṭet-f er ḥeteptu ȧb - f
[and] air to his nostrils to the satisfaction of his heart,

5. *reṭet en ȧb - f meses-nef khut tchef*
germinateth his heart, he produceth the light, the divine food,

setem-nef ḥert sbau sun-nef sbau āāiu
obey him heaven and the star-gods, he maketh to be open the great gates,

neb hennu em pet reset ṭuau em pet meḥtet
lord of praises in the southern heaven, adored in the northern heaven,

ȧukhemu - 6. seku kher ȧst ḥrȧ-f ȧst - f
the stars which never diminish [are] under the seat of his face, his seats

pu ȧukhemu-urṭu per-nef ḥetep em
are the stars which never rest, cometh to him an offering by

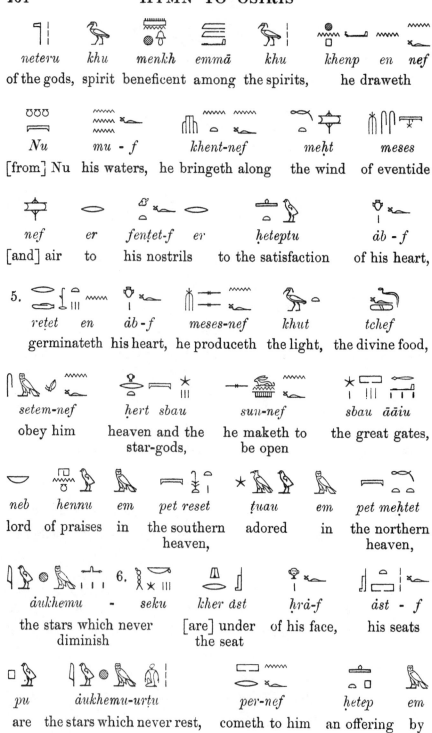

utu en Seb paut neteru ḥer ṭua - f sbau

the order of Seb, the *paut* of the gods praise him, the star gods

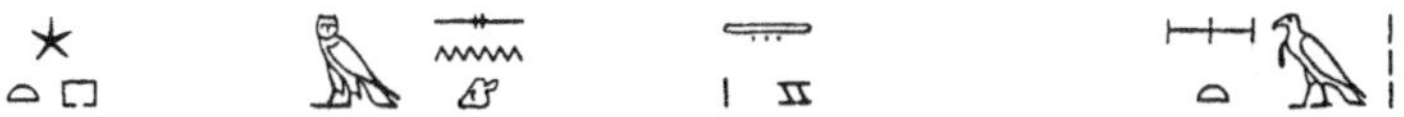

ṭuat em sen ta tchtchati

of the underworld smell the earth [before him], the boundaries [of earth]

em kesu tcherti em thebḥu

bow the back, the limits of heaven make supplication

7. 

maa-sen su naiu ȧm shepsu

[when] they see him. Those who are among the holy ones

ḥer ner-nef taui ṭemt ḥer erṭā nef ȧaiu

fear him, the two lands, all [of them] give to him praises

em khesefu ḥen-f sāḥu khu khent sāḥu

in meeting his majesty, the master glorious, chief of masters,

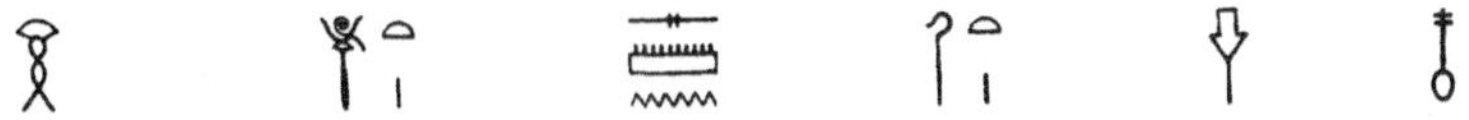

uaḥ ȧat smen ḥeqet sekhem nefer

endowed with divine rank, stablished of dominion. Form beautiful

8. 

en paut neteru am ḥrȧ merer

of the company of the gods, gracious of face, beloved by

maa-nef *erṭā* *senṭ - f* *em* *taiu* *neb* *en*

him that seeth him. He putteth his fear in all lands, through

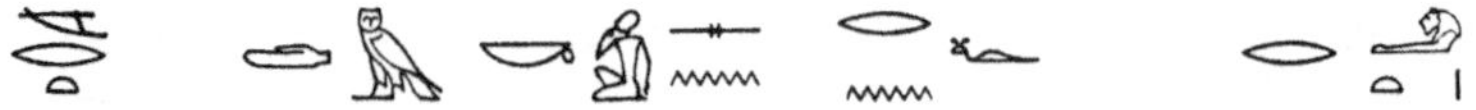

mert *ṭem* *ka - sen* *ren - f* *er* *ḥāt*

love [of him] they all proclaim his name before [every name].

ṭerp - nef *nebu* *neb* *sekhau* *em*

Make offerings to him all men, the lord who is commemorated in

pet *em* *ta* *āsh* *hi* *em* *Uaḳ*

heaven [and] in earth, [he is] greatly praised in the Uaḳ festival;

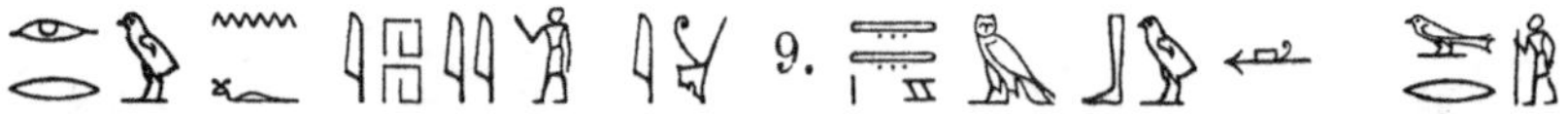

àru - nef *àhhi* *àn* *taui* *em* *bu* *uā* *ur*

make to him cries to joy the two lands all together, the great one,

ṭep *en* *sennu - f* *seru* *en* *paut* *neteru*

first of his divine brethren, prince of the *paut* of the gods,

smen *maāt* *khet* *taui* *erṭā* *sa*

stablisher of right and truth throughout the two lands, placer of the son

ḥer *nest-f* *āa* *en* *àt - f* *Seb* *merer* *mut - f*

upon his throne great of his father Seb, darling of his mother

Nut āa peḥpeḥ sekher-f Sebȧ āḥā sma-f

Nut, great one of two-fold strength, he casts down Sebȧ, he hath slaughtered

10. 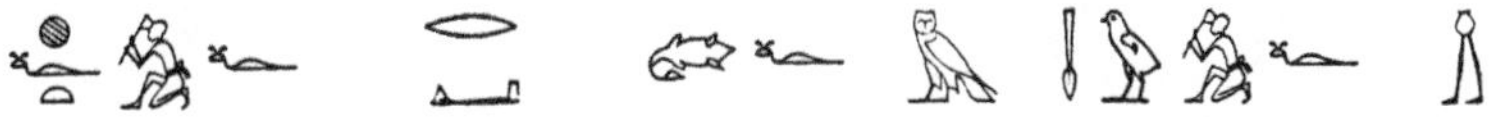

kheft-f erṭā senṭ-f em kheru-f ȧn

his enemy placing his fear in his foe. Bringer

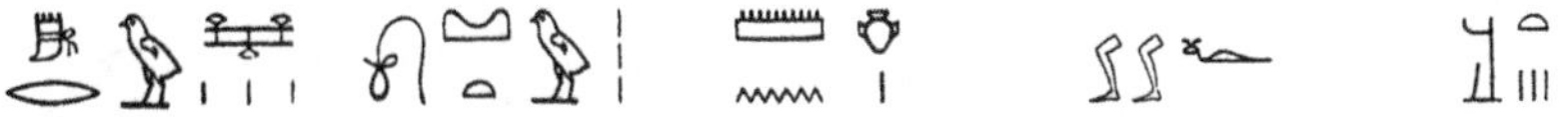

tcheru uaṭu men ȧb reṭui-f thest

of boundaries remote, firm of heart, his two feet are lifted up.

āuāu Seb sutenit taui maa-f khu-f

Heir of Seb and the sovereignty of the two lands. He hath seen his power,

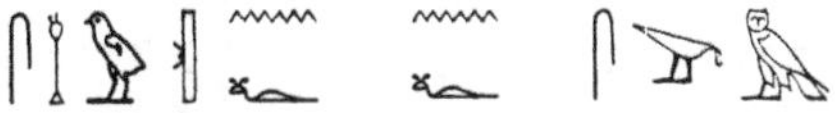 11. 

sutu-nef nef sem taiu en em ā er

he hath given command to him to lead the lands by [his] hand to

uaḥ en sep ȧri-nef ta pen em ā-f

the end of times. He hath made this earth in his hand,

mu-f nef-f sem-f menment-f nebt

its waters, its air, its green herbs, its cattle all,

pait nebt khepanen nebt tchetfet-f āut-f

[its] birds all, [its] fishes all, its reptiles, its quadrupeds,

set smaāu en sa Nut taui heru ḥer

the desert is by right to the son of Nut, the two lands are content

sekhā ḥer nest ent tef mȧ Rā uben - f

to crown [him] on the throne of the father like Rā. He riseth

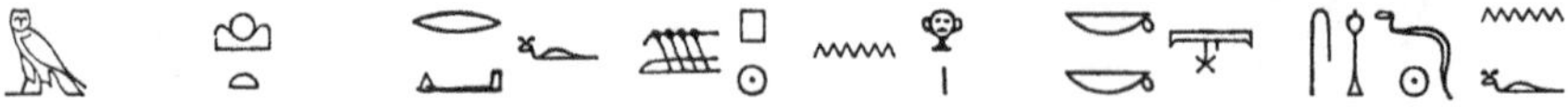

em khut erṭā - f shep en ḥer kek seḥetch-nef

on the horizon, he giveth light through the darkness, he shineth

shu em shuti-f bāḥ-nef taui mȧ ȧthen

with light from his plumes, he floodeth with light the two lands like the Disk

em ṭep ṭuait ḥetch-f ṭem-nes ḥert sensen

at the early sunrise. His crown pierceth heaven, he is a brother

sbau semu en neter neb menkh utu

of the star gods, the guide of god every, operative by command

meṭu ḥesi en paut neteru āat merer

and word, favoured one of the *paut* of the gods great, beloved of

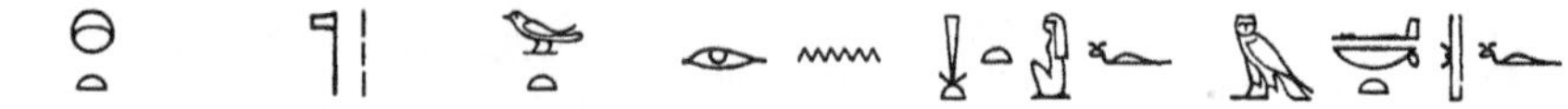

paut neteru netcheset ȧri en sent - f māket - f

the *paut* of the gods little. Hath made his sister his protection,

14.

seḥerit *kheru* *seḥemt* *sep* *sheṭ* *kheru*

driving away foes, turning back evil hap, uttering the word

em *khu* *re-s* *åqert* *nes* *ån* *uh*

with the power of her mouth, perfect of tongue, not erring

en *meṭu* *semenkhet* *utu* *meṭu* *Åst* *khut*

of speech, operating by decree and word Isis, the strong one,

netchet *sen-s* *ḥeḥet* *su* *åtet* *beḳeḳ*

the avenger of her brother. She sought him without weariness,

15.

reret *ta* *pen* *em* *ḥai* *ån* *khen - nes*

she went round about this earth in sorrow, not alighted she

ån *qemtu - s* *su* *årit* *shut* *em* *shut - s*

without finding him, she made light with her hair (or, feathers)

khepert *nef* *em* *ṭenḥui* *årit* *hennu* *menåṭ*

making to become wind with [her] wings, she made cries at the bier

16.

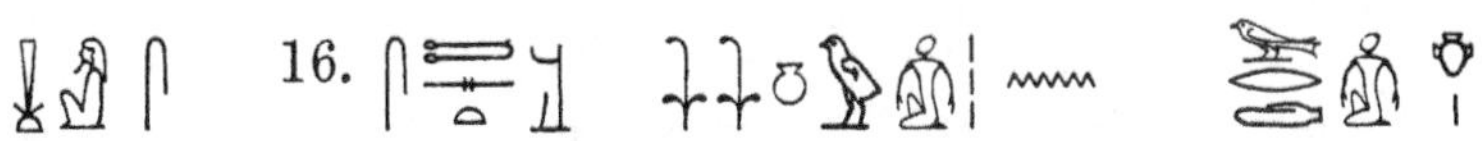

sen - s *setheset* *enenu* *en* *urṭ - åb*

of her brother. She raised up [from] inactivity the one still of heart,

khenpet mu - f ȧrit āuāu sheṭet nekhen

she extracted his seed, she made the heir, she suckled the babe

em uāāu ȧn rekh bu - f ȧm beset

in solitariness, not known is his place wherein she reared

su ā - f nekhtu em khent ḥet 17. *Seb paut*

him, his hand is mighty within the house of Seb. The *paut*

neteru ḥer resh sep sen iui Ȧsȧr sa Ḥeru men ȧb

of gods rejoice, rejoice at the coming of Osiris' son Horus, stablished of heart,

maā kheru sa Ȧst āuāu Ȧsȧr seḥuu - nef

whose word is absolute, son of Isis, heir of Osiris. Gather to him

tchatchat maāt paut neteru Neb-er-tcher tchesef

the sovereign princes of Maāt, the *paut* of the gods [and] Neb-er-tcher himself

nebu Maāt smaiu ȧm - s 18. *māk ḥaiu*

[and] the lords of Maāt assemble therewith. Verily those who repulse

ȧsfet senetchemu em ḥet ent Seb er erṭāt ȧat

faults rejoice in the house of Seb to bestow the rank [of Osiris]

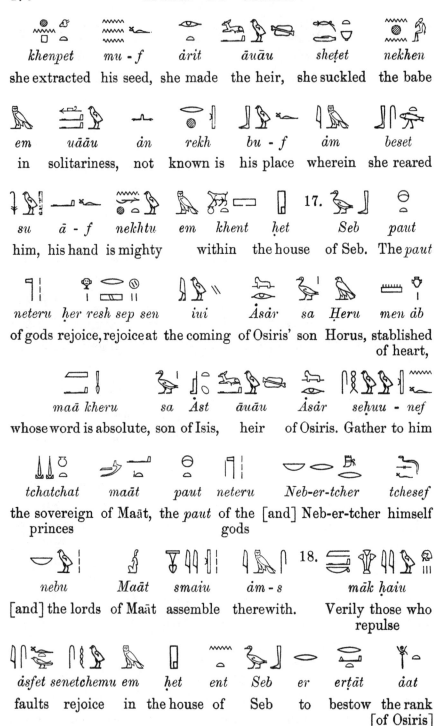

en	*neb-s*	*suteni*	*en*	*maāt-s*	*nef*	*qemen-tu*
upon	its lord,	the sovereignty	of	its right	[is] to him.	Hath found

Ḥeru	*kheru-f*	*māu*	*erṭāu - nef*	*ȧat*	*ent*	*tef*
Horus	his voice	true.	Hath been given to him	the rank	of	his father.

per-nef	*meḥu*	19. *em*	*utu*	*en*	*Seb*
He hath come forth	crowned	by	the command	of	Seb.

shep - nef	*ḥeq*	*taui*	*ḥetch*	*men*
He hath received	the sceptre	of the two lands,	the White Crown	is established

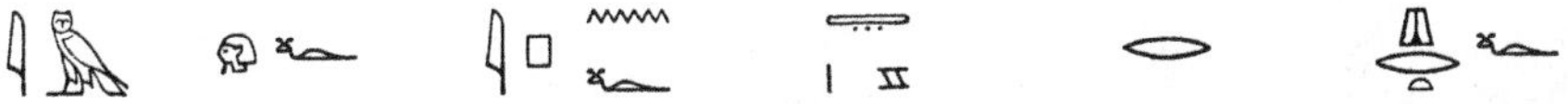

ȧm	*ṭep-f*	*ȧp-nef*	*ta*	*er*	*khert-f*
upon	his head.	He judgeth	the earth	according to	his plan.

pet ta	*kher*	*ȧst*	*ḥrȧ-f*	*s-utu-nef*	*ret*
Heaven and earth	are under	the seat	of his face.	He commandeth	men,

khu	*pāt*	*ḥamemet*	*Ta-merȧ*	*Ḥa-nebu*
spirits,	the dead,	the . . . .,	and Egypt,	the lords of the north,

shentu	20. *ȧthen*	*kher*	*sekheru-f*	*meḥt*	*ȧter*
the circle	of the Disk,	are under	his plans,	and the north wind,	the flood,

ennui khet en ānkh renpet nebt Neprȧ

the celestial waters, the staff of life, herb every. Neprȧ,

ṭā - f sem - f neb tchefau bes - f

he giveth his green herbs, the lord of tchefau food, he leadeth on

21.

sesau ṭā - f su em taiu bu neb khent

abundance, he giveth it in [all] lands. Everywhere is joy,

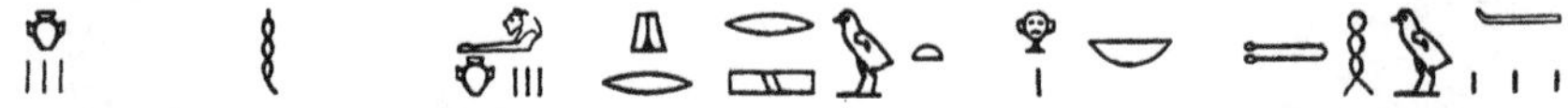

ȧbu netchem ḥātu kher reshut hrȧ-neb theḥu

hearts are glad, hearts rejoice, every face is happy.

ȧu bu-neb ḥer ṭua neferu-f netchemui mert - f

Every place adoreth his beauties. Doubly sweet is his love

kher-n menkhut - f rer - nes ȧbu ur mert-f

to us, his active goodness goeth round hearts, great is his love

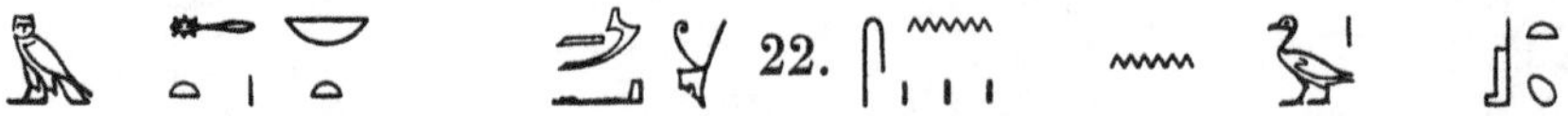

22.

em khat nebt maā en sen en sa Ȧst

in every body, and they do what is right to the son of Isis.

kheft - f kher en qen - f ȧri ṭu

His enemy hath fallen before his wrath, the maker of evil

er shet kheru ut qen sep-f

at the utterance of the voice, shooting forth his wrath in his season,

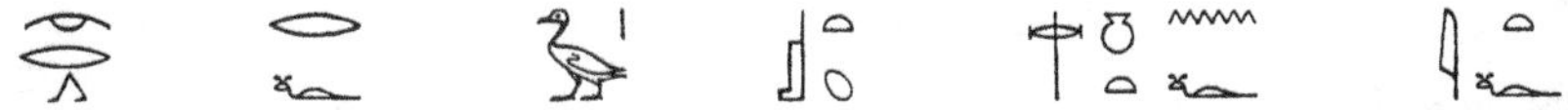

sper eref sa Ȧst netcht-nef ȧt-f

cometh unto him the son of Isis, the avenger of his father.

23.

setcheseru semenkhu ren-f shefit ḥetep-nes ȧst - s

Holy and beneficent is his name; awe resteth in its seat,

fu men er hepu - f uat sesh-thȧ

stablished everywhere are his laws, the path is opened,

māthennu un seherui taui āuit

the roads are opened, content are the two lands, wickedness

shems āui ruu ta em ḥetep kher

departeth, evil goeth away, the earth is at peace beneath

24.

neb-f smen Maāt en neb - s ertāu sa

its lord, established is Maāt by its lord, it giveth the back

er ȧsfet netchem ȧb-k Un-nefer sa Ȧst shep

to iniquity. Glad is thy heart, Un-nefer, son of Isis, he hath

nef *ḥetch* *smaāu* *nef* *ȧat* *ent* *tef*

received the White Crown, is his by right the rank of his father

em khennu *Ḥet - Seb* *Rā* *tcheṭ-f* *Teḥuti*

within the House of Seb, [he is] Rā [when] he speaketh, Thoth

ān - f 25. *tchatchat* *her-thȧ* *utu* *en*

[when] he writeth. The assessors are content; what hath decreed

nek *ȧtf-k* *Seb* *ȧri-entu* *kheft* *tcheṭet-nef*

for thee thy father Seb let be performed even as he spake;

suten ṭā ḥetep *Ȧsȧr* *Khent* *Ȧmenti* *neb* *Ȧbṭu*

may give a royal offering Osiris, governor of Ȧmenti, lord of Abydos,

ṭā - f *per kheru* *ȧḥ* *apṭ* *shesa* *sentra* *merḥet*

may he give sepulchral meals, oxen, fowl, bandages, incense, wax,

māt 26. *renpet* *neb* *ȧri* *kheperu* *sekhem*

gifts of herbs of all kinds, the making of transformations, the mastery

Ḥāp *pert* *em* *ba* *ānkhi* *maa* *em* *ȧthen*

of Nile, appearance as a soul living, the sight of the disk

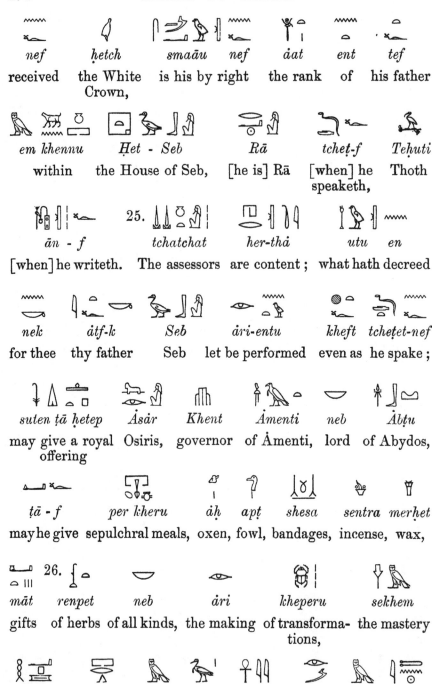

ṭep ṭuait *āq* *pert* *em* *Re-stau* *ȧn* *shenā*

at dawn daily, entrance into and exit from Re-stau, not being repulsed

27.

ba *em* *Neter-khert* *ṭerp - tu - f* *em - mā*

the soul in the Underworld, reception among

ḥesiu *embaḥ* *Un-nefer* *shep sennu* *per*

the favoured ones before Un-nefer, receipt of cakes, coming forth

em-baḥ *ḥer khaut* *ent* *neter* *āa* *sesenet* *nef*

before the altar of the god great, the snuffing of the wind

netchem *meḥt-s*

sweet of the north.

CHAPTER X

"THE NAMES OF OSIRIS IN EVERY SHRINE WHEREIN HE DWELLETH"

(THEBAN RECENSION, ABOUT B.C. 1600)

1. Åsår Un-nefer . . . 
2. Åsår Ānkhti . . . 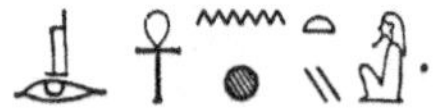
3. Åsår Neb-ānkh . . 
4. Åsår Neb-er-tcher . . 
5. Åsår Khenti-...... . . 
6. Åsår Saḥ . . . . 
7. Åsår Saa . . . . 
8. Åsår Khenti-peru . . 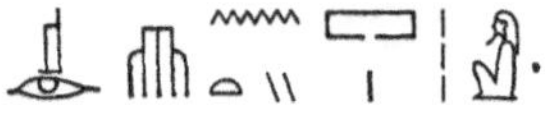
9. Åsår Em Resenet . . 
10. Åsår Em Meḥenet . . 
11. Åsår Nub-ḥeḥ . . . 
12. Åsår Bati erpit . . 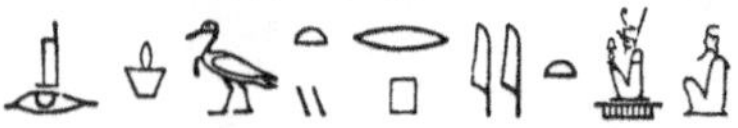
13. Åsår Ptaḥ-neb-Ānkh . 
14. Åsår Khenti Re-stau . 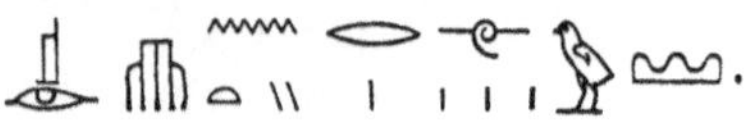
15. Åsår Ḥer-åb semt . . 
16. Åsår Em Åti (Ånetch) . 

17. Åsår Em Seḥtet . . 

18. Åsår Em Netchefet . . 

19. Åsår Em Resu . . . 

20. Åsår Em Pe . . . 

21. Åsår Em Neteru . . 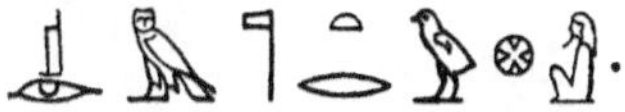

22. Åsår Em Sau-kheri . . 

23. Åsår Em Båket . . 

24. Åsår Em Sunnu . . 

25. Åsår Em Reḥenenet . . 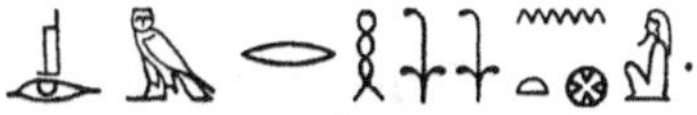

26. Åsår Em Āper . . . 

27. Åsår Qefṭennu . . . 

28. Åsår Sekri Em Peṭ-she . 

29. Åsår Khenti Nut-f . . 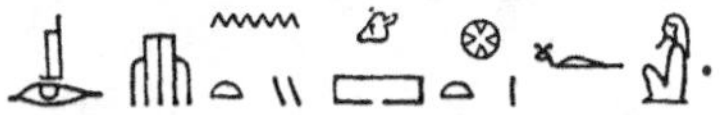

30. Åsår Em Pesek̦-re . . 

31. Åsår Em-åst-f-åmu-Ta-meḥ 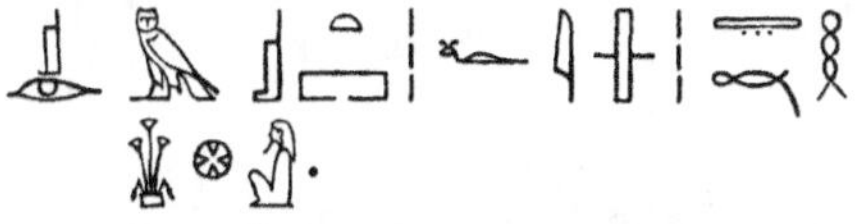

32. Åsår Em Pet . . . 

33. Åsår Em-åst-f-åmu-Re-stau 

34. Åsår Netchesti . . . 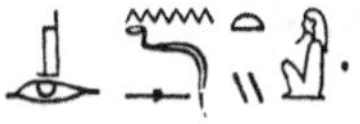

35. Åsår Smam-ur . . . 

36. Åsår Sekri . . . 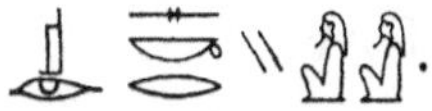

37. Åsår Ḥeq-tchetta . . 

38. Åsår Tua . . . . 

39. Åsår Em Åter . . . 

40. Åsår Em Sek . . . 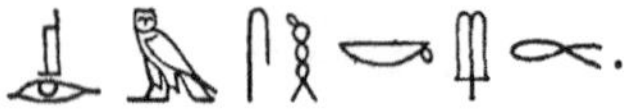

41. Åsår Neb-tchetta . . 

42. Åsår Åthi . . . 

43. Åsår Taiti . . . 

44. Åsår Em Re-stau . . 

45. Åsår Ḥer-shāi-f . . 

46. Åsår Khenti-seḥ-ḥemt . 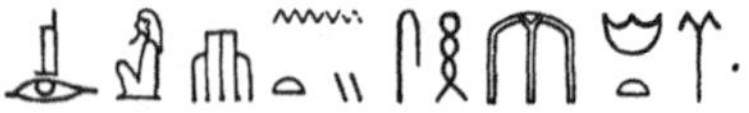

47. Åsår Em Tau-enenet . 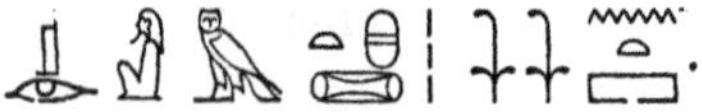

48. Åsår Em Neṭebit . . 

49. Åsår Em Såti . . . 

50. Åsår Em Beṭeshu . . 

51. Åsår Em Ṭepu . . . 

52. Åsår Em Sau-ḥeri . . 

53. Åsår Em Nepert . . 

54. Åsår Em Shennu . . 

55. Åsår Em Ḥenket . . 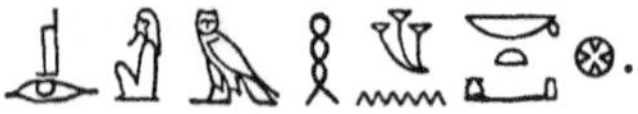

56. Åsår Em Ta-Sekri . . 

57. Åsår Em Shau . . . 

58. Åsår Em Fat-Ḥeru . . 

59. Åsår em Maāti . . . 

60. Åsår Em Henå . . . 

"THE NAMES OF OSIRIS IN EVERY SHRINE IN WHICH HE DWELLETH"

(SAÏTE RECENSION, ABOUT B.C. 300)

1. Ȧsȧr Un-nefer . . .
2. Ȧsȧr Ānkhi . . . .
3. Ȧsȧr Neb Ānkh . .
4. Ȧsȧr Neb-er-tcher . .
5. Ȧsȧr Ȧp- . . . . taui . .
6. Ȧsȧr Khentet Un . .
7. Ȧsȧr Khentet Nepra . .
8. Ȧsȧr Saḥ . . . .
9. Ȧsȧr Seps-baiu-Ȧnnu .
10. Ȧsȧr Khenti-Thenenet .
11. Ȧsȧr Em Resenet . .
12. Ȧsȧr Em Meḥenet . .
13. Ȧsȧr Neb Ḥeḥ . . .
14. Ȧsȧr Sa Erpeti . .
15. Ȧsȧr Ptaḥ Neb Ānkh .
16. Ȧsȧr Khent Re-stau . .
17. Ȧsȧr Ḥeq taiu ḥer-ȧb Ṭaṭṭu
18. Ȧsȧr Ḥer-ȧb set . .
19. Ȧsȧr Ba sheps em Ṭaṭṭu .
20. Ȧsȧr Em Ȧtet . . .
21. Ȧsȧr Em Ḥest, or, Neter-ʒeḥt

22. Åsår Neb ta ānkhtet . . 

23. Åsår Ḿm Sau . . . 

24. Åsår Em Netchet . . 

25. Åsår Em Resu, or, em Tchatchat . . . 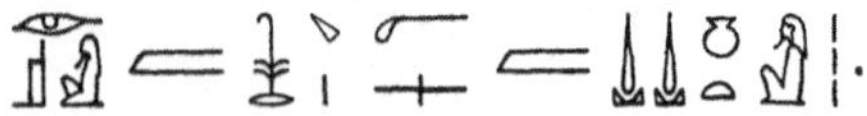

26. Åsår Em Pe . . . 

27. Åsår Em Ṭept . . . 

28. Åsår Em Netrå . . 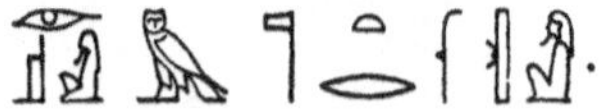

29. Åsår Em Sau Khert . 

30. Åsår Em Sau ḥert . . 

31. Åsår Em Ån-ruṭ-f . . 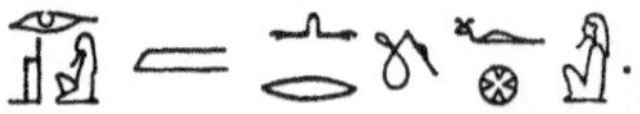

32. Åsår Em Båkui . . 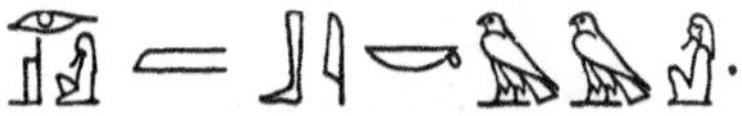

33. Åsår Em Sunnu . . 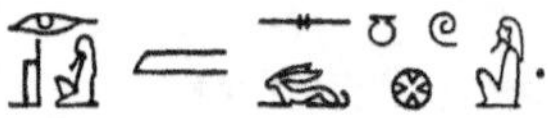

34. Åsår Em Renen . . 

35. Åsår Em Āper . . 

36. Åsår Em Qefennu . . 

37. Åsår Em Sekri . . 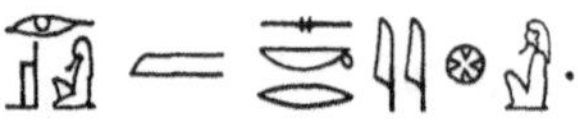

38. Åsår Em Peṭet . . 

39. Åsår Em Ḥet-f em Re-stau 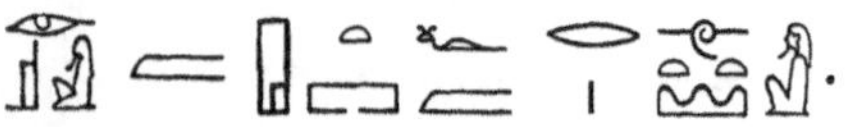

40. Åsår Em Nif-ur . . 

41. Åsår Em Neṭit . . ;

42. Åsår Khenti nut-f . . 

43. Åsår Ḥenti . . . 

44. Åsår Em Peḳes . . 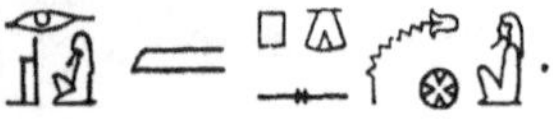

45. Åsår Em ḥet-f åm ta reset.

46. Åsår Em ḥet-f åm ta meḥt

47. Åsår Em pet . . .

48. Åsår Em ta . . .

49. Åsår Em nest . . .

50. Åsår Em Atef-ur . .

51. Åsår Seker em sheṭat .

52. Åsår ḥeq tchetta em Ånnu

53. Åsår Utet . . .

54. Åsår Em Sektet . .

55. Åsår Em Rertu-nifu . .

56. Åsår Neb-tchetta . .

57. Åsår Neb-ḥeḥ . .

58. Åsår Em Ṭesher . .

59. Åsår Em Seshet . .

60. Åsår Em Uḥet-resu . .

61. Åsår Em Uḥet-meḥt .

62. Åsår Em Åat-urt . .

63. Åsår Em Āpert. . .

64. Åsår Em Shennu . .

65. Åsår Em Ḥekennut, or, Ḥesertet . . .

66. Åsår Em Seker . .

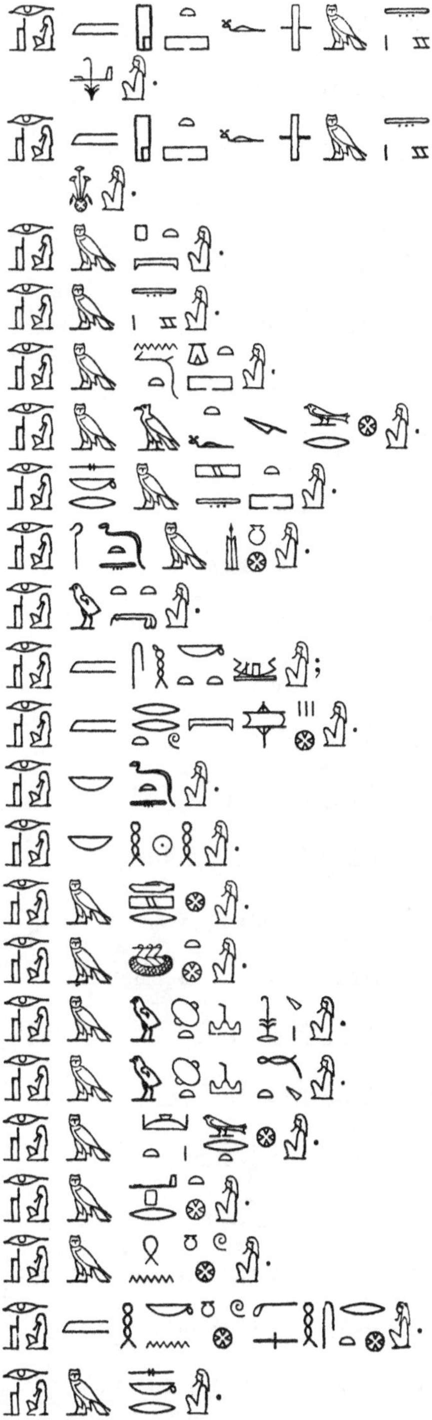

67. Åsår Em Shau
68. Åsår Fa-Ḥeru
69. Åsår Em Uu-Peḳ
70. Åsår Em Maāti
71. Åsår Em Menå
72. Åsår Baiu tef-f
73. Åsår Neb taiu suten neteru
74. Åsår Em Bener
75. Åsår Em Tai
76. Åsår Ḥer shāi-f
77. Åsår Khent seḥet kauit-f
78. Åsår Em Så
79. Åsår Em Såti
80. Åsår Em Asher
81. Åsår Em taui nebu
82. Åsår Khent shet āa-perti
83. Åsår Em Ḥet Benbenet
84. Åsår Em Ånnu
85. Åsår Åau åm Ånnu
86. Åsår Em Ḥemaḳ
87. Åsår Em Ākesh
88. Åsår Em Pe Nu
89. Åsår Em Ḥet-āat
90. Åsår Neb-Ānkh em Åbṭu

91. Åsår Neb-Ṭaṭṭu . .
92. Åsår Khent Ḳa-åst . .
93. Åsår Åthi ḥer-ab Åbṭu .
94. Åsår Åthi ḥer-åb Shetat .
95. Åsår Em ānkh em Ptaḥ-ḥet-kat . . .
96. Åsår neb peḥtet petpet Sebå
97. Åsår Ba ḥer-åb Qemt .
98. Åsår Åḥeti . . .
99. Åsår Seḥ . . .
100. Åsår Ḥeru-khuti . .
101. Tem Ka kha paut neteru āat
102. Åp-uat rest sekhem taui .
103. Åp-uat meḥt sekhem pet
104. Ptaḥ Ṭeṭṭeṭ sheps åst Rā
105. Uā seqeb em Ḥet-Benben
106. Seb erpāt neteru . .
107. Ḥeru-ur . . . .
108. Ḥeru-khentet-ån-maati .
109. Ḥeru-sa-Åst . . .
110. Åmsu (Min)-suten-Ḥeru-nekht . . . .
111. Ån-mut-f āb-perui-urui .
112. Khnemu-Ḥeru-ḥetep .
113. Ḥeru-Sekhai . . .

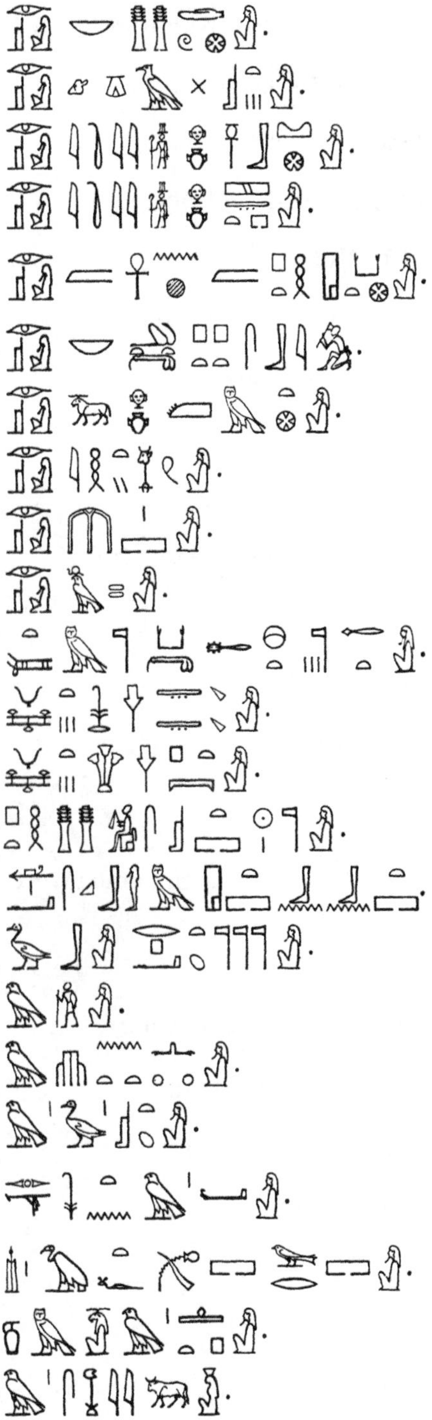

114. Ḥeru-khent-khaṭṭhi . 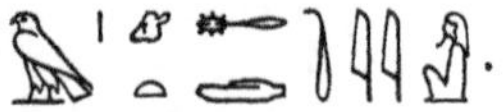

115. Ḥeru-Teḥuti . . . 

116. Ȧn-ḥer . . . . 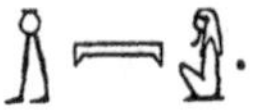

117. Ȧnpu-khent-neter-seḥ . 

118. Nut . . . . . 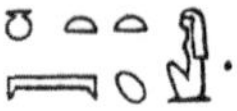

119. Ȧst netert em ren-s nebu 

120. Re-sekhait . . . 

121. Shenthit . . . 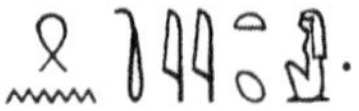

122. Ḥeqtit . . . . 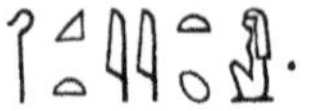

123. Neshmet neb tchetta . 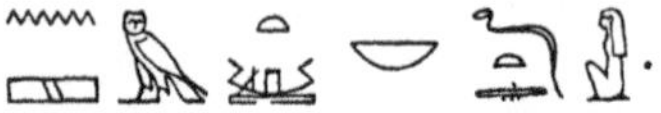

124. Net . . . . . 

125. Serqet . . . . 

126. Maāt . . . . 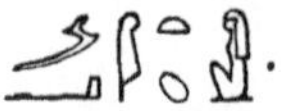

127. Ahit . . . . 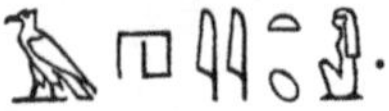

128. Ta fṭu Meskhenu ȧmu Ȧbṭu 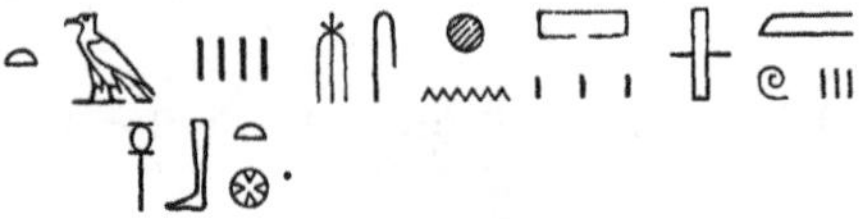

129. Meskhen Āat . . . 

130. Meskhen Seqebet . . 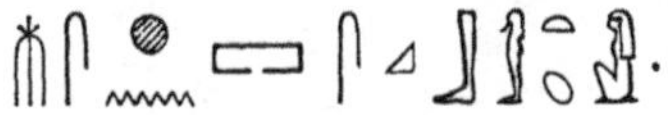

131. Meskhen Ment (?) . . 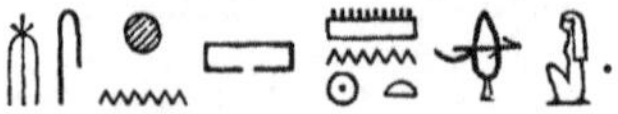

132. Meskhen Nefert . . 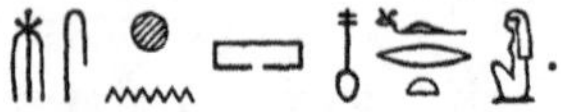

133. Ȧmseth . . . . 

134. Ḥāpi . . . . 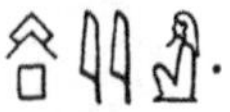

135. Ṭua-mut-f . . . 

136. Qebḥ-sennu-f . . . 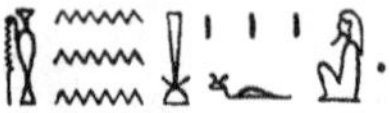

137. Āārāt ḥer-ȧb neter ḥet .
138. Neteru semu Ṭuat . .
139. Neteru Qerti . . .
140. Neteru neterit ȧmu Ȧbṭu
141. Ȧturti Rest Meḥt . .
142. Ȧmkhiu nu Ȧsȧr . .
143. Ȧsȧr Khent Ȧmentet .
144. Ȧsȧr Em ȧst-f nebu. .
145. Ȧsȧr Em ȧst-f em ta rest
146. Ȧsȧr Em āḥāt-f em ta meḥt
147. Ȧsȧr Em ȧst-f neb meri ka-f ȧm . . .
148. Ȧsȧr Em seḥ-f nebu .
149. Ȧsȧr Em qema-f nebu .
150. Ȧsȧr Em ren-f nebu .
151. Ȧsȧr Em ḳer-f neb .
152. Ȧsȧr Em khāu-f nebu .
153. Ȧsȧr Em khakeru-f nebu
154. Ȧsȧr Em āḥāt-f nebu .
155. Ḥeru-netch-tef-f em ren-f neb . . . .
156. Ȧnpu khent neter seḥ em ren-f neb . . .
157. Ȧnpu ȧm Uḥet . . .
158. Neteru ent Neter-khert ent ȧmu Ṭuat . .

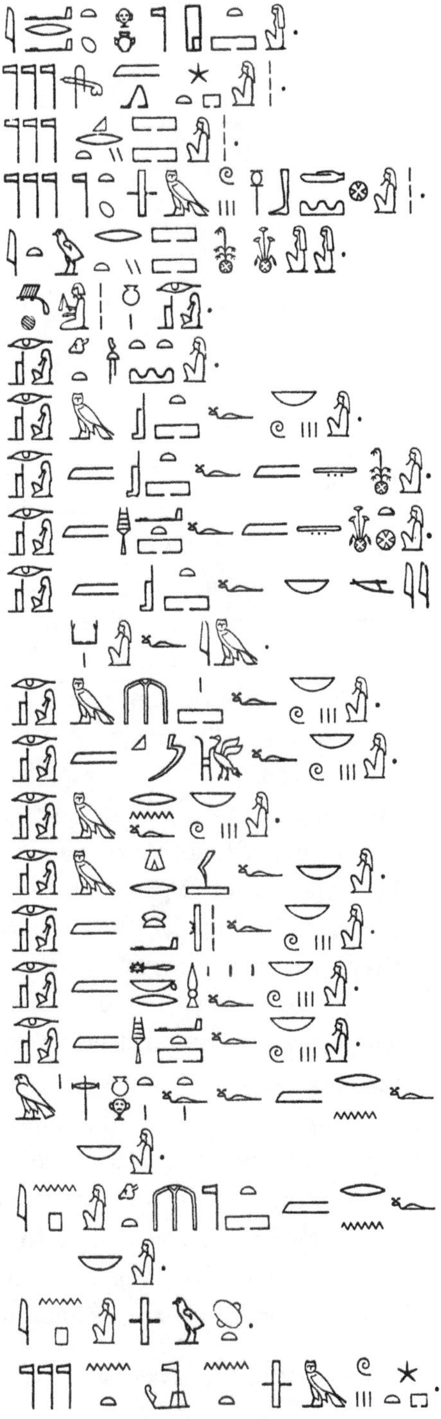

CHAPTER XI

PLUTARCH'S MYTHOLOGICAL HISTORY OF ISIS AND OSIRIS[1]

XII. "NOW the story of Isis and Osiris, its most significant and "superfluous parts omitted, is thus briefly related:— "Rhea, they say, having accompanied with Kronos by stealth, was "discovered by Helios, who hereupon denounced a curse upon her, "'that she should not be delivered in any month or year.' Hermes "however, being likewise in love with the same Goddess, in "recompence of the favours which he had received from her, plays "at tables with Selene, and wins from her the seventieth part of "each of her illuminations; these several parts, making in the "whole five new days, he afterwards joined together, and added to "the three hundred and sixty, of which the year formerly "consisted: which days therefore are even yet called by the "Egyptians the 'Epact' or 'superadded,' and observed by them "as the birth-days of their Gods. For upon the first of them, say "they, was OSIRIS born, just at whose entrance into the world a "voice was heard, saying, 'the lord of all the earth is born.' "There are some indeed who relate this circumstance in a different "manner, as that a certain person named Pamyles, as he was "fetching water from the temple of Jupiter at Thebes, heard a "voice commanding him to proclaim aloud, that 'the good and "great king Osiris was then born'; and for this reason Kronos "committed the education of the child to him, and that in memory "of this event the Pamylia were afterwards instituted, a festival "much resembling the Phallephoria or Priapeia of the Greeks.

[1] See S. Squire, *Plutarch's Treatise of Isis and Osiris*, Cambridge, 1744, p. 15 ff.

"Upon the second of these days was AROUERIS ('Αρουηρις) born; "whom some call Apollo, and others distinguish by the name of "the elder Orus.[1] Upon the third, TYPHO [i.e., Set ] "came into the world, being born neither at the proper time, nor "by the right place, but forcing his way through a wound which "he had made in his mother's side. ISIS was born on the fourth "of them, in the marshes of Egypt; as Nephthys was upon the "last, whom some call Teleute and Aphrodite, and others Nike. "Now as to the fathers of these children, the two first of them are "said to have been begotten by Helios; Isis by Hermes; Typho "and Nephthys by Kronos; and accordingly, the third of these "superadded days, because it was looked upon as the birth-day of "Typho, was regarded by the kings as inauspicious, and consequently "they neither transacted any business in it, or even suffered them-"selves to take any refreshment until the evening. They further "add, that Typho married Nephthys; and that Isis and Osiris, "having a mutual affection, enjoyed each other in their mother's "womb before they were born, and that from this commerce sprang "Aroueris, whom the Egyptians likewise call the 'elder Orus,' and "the Greeks 'Apollo.'"

XIII. "Osiris, being now become king of Egypt, applied "himself towards civilizing his countrymen, by turning them from "their former indigent and barbarous course of life; he moreover "taught them how to cultivate and improve the fruits of the earth; "he gave them a body of laws to regulate their conduct by, and "instructed them in that reverence and worship, which they were "to pay to the gods; with the same good disposition he afterwards "travelled over the rest of the world, inducing the people every-"where to submit to his discipline, not indeed compelling them by "force of arms, but persuading them to yield to the strength of "his reasons, which were conveyed to them in the most agreeable "manner, in hymns and songs accompanied with instruments of "music; from which last circumstance, the Greeks conclude him "to have been the same person with their Dionysos or Bacchus. "During Osiris's absence from his kingdom Typho had no

[1] 'Αρουηρις = ḤERU-UR, .

"opportunity of making any innovations in the state, Isis being "extremely vigilant in the government and always upon her guard. "After his return, however, having first persuaded seventy-two "other persons to join with him in the conspiracy, together with a "certain queen of Ethiopia named Aso, who chanced to be in "Egypt at that time, he contrived a proper stratagem to execute "his base designs. For having privily taken the measure of "Osiris's body, he caused a chest to be made exactly of the same "size with it, as beautiful as might be, and set off with all the "ornaments of art. This chest he brought into his banqueting "room; where, after it had been much admired by all who were "present, Typho, as it were in jest, promised to give it to any one "of them, whose body upon trial it might be found to fit. Upon "this the whole company, one after another, go into it, but as it "did not fit any of them, last of all Osiris lays himself down in it, "upon which the conspirators immediately ran together, clapped "the cover upon it, and then fastened it down on the outside with "nails, pouring likewise melted lead over it. After this, they "carried it away to the river side, and conveyed it to the sea by "the Tanaïtic mouth of the Nile; which for this reason is still held "in the utmost abomination by the Egyptians, and never named "by them but with proper marks of detestation. These things, say "they, were thus executed upon the 17th day of the month Athyr, "when the Sun was in Scorpio, in the 28th year of Osiris's reign; "though there are others who tell us that he was no more than 28 "years old at this time.

XIV. "The first who knew the accident which had befallen "their king, were the Pans and Satyrs who inhabited the country "about Chemmis;[1] and they immediately acquainting the people "with the news gave the first occasion to the name Panic Terrors, "which has ever since been made use of to signifie any sudden "affright or amazement of a multitude. As to Isis, as soon as the "report reached her, she immediately cut off one of the locks of "her hair, and put on mourning apparel upon the very spot where

[1] I.e., Apu, , the Panopolis of the Greeks; the name Χέμμις, the modern Akhmîm, is derived from the old Egyptian name, .

"she then happened to be, which accordingly from this accident "has ever since been called Coptos, or the *City of Mourning*, though "some are of opinion that this word rather signifies *Deprivation.* "After this she wandered everywhere about the country, full of "disquietude and perplexity, in search of the chest, enquiring of "every person she met with, even of some children whom she "chanced to see, whether they knew what was become of it. Now "it so happened that these children had seen what Typho's accom-"plices had done with the body, and accordingly acquainted her by "what mouth of the Nile it had been conveyed into the sea. For "this reason therefore the Egyptians look upon *children* as endued "with a kind of faculty of divining, and in consequence of this "notion are very curious in observing the accidental prattle which "they have with one another whilst they are at play (especially if "it be a sacred place), forming omens and presages from it. Isis, "during this interval, having been informed that Osiris, deceived by "her sister Nephthys who was in love with him, had unwittingly "enjoyed her instead of herself, as she concluded from the melilot "garland (τὸν Μελιλώτινον στέφανον), which he had left with her, "made it her business to search out the child, the fruit of this "unlawful commerce (for her sister, dreading the anger of her "husband Typho, had exposed it as soon as it was born), and "accordingly, after much pains and difficulty, by means of some "dogs that conducted her to the place where it was, she found it "and bred it up; so that in process of time it became her constant "guard and attendant, and from hence obtained the name of "Anubis, being thought to watch and guard the Gods, as dogs do "mankind.

"At length she receives more particular news of the chest, "that it had been carried by the waves of the sea to the coast of "Byblos, and there gently lodged in the branches of a bush of "Tamarisk, which in a short time had shot up into a large and "beautiful tree, growing round the chest and enclosing it on every "side, so that it was not to be seen; and farther that the king of "the country, amazed at its unusual size, had cut the tree down, "and made that part of the trunk, wherein the chest was concealed, "a pillar to support the roof of his house. These things, say they, "being made known to Isis in an extraordinary manner by the "report of demons, she immediately went to Byblos; where, "setting herself down by the side of a fountain, she refused to "speak to anybody, excepting only to the queen's women who "chanced to be there; these indeed she saluted and caressed in "the kindest manner possible, plaiting their hair for them, and "transmitting into them part of that wonderfully grateful odour, "which issued from her own body. This raised a great desire in "the queen their mistress, to see the stranger, who had this "admirable faculty of transfusing so fragrant a smell from herself "into the hair and skin of other people. She therefore sent for "her to court, and after a further acquaintance with her, made her "nurse to one of her sons. Now the name of the king, who "reigned at this time at Byblos,[1] was Melcarthus, as that of his "queen was Astarte, or according to others, *Saosis*, though some "call her Nemanoun, which answers to the Greek name of "*Athenais*.

XVI. "Isis fed the child by giving it her finger to suck "instead of the breast; she likewise put him every night into the "fire in order to consume his mortal part, whilst transforming "herself into a swallow she hovered round the pillar and bemoaned "her sad fate. Thus continued she to do for some time, till the "queen, who stood watching her, observing the child to be all in a "flame, cryed out, and thereby deprived him of that immortality, "which would otherwise have been conferred upon him. The "goddess upon this, discovering herself, requested that the pillar "which supported the roof might be given her; which she accord-"ingly took down, and then easily cutting it open, after she had "taken out what she wanted, she wrapped up the remainder of "the trunk in fine linnen, and pouring perfumed oil upon it, "delivered it again into the hands of the king and queen (which "piece of wood is to this day preserved in the temple of Isis, and "worshipped by the people of Byblos). When this was done she "threw herself upon the chest, making at the same time such a

[1] The Byblos really referred to here is a city in the Papyrus Swamps of the Delta.

"loud and terrible lamentation over it, as frighted the younger of "the king's sons, who heard her, out of his life. But the elder of "them she took with her, and set sail with the chest for Egypt; "and it being now about morning, the river Phaedrus sending "forth a rough and sharp air, she in her anger dried up its "current.

XVII. "No sooner was she arrived at a desert place, where "she imagined herself to be alone, but she presently opened the "chest, and laying her face upon her dead husband's embraced his "corpse, and wept bitterly; but perceiving that the little boy had "silently stolen behind her, and found out the occasion of her "grief, she turned herself about on the sudden, and in her anger "gave him so fierce and stern a look that he immediately died of "the affright. Others indeed say that his death did not happen in "this manner, but, as was hinted above, that he fell into the sea, "and afterwards received the greatest honours on account of the "goddess; for that the *Maneros*, whom the Egyptians so frequently "call upon in their banquets, is none other than this very boy. "This relation is again contradicted by such as tell us, that the "true name of this child was *Palaestinus*, or Pelusius, and that the "city of this name was built by the goddess in memory of him; "adding farther, that the *Maneros* above mentioned is thus "honoured by the Egyptians at their feasts, because he was the "first who invented music. There are others again, who affirm "that *Maneros* is not the name of any particular person, but a "mere customary form, and complimental manner of greeting "made use of by the Egyptians one towards another at their more "solemn feasts and banquets, meaning no more by it than to "wish 'that what they were then about might prove fortunate "and happy to them,' for that this is the true import of the word. "In like manner, say they, the human skeleton, which at these "times of jollity is carried about in a box, and shewn to all the "guests, is not designed, as some imagine, to represent the particular misfortunes of Osiris, but rather to remind them of their "mortality, and thereby to excite them freely to make use of and "to enjoy the good things which are set before them, seeing they "must quickly become such as they there saw; and that this is "the true reason of introducing it at their banquets—but to "proceed in the narration.

XVIII. "Isis intending a visit to her son Orus, who was "brought up at Butos,[1] deposited the chest in the meanwhile in a "remote and unfrequented place; Typho however, as he was one "night hunting in the light of the moon, accidentally met with it; "and knowing the body which was enclosed in it, tore it into "several pieces, 14 in all, dispersing them up and down in different "parts of the country. Upon being made acquainted with this "event, Isis once more sets out in search of the scattered fragments "of her husband's body, making use of a boat made of the reed "Papyrus in order the more easily to pass thro' the lower and "fenny parts of the country—For which reason say they, the "crocodile never touches any persons, who sail in this sort of "vessels, as either fearing the anger of the goddess, or else respect- "ing it on account of its having once carried her. To this occasion "therefore is to be imputed, that there are so many different "sepulchres of Osiris shewn in Egypt; for we are told, that "wherever Isis met with any of the scattered limbs of her husband, "she there buried it. There are others however who contradict "this relation, and tell us, that this variety of sepulchres was owing "rather to the policy of the queen, who, instead of the real body, "as was pretended, presented these several cities with the image "only of her husband; and that she did this, not only to render "the honours, which would by this means be paid to his memory, "more extensive, but likewise that she might hereby elude the "malicious search of Typho; who, if he got the better of "Orus in the war wherein they were going to be engaged, dis- "tracted by this multiplicity of Sepulchres, might despair of being "able to find the true one—we are told moreover, that notwith- "standing all her search, Isis was never able to recover the privy- "member of Osiris, which having been thrown into the Nile "immediately upon its separation from the rest of the body, "had been devoured by the Lepidotus, the Phagrus, and the "Oxyrynchus, fish which of all others, for this reason, the

[1] I.e., Per-Uatchit, .

"Egyptians have in more especial avoidance. In order, how-
"ever, to make some amends for the loss, Isis consecrated the
"Phallus made in imitation of it, and instituted a solemn
"festival to its memory, which is even to this day observed by the
"Egyptians."

"After these things, Osiris returning from the other world
"appeared to his son Orus, encouraged him to the battle, and at
"the same time instructed him in the exercise of arms. He then
"asked him, 'what he thought the most glorious action a man
"could perform?' to which Orus replied, 'to revenge the injuries
"offered to his father and mother.' He then asked him, 'what
"animal he thought most serviceable to a soldier?' and being
"answered 'a horse,' this raised the wonder of Osiris, so that he
"further questioned him, 'why he preferred a horse before a lion?'
"'because,' says Orus, 'tho' the lion be the more serviceable
"creature to one who stands in need of help, yet is the horse more
"useful in overtaking and cutting off a flying adversary.' These
"replies much rejoiced Osiris, as they shewed him that his son
"was sufficiently prepared for his enemy. We are moreover told,
"that amongst the great numbers who were continually deserting
"from Typho's party was his concubine Thueris,[1] and that a serpent
"pursuing her as she was coming over to Orus, was slain by his
"soldiers—the memory of which action, say they, is still preserved
"in that cord, which is thrown into the midst of their assemblies,
"and then chopt into pieces—afterwards it came to a battle between
"them, which lasted many days; but victory at length inclined to
"Orus, Typho himself being taken prisoner. Isis however, to
"whose custody he was committed, was so far from putting him to
"death, that she even loosed his bonds and set him at liberty.
"This action of his mother so extremely incensed Orus, that he
"laid hands upon her, and pulled off the ensign of royalty which
"she wore on her head; and instead thereof Hermes clapt on an
"helmet made in the shape of an oxe's head. After this Typho
"publicly accused Orus of bastardy; but by the assistance of
"Hermes, his legitimacy was fully established by the judgment of

[1] I.e., Ta-urt, .

"the Gods themselves. After this, there were two other battles "fought between them, in both which Typho had the worst. Fur-"thermore, Isis is said to have accompanied Osiris after his death, "and in consequence hereof to have brought forth Harpocrates, "who came into the world before his time, and lame in his lower "limbs."

CHAPTER XII

ÅSÅR-ḤĀPI, , OR SERAPIS.

IN connexion with the history of the god Osiris mention must be made of ÅSÅR-ḤĀPI or SERAPIS, a deity whose cult was wide-spread in Egypt under the Ptolemies, and in many provinces of the Roman Empire after that country had passed under the authority of the Cæsars. The second part of the name, "Ḥāpi," was that which was given to the famous bull which formed the object of worship at Memphis very early in the dynastic period of Egyptian history, and which is commonly known as the "APIS BULL," whilst the first part is, of course, nothing but the name Osiris in its Egyptian form. The Greeks fused the names of the two deities together under the form Σάραπις, and, although the exact nature of the attributes which they assigned to Osiris and Apis united is not quite clear, it seems tolerably certain that they regarded Serapis as the form which Apis took after death. According to the hieroglyphic texts[1] which were found on stelae and other objects in the Serapeum at Ṣaḳḳâra, Apis is called "the life of Osiris, the "lord of heaven, Tem [with] his horns [in] his head,"  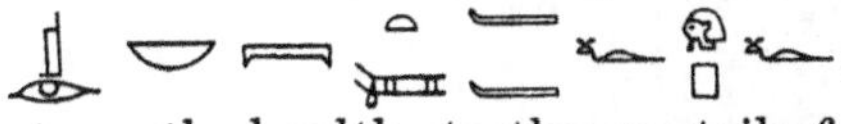, and he is said to "give life, strength, health, to thy nostrils for ever." Elsewhere APIS-OSIRIS is described as, "the great god, Khent Åmentet, the lord of life for ever," , and as this text belongs to the period of the XVIIIth Dynasty, we see that even at the beginning of the New Empire Apis and Osiris were

[1] See Mariette, *Le Sérapéum de Memphis*, Paris, 1882, p. 125 ff.; Mariette, *Mémoire sur cette Représentation gravée en tête de quelques proscynèmes du Sérapéum*, Paris, 1856.

joined together by the priests of Memphis, and that the attributes of Apis had been made to assume a funereal character, and that he was at that time recognized as a god of the Underworld. On a monument of the XIXth Dynasty,[1] Apis is said to be "the renewed life of Ptaḥ," 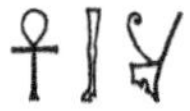 , and in an inscription of the XXVIth Dynasty he is called the "second Ptaḥ," ;[2] in the same text we have a mention of the "temple of Åsår-Ḥāpi,"  , i.e., of Serapis, and we may learn from this fact that Apis had been finally made a god of the Underworld, and that his identity had been merged in that of Osiris. The identification of Apis with Osiris was easy enough, because one of the commonest names of Osiris was "Bull of the West," and the identification once made the shrines of Osiris were regarded as the proper places at which the worship of the double god should be paid. Apis was, in fact, believed to be animated by the soul of Osiris, and to be Osiris incarnate, and the appearance of a new Apis was regarded as a new

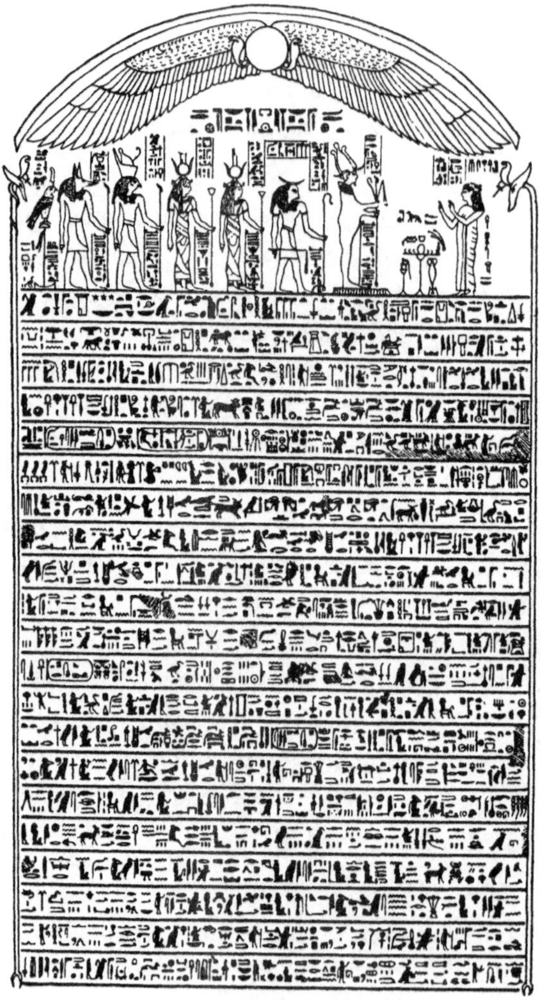

Sepulchral tablet with a scene in which the deceased is seen adoring Osiris, Serapis, and other gods.

[1] Mariette, *Sérapéum*, p. 139.

[2] *Ibid.*, p. 198.

manifestation of Osiris upon earth; but he was also an emanation of Ptaḥ, and he was even called the "son of Ptaḥ,"[1]. The double god Åsår-Ḥāpi or Ḥāpi-Åsår, is depicted in the form of a bull, which has the solar disk and a uraeus between its horns. The peculiar marks on a bull which indicated that he was Apis, and the general history of the god will be found in the Chapter on "Animals sacred to the Gods."

The chief centre of the worship of Serapis in Ptolemaïc times was Alexandria, where it was established, according to tradition, by Ptolemy Soter. This great ruler of Egypt appears to have wished to find some god who could be worshipped both by Greeks and Egyptians at a common shrine, and one whom he could cause to be regarded as the characteristic god of his dynasty in Egypt. The most important Egyptian god at the time was Osiris, that is to say Osiris-Apis, the great god of the Egyptian Underworld, but it was impossible for him to remove the great sanctuary of this god, and he therefore determined either to rebuild some ruined Serapeum at Alexandria, or to found a new one wherein he might set up a statue which should be worshipped both as the god of the Egyptian Underworld and the Greek Hades, and in which would be united the attributes of Osiris Khent Åmenti, and of Dis. Whilst Ptolemy was meditating upon these or similar things he had a dream, wherein a colossal statue of some god appeared to him, and told him to remove it from where it was to Alexandria; according to Plutarch (*De Iside et Osiride*, § 28), he had never seen a similar statue, and he knew neither the place where it stood, nor to whom it belonged. One day he happened to mention his dream to Sosibius, and described the statue which he had seen, whereon this man declared that he had seen a statue like it at Sinope. Tradition says that this was Sinope on the Pontus, and adds that as the inhabitants of the city were extremely unwilling to part with their statue, it, of its own accord, after waiting for three years, entered

[1] In the text of Pepi I. (l. 671) the god UR-SHEPS-F, , is called the "beloved, the son of Ptaḥ," , but we are not justified in assuming him to be an old form of Osiris-Apis.

into a ship and arrived at Alexandria safely after a voyage of only three days. When the Greeks came to see the statue it was introduced to them as the god Hades, and the Egyptian priests were ready to bestow upon him the name Åsår-Ḥāpi, or Serapis, by which name the Greeks were, apparently, quite contented to call him. Thus both the Greeks and Egyptians in Alexandria acquired a god whom they willingly worshipped as the god of the Underworld.

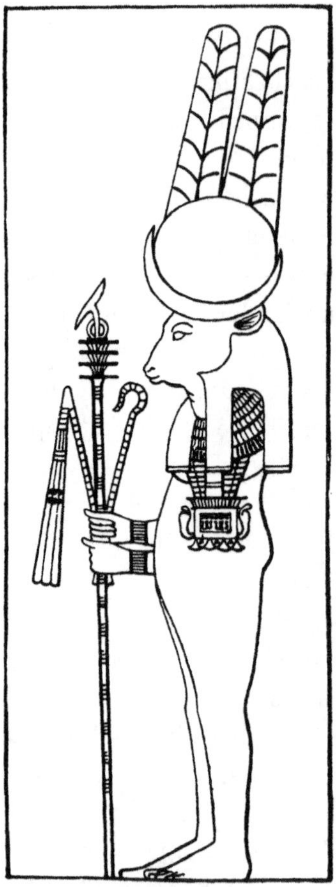

Åsår-Ḥāpi (Serapis).

As soon as the god who was now called Serapis had been established in his new home, his former worship and rites were greatly modified, and his services and processions were made to resemble those of the Egyptians, who naturally expected their main features to be brought into harmony with those of the cult of Osiris, their national god. It appears to have been to the interest of all parties to welcome Serapis, and all must admire the astute action of Ptolemy, who succeeded in making the Greeks think that in worshipping this god they were adoring one of their own native deities, and who persuaded the Egyptians that they were maintaining the supremacy of Osiris-Apis in spite of the fact that the Macedonians were the rulers and masters of the country. Some doubt has been cast upon the identification of the Sinope mentioned by Plutarch with the Sinope of Pontus, but with insufficient reason. The Serapeum which Ptolemy repaired, or founded, was probably near Rāqeṭit , and was a very remarkable building; its main plan seems to have resembled that of the famous Serapeum at Memphis, but parts of it were richly painted and gilded, and it possessed a fine library which was said to contain some 300,000 volumes. The following is Plutarch's account of the introduction of the god of Sinope into Egypt:—

" After this, say they, both Isis and Osiris, on account of their " eminent virtue, were translated from the order of good Demons " to that of Gods, as in after ages were Hercules and Bacchus; and " therefore the honours which are paid them are very properly of " the mixed kind, such as are due both to Gods and Demons, their " power being very great, not only upon earth, but in those regions " likewise which are under the earth. For, say they, Osiris is none " other than Pluto, nor is Isis different from Proserpine, as Arche- " machus the Euboean asserts, and as appears likewise to have " been the opinion of Heraclides of Pontus from his declaring the " oracle at Canopus to belong to Pluto.

XXVIII. " But the following facts will make this point still " more evident. Ptolemy, surnamed the Saviour, had a dream, " wherein a certain Colossean statue, such as he had never seen " before, appeared unto him, commanding him to remove it as soon " as possible from the place where it then stood to Alexandria. " Upon this the king was in great perplexity, as he knew neither " to whom the statue belonged nor where to look for it. Upon his " relating the vision to his friends, a certain person named Sosibius, " who had been a great traveller, declared that he had seen just " such a statue as the king described at Sinope. Soteles and " Dionysius were hereupon immediately dispatched in order to " bring it away with them, which they at length accomplished " though not without much difficulty, and the manifest interposi- " tion of providence. Timotheus the Interpreter, and Manetho, as " soon as the statue was shown to them, from the Cerberus and " Dragon that accompanied it, concluded that it was designed to " represent Pluto, and persuaded the king that it was in reality " none other than the Egyptian *Sarapis;* for it must be observed, " that the statue had not this name before it was brought to " Alexandria, it being given to it afterwards by the Egyptians, as " equipollent, in their opinion, to its old one of Pluto. So again, " when Heraclitus the Physiologist asserts that Pluto and Bacchus " are the same, does not this directly lead to the same conclusion? " For as to those who say that by Pluto is here meant *the body,*

" because the soul, whilst it is in it, is as it were intoxicated and " beside itself, and that from hence springs the relation between " it and Bacchus, this is too subtle and finespun an allegory to " deserve our serious notice. Heraclitus's assertion therefore may " be much more probably accounted for, by supposing the Bacchus " here meant to be the same as Osiris, and Osiris again the same " as Sarapis, this latter appellation having been given him, upon " his being translated from the order of Genii to that of the Gods, " Sarapis being none other than that common name by which all " those are called, who have thus changed their nature, as is well " known by those who are initiated into the mysteries of Osiris.

" Little regard therefore is to be paid to those *Phrygian Tales*, " wherein mention is made of one Sarapis, as the daughter of " Hercules, and of Typho, as born of Isaeacus one of his sons: " nor does Phylarchus better deserve our credit, when he tells us " that 'Bacchus first brought two bullocks with him out of India " into Egypt, and that the name of the one was *Apis*, and that of " the other *Osiris*,' adding moreover, 'that Sarapis, in the proper " meaning of the word, signifies *him who disposed the Universe* " *into its present beautiful order*.' Now though this assertion of " Phylarchus be weak enough, yet it is not quite so absurd as that " of those who assert, that 'Sarapis is no god at all, but the mere " denomination of the sepulchral chest, wherein the body of Apis " after its death is deposited;' much more tolerable than either of " the preceding is their opinion, who would derive this name from " words which in the Greek language import, '*one who first* " *impelled and gave motion to the universe*.' The priests indeed, at " least the greatest part of them, tell us, that Sarapis is none other " than the mere union of Osiris and Apis into one word; declarative " as it were of that opinion, which they are perpetually explaining " and inculcating, 'that the Apis ought ever to be regarded by us, " as a fair and beautiful image of the soul of Osiris.' For my part " I cannot but think, that if this word be of Egyptian extraction, " it ought to be interpreted so as to express *joy and gladness*, seeing " that festival, which we Grecians call Charmosyna, or *the feast of* " *joy*, is by the Egyptians expressly termed *Sarei*. Nor altogether " disagreeable to this last notion of Sarapis, is the explication which

" Plato gives of the corresponding name of Hades or Pluto, stiling " him, ' the son of cheerfulness, and a kind and gentle Deity to all " such as come unto him.' There are likewise many other words, " which when interpreted into Greek, become entire sentences; " such particularly is *Amenthes*, or that subterraneous region " whither they imagine the souls of those who die to go after their " decease, a name which expressly signifies in the tongue, *the receiver* " *and giver*.[1] But whether this likewise be not one of those words, " which were originally transplanted from Greece into Egypt, we " will enquire in another place."

[1] The Egyptian form of the word is  *Amentet*, and the name means " hidden place."

CHAPTER XIII

ȦST, 𓊨, OR 𓊨𓏏, OR 𓊨𓏏𓆇𓁐, ISIS

NOTWITHSTANDING the fact that Ȧs, or Ȧst, i.e., Isis, is one of the goddesses most frequently mentioned in the hieroglyphic texts, nothing is known with certainty about the attributes which were ascribed to her in the earliest times. From the fact that she was regarded as the female counterpart of Osiris in the dynastic period, we may assume that she was also associated with the god in this capacity in the predynastic period, and if he was originally a water spirit or a river-god, she must have possessed the same characteristics. The name Ȧst has, like Ȧsar, up to the present defied all explanation, and it is clear from the punning derivations to which the Egyptians themselves had recourse, that they knew no more about the meaning of her name than we do. The probability is that Ȧs, or Ȧst, is a Libyan name originally, and that it is to be classed with the names of the other Libyan deities, e.g., Net, Bast, etc., who were worshipped by the predynastic Egyptians, and the sounds of whose names were expressed by hieroglyphic symbols as nearly as possible when the people of the country borrowed or invented the art of writing. The symbol of the name of Isis in Egyptian is a seat, or throne, 𓊨, but we have no means of connecting it with the attributes of the goddess in such a way as to give a rational explanation of her name, and all the derivations hitherto proposed must be regarded as mere guesses. Isis is usually depicted in the form of a woman who wears on her head a vulture head-dress, and holds in her hand a papyrus sceptre. The usual ornament or crown on her head consists of a pair of horns, between which is a solar disk, and this is sometimes surmounted by 𓊨, the symbol of the sound of her name. Sometimes she wears the double crowns

The Goddess Isis.

of the South and the North, to the back of which is attached the feather of Maāt, and sometimes she wears with the pair of horns and the solar disk two plumes.[1] Her horns are usually those of the cow of Hathor, or of one of the sister forms of this goddess, , but occasionally[2] she wears a pair of ram's horns, , under her double crown; since, however, Osiris was represented by the Ram of Mendes, and was identified with Khnemu, it is only to be expected that his female counterpart Isis should appear sometimes with the horns which are the peculiar characteristic of the great Ram-god. Isis, as a woman, and not as a goddess, is depicted in the ordinary head-dress of a woman, but even so she has the uraeus over her forehead, for the Egyptians wished it never to be forgotten that she was of divine origin; of the forms which she had the power to take in her character of the "lady of words of power" mention will be made further on.

An examination of the texts of all periods proves that Isis always held in the minds of the Egyptians a position which was entirely different from that of every other goddess, and although it is certain that their views concerning her varied from time to time, and that certain aspects or phases of the goddess were worshipped more generally at one period than at another, it is correct to say that from the earliest to the latest dynasties Isis was the greatest goddess of Egypt. Long before the copies of the Pyramid Texts which we possess were written the attributes of Isis were well-defined, and even when the priests of Heliopolis assigned to her the position which she held in the cycle of their gods between B.C. 4000 and B.C. 3000 the duties which she was thought to perform in connexion with the dead were clearly defined, and were identical with those which belonged to her in the Graeco-Roman period. Isis was the great and beneficent goddess and mother, whose influence and love pervaded all heaven, and earth, and the abode of the dead, and she was the personification of the great feminine, creative power which conceived, and brought forth every living creature, and thing, from the gods in heaven, to man on the earth, and to the insect on the ground; what she brought forth she protected, and cared for, and fed, and nourished, and she

[1] See Lanzone, *Dizionario*, pll. 306 ff.

[2] *Ibid.*, pl. 308, No. 3.

employed her life in using her power graciously and successfully, not only in creating new beings but in restoring those that were dead. She was, besides these things, the highest type of a faithful and loving wife and mother, and it was in this capacity that the Egyptians honoured and worshipped her most. In the section on Osiris a rendering of the Mythological History of Isis and Osiris by Plutarch has already been given, but reference must here be made to one or two passages in it for purposes of comparison with Egyptian texts. According to this document Osiris was slain by the cunning of his brother Typhon, or Set, and the box containing his body was thrown into the river, which carried it to the sea; after long search Isis found it, and set it, as she thought, in a safe hiding place, but it was found by Typhon, who cut it up into a number of pieces. It is nowhere so stated, but it seems that Isis was childless before the death of Osiris, and both the narrative of Plutarch and a passage in the Hymn to Osiris quoted above (p. 150) agree in stating that, by means of certain words of power which had been given to her by Thoth and which she knew how to use, she restored her dead husband to life, and was united to him; as the result of this embrace she conceived her son Horus, and in due course brought him forth.

The incidents of her search for the dead body of Osiris, and of the conception and birth, and rearing of her child powerfully impressed the imagination of the Egyptians, and hieroglyphic literature is full of allusions to them. In the Pyramid Texts the deceased is said (Unȧs, line 181) "to breathe the breath of Isis," and to make his passage in heaven, with Isis, in the Māṭet Boat, i.e., the boat of the rising sun (line 293); moreover, he is declared to be the very son of Isis and of her twin form Nephthys.[1] In a remarkable passage in the text of Tetȧ (line 84) the deceased is introduced to the triad of goddesses, Isis, Nephthys, and ASBET, , as their son, and elsewhere (line 172) Seb, the father of Osiris and Isis, is made to speak of

[1] 
, Unȧs, l. 487.

Isis and Nephthys as his "sisters." These things the Egyptians believed because their ancient traditions told them of all that Isis had done for her husband and child, and they hoped that the goddess would be present at the celebrations of their funeral rites, and that she would secure for them a new birth. In the illustrated Recensions of the *Book of the Dead* Isis frequently appears both as the mother of Horus, the heir to the throne of Osiris, and as the mourning widow of her husband. In the vignette to the clist Chapter Isis kneels at the bier of the deceased, and says to him, "I have come to protect thee with the north wind which "cometh forth from Tem; I have strengthened for thee thy throat; "I have caused thee to be with the god; and I have placed all "thine enemies under thy feet." This speech refers to the air which Isis produced by the beating of her wings when she restored Osiris to life in order that she might conceive an heir by him, and also to the air which she provided for her son Horus after he had been stung to death by a scorpion. Everywhere in the *Book of the Dead* Isis is regarded as a giver of life and of food to the dead, and she appears behind the god in the shrine wherein Osiris is seated in the Judgment Hall, and in one of her aspects she is identified with one of the two Maāt goddesses; she may, in fact, be regarded as one of the judges of the dead.

Now, the *Book of the Dead* supplies us with many interesting allusions to her relations with Osiris, but it says little about her devotion to her son Horus, whom she reared with loving care that he might become the "avenger of his father," and we must have recourse to the texts which are found inscribed on the "Metternich stele,"[1] if we would gain a clearer idea of the troubles which Isis endured after the death of Osiris. In one of these the goddess is made to relate the narrative of her wanderings and sorrows, and she says, "I, even I, am Isis, and I came forth from the house "wherein my brother Set had placed me." From this it is clear that Set was not content with murdering his brother Osiris, but that he must needs shut up the widow and her child in some place

[1] This stele was found in Alexandria in 1828, and was given to Prince Metternich by Muḥammad 'Ali; for a facsimile of it, and renderings of the texts upon it, see Golenischeff, *Die Metternichstele*, Leipzig, 1877.

of restraint. Whilst Isis was thus confined, "Thoth, the great "god, the prince of Law both in heaven and upon the earth," came to her and said, "Come, O thou goddess Isis, it is good to be "obedient, for there is life for him that will follow the advice of "another. Hide thou thy son the child [Horus], and this is what "shall happen: his limbs shall grow, and he will become endowed "with two-fold strength, and then he shall be made to sit upon the "throne of his father, and he shall avenge him and take possession "of the rank of the prince of the Two Lands." Isis took the advice of her friend Thoth and, she says, "I came forth from the "house at eventide, and there also came forth with me Seven "Scorpions, who were to accompany me, and to be my helpers. "Two scorpions, Tefen and Befen, were behind me, two scorpions, "Mestet and Mestetef were by my side, and three scorpions, Petet, "Thetet, and Maatet, shewed me the way. I cried out unto them "in a very loud voice, and my speech entered into their ears even "as into the ears of one who knoweth that obedience is a thing "which is applauded, and that disobedience is the mark of the "person who is of no account, and I said unto them, 'Let your "faces be turned to the ground that ye may [shew me] the way.' "So the leader of this company brought me unto the marshes of "Pa-sui, the city of the two Divine Sandals, which lay at the "beginning of the Papyrus Swamps (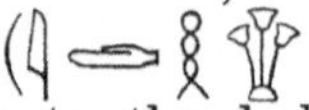 Ȧṭeḥ). When "I had arrived at Ṭeb I came forth to the habitations of the "women who belonged to the overlord of the district, and the chief "woman who had seen me coming along shut her doors in my face, "and was angry with me in her heart because of those (i.e., the "Seven Scorpions) that were with me. Now the scorpions took "counsel on the matter, and they all at one time ejected their "poison on the tip of the tail of Tefen; but as for me, a poor "fen-woman opened her door to me, and I entered into her house. "Meanwhile the Scorpion Tefen entered under the leaves of the "door of the lady [who had shut her doors upon me], and she "stung her son, and fire straightway broke out in the house of the "noble lady; but there was no water forthcoming to put it out, "and the heavens dropped down no rain upon the house of the "noble lady, for it was not the season for rain. And, behold, the

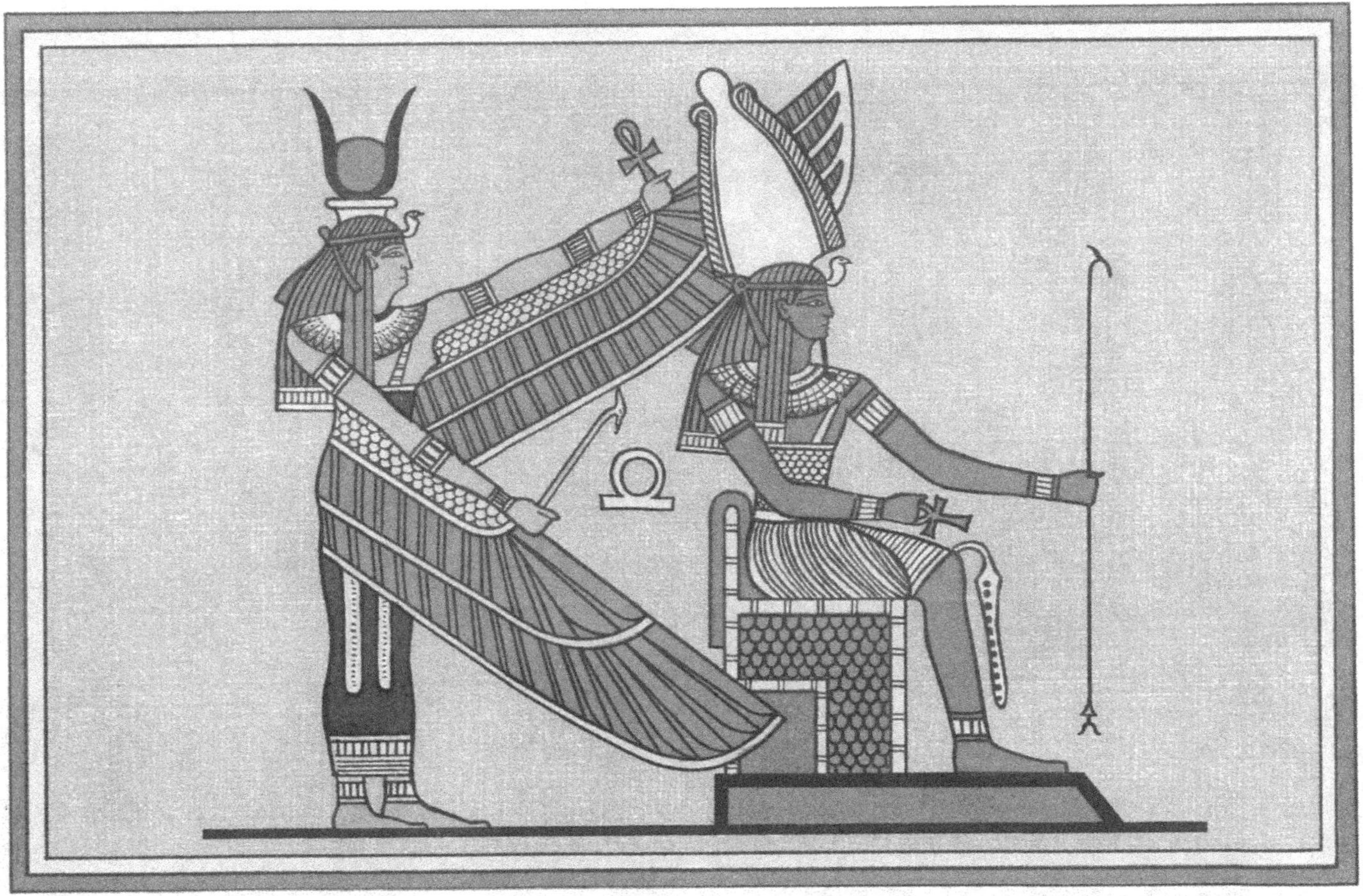

The Goddess Isis. Ptaḥ-Seker-Ausar.

This illustration is reproduced in full color on the
insert attached to the inside back cover of this volume.

ISIS IN THE PAPYRUS SWAMPS SUCKLING HORUS.

"heart of the woman who had not opened her doors to me was "sad, for she knew not whether her son would live, and although "she went round about through her city uttering cries of lamenta- "tion none came at her call. But mine own heart was sad for the "child's sake, and I wished to restore to life him that had com- "mitted no fault. Thereupon I cried out to the noble lady, "'Come to me. Come to me, for my speech hath in it the power "to protect, and it possesseth life. I am a woman who is well- "known in her city, and I can drive the evil out of thy son by one "of my utterances, which my father taught me, for I was the "beloved daughter of his body.'"

The noble lady presumably listened to the words of Isis, who, it seems, either went to her house, or had the dead child brought into her presence, for the narrative continues, "Then Isis laid her "hands upon the child to restore to life him that was without "breath (literally 'him whose throat was foul'), and said, 'O poison "of Tefen, come forth, and appear on the ground; come not in, "approach not! O poison of Befent, come forth, and appear on the "ground! for I am Isis the goddess, and I am the lady of words of "power, and I know how to work with words of power, and most "mighty are [my] words! O all ye reptiles which sting, hearken "unto me, and fall ye down on the ground! O poison of Mestet, "come not hither! O poison of Mestetef, rise not up! O poison of "Petet and Thetet, enter not here! [O poison of] Maatet, fall down!'" Next in the narrative we have the words of the "Chapter of the stinging [of scorpions]" which "Isis, the goddess and great enchantress at the head of the gods," spake on this occasion, and it is said that she learnt her method of procedure from Seb, who had taught her how to drive out poison. At the dawn of day she uttered the words, "O poison, get thee back, turn away, begone, retreat," and added "Mer-Rā;" and at eventide she said, "The Egg of the Goose" cometh forth "from the Sycamore." Then turning to the Seven Scorpions she said, "I speak to you, for I "am alone and am in sorrow which is greater than that of anyone "in the nomes of Egypt. I am like a man who hath become old, "and who hath ceased to search after and to look upon women in "their houses. Turn your faces down to the ground, and find ye "me straightway a way to the swamps and to the hidden places in "Khebet."[1] Following this passage come the exclamation, "The "child liveth and the poison dieth; the Sun liveth and the poison "dieth," and then the wishes, "May Horus be in good case for his "mother Isis! And may he who shall find himself in a similar "state be in good case also!" As the result of the utterances of Isis the fire in the house of the noble lady was extinguished, and "heaven was satisfied with the words which the goddess Isis" had spoken. The narrative is continued by Isis in these words:— "Then came the lady who had shut her doors against me, and "took possession of the house of the fen-woman because she had "opened the door of her house unto me, and because of this the "noble lady suffered pain and sorrow during a whole night, and "she had to bear [the thought] of her speech, and that her son had "been stung because she had closed the doors and had not opened "them to me." Following this come the words, "O, the child "liveth, the poison dieth! Verily, Horus shall be in good case for "his mother Isis! Verily, in like manner shall he be in good case "who shall find himself in a similar position! Shall not the bread "of barley drive out the poison and make it to return from the "limbs? Shall not the flame of the *ḥetchet* plant drive out the fire "from the members?"

"'Isis, Isis, come to thy child Horus, O thou whose mouth is "wise, come to thy son:' thus cried out the gods who were near "her after the manner of one whom a scorpion hath stung, and like "one whom Beḥāt, whom the animal Ȧntesh put to flight, hath "wounded. Then came Isis like a woman who was smitten in her "own body. And she stretched out her two arms, [saying], I will "protect thee, I will protect thee, O my son Horus. Fear thou not, "fear thou not, O son, my glorious one. No evil thing whatsoever "shall happen unto thee, for in thee is the seed whereof things "which are to be shall be created. Thou art the son within the

[1] , Khebet, or Khebit, , is, as Dr. Brugsch has shown, the Egyptian original of the Greek Χέμμις, or Χέμβις, an island in the neighbourhood of the city of Buto (Pe and Ṭep), which, according to Herodotus, floated.

"Mesqet, who hast proceeded from Nu, and thou shalt not die by "the flame of the poison. Thou art the Great Bennu who wast "born on the Incense Trees in the House of the Great Prince in "Heliopolis. Thou art the brother of the Åbṭu Fish, who dost "arrange that which is to be, and who wast nursed by the Cat "within the House of Net. Reret, Ḥåt and Bes protect thy "limbs. Thine head shall not fall before him that is hostile to "thee. The fire of that which hath poisoned thee shall not have "dominion over thy limbs. Thou shalt not fail on land, and thou "shalt not be in peril on the water. No reptile that stingeth shall "have the mastery over thee, and no lion shall crush thee or gain "the mastery over thee. Thou art the son of the holy god and "dost proceed from Seb. Thou art Horus, and the poison which "is in thy limbs shall not have the mastery over thee. And even "so shall it be with him that is under the knife. And the four "noble goddesses shall protect thy limbs."

From the above we see that the gods informed Isis that her son Horus had been stung by a scorpion, and from what follows we shall see in what condition Isis found her son. She says, "I, Isis, "conceived a man child, and I was heavy with Horus. I, the "goddess, bare Horus, the son of Isis, within a nest of papyrus "plants (or, 'Island of Åṭeḥ.') I rejoiced over him with exceedingly "great joy, for I saw in him one who would make answer for his "father. I hid him, and I concealed him, for I was afraid lest he "should be bitten. Now I went away to the city of Åm, and the "people thereof saluted me according to their wont, and I passed "the time in seeking food and provision for the boy; but when I "returned to embrace Horus, I found him, the beautiful one of "gold, the boy, the child, inert and helpless. He had bedewed the "ground with the water of his eye, and with the foam of his lips; "his body was motionless, and his heart was still, and his muscles "moved not, and I sent forth a cry . . . . . Then straightway "the dwellers in the swamps came round about me, and the fen "men came out to me from their houses, and they drew nigh to "me at my call, and they themselves wept at the greatness of my "misery. Yet no man there opened his mouth to speak to me "because they all grieved for me sorely; and no man among them "knew how to restore Horus to life. Then there came unto me a "woman who was well known in her city, and she was a lady at "the head of her district, and she came to me to restore [Horus] to "life. Her heart was filled with her own affairs, according to "custom, but the child Horus remained motionless and moved not. "The son of the goddess-mother had been smitten by the evil of "his brother. The plants [where Horus was] were concealed, and "no hostile being could find a way into them.

"The word of power of Tem, the father of the gods, who is in "heaven, acted as the maker of life, and Set had not entered into "this region, and he could not go round about the city of Kheb "(Khemmis); and Horus was safe from the wickedness of his "brother. But Isis had not hidden those who ministered unto him "many times each day, and these said concerning him, 'Horus "liveth for his mother;' they found out where he was, and a "scorpion stung him, and ĀUN-ÁB (i.e., Slayer of the Heart) "stabbed him."

Then "Isis placed her nose in the mouth of Horus to learn if "there was any breath in him that was in his coffin, and she opened "the wound of the divine heir, and she found poison therein. "Then she embraced him hurriedly and leaped about with him like "a fish when it is placed over a hot fire, and she said, 'Horus is "stung, O Rā, thy son is stung. Horus, thy very heir, and the "lord of the . . . . . of Shu is stung. Horus, the child of the "Papyrus Swamps, the child in Ḥet-ser is stung; the beautiful "Child of gold is stung, and the Child, the Babe, hath become a "thing of nothingness. Horus, the son of Un-nefer, is stung,' etc. "Then came Nephthys shedding tears, and she went about the "Papyrus Swamps uttering cries of grief, and the goddess SERQET "said, 'What is it? What is it? What hath happened to the "child Horus?'

"'O Isis, pray thou to heaven so that the sailors of Rā may "cease rowing, so that the Boat of Rā may not depart from the "place where the child Horus is.' Then Isis sent forth a cry to "heaven, and addressed her prayer to the Boat of Millions of "Years; and the Disk stood still, and moved not from the place "where he was. And Thoth came, and he was provided with

MERSEKERT SUCKLING HORUS.

The Goddess ISIS-SEPT.

"magical powers and possessed the great power which made [his] "word to become Maāt (i.e., Law), and he said: 'O Isis, thou "goddess, thou glorious one, who hast knowledge how to use thy "mouth, behold, no evil shall come upon the child Horus, for his "protection cometh from the Boat of Rā. I have come this day in "the Boat of the Disk from the place where it was yesterday. "When the night cometh the light shall drive [it] away for the "healing of Horus for the sake of his mother Isis, and every person "who is under the knife [shall be healed] likewise.'" In answer to this speech Isis told Thoth that she was afraid he had come too late, but she begged him, nevertheless, to come to the child and to bring with him his magical powers which enabled him to give effect to every command which he uttered. Thereupon Thoth besought Isis not to fear, and Nephthys not to weep, for said he, "I have "come from heaven in order to save the child for his mother," and he straightway spake the words of power which restored Horus to life, and served to protect him ever afterwards in heaven, and in earth, and in the Underworld.

The region where all these things took place was situated in the Delta, and the Island in the Papyrus Swamps, where Isis brought forth her child and hid him, was near the famous double city of Pe-Ṭep, which was commonly called Buto by the Greeks. It is impossible to assign a date to the composition of the story briefly narrated above, but it is, no doubt, as old as the legends about the death and resurrection of Osiris, and it must form an integral portion of them, and date from the period when Libyan gods and goddesses were worshipped in the Delta and in certain parts of Upper Egypt before the great development of Sun-worship. The chief importance of the story consists in the fact that it makes Isis to be both woman and goddess, just as the story of Osiris makes that deity to be both god and man, and it is quite conceivable that in the predynastic times the sorrows of Isis, like those of Osiris, formed the subject of miracle plays which were acted annually in all the centres of the worship of Isis. Isis as the faithful and loving wife, and as the tender and devoted mother won the hearts of the Egyptians in all periods of their history, and we can only regret that the narrative of the wanderings and sorrows of the goddess is not known to us in all its details. Her persecution by Set after her husband's death was a favourite theme of ancient writers, who delighted in showing how the goddess outwitted her terrible adversary; thus on one occasion she was so hard pressed by him that she changed her body into that of the cow-goddess Ḥeru-sekha, , and her son Horus into an Apis Bull, ,[1] and went away with him to the Apis temple, 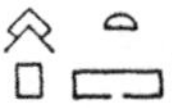, in order that she might see his father Osiris, who was therein.

Another great human element in the story of Isis which appealed strongly to the Egyptians was the desire of the goddess to be avenged on the murderer of her husband, and it is this which is referred to in the words of Isis, who says, "I rejoiced over him "with exceedingly great joy, for I saw in him one who would make "answer for his father." The manner in which Horus "made answer for" and avenged his father is told in the Sallier Papyrus (translated by Chabas,[2]) where it is said that Horus and Set fought together, standing on their feet, first in the forms of men and next in the forms of two bears. For three days and for three nights the fight between them raged, and Horus gained the victory over Set, but when Isis saw that Set was being overpowered her heart was touched on his account, and she cried out and ordered the weapons which her son was wielding against her brother to fall down, and they did so, and Set was released. When Horus saw that his mother had taken his adversary's part he raged at her like a panther of the south, and she fled before his wrath; a fierce struggle between Isis and Horus then took place, and Horus cut off his mother's head. Thoth, by means of his words of power, transformed her head into that of a cow which he attached to her body straightway.

Isis, though worshipped all over Egypt, was specially venerated in certain cities, and the following are among the commonest of her titles[3]:—"The great lady, the God-mother, lady

[1] Brugsch, *Aeg. Zeit.*, 1879, p. 19.
[2] *Le Calendrier*, p. 28.
[3] See Lanzone, *Dizionario*, pp. 829, ff.

"of Re-a-nefer; Isis-Nebuut, , lady of Sekhet; lady "of Besiṭet; Isis in Per Pakht, ; the queen of Mesen, " ; Isis of Ta-āt-nehepet, ; Isis, "dweller in Netru, ; Isis, lady of Ḥebet, ; "Isis in P-she-Ḥert, ; Isis, lady of Khebt, ; "Usert-Isis, , giver of life, lady of Abaton, lady of "Philae, lady of the countries of the south," etc. From a list of titles of the goddess collected by Dr. Brugsch,[1] it is clear that Isis was called Usert, , in Thebes, Āāt, , in Heliopolis, Menkhet, , in Memphis, God-mother, , in Coptos, Ḥert, , in Letopolis; and "Ḥent," i.e., "Queen," in every nome;[2] and another important list tells us that Isis was called Ȧment, , in Thebes, Menḥet, , in Heliopolis, Renpet, , in Memphis, Sepṭ, , in Abydos, Ḥeṭeṭ, , in Beḥuṭet, Ḥurt, , in Nekhen, Thenenet, , in Hermonthis, Ȧnt, , in Dendera, Sesheta, , in Hermopolis, Ḥeqet, , in Hibiu, Uatchit, , in Hipponus, Mersekhen, , in Herakleopolis, Renpet, , in Crocodilopolis, Neb-ṭept, , in Arsinoë, Thȧt, , or Tcheṭut, , in Aphroditopolis, and Shetat, , in Bubastis. Among her general titles may be mentioned those of "the divine one, the only one, the greatest of the gods "and goddesses, the queen of all gods, the female Rā, the female "Horus, the eye of Rā, the crown of Rā-Ḥeru, Sepṭ, opener of the "year, lady of the New Year, maker of the sunrise, lady of heaven, "the light-giver of heaven, lady of the North Wind, queen of the "earth, most mighty one, queen of the South and North, lady of "the solid earth, lady of warmth and fire, benefactress of the Ṭuat,

[1] *Religion*, p. 646.

[2] Brugsch, *Thesaurus*, p. 773.

"she who is greatly feared in the Ṭuat, the God-mother, the God-"mother of Ḥeru-ka-nekht, the mother of the Horus of gold, the "lady of life, lady of green crops, the green goddess (Uatchet), "lady of bread, lady of beer, lady of abundance, lady of joy and "gladness, lady of love, the maker of kings, lady of the Great "House, lady of the House of fire, the beautiful goddess, the lady "of words of power, lady of the shuttle, daughter of Seb, daughter "of Neb-er-tcher, the child of Nut, wife of Rā, wife of the lord "of the abyss, wife of the lord of the Inundation, the creatrix of "the Nile flood."

From a number of passages in the texts of various periods we learn that Isis possessed great skill in the working of magic, and several examples of the manner in which she employed it are well known. Thus when she wished to make Rā reveal to her his greatest and most secret name, she made a venomous reptile out of dust mixed with the spittle of the god, and by uttering over it certain words of power she made it to bite Rā as he passed. When she had succeeded in obtaining from the god his most hidden name, which he only revealed because he was on the point of death, she uttered words which had the effect of driving the poison out of his limbs, and Rā recovered.[1] Now Isis not only used the words of power, but she also had knowledge of the way in which to pronounce them so that the beings or things to which they were addressed would be compelled to listen to them and, having listened, would be obliged to fulfil her behests. The Egyptians believed that if the best effect was to be produced by words of power they must be uttered in a certain tone of voice, and at a certain rate, and at a certain time of the day or night, with appropriate gestures or ceremonies. In the Hymn to Osiris, of which a rendering has already been given (see p. 150), it is said that Isis was well skilled in the use of words of power, and it was by means of these that she restored her husband to life, and obtained from him an heir. It is not known what the words were which she uttered on this occasion, but she appears to have obtained them from Thoth, the "lord of divine words," and it was to him that

[1] See the translation of the Legend of Rā and Isis given in vol. i., p. 372 ff.

The Goddess RENNUT.

she appealed for help to restore Horus to life after he had been stung to death by a scorpion.

In the Theban Recension of the *Book of the Dead* is found a Chapter (No. clvi.) which was composed for the purpose of bestowing upon the deceased some of the magical power of the goddess. The Chapter was intended to be recited over an amulet called *thet* , made of carnelian, which had to be steeped in water of *ānkhami* flowers, and set in a sycamore plinth, and if this were laid on the neck of a dead person it would place him under the protection of the words of power of Isis, and he would be able to go wheresoever he pleased in the Underworld. The words of the Chapter were:—
"Let the blood ( ) of
"Isis, and the magical powers
"(or spirits) of
"Isis, and the words of power
"( ) of Isis, be mighty
"to protect and keep safely
"this great god (i.e., the
"deceased), and to guard him
"from him that would do unto
"him anything which he abomi-
"nateth."

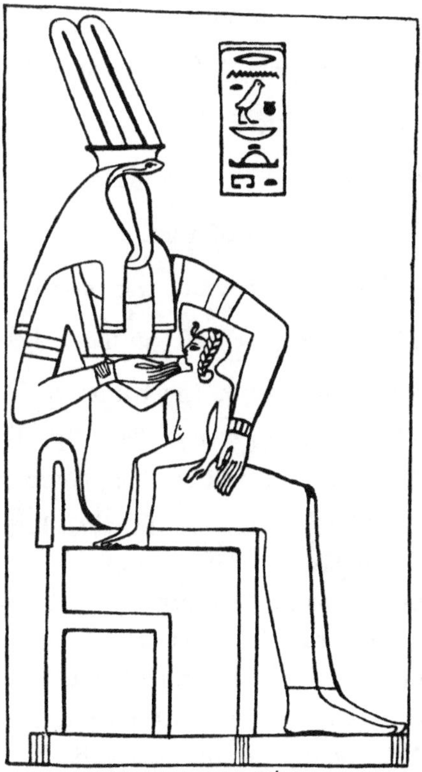
Rennut, lady of Àat.

The symbol of Isis in the heavens was the star Sepṭ, , which was greatly beloved because its appearance marked not only the beginning of a new year, but also announced the advance of the Inundation of the Nile, which betokened renewed wealth and prosperity of the country. As such Isis was regarded as the companion of Osiris, whose soul dwelt in the star Sah, , i.e., Orion, and she was held to have brought about the destruction of the fiend Apep, , and of his hosts of darkness by means of the might of her words of power. As the light-giver at this season of the year she was called KHUT, , as the mighty earth-goddess her name was USERT, , as the Great Goddess of the Underworld she was THENENET, , as the power which shot forth the Nile flood she was SATI, , and SEPṬ, as the embracer of the land and producer of fertility by her waters she was Ānqet, , as the producer and giver of life she was Ānkhet, , as the goddess of cultivated lands and fields she was SEKHET, , as the goddess of the harvest she was RENENET, , as the goddess of food which was offered to the gods she was TCHEFT, , and lived in the Temple of TCHEFAU, , and as the great lady of the Underworld, who assisted in transforming the bodies of the blessed dead into those wherein they were to live in the realm of Osiris, her name was ÅMENT, , i.e., the "hidden" goddess. In this last capacity she shared with Osiris the attribute of "giver of life," and she provided food for the dead as well as for the living; as ÅMENT also she was declared to be the mother of Rā. In fact, at a comparatively early period in Egyptian history Isis had absorbed the attributes of all the great primitive goddesses, and of all the local goddesses such as Nekhebet, Uatchet, Net, Bast, Hathor, etc., and she was even identified as the female counterpart of the primeval abyss of water from which sprang all life. From what has been said above it is manifestly impossible to limit the attributes of Isis, for we have seen that she possesses the powers of a water goddess, an earth goddess, a corn goddess, a star goddess, a queen of the Underworld, and a woman, and that she united in herself one or more of the attributes of all the goddesses of Egypt known to us.

From the works of classical writers we know that her worship spread from Egypt into several places in Western Europe, and she was identified with Persephone, Tethys, Athene, etc., just as Osiris was identified with Hades or Pluto, Dionysos-Bacchus, and other foreign gods. According to Herr August Mau,[1] various causes contributed to the rapid extension of the cult of Isis and Serapis. "The worship of Isis, associated with Mysteries from an "early period, was reorganized by the first Ptolemy with the help "of Manetho an Egyptian priest, and Timotheus, a Greek skilled "in the Eleusinian Mysteries . . . . It had the charm of some-"thing foreign and full of mystery. Its doctrine, supported by "the prestige of immemorial antiquity, successfully opposed the "mutually destructive opinions of the philosophers, while at the "same time its conception of deity was by no means inconsistent "with philosophic thought; and it brought to the initiated that "expectation of a future life to which the Eleusinian Mysteries "owed their attractive power. The ascetic side of the worship "too, with its fastings and abstinence from the pleasures of sense, "that the soul might lose itself in the mystical contemplation of "deity, had a fascination for natures that were religiously suscep-"tible; and the celebration of the Mysteries, the representation of "the myth of Isis in pantomime with a musical accompaniment, "appealed powerfully to the imagination." A college of the servants of Isis, who were called Pastophori, was founded in Rome in the time of Sulla, about B.C. 80 (Apuleius, *Met.* xi.), but after a very few years the worship of Isis was proscribed by the authorities, and the temples of the goddess were pulled down in the years 58, 53, 50, and 48. In B.C. 43, however, the triumvirs, seeing that it was the only way to win the affections of the people, built temples in honour of Isis and Serapis, and publicly sanctioned their worship, and in a short time several temples of these gods were in existence outside the city; all these were under the control of the Government, which had frequently to be exercised in a vigorous fashion on account of the orgies and debaucheries which took place in connexion with the celebration of the festivals of Isis. From the time of Vespasian, however, the worship of Isis and Serapis grew and flourished until the general introduction of

[1] *Pompeii, its Life and Art*, London, 1899, p. 162.

Christianity, and the festival of these gods was recognized in the public Calendar.

The chief temple of Isis in Rome stood in the Campus Martius, where the goddess was called "Isis Campensis"; and an inscription of the year 105 B.C. found at Puteoli proves that a temple of Serapis was then standing in that city.[1] The important temple of Isis at Pompeii appears to have been built soon after this date, and an inscription over the door states that it was rebuilt by Numerius Popidius Celsinus after the earthquake (that of the year 63). It has architecturally nothing suggestive of the Egyptian style, yet the plan presents a marked deviation from ordinary types. In his Eleventh Book Apuleius gives a very interesting description of the manner in which Isis was worshipped in Rome in the latter half of the second century A.D., and adds some curious details about the attributes of the goddess herself. Thus in his prayer to her he calls her "queen of heaven," *regina coeli*,[2] and he identifies her with Ceres, and Venus, and Proserpine, and refers to her in her capacity as goddess of wheat and crops. At daybreak on the day of the festival of the goddess the priest went into her temple, and threw open the doors, leaving nothing but white linen curtains across the doorway to screen the interior. When the courts were filled with people, these curtains were drawn, and the worshippers were permitted to gaze upon the image of the goddess; to it at once the people began to pray, and the women rattled their sistra, and the prayers were followed by an interval, during which the devout crowd engaged in silent prayer and contemplation of the goddess. About one hour after daybreak, i.e., when the sun had risen, the multitude sang a hymn to the newly risen god, and then departed to their homes. In the afternoon another service was held, at which sistra were shaken, and sacrifices were offered up, and incense was burnt, and an elaborate ceremony in connexion with the use of a vessel of holy Nile water was performed.

The holiest of all the sanctuaries of Isis known to the Greeks was that at Tithorea, and Pausanias tells us[3] that festivals were

[1] *Mau*, op. cit., p. 163.

[2] The Egyptian 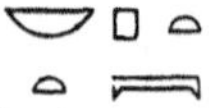.

[3] Book x., chap. xxxii., § 9 (J. G. Frazer's translation).

held there in honour of the goddess twice a year, one in spring and one in autumn. He says, "Two days before each festival the "persons who are free to enter the shrine clean it out in a certain "secret way; and whatever remains they find of the sacrificial "victims which were cast in at the previous festival, they always "carry them to the same spot and bury them there. The distance "of this spot from the shrine we judged to be two furlongs. That "is what they do to the sanctuary on this day. On the next day "the hucksters set up booths of reeds and other improvised "material; and on the last of the three days they hold a fair for "the sale of slaves and all kinds of cattle, also garments, and silver "and gold. After noon they betake themselves to sacrificing. "The richer people sacrifice oxen and deer, the poorer folk "sacrifice geese and guinea fowl. But it is against the custom to "use swine, sheep, and goats for this sacrifice. Those whose (duty "it is) to burn the victims, and bring them into the shrine . . . . "must wrap the victims in bandages of linen, either common linen "or fine linen; the mode of dressing them is the Egyptian. All "the animals sacrificed are led in procession; some convey the "victims into the shrine, others burn the booths in front of it and "depart in haste. They say that once upon a time, when the pyre "began to burn, a profane fellow who had no right to go down "into the shrine rashly entered it out of curiosity. The whole "place seemed to him full of spectres; and scarcely had he "returned to Tithorea and told what he had beheld when he gave "up the ghost. I have heard a like story from a Phoenician man. "He said that the Egyptians hold the festival of Isis at the time "when they say she is mourning for Osiris. At that time the Nile "begins to rise, and it is a common saying among the natives that "it is the tears of Isis that cause the river to rise and water the "fields. Well, then, my informant said that at that season the "Roman governor of Egypt bribed a man to go down to the "shrine of Isis at Coptos. The man who was thus sent in returned "from the shrine; but after he had told us all that he had beheld, "he, too, I was informed, immediately expired. Thus it appears to "be a true saying of Homer's that it is ill for mankind to see the "gods in bodily shape."

Among the various peoples by whom Isis is venerated must be mentioned those of Syria, who identified her with certain of their local goddesses, and it is clear that the early Christians bestowed some of her attributes upon the Virgin Mary. There is little doubt that in her character of the loving and protecting mother she appealed strongly to the imagination of all the Eastern peoples among whom her cult came, and that the pictures and sculptures wherein she is represented in the act of suckling her child Horus formed the foundation for the Christian figures and paintings of the Madonna and Child. Several of the incidents of the wanderings of the Virgin with the Child in Egypt as recorded in the Apocryphal Gospels reflect scenes in the life of Isis as described in the texts found on the Metternich Stele, and many of the attributes of Isis, the God-mother, the mother of Horus, and of Neith, the goddess of Saïs, are identical with those of Mary the Mother of Christ. The writers of the Apocryphal Gospels intended to pay additional honour to Mary the Virgin by ascribing to her the attributes which up to the time of the advent of Christianity they had regarded as the peculiar property of Isis and Neith and other great indigenous goddesses, and if the parallels between the mythological history of Isis and Horus and the history of Mary and the Child be considered, it is difficult to see how they could possibly avoid perceiving in the teaching of Christianity reflections of the best and most spiritual doctrines of the Egyptian religion. The doctrine of partheno-genesis was well known in Egypt in connexion with the goddess Neith of Saïs centuries before the birth of Christ; and the belief in the conception of Horus by Isis through the power given her by Thoth, the Intelligence or Mind of the God of the universe, and in the resurrection of the body and of everlasting life, is coeval with the beginnings of history in Egypt. We may note too in passing the probability that many of the heresies of the early Christian Church in Egypt were caused by the survival of ideas and beliefs connected with the old native gods which the converts to Christianity wished to adapt to their new creed. Be this, however, as it may, the knowledge of the ancient Egyptian religion which we now possess fully justifies the assertions that the rapid growth and progress of Christianity in

THE GODDESS MENQET.

Egypt were due mainly to the fact that the new religion, which was preached there by Saint Mark and his immediate followers, in all its essentials so closely resembled that which was the outcome of the worship of Osiris, Isis, and Horus that popular opposition was entirely disarmed. In certain places in the south of Egypt, e.g., Philae, the worship of Osiris and Isis maintained its own until the beginning of the fifth century of our era, though this was in reality due to the support which it received from the Nubians, but, speaking generally, at this period in all other parts of Egypt Mary the Virgin and Christ had taken the places of Isis and Horus, and the "God-mother," or "mother of the god," , was no longer Isis, but Mary whom the Monophysites styled Θεοτοκος.

CHAPTER XIV

THE SORROWS OF ISIS[1]

48. 

nuk Ȧst per-kuȧ em na ȧt erṭā-nuȧ

I am Isis. I came forth from the house placed me

senȧ-ȧ 49. *Set er-s ȧs tcheṭ-nȧ Teḥuti ur*

my brother Set in it. Behold, said to me Thoth, the great one,

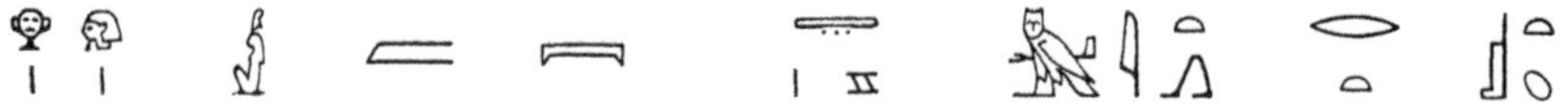

ḥer ṭep Maāt em pet ta māāt ert Ȧst

chief of Maāt in heaven and earth, "Come, thou Isis,

netert nefer kher pu setem ānkh uā sems

goddess, good (it is) to possess obedience; life (is to the) one (who is) led

ki seṭeḳa ert kher sa nekhen 50.

(by) another. Hide thyself with the son child,

iu - f enen ḥāu-f ruṭ peḥpeḥ-f neb

will happen these things, his limbs (will) grow, he will grow strong wholly,

[1] See Golenischeff, *Die Metternichstele*, Leipzig, 1877, pl. 3, l. 48, ff.

khep ṭāt ḥetep-f	*ḥer*	*nest*	*tef - f*	*netchet-nef*
and he shall be made to rest	upon	the throne	of his father,	he will obtain

àat	*ḥeq*	*taui*	*per-kuà*	*ḥer*	*tràt*	*en*
the dignity	of prince	of the two lands."	I came forth	at	the season	of

mesher	*pert*	*matet* vii.	51. *khert ḥāt-à*	*maā-sen*
evening,	and came forth	seven scorpions	before me,	they continued

nà	*ā*	*Tefen*	*Befen*	*ḥa-à*	*sep sen*	*Mestet*
with me at my side.		Tefen and	Befen were	behind me,	twice,	Mestet and

Mestetef	*kher māt-à*	*Petet*	*Thetet*	*Maatet*
Mestetef were	near me,	and Petet,	and Thetet,	and Maatet

ḥer tcheser-nà	*uat*	*ḥen-à*	*en*	*sen*	*ur* 52. *sep sen*
showed to me	the way.	I cried out	to	them	loudly, loudly,

meṭ-à	*sekhep*	*em*	*ānkhui-sen*	*em*	*rekh*	*setem*
my word	entered	into	their ears,	as in	(those of) a wise man;	obedience

usheṭ	*ṭesher*	*em*	*sa*	*sa*
is praiseworthy,	disobedience	(is) as	the mark	of the son

sa er netches	*ḥrȧ-then*	*em kher*	*ḥer-ā*	*uat*
of a man of low estate,	" Let your faces be	bent down	on	the way."

ȧri sem	*ḥeḥ-nuȧ*	*er*	*peḥ n (sic)* 53.	*Pasui*
The leader of the company	brought me	to	the swamps	of Pasui,

nut	*ent*	*Thebt*	*ḥāt*	*ȧṭ*
the city	of the	two Sandal-goddesses	at the beginning	of the Papyrus Swamps.

peḥ-iu	*Ṭeb*	*sper-nȧ*	*ḥem*	*ketut*
Having arrived at	Ṭeb	I came forth to	the houses	of the women

hai	*ȧu ṭeḳa - nuȧ*	*sheps*	*em ua*
of the governor.	Had seen me	the chief woman	on the march,

54. *ȧn-nes*	*āāiu-s*	*ḥer-ȧ*	*men-s*	*ḥer-ȧb*	*en*
she closed	her doors	upon me,	she was angry	in her heart	at

entet	*er ḥen-ȧ*	*netch-sen re*	*ḥer-s*	*erṭā-sen*
those who	were with me.	They decreed	about it	(and) they placed

metu-sen	*en sep*	*ḥer ṭep*	*set*	*en*	*Tefen*	*un-nȧ*
their poison	all at one time	on	the tail	of	Tefen.	Opened to me

55.

taḥ sba-s āq-tu er pa-s senen

a poor woman her door, (I) entered into her house. Cunningly

Tefen āqet kher āāiu en sba tcheṭeb-nes

Tefen entered under the leaves of the door, smote she

sa usert khet pertu em pa usert

the son of the noble lady, fire broke out in the house of the noble lady,

àn un mu àm er ākhem-s àn pet ḥi

not was water there to quench it, not did heaven let fall

mu-s em pa usert àn tràt àru

its rain in the house of the lady, not being it the season thereof.

56. *às pu tem-s un-nà àb-s ànṭ er*

And behold, she who had not opened to me, her heart (was) sad

àn rekh ānkh-f serer-nes nut-s em àmem

not knowing if he lived. She went round her city with lamentation, through

àn un i en kheru-s àb-à ànṭ en sher

not came [any] at her call. My heart was sad about the child

ḥer-s — *er seānkh* — *shu em bet - f* — *nȧs-ȧ*

for her sake, (I wished) to revive (him that was) without fault. I cried out

nes ḥer — *māȧ* — *nȧ* — *sep sen* — *māk* — *ret-ȧ* — *kher* — *ānkh*

to her, Come to me, twice. A charm is my word having life.

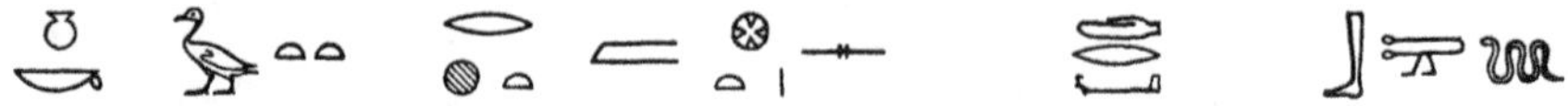

nuk — *satet* — *rekht* — *em* — *nut-s* — *ṭer* — *bethet*

I am a daughter known in her city, who driveth away evil

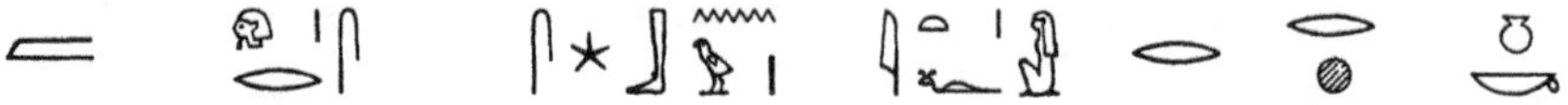

em — *ṭep-re-s* — *sba-nuȧ* — *ȧtf-ȧ* — *er* — *rekh* — *nuk*

by her utterance. Taught me my father to know. I am

58.

satet-f — *mer* — *khat-f* — *uaḥ en* — *Ȧst* — *āāui-s* — *ḥer*

the daughter beloved of his body. Laid Isis her hands upon

nekhen — *er* — *seānkh* — *entet em* — *ḳa* — *ȧḥet* — *met*

the child to vivify that of which had closed the throat. O poison

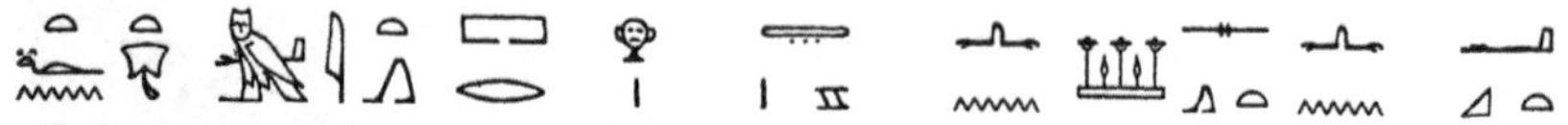

Tefen — *māȧt* — *per* — *ḥer* — *ta* — *ȧn* — *shaset* — *ȧn* — *āqet*

of Tefen, come, appear on the earth, not advance, not enter in.

59.

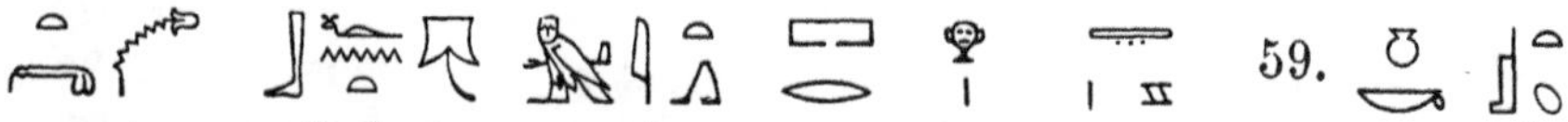

met — *Befent* — *māȧt* — *per* — *ḥer* — *ta* — *nuk* — *Ȧst*

O poison of Befent, come, appear on the earth. I am Isis

netert	*nebt*	*ḥeka*	*āri*	*ḥeka*	*khu*
the goddess,	lady	of words of power,	worker with	words of power,	mighty

tcheṭ kheru	*setem-nā*	*re neb*	*pesḥu*	*khert er kher*
in utterance of speech.	Hearken to me,	mouth every	(which) biteth,	fall downwards.

met	*en*	*Mestet*	*ān*	*sekheset*	*met*	*en*	*Mestetef*
Poison	of	Mestet,	not	advance,	poison	of	Mestetef

ān	*theset*	*met*	*en*	*Petet*	*Thetet*	*ān*	*āqet*
not	rise up.	Poison	of	Petet	and Thetet	not	enter.

60. *Matet*	*kher kher*	*re*	*en*	*peḥes*	*tcheṭ en*	
Maatet	fall down.	Chapter	of	stinging	(which) spake	

Āst	*netert*	*urt*	*ḥeka*	*khent*	*neteru*
Isis,	the goddess,	the great one	of words of power,	head	of the gods.

erṭāt-nes	*Seb*	61. *khu - f*	*er*	*khesef*	*met*	*em*
Had given to her	Seb	his powers	to	repulse	poison	from

sekhem-s	*khesef*	*khet*	*ḥem*	*ḥat*	*met*	*em*
her form (?),	repulsing,	turning away,	driving back,	away back,	poison	at

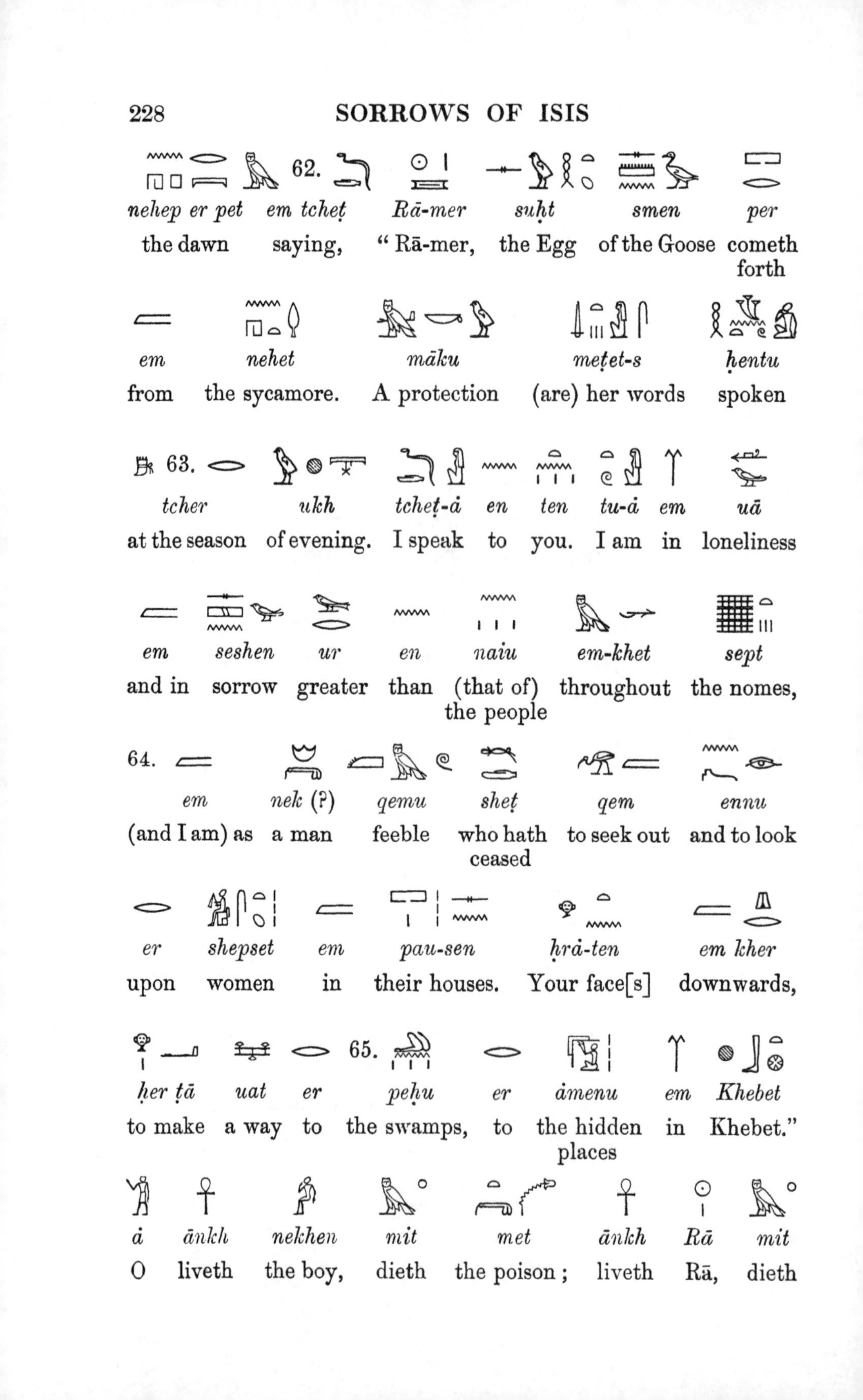

				62.				
nehep er pet		*em tcheṭ*		*Rā-mer*	*suḥt*	*smen*		*per*
the dawn		saying,		" Rā-mer,	the Egg	of the Goose		cometh forth

em	*neḥet*	*māku*	*meṭet-s*	*ḥentu*
from	the sycamore.	A protection	(are) her words	spoken

63.							
tcher		*ukh*	*tcheṭ-ȧ*	*en*	*ten*	*tu-ȧ em*	*uā*
at the season		of evening.	I speak	to	you.	I am in	loneliness

em	*seshen*	*ur*	*en*	*naiu*	*em-khet*	*sept*
and in	sorrow	greater	than	(that of) the people	throughout	the nomes,

64.					
em	*nek* (?)	*qemu*	*sheṭ*	*qem*	*ennu*
(and I am) as	a man	feeble	who hath ceased	to seek out	and to look

er	*shepset*	*em*	*pau-sen*	*ḥrȧ-ten*	*em kher*
upon	women	in	their houses.	Your face[s]	downwards,

			65.				
ḥer ṭȧ	*uat*	*er*	*peḥu*	*er*	*ȧmenu*	*em*	*Khebet*
to make	a way	to	the swamps,	to	the hidden places	in	Khebet."

ȧ	*ānkh*	*nekhen*	*mit*	*met*	*ānkh*	*Rā*	*mit*
O	liveth	the boy,	dieth	the poison;	liveth	Rā,	dieth

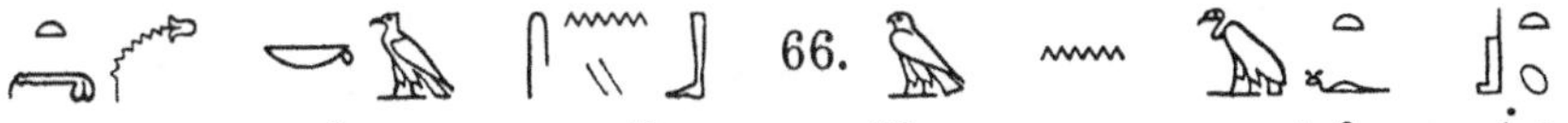

met ka snib 66. *Ḥeru en mut-f Ȧst*

the poison. Verily, healthy be Horus for his mother Isis.

ka snib enti kher meṭes mȧtet khet

Verily, healthy be he who is under the knife also. The fire

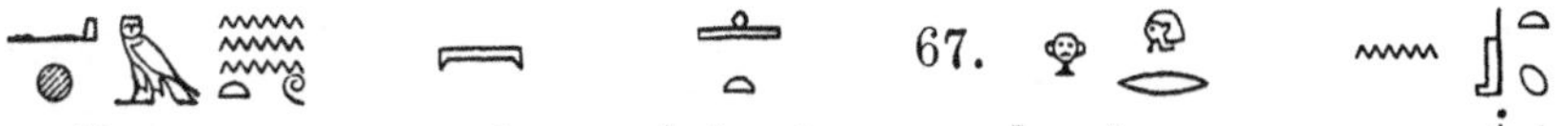

āḳhem-tu pet ḥetepet 67. *ḥer ṭep re en Ȧst*

is extinguished, heaven is content at the utterance of Isis,

netert usert it ȧn-s-nȧ khet-s

the goddess. The lady (who) came, (she who) had shut on me her house,

meḥ-nes pa en taḥ en ka en taḥ

she seized the house of the poor woman because the poor woman

68. *er un - nȧ sa - s er usert ḥer men*

had opened to me her door. Wherefore the lady was in pain

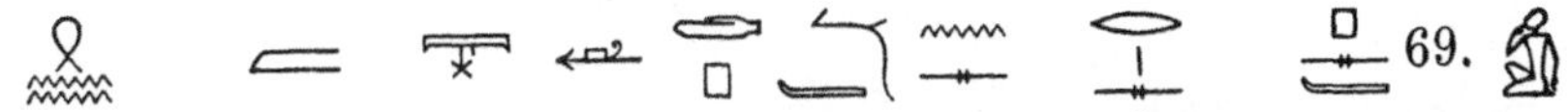

shenen em ḳerḥ uā ṭep - nes re-s 69. *peshu*

and sorrow during night one, she tasted her speech. Was stung

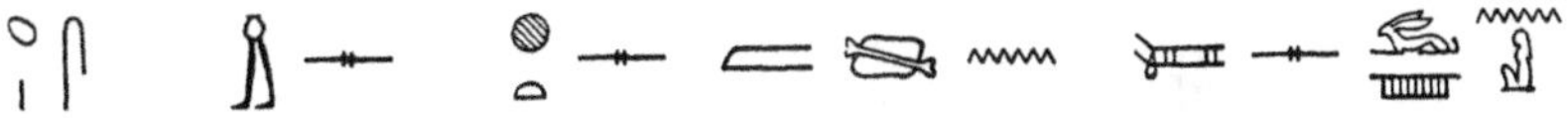

sa-s ȧn-s khet-s em ȧsu en tem-s un-nȧ

her son, was closed for her her house in return for her not having opened to me.

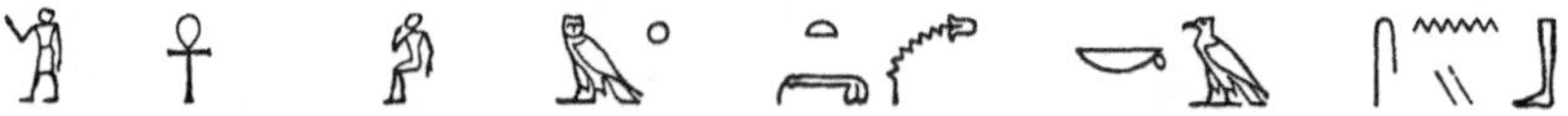

ȧ ānkh nekhen mit met ka senib

O liveth the child, dieth the poison. Verily shall be sound

70. 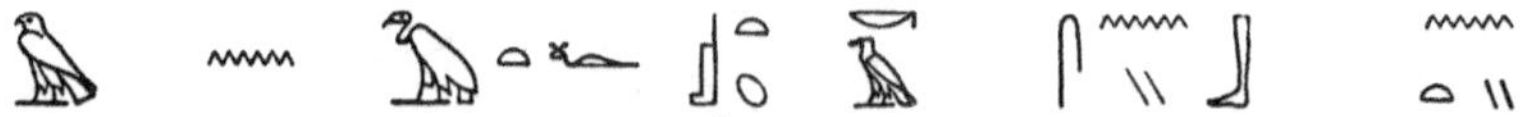

Ḥeru en mut - f Ȧst ka snib enti

Horus through his mother Isis. Verily shall be sound he who is

kher meṭes neb mȧtet ȧn ta en beti

under the knife every one likewise. Shall not bread of barley

 71. 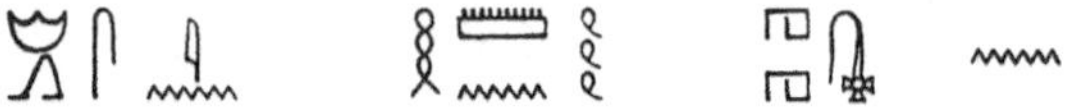

ṭer - f met ḥem-s ȧn ḥemen ḥāu heh en

drive out poison? It shall return through all the limbs the flame of

ḥetchet ṭer - f neb em ḥāu en Ȧst sep sen

ḥetchet and drive out the fire from the members Isis. Twice.

 72. 

māȧ-t net Ḥeru rekh re-s māȧ-t en

Come thou to Horus. Thou whose mouth is wise come thou to

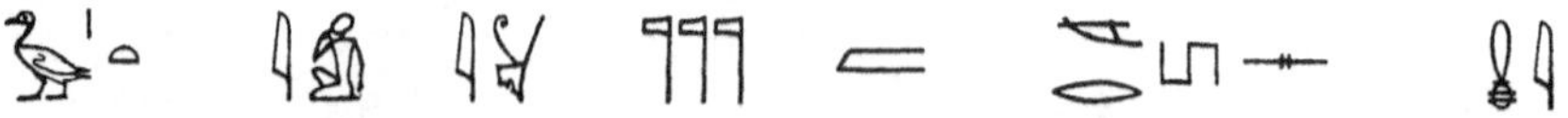

sa-t ȧ ȧn neteru em mer - s mȧ

thy son. "Hail," say the gods in her neighbourhood, like

73. 

entet tcheṭeb nes Tchart beḥā-nes

one whom has stung the scorpion Tchart, whom hath pierced

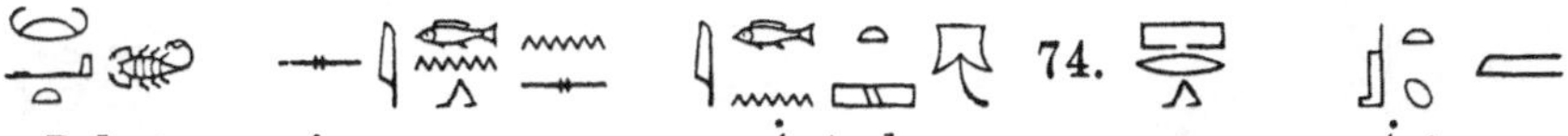

Behāt sȧn - nes Ȧntesh 74. *per Ȧst em*

Behāt, whom hath put to flight Ȧntesh. Appeared Isis as

seṭ ḥer shebenet-s peṭ-nes āāui-s

one who was wounded in her body. She stretched out her arms,

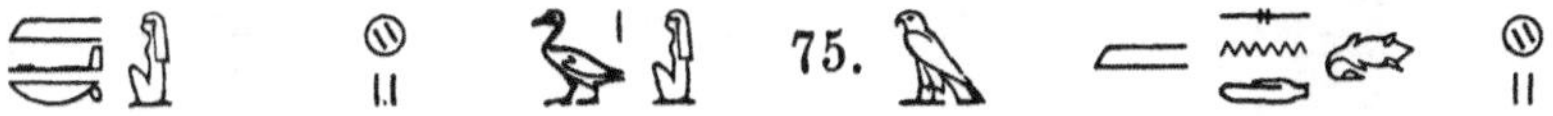

māk-ȧ sep sen sa-ȧ 75. *Ḥeru em senṭ sep sen*

I will protect, twice, my son Horus. Fear not, twice,

sa khut-ȧ ȧn kheper khet neb ṭu erek

O son, my glory. Not shall happen thing any evil unto thee.

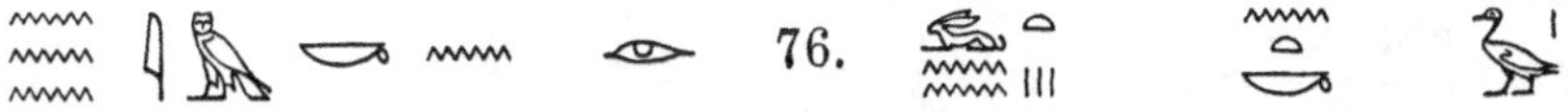

mu ȧm-k en ȧri 76. *unnet entek sa*

Seed is in thee for making things which are to be. Thou art the son

ḥer-ȧb Mesqet per em Mu ȧn mit-k em

within Mesqet, proceeding from Nu, not shalt thou die by

ta na met entek Bennu āā mes

the flame of the poison. Thou art the Bennu Great born

ḥer ṭep trȧ em Ḥet-ser ur em Ȧnnu entek

on the incense trees in the House of the Prince great in Ȧnnu. Thou art

78. 

senȧ en Ȧbṭ ser kheper menāt

the brother of the Ȧbt Fish, the disposer of what is to be, nursed

 79. 

nu mȧut em khen en Ḥet Net Rert Ḥȧt

by the cat within the House of Net. Rert, and Ḥȧt,

Bes em sa en ḥāu-k ȧn kher ṭep-k en

and Bes, protect thy limbs. Not shall fall thy head before

 80. 

tchat ȧm-k ȧn shep ḥāu-k tai

him that is hostile to thee. Not shall conquer thy limbs the fire

en metu-k ȧn ḥen-k ḥer ta ȧn

of thy poison. Not shalt thou fall on the ground, not

81. 

khas-k ḥer mu ȧn sekhem re neb

shalt thou be in peril on water. Not shall have the mastery reptile any

pesḥ ȧm-k ȧn rehen mai neb

stinging over thee. Not shall crush thee lion any

sekhemet ȧm-k entek sa neter tchesert

(or) be master over thee. Thou art the son of a god holy

82. 

per em Seb entek Ḥeru ȧn sekhem

proceeding from Seb. Thou art Horus, not shall have the mastery

metu em ḥāu-k entek sa neter tchesert

the poison in thy limbs. Thou art the son of a god holy

per em Seb pa entet kher ṭem mȧtet

proceeding from Seb. (With him) that is under the knife likewise (is it).

 83. 

ȧu iv. shepset em sa en ḥāu-k

The four holy goddesses protect thy limbs. . . . .

168. 

nuk Ȧst āuur-th em tcha-s baka-th em Ḥeru

I am Isis, who conceived her male child, and was heavy with Horus.

netert mes-nȧ Ḥeru sa Ȧsȧr em khen sesh en

A goddess I bore Horus, son of Osiris, within a nest of

 169. 

ȧṭeḥ ḥāā-nȧ ḥer-s ur sep sen ḥer maa-nȧ

papyrus plants. I rejoiced over it greatly, twice, because I saw (in him)

usheb ḥer ȧt-f ȧmen-ȧ su seṭeḳ-ȧ su

one who would answer for his father. I hid him, I concealed him

kher sent netep-f shema-à àm tuà

having fear of his being bitten. I went to the city Àm, (the people) saluted

em sent àri . . . . ursh-à her heh nekhen

according to custom. I spent the time in seeking for the boy

her àri kher-f hem net er sekhen Heru qem-nà

to make his food. I returned to embrace Horus, I found

 170. 

su Heru nefer en nub nekhen suk

him, Horus, the beautiful one of gold, the boy, the child,

àtet-f netef-nef taiu em mu nu

he was nothing. He had bedewed the ground with the water of

maat-f em netet nu septi-f tchet-f urt

his eye, and with the foam of his lips; his body was motionless,

àb-f betesh àn pa metu nu hāu-f utu-nà

his heart still, not moved the muscles of his body. I sent forth

 . . . . 177. 

tàa her àmu ateh rer-sen nà

a cry . . . . The dwellers in the swamp they came round me

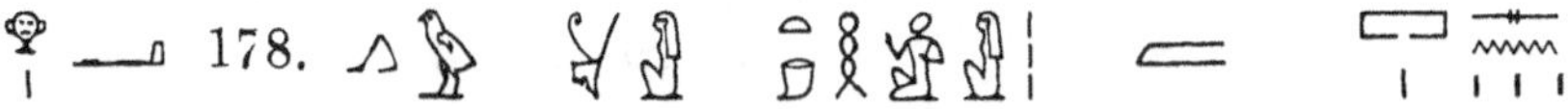

ḥer ā 178. *iu nȧ taḥu em pau-sen*

at once, came to me the fenmen from their houses,

nehep - sen net 179. *ḥer kheru-ȧ aḳeb - sen ȧru*

they drew nigh to me at my call, they wept, even they,

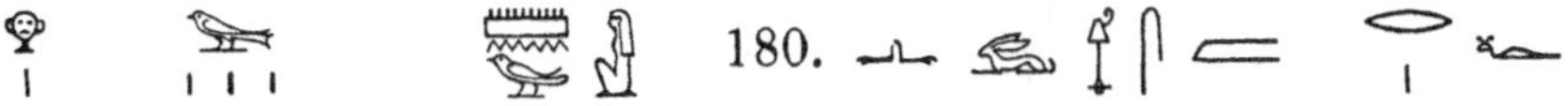

ḥer uru men-ȧ 180. *ȧn un s em re - f*

at the greatness of my misery. There was none who opened his mouth

ȧm er sa neb ȧm-sen ḥer āun 181. *sep sen ȧn un rekh*

there, man every among them grieved greatly. There was none knowing

ȧm er seānkh iu-nȧ set rekht

there to make to live (Horus). Came to me a woman well known

182. *em nut-s erpet khent uu-s iu-s*

in her city, a lady at the head of her district. She came

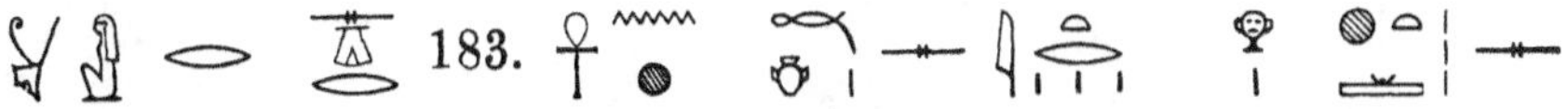

nȧ er se-ḳer 183. *ānkh meḥ ȧb-s ȧteru ḥer khet - s*

to me to restore life, her heart was filled with her affairs

em senṭ sep sen sa Ḥeru 184. *em beṭesh*

according to wont. Twice. The son Horus (was) in inactivity.

sep sen — neter mut nekhen — baq er — ṭu — en — sen - f

Twice. The son of the mother of the god was safe from the evil of his brother.

185. 

ba — åmen-tu — ån āq — em — khefti

The plants were hidden, not could enter there an enemy

er-es — ḥeka — en — Tem — tef — neteru

into them. The word of power of Tem father of the gods,

186. 

enti — em — pet — em — åri — ānkhet — ån — āq

who is in heaven, was as the maker of life, not entered

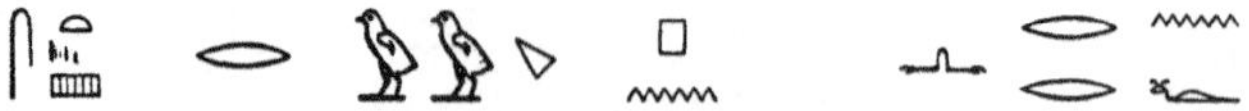 187. 

Set — er — uu — pen — ån rer-nef — Kheb

Set into region this, not could he go about Kheb.

Ḥeru — baq — er — ṭu — en — senå-f — ån ṭekhen-s

Horus was smitten by the wickedness of his brother. Not had she hidden

 188. 

åmu — shesu - f — ḥeḥ — sep — hru — enen

those who were in his service many time[s] a day. These (said)

 189. 

ḥer-f — ānkh — Ḥeru — en — mut-f s — em un-eref

concerning him, "Shall live Horus for his mother?" they found where he was,

tchart ḥer tcheṭem - f āun-ȧb ḥer 190. *khun - f*

and a Scorpion stung him, and the slayer of the heart hath stabbed him.

erṭā en Ȧst fenṭ-s em re-f ḥer rekh set ȧru

Placed Isis her nose in his mouth to know if had breath

em 191. *khen en sheta - f ȧp - s men nu āuāā*

he who was in his coffin. She opened the wound of the heir

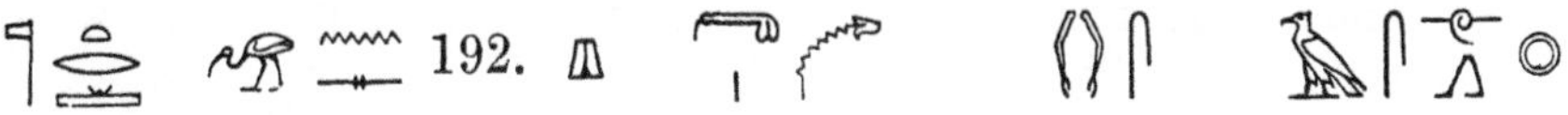

netert qem-nes 192. *kher met sekhen-s asta*

divine, she found it possessing poison. She embraced him hurriedly

ḥer perper kher - f mȧ remu khaā 193. *ḥer tchā*

and leaped about with him like a fish laid upon a fire

pesḥ Ḥeru Rā pesḥ sa-k 194. *pesḥ*

(saying,) Stung is Horus, O Rā, stung is thy son. Stung is

Ḥeru āā en āu neb . . . . en Shu

Horus, heir of heir, lord of the [pillars ?] of Shu.

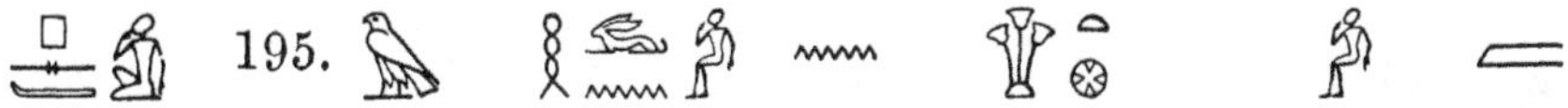

pesḥ 195. *Ḥeru ḥun en Ȧtḥet nekhen em*

Stung is Horus, the child of the papyrus swamp, the child in

Ḥet-ser *pesḥ* 196. *nekhen* *nefer* *en* *nub* *nu*

Ḥet-ser. Stung is the child beautiful of gold. The child,

suḳ *ȧtet - f* *pesḥ* *Ḥeru* *sa* *Un-nefer* ......

the babe, he is nothing. Stung is Horus, son of Un-nefer.

202. *iu eref* *Nebt-ḥet* 203. *ḥer rem* *tȧau-s* *rer*

Then came Nephthys weeping, she cried, going about

ȧaṭeḥ *Serq ḥer* 204. *petrȧ* *sep sen* *nimā trȧ*

the swamp, and Serqet (who said), What, twice, what then is

er *sa* *Ḥeru* *Ȧst* *ṭua* *ert* *er* *pet*

to the child Horus, Isis? pray thou therefore to heaven

205. *kheper* *āḥā* *qeti* *Rā* *ȧn* *nā* *uȧa*

so that may come a stop to the sailors of Rā, not will travel the boat

en *Rā* *er* *sa* *Ḥeru* 206. *ḥer ḳes-f* *utu*

of Rā from the son Horus from where he is. Sent forth

Ȧst kheru-s er pet sebeḥ-s er uȧa en

Isis her cry to heaven, her prayer (was) to Boat of

ḥeḥ sekhen 207. *ȧten em āq-s ȧn menmen-f*

Millions of years. Stood still the disk at her coming, not moved he

ḥer ȧst-f Teḥuti iu āper em 208. *peḥ-f*

on his seat. Thoth came provided with his magic power,

kher utu āat en maākheru peter sep sen Ȧst

possessing command great of *maā-kheru*. What, twice, Isis,

netert khut 209. *rekh re-s ȧn ṭu*

goddess, mighty one, understanding (with) her mouth, not evil

ȧs er sa Ḥeru sa-f en uȧa

behold shall be to the son Horus, his protection is from the boat

en Rā 210. *i-nȧ mȧn em ṭept ȧten*

of Rā. I have come to-day in the boat of the disk

 211. 

em	*ȧst - f*	*en*	*sef*	*kek*	*kheper*
from	its place	of	yesterday.	When the night	cometh

seshep	*ṭer*	*er*	*senb*	*Ḥeru*	*en*	*mut - f*
the light	driveth (it) away	to	heal	Horus	for	his mother

212. 

Ȧst	*sa*	*neb*	*ent*	*kher*	*maten*	*mȧtet*
Isis	(and) person	every	who is	under	the knife	likewise.

CHAPTER XIV

SET, 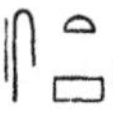, , OR SUTI, , AND NEPHTHYS

SET, the Σήθ of Plutarch, and the god who was identified with Typhon in late times, was, according to the Heliopolitan system of mythology, the son of Seb and Nut, the brother of Osiris, Isis, and Nephthys, the husband of Nephthys, and the father of Anubis; the worship of the god is, however, very much older than this system, and in primitive times the attributes of the god were very different from those which are usually ascribed to him in the late dynastic period. In the Pyramid Texts we find Set associated very closely with Horus, and he always appears in them in the character of a god who is a friend and helper of the dead. It will be remembered that according to one myth the floor of heaven was made of a vast, rectangular plate of iron, the four corners of which rested upon four pillars which served to mark the cardinal points. At certain places this iron plate was thought to be so near the tops of the mountains that the deceased might easily clamber on to it and so obtain admission into heaven, but at others the distance between it and the earth was so great that he needed help to reach it. A legend current in early times asserted that Osiris experienced some difficulty in getting on to the iron plate, and that he only succeeded in doing so by means of a ladder with which Rā provided him. Even then Osiris appears to have found some difficulty in mounting the ladder, and he was finally helped to ascend it by Ḥeru-ur and Set, who were twin gods. Thus in the text of Pepi I. (line 192), the deceased is made to say, "Homage "to thee, O divine Ladder! Homage to thee, O Ladder of Set! "Stand thou upright, O divine Ladder! Stand thou upright, O

"Ladder of Set! Stand thou upright, O Ladder of Horus, whereby "Osiris came forth into heaven." In the text of Unȧs (line 493) it is said, "Unas cometh forth upon the Ladder which his "father Rā hath made for him, and Horus and Set take the hand "of Unȧs, and they lead him into the Ṭuat."[1] On the other hand, in another passage Rā and Horus are said to set up the Ladder for Osiris (line 579 ff.), but even so when the dead king "standeth up "he is Horus, and when he sitteth down he is Set."

The association of Set with Horus in these and many other passages well illustrates the antiquity of the cult of Set, and helps us to understand his attributes. Here we find him regarded as the equal in every respect of Ḥeru-ur, i.e., "Horus the Elder," who was admittedly one of the oldest gods in Egypt, and it was considered necessary for the welfare of the deceased that Set should be propitiated, and his favour secured. From other passages, however, it is clear that there existed opposition and hostility between Ḥeru-ur and Set, and that the destruction of one god by the other was only prevented by Thoth, who in his capacity as regulator of the strife which existed between the two gods, was called Ȧp-reḥu, , or Ȧp-reḥui, , or 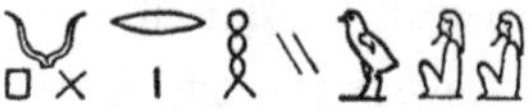, i.e., "Judge of the two opponent gods," and thus it is clear that even in the period of the Early Empire Set was regarded both as the enemy of Ḥeru-ur and as a god who could be of service to the dead in the Underworld, and who if he were not a friend to him would certainly be a foe. From the fact that Ḥeru-ur and Set were thought to be always in opposition we are justified in assuming that the attributes of the former god were exactly contrary to those of the latter, and the assumption is supported by the evidence of the hieroglyphic texts. Ḥeru-ur, as we have already seen, was the god of the sky by day, and Set was the god of the sky by night; this fact is proved by the figures

1 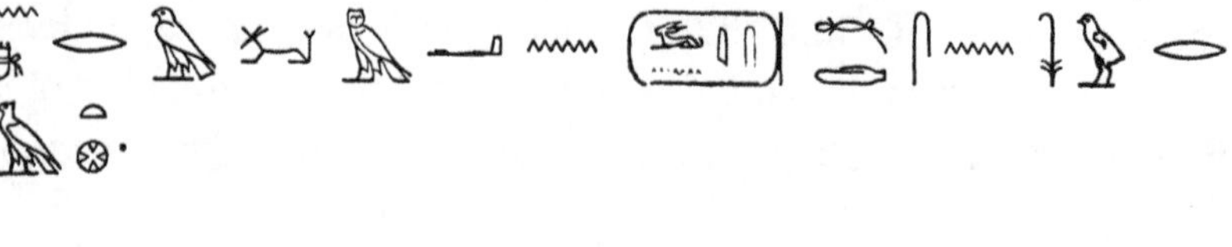

THE DUAL GOD HORUS-SET.

of the double god which are found in mythological scenes whereon the head of Ḥeru-ur and the head of Set are seen upon one body. The attributes of Ḥeru-ur changed somewhat in early dynastic times, but they were always the opposite of those of Set, whether we regard the two gods as personifications of two powers of nature, i.e., Light and Darkness, Day and Night, or as Kosmos and Chaos, or as Life and Death, or as Good and Evil.

The signification of the name of Set is not easy to determine. Ḥeru, or Horus, certainly means "he who is above," and by analogy the name Set ought to mean something like "he who is below;" and in proof of this Dr. Brugsch calls attention[1] to the well-known Coptic words, ϩⲣⲁⲓ "above," and ⲉⲥⲏⲧ "below." The hieroglyphic form of the name Set, 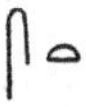, or , has for its determinative either a stone,  (), or the figure of an animal, , or  (, or 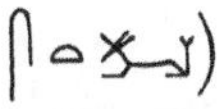); the former of these indicates that the god was the personification of the stony or desert land and the regions of death, but the signification of the latter is not so easy to understand because the animal has not yet been identified. The pictures of the animal which was supposed to be the incarnation of Set represent it with a head something like that of a camel, with curious, pricked ears, and a straight tail, bifurcated at the end. In the absence of any facts on the subject we must assume that the animal which was the symbol of Set was one that prowled about by night in the deserts and in waste places of the towns and cities, and that his disposition was hostile to man, and wicked generally, and that owing to his evil reputation he was hunted and slain with such diligence that he became extinct in comparatively early times.

The region in which the Set animal lived appears to have been situated in the South, and the god Set became, in consequence, the god of the South, just as Ḥeru-ur became the god of the North, and as such he assisted at the coronation ceremonies of kings. Thus a relief[2] at Thebes represents Horus and Set standing one on each side of Seti I., and each god is pouring out a libation

[1] *Religion*, p. 702. [2] Lanzone, *Dizionario*, pl. 375.

of "life" over the head of the king; and in another scene[1] Horus and Set are represented in the act of placing the double crown of the South and the North upon the head of Rameses II. Horus says to the king, "I will give thee a life like unto that of Rā, and years even as the years of Tem," and Set says, "I stablish the "crown upon thy head even like the Disk () [on the head of] "Åmen Rā, and I will give thee all life, and strength, and health;" in his character of giver of life each god holds in his hand the notched palm branch, , symbol of "years," which rests upon a frog, , and Ω, the emblem of the Sun's path in the heavens and of eternity. In yet another scene[2] we find Set teaching Thothmes III. the use of the bow in connexion with the emblem of the goddess Neith, whilst Horus instructs him how to wield some weapon, which appears to be a staff. According to Dr. Brugsch,[3] Set was the god of the downward motion of the sun in the lower hemisphere, in a southerly direction, and for this reason he was the source of the destructive heat of summer; and since the days began to diminish after the summer solstice, it was declared that he stole the light from Horus or Rā, and he was held to be the cause of all the evil, both physical and moral, which resulted therefrom. The light which Thoth brought with the new moon was withdrawn by Set as soon as it was possible for him to obtain power over that luminary, and he was, naturally, thought to be the cause of clouds, mist, rain, thunder and lightning, hurricanes and storms, earthquakes and eclipses, and in short of every thing which tended to reverse the ordinary course of nature and of law and order. From a moral point of view he was the personification of sin and evil.

The mythological and religious texts of all periods contain many allusions to the fight which Set waged against Horus, and more than one version of the narrative is known. In the first and simplest form the story merely records the natural opposition of Day to Night, or Night to Day, and the two Combatant gods were Ḥeru-ur, or Horus the Elder, and Set. In its second form the two Combatant gods are Rā and Set, and the chief object of the

[1] Lanzone, *Dizionario*, pl. 374. [2] *Ibid.*, pl. 376. [3] *Religion*, p. 703.

latter is to prevent Rā from appearing in the East daily. The form which Set assumed on these occasions was that of a monster serpent, and he took with him as helpers a large number of small serpents and noxious creatures of various kinds. The name of the serpent was Āpep, 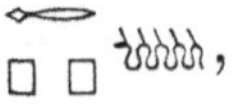, or Āāapef, , which is preserved in Coptic under the form ⲁⲡⲱⲫ, but he was also called Rerek, , and since he was identified with a long series of serpent monsters he had as many names as Rā. The weapons with which Āpep fought were cloud, mist, rain, darkness, etc., and Rā, his opponent, was armed with the burning and destroying heat of the sun, and the darts and spears of light. The result of the fight was always the same; Āpep was shrivelled and burnt up by Rā, but he was able to renew himself daily, and at the end of each night he collected his fiends, and waged war against Rā with unabated vigour. In the third form of the story the Combatant gods are Osiris and Set, and we have already seen how Set slew his brother and persecuted his widow and child, and how he escaped punishment because Osiris had, at the time of his death, none to avenge his cause. In the fourth form of the story the Combatant gods are Horus, the son of Osiris and Isis, and Set, and the avowed intention of Horus is to slay him that slew his father Osiris.

The two gods fought in the forms of men, and afterwards in the forms of bears, and Horus would certainly have killed Set, whom he had fettered, had not Isis taken pity upon her brother and loosed his bonds and set him free. The fight between Horus, son of Osiris and Isis, and Set, had a very important bearing on the destinies of the dead, for to it was attached the moral idea of the victory of Good over Evil, and the deceased was believed to conquer Set even as Osiris had done. Thus in the *Book of the Dead* (ix. 3), he says, "I have come, I have seen my divine father Osiris. "I have stabbed the heart of Suti" (i.e., Set); and from Chapter xviii.H 1 ff., we may see that although the fiends of Set changed themselves into wild beasts on the night of the breaking and turning up of the earth in Ṭaṭṭu, Osiris, by the help of Thoth, slew them, and mixed their blood with the sods. In Chapter

xxiii. 2, we find the deceased praying that Thoth will come to him, and will by means of his words of power loose the bandages wherewith Set has fettered his mouth; and in Chapter xxxix. 15, we find him declaring that he is Set who "letteth loose the storm-clouds "and the thunder in the horizon of heaven, even as doth the god "Netcheb-àb-f, (). Elsewhere (xl. 1 ff.) Āpep is called both Hai, , and Ām-āau, , i.e., the "Eater of the Ass," and he is declared to be a being abominable both to Osiris and to the god Ḥaàs, 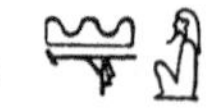, or ; the Ass referred to here is, of course, Rā; the Ass was regarded in one aspect as a solar animal because of his great virility. On the other hand, certain passages prove that even in the XVIIIth Dynasty Set was regarded as a god who was friendly towards the deceased, for we read (xvii. 131), "Tem hath "built thy house, Shu and Tefnut have founded thy habitation; lo! "drugs are brought, and Horus purifieth and Set strengtheneth, "and Set purifieth and Horus strengtheneth." In the Chapter of the deification of members, the backbone of the deceased is identified with the backbone of Set (xlii. 12), and elsewhere the deceased says (l.B 2) "Suti and the company of the gods have joined together "my neck and my back strongly, and they are even as they were "in the time that is past; may nothing happen to break them "apart." But in Chapter lxxxvi. 6, the deceased says, "Set, son of Nut, [lieth] under the fetters which he had made for me;" and elsewhere (cviii. 8), he is said "to depart, having the harpoon "of iron in him," and to have thrown up everything which he had eaten and to have been put in a place of restraint.

A statement in Plutarch's *De Iside et Osiride* (§ 62), informs us that Typhon was called Seth, and Bebo, and Smy, "all of them "words of one common import, and expressing certain violent and "forcible restraint and withholding, as likewise contrariety and "subversion; we are, moreover, informed by Manetho that the "load-stone is by the Egyptians called the 'bone of Horus,' as "iron is, the 'bone of Typho.'" This information is of considerable interest, for it makes the identity of Set and

Typhon[1] certain, and it is, moreover, supported by the evidence of the inscriptions. The name Seth is, of course, Set, 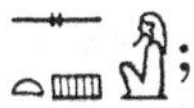; Bebo is the Egyptian , BABA, and Smy is , SMAI, the well-known Egyptian name for Set as the Arch-Fiend. The associates of Set were called SMAIU, , and the determinative , shows that the idea of "violence" was implied in the name. That iron was connected with Set or Typhon is quite clear from the passage quoted by Dr. Brugsch[2] in which Thoth is said to have obtained from Set the knife with which he cut up the bull.

It has been said above that the serpent and the Set animal were the common symbols of Set, but instances are known in which he is represented in the form of a man, wearing a beard and a tail, and holding the usual symbols of divinity. In the example figured by Lanzone[3] the god is called "mighty-one of two-fold strength," , and is accompanied by Nephthys, who wears upon her head a pair of horns and a disk. Now, as Set was the personification of the powers of darkness, and of evil, and of the forces of the waters which were supposed to resist light and order, a number of beasts which dwelt in the waters, or at least partly on land and partly in the water, were regarded as symbols of him and as beings wherein he took up his habitation. Among these were the serpent Āpep, the fabulous beast, ĀKHEKH, , which was a species of antelope with a bird's head surmounted by three uraei, and a pair of wings, the hippopotamus, the crocodile, the pig, the turtle, the ass, etc. These animals were, however, not the only ones which were regarded as types of Set, for as Dr. Brugsch has rightly observed, every creature which was snared or caught in the waters or hunted in the desert, was treated as an incarnation of Set; and animals with red, or reddish-brown hair or skins, and even red-haired men were supposed to be especially

1 TAWFÂN, طُوفَان, or طوفان, the Arabic word for "storm, deluge, inundation, whirlwind," etc., appears to be derived from the name Typhon.

2 *Religion*, p. 707. 3 *Dizionario*, pl. 377.

under the influence of Set. On the other hand, the animals which were used by man in the chase, i.e., dogs, cheetas, etc., and certain other animals, e.g., lions, cats, etc., were held to be sacred to the gods, and according to Plutarch (*De Iside*, § 72), "the gods, "through a dread of Typho, metamorphosed themselves into these "animals, concealing themselves as it were from his purpose in "the bodies of ibises, dogs and hawks." The sacrifice of certain animals associated with Set played a prominent part in the ritual of the Egyptian religion, and at the seasons of the year when Set's influence was supposed to be the greatest earnest attempts were regularly made to propitiate him by means of offerings.

Thus in order to drive away Set from attacking the full moon of the month Pachons an antelope was sacrificed, and a black pig was hacked in pieces upon an altar made of sand, which was built on the bank of the river. On the twenty-sixth day of the month Choiak, which was the time of the winter solstice, an ass was slain, and a model of the serpent-fiend was hewn in pieces. On the first day of Mesore, which was the day of the great festival of Ḥeru Beḥuṭet, large numbers of birds and fish were caught, and those which were considered to be of a Typhonic character were stamped upon with the feet, and those who did this cried out, "Ye shall be "cut in pieces, and your members shall be hacked asunder, and each "of you shall consume the other; thus doth Rā triumph over all his "enemies, and thus doth Ḥeru-Beḥuṭet, the great god, the lord of "heaven, triumph over all his enemies." On such occasions, we learn from Plutarch (*De Iside*, § 63), sistra[1] were shaken in the temples, "for, say they, the sound of these Sistra averts and drives away "Typho; meaning hereby, that as corruption clogs and puts a

[1] The sistrum is thus described by Plutarch:—"Now the outer surface of this "instrument is of a convex figure, as within its circumference are contained those "four chords or bars, which make such a rattling when they are shaken—nor is "this without its meaning; for that part of the universe which is subject to "generation and corruption is contained within the sphere of the moon; and "whatever motions or changes may happen therein, they are all effected by the "different combinations of the four elementary bodies, fire, earth, water, and air. "Moreover, upon the upper part of the convex surface of the sistrum is carved the "effigies of a Cat with a human visage, as on the lower edge of it, under those "moving chords, is engraved on the one side the face of Isis, and on the other that "of Nephthys," etc.

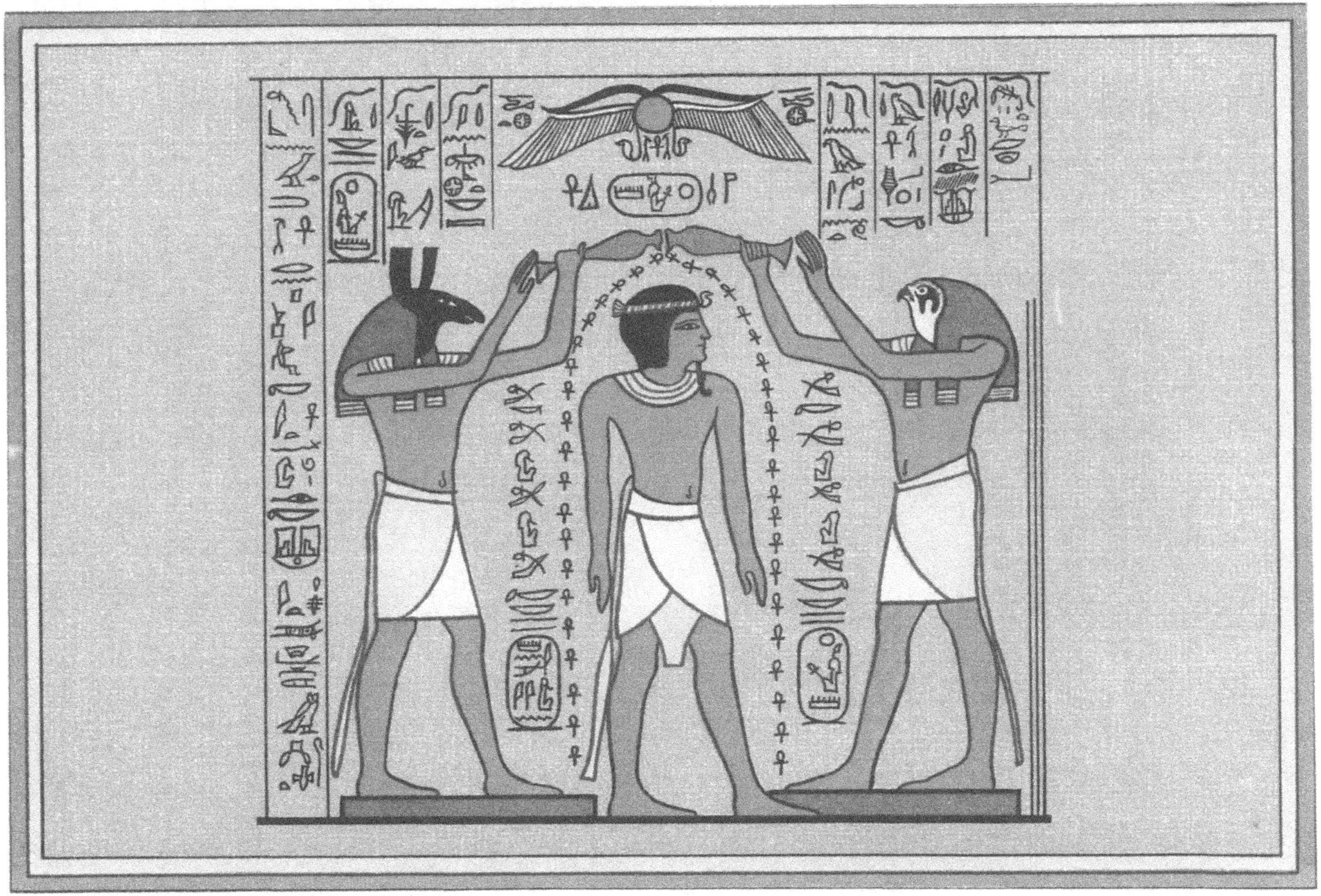

SET AND HORUS POURING OUT LIFE OVER SETI I.

"stop to the regular course of nature, so generation, by the means "of motion, loosens it again, and restores it to its former vigour."

The kingdom of Set was supposed to be placed in the northern sky, and his abode was one of the stars which formed the constellation of Khepesh, , or the "Thigh," which has been identified with the Great Bear, and it was from this region that he made use of his baleful influence to thwart the beneficent designs of Osiris, whose abode was Saḥ or Orion, and of Isis, whose home was Sepṭ, or Sothis. A little consideration will show that the northern sky was the natural domain of Set, for viewed from the standpoint of an Egyptian in Upper Egypt the north was rightly considered to be the place of darkness, cold, mist, and rain, each of which was an attribute of Set; and we may note in passing that the Hebrews called the region of darkness, or the winter hemisphere, SÊPHÔN, a name which appears to be connected beyond a doubt with ṢÂPHÔN, "North." The chief opponent of Set was the hippopotamus goddess RERET, , who was believed to keep this power of darkness securely fettered by a chain; this goddess is usually represented with the arms and hands of a woman which are attached to the body of a hippopotamus, and in each she holds a knife. Her temple was called Ḥet-Khāat, . The duty of the goddess was to keep in restraint the evil influence of Set and to make clear a way in the sky for the birth of ḤERU-SMA-TAUI, whom Dr. Brugsch identified with the spring sun; the texts, however, make it clear that Reret was nothing but a form of Isis.

The seven stars of the Great Bear.

From a passage in the *Book of the Dead* (xvii. 89) we learn that Set was accompanied by the four children of Horus, Mesthȧ, Ḥāpi, Ṭuamutef, and Qebḥsennuf, who were said to be "behind the Thigh in the northern sky," and were believed to take part in curbing the evil deeds of Set. They may be identified with the four ÅF gods, , "who are the four gods of the Followers

"who do battle against the evil of Set ( ), who is a mighty "warrior," and it was their duty to be with the sailors of the Boat of Rā, that is to say, with the Åkhemu-seku, , of the North, and with the four stars of the Meskheti, , or Great Bear. In the text from which these details are quoted it is said definitely that the "Meskheti is the Thigh of Set," .[1] In early dynastic times it is tolerably certain that the worship of Set was widespread, and his cult seems to have flourished until the period which lies between the XIIth and the XVIIIth Dynasties; but about B.C. 1700 a change came over his fortunes, and the Egyptians began to show the greatest detestation for him. He had, of course, always been connected with evil, but it appears that the popularity of his cult suffered greatly at this period because he was associated with the occupation of Northern Egypt by the Hyksos, who identified him with certain Semitic, Syrian gods. At Kom Ombo and in the south of Egypt a common name of Set was Nubti, , or Set-Nubti, , and as such he is usually represented with one body and two heads, one being that of a hawk, and the other that of the remarkable animal which was the symbol of the god.[2] In the North and South of Egypt Set was called both Nubti and Sutekh, , or , and there is no doubt whatsoever that he was endowed by the peoples in the Delta with all the attributes of the Semitic god Baal, בַּעַל, whose name appears in Egyptian under the form Bār, or Bālu, .

That the name of Bār was common in Egypt, at all events among settlers from Syria, is proved by its occurrence in proper names, e.g., Bāri-Menthu, , and Bāri-Rumāu, , the last being the equivalent of the Semitic name Ba'al Râm, בַּעַל־רָם.[3] In Middle Egypt the centre of the

[1] Brugsch, *Thesaurus*, p. 122; *Religion*, p. 712.

[2] See Lanzone, op. cit., pl. 378.

[3] See Müller, *Asien und Europa*, p. 309; *Recueil*, tom. xii. 17.

worship of Set was at Sept-Mert-et, , which is commonly known as Oxyrhynchus,[1] and other prominent places of his worship were one of the Oases, , and Sennu, , and Unnu, , Hermopolis. In the Delta the centre of his worship was the famous city Ḥet-uārt, or Avaris, where the Hyksos king Ȧpepȧ made him to be the greatest of all the gods of his dominions, and at one time Set was to all intents and purposes the national god of the Delta.

In the narratives of their prowess in battle which kings caused to be inscribed on stelae and on the walls of their temples, they delighted to have it stated that they were as terrible as Bār in the attacks which they made upon their foes. Under the XVIIIth Dynasty we hear little of Set, for Ȧmen, the god of the Upper Country, had the pre-eminence, but the cult of Set appears to have been revived under the XIXth Dynasty, for the second king thereof called himself Seti, after the name of the god, and this king caused bas-reliefs to be set up in his temples wherein Set is represented in the act of performing the coronation ceremonies. Under this Dynasty we have another king called after the name of the god, i.e., Seti II., Menephthah, but after that period the figure of Set appears in no cartouche, and his evil reputation increased. To the XXth Dynasty probably belongs the very interesting bronze figure of Set in the British Museum (No. 18,191), which was worn as a pendant, and was originally plated with gold; the god stands upright and wears the double crown of the South and the North and a uraeus. When found the figure was bent double, a position which it was made to take by violence, probably by someone who detested the god, but the body has been straightened out and it is now possible to examine the head of the Set animal, which in this specimen is finely shaped. Another interesting figure of Set is No. 22,897, which is of good workmanship; this, like the preceding, was also gilded and worn as a pendant. Belonging to a much later period we have the small wooden figure of the Set animal (No. 30,460), and the upper part of a

[1] Brugsch, *Dict. Géog.*, p. 275.

two-headed bronze figure of Åmen-Ḥeru-pa-kharṭ (No. 16,228). The former stands on a pedestal on which is a sepulchral inscription, addressed to Set, "the great god, lord of heaven," who is asked to give "life, strength, and health" to him that had it made; and the latter represents Åmen under the form of a ram-headed man, who wears on his head the plumes of Shu, the disk of Rā, and a uraeus, and the head of Set, with characteristic ears. The above four figures are when taken together of great interest, and, as they all have been acquired by the Trustees of the British Museum since Signor Lanzone issued the last part of his *Dizionario*, they form a valuable addition to the examples registered by him in it.

The ideas which were held by the Egyptians about Set in the late times are well illustrated by the following extract from Plutarch (*De Iside*, § 30), who says that it is evident from many of their rites and ceremonies "that they hold him in the greatest "contempt, and do all they can to vilify and affront him. Hence "their ignominious treatment of those persons, whom from the "redness of their complexions they imagine to bear a resemblance "to him; and hence likewise is derived the custom of the Coptites "of throwing an Ass down a precipice; because it is usually of "this colour. Nay, the inhabitants of Busiris and Lycopolis "carry their detestation of this animal so far, as never to make any "use of trumpets, because of the similitude between their sound "and the braying of the ass. In a word, this animal is in general "regarded by them as unclean and impure, merely on account of "the resemblance which they conceive it bears to Typho; and in "consequence of this notion, those cakes which they offer with "their sacrifices during the last two months Paüni and Phaophi, "have the impression of an Ass bound stamped upon them. For "the same reason likewise, when they sacrifice to the Sun, they "strictly enjoyn all those who approach to worship the God, "neither to wear any gold about them, nor to give provender to "any ass. It is moreover evident, say they, that even the "Pythagoreans looked upon Typho to have been of the rank or "order of Demons, as, according to them, 'he was produced in the "even number fifty-six.' For as the power of the Triangle is "expressive of the nature of Pluto, Bacchus, and Mars, the "properties of the Square of Rhea, Venus, Ceres, Vesta, and Juno; "of the Dodecagon of Jupiter; so, as we are informed by Eudoxus "is the figure of 56 angles expressive of the nature of Typho: as "therefore all the others above-mentioned in the Pythagorean "system are looked upon as so many Genii or Demons, so in like "manner must this latter be regarded by them. 'Tis from this "persuasion likewise of the red complexion of Typho, that the "Egyptians make use of no other bullocks in their sacrifice but "what are of this colour. Nay, so extremely curious are they in "this respect, that if there be so much as one black or white hair "in the beast, 'tis sufficient to render it improper for this service. "For 'tis their opinion, that sacrifices ought not to be made of such "things as are in themselves agreeable and well-pleasing to the "Gods, but, on the contrary, rather of such creatures wherein the "souls of wicked and unjust men have been confined during the "course of their transmigration. Hence sprang that custom, "which was formerly observed by them, of pronouncing a solemn "curse upon the head of the beast which was to be offered in "sacrifice, and afterwards of cutting it off and throwing it into the "Nile, though now they dispose of it to foreigners. No bullock "therefore is permitted to be offered to the Gods, which has not "the seal of the Sphragistae first stamped upon it, an order of "priests peculiarly set apart for this purpose, from whence likewise "they derive their name. Their impress, according to Castor, is "'a man upon his knees with his hands tied behind him and a "sword pointed at his throat.' Nor is it from his colour only that "they maintain a resemblance between the Ass and Typho, but "from the stupidity likewise and sensuality of his disposition; and "agreeably to this notion, having a more particular hatred to "Ochus than to any other of the Persian monarchs who reigned "over them, looking upon him as an exsecrable and abominable "wretch, they gave him the nick-name of the Ass, which drew the "following reply from that prince, 'But this ass shall dine upon "your ox,' and accordingly he slew the Apis: this story is thus "related by Dino. Now as to those who pretend that Typho "escaped out of the battle upon an Ass after a flight of seven days, "and that, after he had got into a place of security, he begat two "sons, Hierosolymus and Judaeus, 'tis obvious from the very face "of the relation, that their design is to give an air of fable to "[what] the Jewish history [relates] of the flight of Moses out of "Egypt, and of the settlement of the Jews about Hierusalem and "Judaea" (Squire's Translation).

As a proof of the correctness of Plutarch's statements may be mentioned the figure of Set, which is reproduced from a Demotic papyrus at Leyden by Signor Lanzone,[1] and which represents the god as having the head of an ass; on his breast, which is that of a man, is inscribed the name **ⲤⲎⲐ**. We have now seen how the god Set was the opponent first of Ḥeru-ur, then of Rā, andfi nally of Osiris and his son Horus, and that during the long period of Egyptian history his attributes changed according to the various modifications which took place in the beliefs concerning this god in the minds of the Egyptians, and that from being a power of nature, the darkness, he became the symbol and personification of both physical and moral evil. We have now to consider briefly the female counterpart of Set, that is to say the goddess Nephthys, and to describe the part which she played in the Great Company of the gods of Heliopolis.

NEBT-ḤET 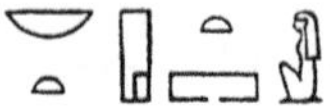, or 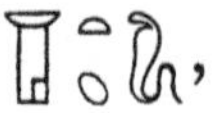, NEPHTHYS.

NEBT-ḤET, or Nephthys, was the daughter of Seb and Nut, and the sister of Osiris, and Isis, and Set, and the wife of Set, and the mother of Ȧnpu, or Anubis, either by Osiris or Set. The name "Nebt-ḥet" means the "lady of the house," but by the word "house" we must understand that portion of the sky which was supposed to form the abode of the Sun-god Horus; in fact "ḥet" in the name of Nebt-ḥet is used in exactly the same sense as "ḥet" in the name "Ḥet-Ḥert," or Hathor, i.e., the "house of Horus." In the earliest times Nephthys was regarded as the female counterpart of Set, and she was always associated with him; nevertheless

[1] *Dizionario*, pl. 378.

THE GODDESS NEBT-ḤET (NEPHTHYS).

she always appears as the faithful sister and friend of Isis, and helps the widowed goddess to collect the scattered limbs of Osiris and to reconstitute his body. In the Pyramid Texts she appears as a friend of the deceased, and she maintains that character throughout every Recension of the *Book of the Dead;* indeed, she seems to perform for him what as a nature goddess she did for the gods in primeval times when she fashioned the "body" of the "Company of the Gods," and when she obtained the name NEBKHAT, ,[1] i.e., "Lady of the body [of the Gods]." The goddess is represented in the form of a woman who wears upon her head a pair of horns and a disk which is surmounted by the symbol of her name, , or the symbol only; and her commonest titles are, "dweller within Senu," "lady of heaven," "mistress of the gods," "great goddess, lady of life," "sister of the god, eye of Rā, lady of heaven, mistress of the gods," "lady of heaven, mistress of the two lands," "sister of the god, the creative goddess who liveth within Ȧn," etc. The chief centres of her worship were Senu , Ḥebet, (Behbit), Per-mert, , Re-nefert, , Ḥet-sekhem, Ḥet-Khas, Ta-keḥset, and Diospolites.

In the vignettes of the Theban Recension of the *Book of the Dead* we find Nephthys playing a prominent part in connexion with Isis, whose efforts it seems to be her duty to second and to forward. She stands in the shrine behind Osiris when the hearts of the dead are weighed in the Great Scales in the presence of the god; she is seen kneeling on , by the side of the Ṭeṭ, from which the disk of the Sun is thrust upwards by the "living Rā," , at sunrise; she is one of the "great sovereign chiefs in Ṭeṭṭu," with Osiris, Isis, and Ḥeru-netch-ḥrȧ-f; and she kneels at the head of the bier of Osiris and assists him to arise. In the address which she makes (Chap. cli.A), she says, "I go round about behind "Osiris. I have come that I may protect thee, and my strength "which protecteth shall be behind thee for ever and ever. The god "Rā hearkeneth unto thy cry; thou, O son of Hathor, art made to

[1] See *Aeg. Zeitschrift*, 1864, p. 65.

"triumph, thy head shall never bc taken away from thee, and "thou shalt be made to rise up in peace." Like Isis, Nephthys was believed to possess magical powers, and URT-ḤEKAU, , i.e., "mighty one of words of power," was as much a title of the goddess as of her husband, SET-NUBTI, the great one of two-fold strength, . Nephthys also, like Isis, has many forms, for she is one of the two Maāt goddesses, and she is one of the two Mert goddesses, and she is one of the two plumes which ornamented the head of her father Rā. In her birth-place[1] in Upper Egypt, i.e., Ḥet-Sekhem, or "the house of the Sistrum," the goddess was identified with Hathor, the lady of the sistrum, but the popular name of the city, "ḤET," i.e., the "House," seems to apply to both goddesses. In the Serapeum which belonged to the city, or the House of the Bennu, Osiris was re-born under the form of Horus, and Nephthys was one of his "nursing mothers." The form in which Osiris appeared here was the Moon, and as such he represented the left eye of the Bennu or Rā, and as he thus became closely associated with Khensu and Thoth, to his female counterparts were ascribed the attributes of SESHETA and Maāt, who were the female counterparts of Thoth. Nephthys, as the active creative power which protected Osiris, the Moon-god, was called MENKHET, , and in allusion to her beneficent acts in connection with him the names of BENRA-MERIT and KHERSEKET were bestowed upon her, and the former appears to belong to the goddess when she made herself manifest under the form of a cat.

From Plutarch's treatise on Isis and Osiris we may gather many curious facts about the Egyptian beliefs concerning Nephthys. Thus he tells us (§ 38) that the Egyptians call the "extreme limits of their country, their confines and sea-shores, "Nephthys (and sometimes Teleute, a name expressly signifying "the *end of anything*), whom they suppose likewise to be married "to Typho. Now as the overflowings of the Nile are sometimes "very great, and extend even to the remotest boundaries of the "land, this gave occasion to that part of the story, which regards

[1] Nephthys was born on the last of the five epagomenal days.

"the secret commerce between Osiris and Nephthys; and as the "natural consequence of so great an inundation would be perceived "by the springing up of plants in those parts of the country, which "were formerly barren, hence they supposed, that Typho was first "made acquainted with the injury which had been done his bed by "means of a Mellilot-garland which fell from the head of Osiris "during his commerce with his wife, and afterwards left behind "him; and thus, they say, may the legitimacy of Orus the son of "Isis be accounted for, as likewise the spuriousness of Anubis, "who was born of Nephthys. So again, when they tell us, that "it appears from the tables of the successions of their ancient "kings, that Nephthys was married to Typho, and that she was at "first barren, if this indeed is to be understood, not as spoken of a "mortal woman, but of a goddess, then is there design to insinuate "the utter infertility of the extreme parts of their land, occasioned "by the hardness of the soil and its solidity." Plutarch tells us, moreover, that "on the upper part of the convex surface of the "sistrum is carved the effigies of a Cat with a human visage, as on "the lower edge of it, under those moving chords, is engraved on "the one side the face of Isis, and on the other that of Nephthys." The face of Isis represents Generation, and that of Nephthys Corruption, and Plutarch says (§ 63) that the Cat denotes the moon, "its variety of colours, its activity in the night, and "the peculiar circumstances which attend its fecundity making "it a proper emblem of that body. For it is reported of "this creature, that it at first brings forth one, then two, after-"wards three, and so goes on adding one to each former birth till "it comes to seven; so that she brings forth twenty-eight in all, "corresponding as it were to the several degrees of light, which "appear during one of the moon's revolutions. But though this "perhaps may appear to carry the air of fiction with it, yet may "it be depended upon that the pupills of her eyes seem to fill up "and to grow larger upon the full of the moon, and to decrease "again and diminish in their brightness upon its waining—as to "the human countenance with which this Cat is carved, this is "designed to denote that the changes of the moon are regulated "by understanding and wisdom."

From the above paragraphs it is clear that Nephthys is the personification of darkness and of all that belongs to it, and that her attributes were rather of a passive than active character. She was the opposite of Isis in every respect; Isis symbolized birth, growth, development and vigour, but Nephthys was the type of death, decay, diminution and immobility. Isis and Nephthys were, however, associated inseparably with each other, even as were Horus and Set, and in all the important matters which concern the welfare of the deceased they acted together, and they appear together in bas-reliefs and vignettes. Isis, according to Plutarch (§ 44), represented the part of the world which is visible, whilst Nephthys represents that which is invisible, and we may even regard Isis as the day and Nephthys as the night. Isis and Nephthys represent respectively the things which are and the things which are yet to come into being, the beginning and the end, birth and death, and life and death.[1] We have, unfortunately, no means of knowing what the primitive conception of the attributes of Nephthys was, but it is most improbable that it included any of the views on the subject which were current in Plutarch's time. Nephthys is not a goddess with well-defined characteristics, but she may, generally speaking, be described as the goddess of the death which is not eternal. In the *Book of the Dead* (Chap. xvii. 30), the deceased is made to say, "I am the god Åmsu (or, Min) in his coming "forth; may his two plumes be set upon my head for me." In answer to the question, "Who then is this?" the text goes on to say, "Åmsu is Horus, the avenger of his father, and his coming "forth is his birth. The plumes upon his head are Isis and "Nephthys when they go forth to set themselves there, even as his "protectors, and they provide that which his head lacketh, or (as "others say), they are the two exceeding great uraei which are "upon the head of their father Tem, or (as others say), his two "eyes are the two plumes which are upon his head."

This passage proves that Nephthys, although a goddess of death, was associated with the coming into existence of the life which springs from death, and that she was, like Isis, a female counterpart of Åmsu, the ithyphallic god, who was at once the type

[1] *Religion*, p. 735.

of virility, and reproduction, and regeneration. Isis and Nephthys prepared the funeral bed for their brother Osiris, and together they made the swathings wherewith his body was swathed after death; they assisted at the rising of the Sun-god when he rose upon this earth for the first time, they assisted at the resurrection of Osiris, and similarly, in all ages, they together aided the deceased to rise to the new life by means of the words which they chanted over his bier. In late dynastic times there grew up a class of literature which is now represented by such works as the "Book of Respirations," the "Lamentations of Isis and Nephthys," the "Festival Songs of Isis and Nephthys," the "Litanies of Seker," etc., works which supply us with the very words which were addressed to Osiris and to all those who were his followers. The goddesses were personified by two priestesses who were virgins and who were ceremonially pure; the hair of their limbs was to be shaved off, they were to wear ram's wool garlands upon their heads, and to hold tambourines in their hands; on the arm of one of them was to be a fillet inscribed "TO Isis," and on the arm of the other was to be a fillet inscribed "TO Nephthys." On five days during the month of December these women took their places in the temple of Abydos and, assisted by the KHER ḤEB, or precentor, they sang a series of groups of verses to the god, of which the following are specimens:—

"Hail, lord Osiris. Hail, lord Osiris. Hail, lord Osiris. Hail, "lord Osiris. Hail, beautiful boy, come to thy temple straight-"way, for we see thee not. Hail, beautiful boy, come to thy "temple, and draw nigh after thy departure from us. Hail, "beautiful boy, who leadest along the hour, who increasest except "at his season. Thou art the exalted image of thy father Tenen, "thou art the hidden essence who comest forth from Ȧtmu. O "thou lord, O thou lord, how much greater art thou than thy "father, O thou eldest son of thy mother's womb. Come thou "back again to us with that which belongeth unto thee, and we "will embrace thee; depart not thou from us, O thou beautiful "and greatly loved face, thou image of Tenen, thou virile one, "thou lord of love. Come thou in peace, and let us see thee, O "our lord, and the two sisters will join thy limbs together, and "thou shalt feel no pain, and they shall put an end unto all that "hath afflicted thee, even as if it had never been . . . . . . Hail, "Prince, who comest forth from the womb. Hail, Eldest son of "primeval matter. Hail, Lord of multitudes of aspects and created "forms. Hail, Circle of gold in the temples. Hail, Lord of time, "and Bestower of years. Hail, Lord of life for all eternity. Hail, "Lord of millions and myriads. Hail, thou who shinest both in "rising and setting. Hail, thou who makest throats to be in good "case. Hail, thou Lord of terror, thou mighty one of trembling. "Hail, lord of multitudes of aspects, both male and female. Hail, "thou who art crowned with the White Crown, thou lord of the "Urerer Crown. Hail, thou holy Babe of Ḥeru-ḥekennu. Hail, "thou son of Rā, who sittest in the Boat of Millions of Years. "Hail, thou Guide of rest, come thou to thy hidden places. Hail, "thou lord of fear, who art self-produced. Hail, thou whose "heart is still, come to thy city. Hail, thou who causest cries "of joy, come to thy city. Hail, thou beloved one of the gods "and goddesses. Hail, thou who dippest thyself [in Nu], come to "thy temple. Hail, thou who art in the Ṭuat, come thou to thy "offerings. . . . Hail, thou holy flower of the Great House. Hail, "thou who bringest the holy cordage of the Sekti Boat. Hail, "thou Lord of the Ḥennu Boat, who renewest thy youth in the "secret place. Hail, thou Perfect Soul in Neter-khert. Hail, "thou holy Judge (?) of the South and of the North. Hail, thou "hidden one, who art known to mankind. Hail, thou who dost "shine upon him that is in the Ṭuat and dost show him the "Disk. Hail, lord of the Atef Crown, thou mighty one in Suten-"ḥenen. Hail, mighty one of terror. Hail, thou who risest in "Thebes, who dost flourish for ever. . . . Hail, thou living Soul "of Osiris, who art diademed with the moon. Hail, thou who "hidest thy body in the great coffin at Heliopolis."

CHAPTER XV

ÀNPU , OR ANUBIS

IT has been said above that Nephthys gave birth to a son called ÀNPU, or Anubis, and that his father was, according to some, Osiris, and according to others, Set; from another point of view he was the son of Rā. The animal which was at once the type and symbol of the god was the jackal, and this fact seems to prove that in primitive times Anubis was merely the jackal god, and that he was associated with the dead because the jackal was generally seen prowling about the tombs. His worship is very ancient, and there is no doubt that even in the earliest times his cult was general in Egypt; it is probable that it is older than that of Osiris. In the text of Unȧs (line 70) he is associated with the Eye of Horus, and his duty as the guide of the dead in the Underworld on their way to Osiris was well defined, even at the remote period when this composition was written, for we read, "Unas standeth with the Spirits, get thee onwards, Anubis, into "Àmenti (the Underworld), onwards, onwards to Osiris." In the lines that follow we see that Anubis is mentioned in connexion with Horus, Set, Thoth, Sep, and Khent-ȧn-maati. From another passage of the same text we find (line 207 ff.) that the hand, and arms, and belly, and legs of the deceased are identified with Temu, but his face is said to be in the form of that of Anubis, . The localities in which Anubis was specially worshipped are Ābt, the Papyrus Swamps, 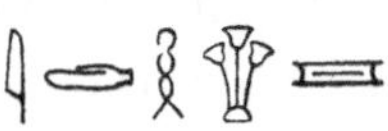, Sep, , Re-āu, 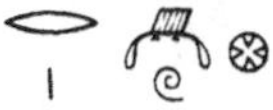, Ḥeru-ṭi, 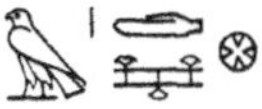, Ta-ḥetchet, , Saiut,

 (Lycopolis), Sekhem,  (Letopolis),[1] etc. In the Theban Recension of the *Book of the Dead* he plays some very prominent parts, the most important of all being those which are connected with the judgment and the embalming of the deceased. Tradition declared that Anubis embalmed the body of Osiris, and that he swathed it in the linen swathings which were woven by Isis and Nephthys for their brother; and it was believed that his work was so thoroughly well performed under the direction of Horus and Isis and Nephthys, that it resisted the influences of time and decay. In the vignette of the Funeral Procession the mummy is received by Anubis, who stands by the side of the tomb door; and in the vignette to Chapter cli. of the *Book of the Dead* the god is seen standing by the side of the mummy as it lies on its bier, and he lays his protecting hands upon it. In the speech which is put into the mouth of Anubis, he says, "I have come to protect Osiris." In the text of Unȧs (line 219) the nose of the deceased is identified with the nose of Anubis, but in the xliind Chapter of the *Book of the Dead* the deceased declares, "My lips are the lips of Ȧnpu." From various passages it is clear that in one part of Egypt at least Anubis was the great god of the Underworld, and his rank and importance seem to have been as great as those of Osiris. (See Chapter liii.)

In the Judgment Scene Anubis appears to act for Osiris, with whom he is intimately connected, for it is he whose duty it is to examine the tongue of the Great Balance, and to take care that the beam is exactly horizontal. Thoth acts on behalf of the Great Company of the gods, and Anubis not only produces the heart of the deceased for judgment, but also takes care that the body which has been committed to his charge shall not be handed over to the "Eater of the Dead" by accident. The vignette of the xxvith Chapter of the *Book of the Dead*, as given in the Papyrus of Ani, represents the deceased in the act of receiving a necklace and pectoral from Anubis, who stands by grasping his sceptre; in the vignette of the Chapter in the Papyrus of Nebseni Anubis is seen presenting the heart itself to the deceased, and in the text below

[1] Lanzone, op. cit., p. 68.

This illustration is reproduced in full color on the insert attached to the inside back cover of this volume.

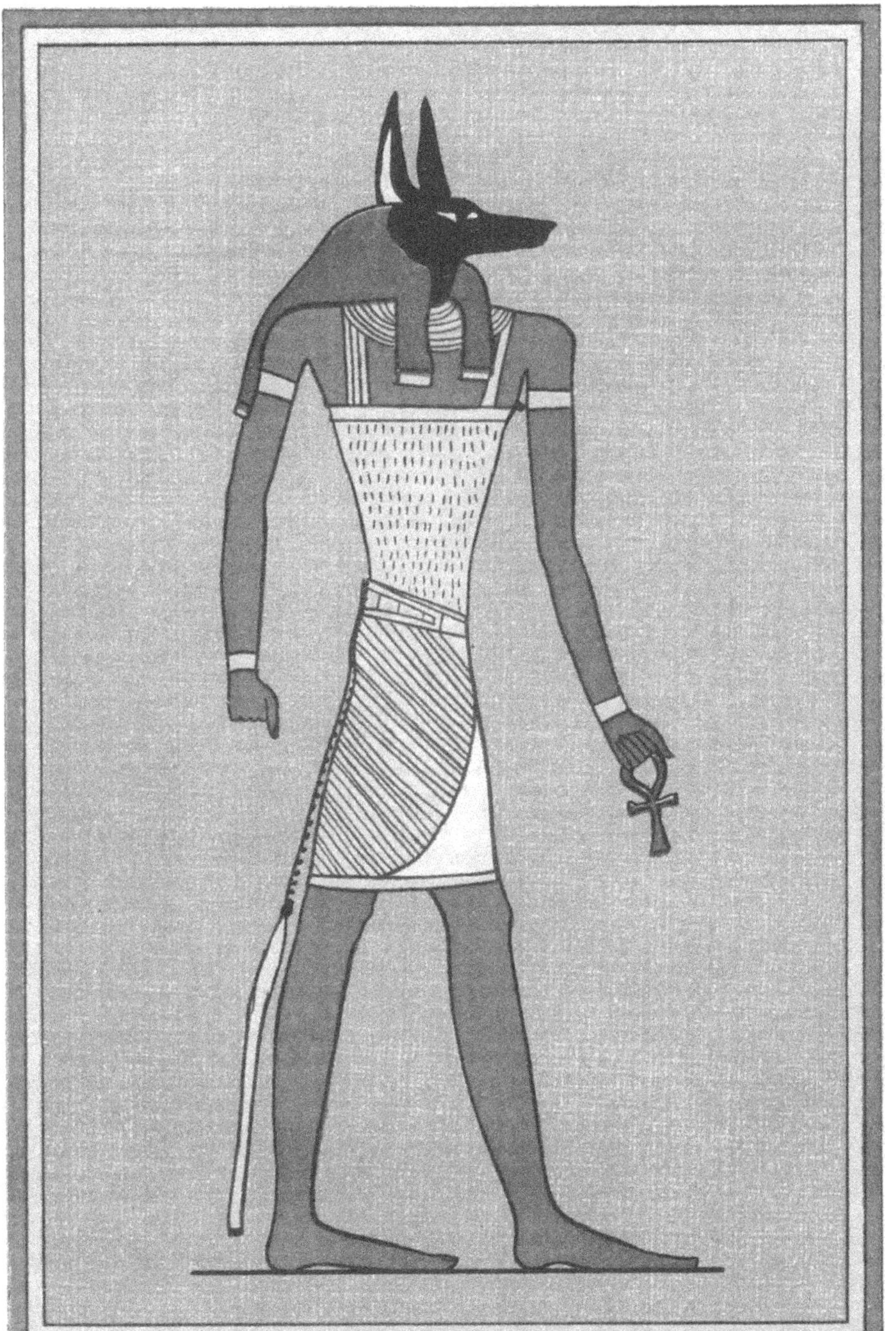

ANUBIS, THE GOD OF THE DEAD.

The Deceased holding a Necklace and Pectoral before Anubis.

Nebseni prays, saying, "May Anubis make my thighs firm so that "I may stand upon them." In allusion to his connexion with the embalmment of Osiris the god Anubis is called Ȧm Ut, , i.e., "Dweller in the chamber of embalmment;" as the watcher in the place of purification wherein rested the chest containing the remains of Osiris he was called Khent Seḥet, , i.e., "Governor of the Hall of the God;" and one of his names as the god of the funeral mountain was "Ṭep-ṭu-f," , i.e., "he who is upon his hill." In the cxlvth Chapter of the *Book of the Dead* the deceased says, "I have washed myself "in the water wherein the god Ȧnpu washed when he had "performed the office of embalmer and bandager;" and elsewhere the deceased is told (clxx. 4) that "Ȧnpu, who is upon his hill, "hath set thee in order, and he hath fastened for thee thy "swathings, thy throat is the throat of Anubis (clxxii. 22), and "thy face is like that of Anubis" (clxxxi. 9).

The duty of guiding the souls of the dead round about the Underworld and into the kingdom of Osiris was shared by Anubis with another god whose type and symbol was a jackal, and whose name was Ȧp-uat, , or , i.e., the "Opener of the ways;" formerly Anubis and Ȧp-uat were considered to be two names of one and the same god, but there is no longer any reason for holding this view. In the vignette to the cxxxviiith Chapter of the *Book of the Dead* we find represented the scene of setting up the standard which supports the box that held the head of Osiris at Abydos. On each side of it are a standard with a figure of a jackal upon it and a pylon, on the top of which lies a jackal; and as it is quite clear from the groups of objects on each side of the standard that we are dealing with symbols either of the South and the North, or of the East and the West, we are justified in thinking that one jackal represents Ȧp-uat and the other Anubis. Moreover, from the cxlvth Chapter we find that the xxist Pylon of the House of Osiris was presided over by seven gods, among whom were Ȧp-uat and Ȧnpu,[1] and as in the xviiith

[1] The others were Tcher or Āṭ, Ḥetep-mes, Mes-sep, Utch-re, and Beq.

Chapter (F., G.) we have both gods mentioned, and each is depicted in the form of a jackal-headed man, we may conclude that each was a distinct god of the dead, although their identities are sometimes confused in the texts. The function of each god was to "open the ways," and therefore each might be called ȦP-UAT, but, strictly speaking, Anubis was the opener of the roads of the North, and Ȧp-uat the opener of the roads of the South; in fact, Anubis was the personification of the Summer Solstice, and Ȧp-uat of the Winter Solstice.

Anubis is called in the texts SEKHEM EM PET, and is often said to be the son of Osiris, and Ȧp-uat bore the title SEKHEM TAUI, and was a form of Osiris himself. When, therefore, we find the two jackals upon sepulchral stelae, we must understand that they appear there in their character of openers of the ways of the deceased in the kingdom of Osiris, and that they assure to the deceased the services of guides in the northern and southern parts of heaven; when they appear with the two Utchats thus, 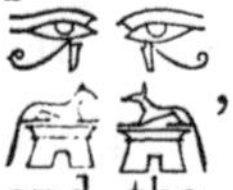, they symbolize the four quarters of heaven and of earth, and the four seasons of the year. On the subject of Anubis Plutarch reports (§§ 44, 61) some interesting beliefs. After referring to the view that Anubis was born of Nephthys, although Isis was his reputed mother, he goes on to say, "By Anubis they "understand the horizontal circle, which divides the invisible part "of the world, which they call Nephthys, from the visible, to which "they give the name of Isis; and as this circle equally touches "upon the confines of both light and darkness, it may be looked "upon as common to them both—and from this circumstance arose "that resemblance, which they imagine between Anubis and the Dog, "it being observed of this animal, that he is equally watchful as "well by day as night. In short, the Egyptian Anubis seems to "be of much the same power and nature as the Grecian Hecate, a "deity common both to the celestial and infernal regions. Others "again are of opinion that by Anubis is meant Time, and that his "denomination of *Kuon* does not so much allude to any likeness, "which he has to the dog, though this be the general rendering of "the word, as to that other signification of the term taken from "*breeding;* because Time begets all things out of it self, bearing "them within itself, as it were in a womb. But this is one of those "secret doctrines which are more fully made known to those who "are initiated into the worship of Anubis. Thus much, however, "is certain, that in ancient times the Egyptians paid the greatest "reverence and honour to the Dog, though by reason of his devour- "ing the Apis after Cambyses had slain him and thrown him out, "when no other animal would taste or so much as come near him, "he then lost the first rank among the sacred animals which he had "hitherto possessed." Referring to Osiris as the "common Reason "which pervades both the superior and inferior regions of the "universe," he says that it is, moreover, called "Anubis, and "sometimes likewise Hermanubis (i.e., , Ḥeru- "em-Ànpu); the first of these names expressing the relation it has "to the superior, as the latter, to the inferior world. And for "this reason it is, they sacrifice to him two Cocks, the one white, "as a proper emblem of the purity and brightness of things above, "the other of a saffron colour, expressive of that mixture and "variety which is to be found in those lower regions."

Strictly speaking, Anubis should be reckoned as the last member of the Great Company of the gods of Heliopolis, but as a matter of fact his place is usually taken by Horus, the son of Isis and of Osiris, who generally completes the divine *paut*; it is probable that the fusion of Horus with Anubis was a political expedient on the part of the priesthood who, finding no room in their system for the old god of the dead, identified him with a form of Horus, just as they had done with his father Set, and then mingled the attributes of the two gods. Horus and Anubis thus became in the new theology a duplicate of the Horus and Set in the old, and the double god possessed two distinct and opposite aspects; as the guide of heaven and the leader of souls to Osiris he was a beneficent god, but as the personification of death and decay he was a being who inspired terror. From an interesting passage in the "Golden Ass" of Apuleius (Book xi.) we find that the double character of Anubis was maintained by his votaries in Rome even in the second century of our era, and in describing the

Procession of Isis he says, "Immediately after these came the "Deities, condescending to walk upon human feet, the foremost "among them rearing terrifically on high his dog's head and "neck—that messenger between heaven and hell displaying "alternately a face black as night, and golden as the day; in his "left the caduceus, in his right waving aloft the green palm "branch. His steps were closely followed by a cow, raised into "an upright posture—the cow being the fruitful emblem of the "Universal Parent, the goddess herself, which one of the happy "train carried with majestic steps, supported on his shoulders. "By another was borne the coffin containing the sacred things, "and closely concealing the deep secrets of the holy religion."

This extract shows that even in the second century at Rome the principal actors in the old Egyptian Osiris ceremonial were represented with scrupulous care, and that its chief characteristics were preserved. The cow was, of course, nothing less than the symbol of Isis, "the mother of the god," and the coffin containing the "sacred things" was the symbol of the sarcophagus of Osiris which contained his relics. Before these fitly marched Anubis in his two-fold character, and thus we have types of Osiris and his mysteries, and of Isis who revivified him, and of Anubis who embalmed him. Had Apuleius understood the old Egyptian ceremonies connected with the Osiris legend and had he been able to identify all the characters who passed before him in the Isis procession, he would probably have seen that Nephthys and Horus and several other gods of the funeral company of Osiris were duly represented therein. On the alleged connexion of Anubis with Christ in the Gnostic system the reader is referred to the interesting work of Mr. C. W. King, *Gnostics and their Remains*, Second Edition, London, 1887, pp. 230, 279.

CHAPTER XVI

CIPPI OF HORUS

IN connexion with the god Horus and his forms as the god of the rising sun and the symbol and personification of Light must be mentioned a comparatively numerous class of small rounded stelae on convex bases, on the front of which are sculptured in relief figures of the god Horus standing upon two crocodiles. These curious and interesting objects are made of basalt and other kinds of hard stone, and of calcareous stone, and they vary in height from 3 ins. to 20 ins.; they were used as talismans by the Egyptians, who placed them in their houses and gardens, and even buried them in the ground to protect themselves and their property from the attacks of noxious beasts, and reptiles, and insects of every kind. In addition to the figures of Horus and of the animals over which he gained the victory, and the sceptres, emblems, etc., which are sculptured upon cippi of Horus, the backs, sides, and bases are usually covered with magical texts. The ideas suggested by the figures and the texts are extremely old, but the grouping and arrangement of them which are found on the stelae under consideration are not older than the XXVIth Dynasty; it is doubtful if this class of objects came into general use very much earlier than the end of the period of the Persian occupation of Egypt. The various museums of Europe contain several examples of cippi, but the largest, and finest, and most important, is undoubtedly that which is commonly known as the "Metternich Stele;"[1] it was found in the year 1828 during the building of a cistern in a Franciscan monastery in Alexandria, and was presented by Muḥammad 'Ali Pâsha to Prince Metternich. We are, fortunately, enabled to date the stele, for the name of Nectanebus I.,

[1] See *Metternichstele,* ed. Golénischeff, Leipzig, 1877, pl. 3, l. 48 ff.

Side of the Stele.

the last but one of the native kings of Egypt, who reigned from B.C. 378 to B.C. 360, occurs on it, and it is clear from several considerations that such a monument could have been produced only about this period. On the front of the stele (see page 271) we have the following figures and scenes:—

1. The solar disk wherein is seated the four-fold god Khnemu, who represents the gods of the four elements, earth, air, fire, and water, resting between , which is supported on a lake of water; on each side of it stand four apes, with their paws stretched out in adoration. No names are given to the apes here, but we may find them in a text at Edfû[1] where they are called:—1. Aāān, . 2. Bentet, . 3. Hetet-Sept, . 4. Qefṭen, . 5. Åp, . 6. Åsṭen, . 7. Keḥkeḥ, . 8. Uṭennu, . The Bentet apes praised the morning sun, and the Uṭennu apes praised the evening sun, and the Sun-god was pleased both with their words and with their voices. On the right hand side is a figure of king Nectanebus kneeling before a lotus standard, with plumes and *menàts*, and on the left is the figure of

[1] Duemichen, *Tempelinschriften*, i., 26.

the god Thoth holding a palette in his left hand.

2. In this register we have (*a*) Ptaḥ-Seker-Åsår standing on crocodiles, the gods Åmsu and Kheperå standing on  pedestals, Khas, a lion-headed god, Thoth, Serqet and Hathor grouped round a god who is provided with the heads of seven birds and animals, and four wings, and two horns surmounted by four uraei and four knives, and who stands upon two crocodiles. (*b*) Ta-urt holding a crocodile by a chain or rope which a hawk-headed god is about to spear in the presence of Isis, Nephthys, and four other deities, etc.

3. Isis holding Horus in her outstretched right hand, and standing on a crocodile. Thoth. Standard of Nekhebet. Horus, with a human phallus, and a lion, on a lake (?) containing two crocodiles. Seven halls or lakes, each guarded by a god. A lion treading on a crocodile, which lies on its back, four gods, a lion standing on the back of a crocodile, a vulture, a god embracing a goddess, and three goddesses.

4. Horus spearing a crocodile which is led captive by Ta-urt. The four children of Horus. Neith and the two crocodile gods. Harpocrates seated upon a crocodile under a serpent. A lion, two scorpions and an oryx, symbols of Set. Seven

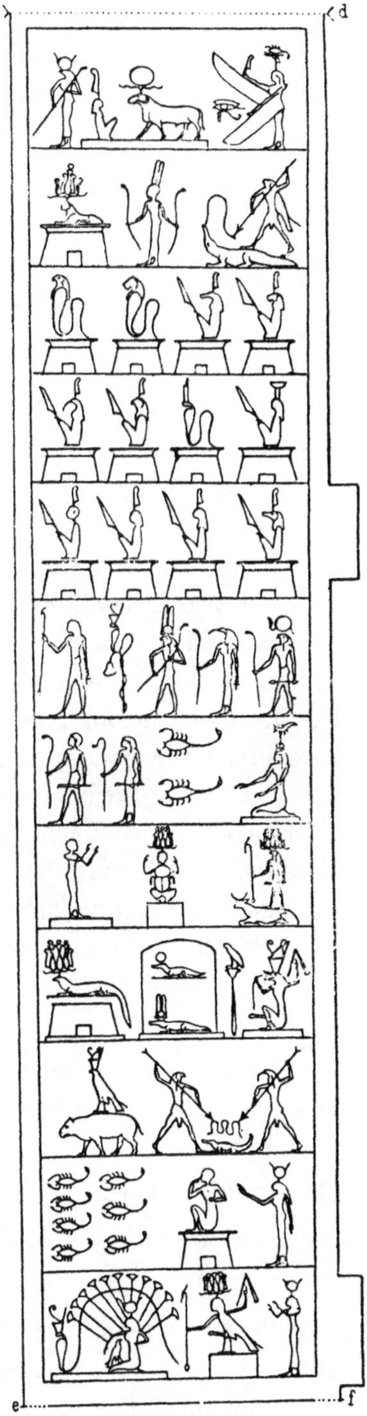

Side of the Stele.

serpents having their tails pierced by arrows or darts. A king in a chariot drawn by the fabulous AKHEKH animal which gallops over two crocodiles. Horus standing on the back of the oryx, emblem of Set.

5. A miscellaneous group of gods, nearly all of whom are forms of the Sun-god and are gods of reproduction and regeneration.

6. A hawk god, with dwarf's legs, and holding bows and arrows. Horus standing on an oryx (Set). A cat on a pedestal. Ån-ḥer spearing an animal. Uraeus on the top of a staircase. The ape of Thoth on a pylon. Two Utchats, the solar disk, and a crocodile. Ptaḥ-Seker-Åsår. The Horus of gold. Serpent with a disk on his head. A group of solar gods followed by Ta-urt and Bes.

7. In this large scene Horus stands with his feet upon the backs of two crocodiles, and he grasps in his hands the reptiles and animals which are the emblems of the foes of light and of the powers of evil. He wears the lock of youth, and above his head is the head of the old god Bes, who here symbolizes the Sun-god at eventide. The canopy under which he stands is held up by Thoth and Isis, each of whom stands upon a coiled up serpent, which has a knife stuck in his forehead. Above the canopy are the two Utchats, with human hands and arms attached, and within it by the sides of the god are:—1. Horus-Rā standing on a coiled up serpent. 2. A lotus standard, with plumes and *menàts*. 3. A papyrus standard surmounted by a figure of a hawk wearing the  Crown.

On the back of the Stele we have a figure of the aged Sun-god in the form of a man-hawk, and he has above his head the heads of a number of animals, e.g., the oryx and the crocodile, and a pair of horns upon which rest , and eight knives. He has four human arms, to two of which wings are attached, and in each hand he grasps two serpents, , two knives, , and "life," , "stability," , and "power," ; and numbers of figures of gods. His two other human arms are not attached to wings, and in one hand he holds the symbol of "life," and in the other a sceptre.

From the head of the god proceed jets of fire, , and on each side of him is an Utchat, which is provided with human hands and

The Metternich Stele (Obverse).

arms. The god stands upon an oval, within which are figures of a lion, two serpents, a jackal, a crocodile, a scorpion, a hippopotamus, and a turtle. Below this relief are five rows of figures of gods and mythological scenes, many of which are taken from the vignettes of the *Book of the Dead.* The gods and goddesses are for the most part solar deities who were believed to be occupied at all times in overcoming the powers of darkness, and they were sculptured on the Stele that the sight of them might terrify the fiends and prevent them from coming nigh unto the place where it was set up. There is not a god of any importance whose figure is not on it, and there is not a demon, or evil animal, or reptile who is not depicted upon it in a vanquished state.

The texts inscribed upon the Stele are as interesting as the figures of the gods, and relate to events which were believed to have taken place in the lives of Isis, Horus, etc. The first composition is called the "Chapter of the incantation of the Cat,"[1] and contains an address to Rā, who is besought to come to his daughter, for she has been bitten by a scorpion; the second composition, which is called simply "another Chapter," has contents somewhat similar to those of the first. The third text is addressed to the "Old Man who becometh young in his season, the Aged One who "maketh himself a child again." The fourth and following texts contain a narrative of the troubles of Isis which were caused by the malice of Set, and of her wanderings from city to city in the Delta, in the neighbourhood of the Papyrus Swamps. The principal incident is the death of her son Horus, which took place whilst she was absent in a neighbouring city, and was caused by the bite of a scorpion; in spite of all the care which Isis took in hiding her son, a scorpion managed to make its way into the presence of the boy, and it stung him until he died. When Isis came back and found her child's dead body she was distraught and frantic with grief, and was inconsolable until Nephthys came and advised her to appeal to Thoth, the lord of words of power. She did so straightway, and Thoth stopped the Boat of Millions of Years in which Rā, the Sun-god, sailed, and came down to earth in answer to her cry; Thoth had already provided her with the words of power which enabled her to raise up Osiris from the dead, and

1 

he now bestowed upon her the means of restoring Horus to life, by supplying her with a series of incantations of irresistible might.

The Metternich Stele (Reverse).

These Isis recited with due care, and in the proper tone of voice, and the poison was made to go forth from the body of Horus, and his strength was renewed, his heart once more occupied its throne, and all was well with him. Heaven and earth rejoiced at the sight of the restoration of the heir of Osiris, and the gods were filled with peace and content.

The whole Stele on which these texts and figures are found is nothing but a talisman, or a gigantic amulet engraved with magical forms of gods and words of power, and it was, undoubtedly, placed in some conspicuous place in a courtyard or in a house to protect the building and its inmates from the attacks of hostile beings, both visible and invisible, and its power was believed to be invincible. The person who had been stung or bitten by a scorpion or any noxious beast or reptile was supposed to recite the incantations which Thoth had given to Isis, and which had produced such excellent results, and the Egyptians believed that because these words had on one occasion restored the dead to life, they would, whensoever they were uttered in a suitable tone of voice, and with appropriate gestures and ceremonies, never fail to produce a like effect. A knowledge of the gods and of the magical texts on the Stele was thought to make its possessor master of all the powers of heaven, and of earth, and of the Underworld.

CHAPTER XVIII

FOREIGN GODS

IF we consider for a moment it will at once be apparent from the geographical position of Egypt that her people must have been brought in contact with a large number of foreign gods, and that in certain places a few must have become more or less identified with Egytian gods of similar attributes and characteristics. As a rule Orientals have always been exceedingly tolerant of alien gods, and the Egyptians formed no exception to the rule; there is, moreover, in the Egyptian inscriptions, no evidence that they ever tried to suppress the gods of the races they conquered, though we may assume that they never failed, whenever it was possible, to carry off the images of foreign gods, because in so doing they displayed the superior power of the gods of Egypt, and destroyed the religious and political importance of the cities and towns wherein the shrines of the foreign gods were situated. It is not at present possible to decide which gods were indigenous to the Valley of the Nile, and which were of Libyan origin, but there is no doubt that a number of Libyan gods were adopted by the dwellers in the Western Delta, in predynastic times, and that they had become to all intents and purposes Egyptian gods under the rule of the kings of the Ist Dynasty. Among such deities may be mentioned Net, or Neith, of Saïs, Bast of Bubastis, and it is very probable that Osiris and his cycle of gods, though perhaps under different names, were also of Libyan origin. Under the IVth and Vth Dynasties the cult of Rā, the Sun-god, spread with great rapidity in the Delta and in the neighbourhood of Heliopolis, and his priests, as we have seen, obtained almost kingly influence in the country. There is no reason for doubting that the Sun was worshipped in the earliest times in Egypt, but the form of his worship, as approved and promulgated by the priests of Heliopolis, appears to have differed from that which was current in other parts of the country, and it is probable that it possessed something of an Asiatic character. The foreign gods who succeeded in

The goddess Qeṭesh standing on a lion between Min and Reshpu.

obtaining a place in the affections of the Egyptians were of Libyan and Semitic origin, and there is no evidence that they borrowed any deity, except Bes, from Nubia, or the country still further to the south of Egypt.

First among the foreign deities who are made known to us

by the Egyptian inscriptions is ĀNTHȦT,[1] a goddess who is called the lady of heaven, and the mistress of the gods, and who was said to conceive offspring but not to bring them to the birth; she is declared to have been produced by Set, but it is probable that this origin was assigned to her only after her cult was well established in Egypt. She is depicted in the form of a woman seated on a throne or standing upright; in the former position she grasps a shield and spear in her right hand and wields

Ānthȧt.

a club in her left, and in the latter she wears a panther skin and holds a papyrus sceptre in the right hand and the emblem of "life" in her left. She wears the White Crown with feathers attached, and sometimes this has a pair of horns at the base. Ānthȧt was, undoubtedly, a war goddess, and her cult seems to have extended throughout Northern and Southern Syria, where certain cities and

[1] Variant forms of her name are Ānnuthȧt, , and Āntit, .

towns, e.g., Bath-Ānth, , and Qarth-Anthu, , were dedicated to her worship.[1] The worship of the goddess Ānthȧt appears to have made its way into Egypt soon after the Egyptians began to form their Asiatic Empire, and from an inscription published by Virey[2] we learn that a shrine was built in her honour at Thebes in the reign of Thothmes III. This, however, is only what might be expected, for Thothmes III. must have brought large numbers of Syrians with him into Egypt, and many of them undoubtedly found a home at Thebes. The goddess was honoured by Rameses II. of the XIXth Dynasty, and this monarch went so far as to call one of his daughters Banth-Ānth, , i.e., daughter of Ānth. Finally we may note in passing that a goddess called Ānthrethȧ, , is mentioned with Sutekh in the great treaty between the Kheta and the Egyptians, and it is probable that she and Ānthȧt are one and the same goddess.

In connexion with Ānthȧt the goddess Āsthȧrthet, , i.e., 'Ashtoreth, is sometimes mentioned in Egyptian texts, and she is called "mistress of horses, lady of the chariot, dweller in Apollinopolis Magna" (Edfû), .[3] Conformably to this description the goddess is represented in the form of a woman with the head of a lioness, which is surmounted by a disk, and she stands in a chariot drawn by four horses and drives over her prostrate foes. The cult of Āsthȧrthet was comparatively widespread in Egypt at the time when the priest-kings began to reign, and it flourished in the Delta, at least, until Christian times. It cannot, however, have been introduced into Egypt much earlier than the beginning of the XVIIIth Dynasty, and it was probably not well established until the reign of Ȧmen-ḥetep III. In a letter from

[1] See Müller, W. M., *Asien und Europa*, p. 195.

[2] *Tombeau de Khem* (*Mémoires Miss. Arch. Fr.*, tom. v., p. 368).

[3] See *Aeg. Zeitschrift*, 1869, p. 3 ff.; Naville, *Mythe d'Horus*, pl. 4.

Tushratta, king of Mitani, to this king he refers to the going down of "Ishtar of Nineveh (i.e., Ashtoreth, or Āsthårthet), lady of the world," into Egypt, both during his own reign and that of his father,[1] and he seems to indicate that her worship in Egypt had declined, and begs Åmen-ḥetep to make it to increase tenfold. From this it would appear that the Egyptians adopted the worship of the Syrian goddess at or about the time when Thothmes III. was engaged in conquering Ruthennu and Palestine and Syria. In Egypt Āsthårthet, or Ashtoreth, or Ishtar, was identified with one of the forms of Hathor, or Isis-Hathor, early in the XVIIIth Dynasty, and she was regarded both as a Moon-goddess, and as a terrible and destroying goddess of war. As a war-goddess she was the driver of the rampant war-maddened horses and the guide of the rushing chariot on the field of battle, and this consideration shows that as a goddess of horses she was unknown in Egypt before the XVIIIth Dynasty. The Egyptians learned to employ the horse in war from the Semites of the Eastern Desert, and their knowledge of the value of that animal for charging and for drawing war-chariots is not older than about B.C. 1800.

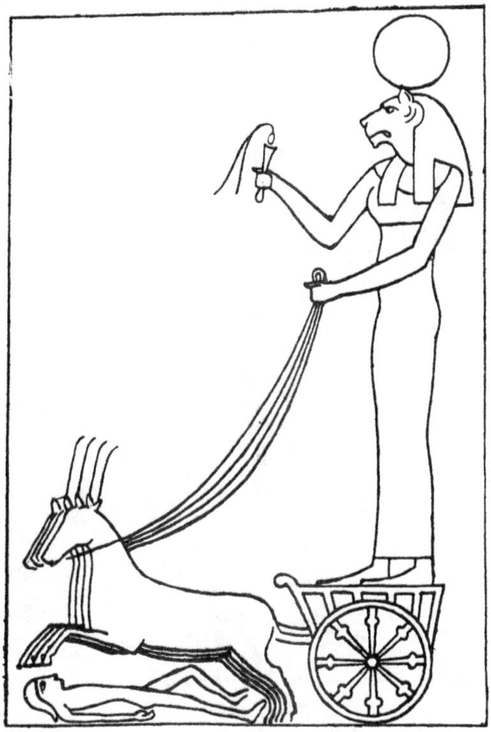

'Ashtoreth.

Closely akin to Āsthårthet was the goddess QEṬESH, ,[2] who was also called the "mistress of all the gods, the eye of Rā,

[1] *The Tell el-Amarna Tablets in the British Museum*, p. xlii.

[2] Variant, , QEṬSHU.

without a second,"
She, like Åsthårthet, was regarded in Egypt as a form of Hathor, the goddess of love and beauty, and as a Moon-goddess. She is represented in the form of an absolutely naked woman, who stands upon a lion; on her head she wears a crescent and disk, which prove her connexion with the Moon. The later representations of Qeṭesh depict her in the same attitude, but they give her the peculiar headdress of Hathor, and she wears a deep necklace or collar and a tight-fitting garment which is held up on her shoulders by two straps, and which extends to her ankles. In her right hand she holds lotus flowers and a mirror (?), and in her left two serpents. It is important to note that, like Bes, she is always represented full face. On a stele in the British Museum (No. 191), we see the goddess, who is here called "KENT ( ), lady of heaven," standing on a lion between Åmsu, , or Min, and Reshpu, and with these gods she appears to form a Semitic triad, but it is not clear which of these two gods was her son, and which was her husband. In any case, Qeṭesh must have been worshipped as a nature goddess, and it was probably the licentiousness of her worship, at all events in Syria, which gave to the Hebrew word קְדֵשָׁה the meaning which it bears in the Bible.[1]

Qeṭesh.

Another foreign goddess of interest is ĀĀSITH, , who is represented in the form of a woman, armed with shield and club, riding a horse into the battle field. In her Müller[2] sees a

[1] Gen. xxxviii. 21, 22; Deut. xxiii. 18; Numbers xxv. 1; Hosea iv. 14.

[2] *Asien und Europa*, p. 316.

female form of the hunter Esau, עֵשָׂו, who, under the form Usoos, was regarded as a god who wore skins and was appeased by means of blood offerings. That she was a goddess of war and of the desert is clear from a relief, which is found on a stele near the building beside the temple set up by Seti I. at Redêsîyeh in the Eastern Desert, on the road to the gold mines of Mount Zâbărâ.

The greatest of all the Syrian gods known to the Egyptians was Bār, , or Pa-Bār, 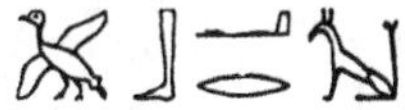, i.e., Baal, the הַבַּעַל, of the Hebrews. Bār appears to have been a god of the mountain and the desert, and his worship was introduced into Egypt under the XVIIIth Dynasty. Like most of the Semitic gods and goddesses he was primarily a god of war and battle, and he may have been a personification of the burning and destroying heat of the sun and blazing desert wind. To the Egyptians of the Delta he soon became familiar, and as he was supposed to be the god who supported their foes the Syrians in many a hard-fought battle they regarded him with a certain awe and reverence. Of his form and worship we know nothing, but the Egyptians placed after their transliterations of his name a figure of the fabulous animal in which the god Set became incarnate, and it is clear that they must have believed Bār and Set to have qualities and attributes in common. Rameses II. boasts in his triumphal inscriptions that when he put on his panoply of war, and mounted his chariot, and set out to attack the Kheta soldiery he was like the god Bār, and we are justified in assuming from this and similar passages that the king of Egypt was proud to compare himself to the mighty Syrian war-god. Bār was worshipped in the Delta, chiefly in the neighbourhood of Tanis, where Rameses II. carried out such extensive building operations, and where a temple of the god existed.

Here for the sake of convenience may be mentioned the goddess Bāirthȧ, 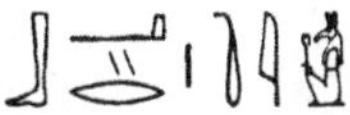, i.e., Ba'alath, or Bêltis, of Tchapuna, , in full Bāirthȧ Tchapuna or Ba'alath-Sĕphôn, who may be regarded as the female counterpart of the Ba'al-Sĕphôn of the Hebrew Scriptures, but not as the wife of Bār.

The city here referred to is on the borders of Egypt (see Exodus xiv. 2). Another city or district of the same name was situated in "Northern Phoenicia,"[1] and is mentioned in an inscription of Tiglath-Pileser II. under the form Ba-'-li Ṣa-pu-na. In a fragmentary inscription of Esarhaddon (Kuyunjik fragment, No. 3500, col. iv., line 10) the god Ba'al-Sĕphôn is mentioned, together with other Phoenician gods, in a series of curses, and these are invoked to bring down upon the ships an evil wind which shall destroy both them and their rigging.

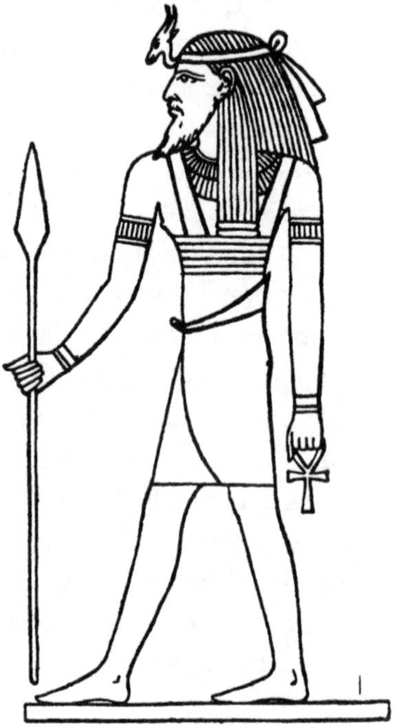

Reshpu.

In this fragment allusion is also made to Baal Sameme (בַּעַל שָׁמַיִם) and Baal Malagî, and all three are said to be the "gods across the river," *ilâni ebir nâri.*[2]

On the stele in the British Museum, No. 191, as has already been said, we meet with another Syrian god called RESHPU; his cult enjoyed a wide popularity in Syria, where he was regarded as a god of war. Signor Lanzone compares him to the Apollo Amyclaeus of the Greeks.[3] In the Egyptian texts he is described as the "great god, the lord of eternity, "the prince of everlastingness, the "lord of two-fold strength among "the company of the gods; great god, lord of heaven, governor of "the gods. The chief centre of his wor-

[1] Müller, *Asien und Europa*, p. 315.

[2] I owe this reference to Mr. R. C. Thompson of the British Museum.

[3] *Dizionario*, p. 483.

ship was at Ḥet-Reshp, 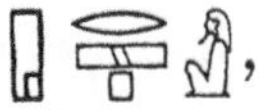, in the Delta, but it is very probable that he was specially worshipped at many small provincial shrines on the eastern frontier of Egypt. He is represented in the form of a warrior who holds a shield and spear in his left hand, and a club in his right; on his head he wears the White Crown, round the base of which is bound a turban. Above his forehead, projecting from his turban, is the head of a gazelle, which appears to be a very ancient symbol of the god, and to indicate his sovereignty over the desert. Reshpu is connected with the god who was known to the Phoenicians under the name of רֶשֶׁף, and was, no doubt, a god of burning and destructive fire, and of the lightning. Opinions differ as to the pronunciation of the name רֶשֶׁף, some reading "Reshef," i.e., "lightning," and others "Rashshâf," i.e., "he who shoots out fire and lightning"; the Egyptian transcription Reshpu supports the first opinion, and from every point of view it seems to be the correct one.

The existence of yet another Syrian god has been pointed out by Müller,[1] who in the Egyptian Åtumā, , or Åthumā, , sees the equivalent of the אֱדֹם of the Hebrew Scriptures; the female counterpart of the god appears under the form of Åtumā, . Finally, among the Western Syrians Müller has quoted the existence of two goddesses called Ennukaru, , and Åmāit, .

In the list of the gods whose names are found at the end of the copy of the treaty which Rameses II. made with Kheta-sar, the prince of the Kheta, are found a number of Sutekh, , gods of various cities, among them being Sutekh of Årenna, Sutekh of Thapu-Årenuta, Sutekh of Paireqa, Sutekh of Khisasapa, Sutekh of Saresu, Sutekh of Khirepu (Aleppo), Sutekh of Rekhasua, and Sutekh of Mukhipaina. In the paragraphs on the god Set it has been shown that for all practical purposes Sutekh and Set were one and the same god in the eyes of the Egyptians, and the fabulous Set animal was as much a symbol of Sutekh as he was of

[1] *Asien und Europa*, p. 316.

Set. Sutekh was supposed to be, more or less, a god of evil, but the Egyptians attempted to obtain his favour, even as they did that of Set, by means of offerings and prayers.

Among the foreign gods known to the Egyptians is usually mentioned Bes, , who according to some is of Semitic, and according to others of African origin;[1] we may note, however, that the name of the god appears to be Egyptian, and it seems to have been bestowed upon him in very early times because of the animal's skin which he wore; the animal itself was called "Besa" or "Basu."[2] He is usually depicted in the form of a dwarf with a huge bearded head, protruding tongue, flat nose, shaggy eyebrows and hair, large projecting ears, long but thick arms, and bowed legs; round his body he wears the skin of an animal of the panther tribe, and its tail hangs down and usually touches the ground behind him; on his head he wears a tiara of feathers, which suggests a savage or semi-savage origin. He is sometimes drawn in profile, like the other Egyptian gods, but usually he appears full face, like the goddess Qeṭesh. As a god of music and the dance he is sometimes represented playing upon a harp;[3] as a god of war and slaughter, and as a destroying force of nature he carries two knives in his hands; as a warrior he appears in a short military tunic, which is fastened round his body by a belt, and he

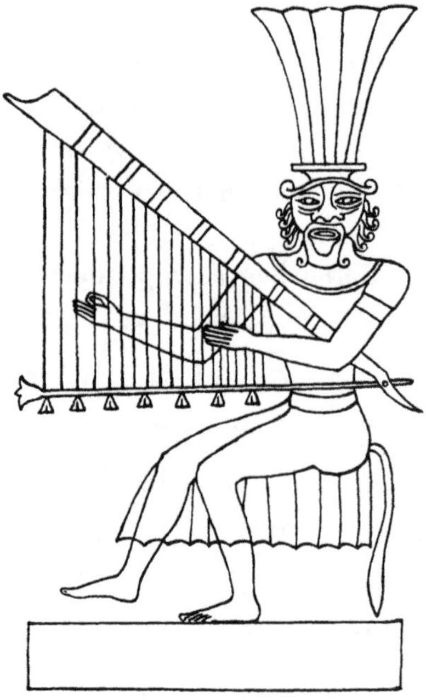

Bes.

[1] Müller, *Asien und Europa*, p. 310; Wiedemann, *Religion of the Ancient Egyptians*, p. 159.

[2] , Bes, , Basu = Felis Cynailurus; see *Aeg. Zeit.* ii. 10.

[3] Lanzone, *Dizionario*, pll. 76, 77.

holds in his left hand a shield and a short sword in his right. Figures of Bes are found carved upon the handles of mirrors, on *kohl* vessels, and on pillows, all of which indicate that in one aspect at least he was associated with rest, and joy, and pleasure. From a number of scenes on the walls of the temples and from bas-reliefs we see that Bes was supposed to be present in the chambers and places wherein children were born, and he seems to have been regarded as a protector of children and youths, and a god who studied to find them pleasure and amusement.

According to Müller,[1] two figures of the god were found at Kahûn, and, if these really belong to the period when that city was flourishing, Bes must have been honoured there as early as the XIIth Dynasty. Taken by itself, however, this evidence is not worth a great deal, because the figures may have been placed in the tombs at Kahûn during burials of a much later date. One of the oldest representations of Bes, as Prof. Wiedemann has pointed out, is found in a relief in the famous temple of Ḥātshepset at Dêr al-Baḥarî, where he appears in the chamber wherein the birth of the great queen is supposed to be taking place. In this chamber MESKHENT, the goddess of birth, presides, and we see the goddesses who act as midwives to the queen of Thothmes I., and those who are nurses, and the gods of the four quarters of the earth, etc., waiting to minister to Ḥātshepset and to her KA, or double, which was, of course, born when she was. By the side of the couch stand Bes and TA-URT, the former with his well-known attributes, and the latter represented in the form of a hippopotamus standing on her hind legs, and leaning with her fore legs upon the emblem of magical protection, . What Bes and Ta-urt were to do for the princess is not apparent, but as we find one or both of these deities

Bes.

[1] Lanzone, *Dizionario*, p. 310.

represented in the lying-in rooms of Egyptian queens, it is clear that their presence was considered to be of great importance both to mother and child. In the Heliopolitan and Theban Recensions of the *Book of the Dead* the name of Bes does not occur, but in one of the vignettes to the cxlvth Chapter (§ xxi.) of the Saïte Recension this god is seen guarding one of the pylons of the house of Osiris in the Underworld. At some period under the New Empire the original attributes of Bes were modified, and he assumed the character of a solar god and became identified with Horus the Child, or Harpocrates; little by little he was merged in other forms of the Sun-god, until at length he absorbed the characteristics of Horus, Rā, and Temu. As Horus, or Harpocrates, he wore the lock of hair, which is symbolic of youth, on the right side of his head, and as Rā-Temu he was given the withered cheeks and attributes of an old man. On the Metternich Stele we see the head of the "Old Man who renews his youth, and the Aged One "who maketh himself once again a boy," placed above that of Horus, the god of renewed life and of the rising sun, to show that the two heads represent, after all, only phases of one and the same god.

After the XXVIth Dynasty and during the Ptolemaïc period we find from certain bronze figures, numerous examples of which are found in the various Museums of Europe, that Bes was merged wholly in Horus, and that the Egyptians bestowed upon him the body and wings of a hawk united to the body of a vigorous young man, who, however, had the head of a very aged man surmounted by the group of heads with which we are familiar from the Cippi of Horus. On the Metternich Stele (see above, p. 273) we see him wearing the plumes of Shu and of the other gods of light and air, and the horns of Åmen or of the Ram of Mendes, and above these are eight knives and the emblem of million of years, and he holds in his hands all the emblems of sovereignty and dominion which Osiris holds, besides serpents, which he crushes in his grasp. He stands upon an oval wherein are grouped specimens of all the Typhonic beasts, and we may gather from his attitude that he is lord of them all. In the vignette to the xxviiith Chapter of the *Book of the Dead* a monster, who somewhat resembles Bes, is

THE GOD BES.

seen standing before the deceased, though apparently not in a threatening attitude; he holds a knife close to his breast in his right hand, and he clasps the root of his tail with his left. There is no indication in the text to show who this monster is, but it seems very probable that it is Bes. In the vignette under consideration the creature has a huge head with long and shaggy hair, but, although his body is large and his limbs massive, he is not represented as a dwarf; he has, apparently, come with his knife to cut out the heart of the deceased, and to carry it away from him. The papyrus in which it is found, viz., that of Nefer-uben-f, which is preserved in Paris, probably dates from the XVIIIth Dynasty, and if the monster be really Bes, or some such form of him as Ḥit, 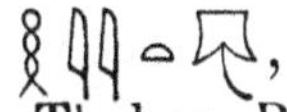, it is important to note that he had found a place in the Theban Recension of the *Book of the Dead* at that early period of its history.

It is difficult to understand the change of view on the part of the Egyptians which turned the god of mirth, and laughter, and pleasure into an avenging deity, but it may be explained by assuming that he only exhibited his terror and ferocity to the wicked, while to the good in the Underworld he was a true friend and merry companion. In the texts, especially those of the late period, Bes is sometimes mentioned in connexion with Neter Ta, or the "Divine Land," or "Land of the God," i.e., Arabia, and as this name is also used in connexion with Punt, and is applied to the adjacent lands, attempts have been made to prove that the god is of Arabian origin. This is, however, extremely improbable, for his characteristics are much more those of an African than Asiatic deity. The figure of Bes suggests that his home was a place where the dwarf and pygmy were held in esteem, whilst his head-dress resembles those head-dresses which were, and still are, worn by the tribes of Equatorial Africa, and this would lead us to place his home in that portion of it which lies a few degrees to the north of the Equator. The knowledge of the god, and perhaps figures of him, were brought from this region, which the Egyptians called the "Land of the Spirits," to Egypt in the early dynastic period, when kings of Egypt loved to keep a pygmy at their courts. The earthly kinsmen of the god who lived to the south of Egypt were, no doubt, well known even to the predynastic Egyptians, and as the dynastic Egyptians were at all times familiar with the figure of Bes those of the late period may be forgiven for connecting him with the "Land of the God," or Punt, whence, according to tradition, came the early people who invaded the Nile Valley from the east, or south-east, and settled in Egypt at no great distance from the modern city of Ḳena. Bes wears an animal's tail, which is a striking characteristic of the early men of Punt, but so does every Egyptian god, and every god, when once he had been included among the gods of Egypt, whether originally Libyan, or Syrian, or Nubian, was endowed with an animal's tail and a plaited beard, which are the traditional attributes of the people of Punt. In his original conception Bes is certainly African, and his cult in Egypt is coeval with dynastic civilization; the name of the god continued in use long after he himself was forgotten, and some famous Copts bore it, among them being Bêsa, the disciple of the great monk Shenûti, ϣⲉⲛⲟⲩϯ.

A Nubian god of interest and of some local importance is MERUL or MERIL, , or 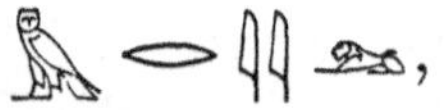, who was the son of Horus and Isis; he was the third member of the triad of the city of Termes, or Telmes, , a city the site of which is marked by the modern village of Kalâbsheh in Nubia, situated about thirty-five miles to the north of Syene. At Dabôd also he was the third member of the local triad, which consisted of Seb, Nut, and Merul. In the figures of the god reproduced by Lanzone[1] he is depicted in the form of a man, with or without a beard, and he wears the White Crown with plumes, or the triple crown with horns and uraei, or a crown composed of a pair of horns, with two plumes and a solar disk between them, and uraei. His titles are:—"Great god, governor (or dweller in) the White Mountain," 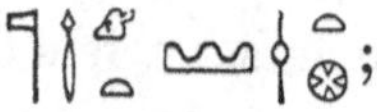; "son of Horus, great god, lord of Telmes," ; "Great Sekhem, governor of the two lands of the West," 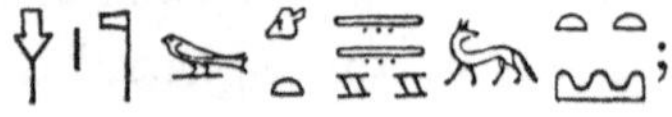; "Beautiful

[1] *Dizionario*, pll. 122, 123.

boy who proceedeth from the son of Isis," ; and "holy child of the son of Osiris," . A text quoted by Brugsch[1] speaks of Merul as coming from Ta-neter, , i.e., the land on both sides of the southern end of the Red Sea, and the coast of Africa which is further to the south. Thus it seems that Merul is not of Egyptian origin, and it is probable that the worship of the god is very ancient. The variant forms of his name are:— , or , , and , i.e., Menruil, Menlil, and Mer-uter; from the first two of these was formed the classical name of the god—Mandulis. The centres of the worship of the god were at Telmes and Philae; at the former place the temple of Merul was rebuilt by Augustus on the site of an earlier building, but the ruins of the little shrine of the god at Philae, which stood behind the colonnade of the Temple of Ȧri-ḥes-nefer, suggests that the building was the work of one of the early Ptolemies, perhaps of Philadelphus.

In connexion with the question of the cult of foreign gods in Egypt, and of the gods of Egypt in foreign lands, reference may here be made to a theory which has recently been put forward[2] to the effect that several of the gods of Egypt were worshipped as idols by the Arabs of the pre-Islamic times. According to this the Egyptian god Tem, , = the Arabic idol Tîm, تيم; Teḥuti (Thoth), , = Ṭâ'ût, طاغوت; Ȧusāās, , = Ya'ûth, يعوث; Reret, , = Lât, اللات; Uatchit, , = 'Azza, العزى; Menȧt, , = Menāt, مناة; Meṭeni, , = Medân, المدان; Ḥāp-re, , = Habal, هبل; Bes, , = Buss, بس; Bennu, , = Buwânat, بوانة; Bār, , = Ba'al, بعل; and so on. The theory is of interest, but beyond a

[1] See Brugsch, *Géographie*, p. 954.

[2] See Ahmed-Bey Kamal, *Les Idoles Arabes et les Divinités Égyptiennes* (Recueil, xxiv., p. 11 ff.).

certain similarity between the Egyptian and Arabic names little proof has been brought forward in support of it. It is, of course, quite possible that the knowledge of several of the gods and goddesses of Egypt should have found its way into Arabia in early times; indeed this is only what is to be expected. We know that already in the IIIrd Dynasty the turquoise mines of Sinai were worked for the benefit of the kings of Egypt, and that the goddess Hathor was especially worshipped in the Peninsula of Sinai long before the close of the VIth Dynasty. From Sinai the knowledge of Hathor, and Sepṭ, and of other Egyptian gods worshipped at Ṣarbût al-Khâdem and other mining centres would spread to the north and south, and it is tolerably certain that it would reach every place where the caravans carried torquoises for barter. Under the Middle and New Empires this knowledge would become very widespread, and might have reached the tribes in the extreme south of the Arabian Peninsula. On the other hand, we have no proof that the pre-Islamic Arabs adopted Egyptian gods, or that they even attempted to understand their attributes and cult. Before the theory already referred to can be accepted it must be shown that the Egyptian and Arabian gods whose names are quoted above are really identical, and that it has more to rest upon than similarities of names. The pre-Islamic gods were probably indigenous, and the pre-Islamic tribes being Semitic, their gods would be, naturally, of a character quite different from that of the gods of Egypt, and the attributes of the Semitic gods would be entirely different from those of the Egyptian gods. Whatsoever borrowing of gods took place under the early dynasties was from Egypt by Arabia and not from Arabia by Egypt, and this is true for all periods of Egyptian history, with the exception of the late Ptolemaïc period, when a few local and unimportant Arabian gods appear to have been adopted at certain places in Egypt. The pre-Islamic Arabs were worshippers of stocks and stones, and it is exceedingly doubtful if they were sufficiently developed, either mentally or spiritually, before the period of the XXVIth Dynasty to understand the gods of Egypt and their attributes, or to adopt their cult to their spiritual needs which, after all, can only have been those of nomadic desert tribes.

CHAPTER XIX

MISCELLANEOUS GODS

I.—The Gods of the Twenty-eight finger-breadths of the Royal Cubit

1. Rā, .
2. Shu, .
3. Khent, .
4. Seb, .
5. Nut, .
6. Åsår, .
7. Åst, .
8. Set, .
9. Nebt-ḥet, .
10. Ḥeru, .
11. Mest, 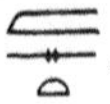.
12. Ḥāp, .
13. Ṭuamātef, .
14. Qebḥsennu-f, 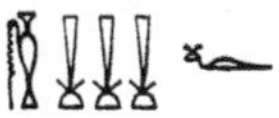.
15. Teḥuti, .
16. Sep, .
17. Ḥeq, 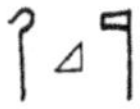.
18. Årmāua, 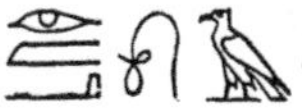.
19. Maa-en-tef, .
20. År-ren-f-tchesef, 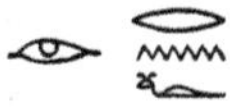
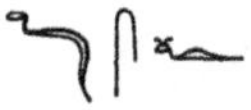
21. Ḥak (?) .
22. Sepṭu, .
23. Seb, .
24. Ån-Ḥer, .
25. Ḥer-åua, .
26. Sheps, .
27. Åmsu (or Min), .
28. Uu, .

II.—The Gods and Goddesses of the Days of the Month.

1. Ist hour of the Ist day of the Moon: Shu.
2. IInd „ „ IInd „ „ Ḥeru-sa-Ȧst.
3. IIIrd „ „ IIIrd „ „ Ȧst.
4. IVth „ „ IVth „ „ Sekhet.
5. Vth „ „ Vth „ „ Uatchit.
6. VIth „ „ VIth „ „ Menḥit.
7. VIIth „ „ VIIth „ „ Ur-ḥeket.
8. VIIIth „ „ VIIIth „ „ Āā [n].
9. IXth „ „ IXth „ „ Ȧp.
10. Xth „ „ Xth „ „ Sa.
11. XIth „ „ XIth „ „ Hetet.
12. XIIth „ „ XIIth „ „ Ba-neb-Ṭeṭṭu.

1. Ist hour of the night of the XIIIth day of the Moon: Shu.
2. IInd „ „ XIVth „ „ [Tefnut].
3. IIIrd „ „ XVth „ „ Seb (Qeb).
4. IVth „ „ XVIth „ „ Nut.
5. Vth „ „ XVIIth „ „ Ȧnpet.
6. VIth „ „ XVIIIth „ „ Khent.

III.—The Gods and Goddesses of the Months of the Year.

Month		Deity
1. ⲑⲱⲟⲩⲧ	=	Goddess Tekhi[1].

[1] Var., , Tekh-ḥeb.

Month		Deity		
2. ⲡⲁⲟⲡⲓ	= .	God	Ptaḥ-àneb-res-f[1]	.
3. ⲁⲑⲱⲣ	= .	Goddess	Ḥet-ḥert	
4. ⲭⲟⲓⲁⲕ	= .	Goddess	Sekhet[2]	.
5. ⲧⲱⲃⲓ	= .	God	Àmsu, or Min[3]	.
6. ⲙⲉⲭⲓⲣ	= .	God	Rekeḥ-ur[4]	.
7. ⲫⲁⲙⲉⲛⲱⲑ	= .	God	Rekeḥ-netches	.
8. ⲫⲁⲣⲙⲟⲩⲑⲓ	= .	Goddess	Rennutet	.
9. ⲡⲁⲭⲱⲛ	= .	God	Khensu	.
10. ⲡⲁⲱⲛⲓ	= .	God	Khenthi[5]	.
11. ⲉⲡⲏⲡ	= .	Goddess	Àpt[6]	.
12. ⲙⲉⲥⲱⲣⲏ	= .	God	Ḥeru-khuti[7]	.

IV.—The Birthdays of the Gods and Goddesses of the Five Epagomenal Days.

1. Day I. . , The Birthday of Osiris.
2. Day II. . , The Birthday of Horus.

[1] Variants, , Menkhet and , Ḥeb-Àpt.

[2] Var., , Ka-ḥer-ka-ḥeb. [3] Var., , Shef-beti.

[4] Var., , Mākhiàr.

[5] Variants, , Ḥeru-khent-khaṭith and , Ḥeb-Àntet.

[6] Variants, , Àpt-ḥent and , Ḥeb-Àpi-ḥent-s.

[7] Variants, , Àpt-Renpit and , Ḥeb-ṭep.

3. Day III. .	⊙ III,	The Birthday of Set.
4. Day IV. .	⊙ IIII,	The Birthday of Isis.
5. Day V. .	⊙ IIIII,	The Birthday of Nephthys.

V.—The Gods and Goddesses of the Hours of the Day.

1. First Hour . .	Ȧmseth . . .	
2. Second Hour .	Ḥāp	
3. Third Hour . .	Ṭua-māt-f . .	
4. Fourth Hour .	Qebḥ-sennu-f .	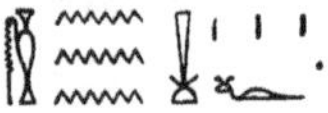
5. Fifth Hour . .	Ḥeq	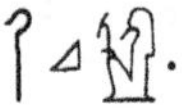
6. Sixth Hour . .	Ȧrmai . . .	
7. Seventh Hour .	Maa-tef-f . .	
8. Eighth Hour .	Ȧr-ren-f-tchesef .	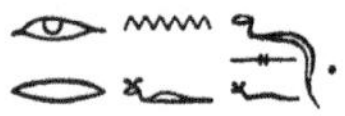
9. Ninth Hour . .	Ḥentch-ḥentch .	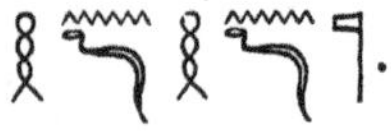
10. Tenth Hour . .	Qeṭ	
11. Eleventh Hour .	Ȧri-nef Nebȧt.[1] .	
12. Twelfth Hour .	Mātcheṭ . . .	

VI.—The Gods and Goddesses of the Hours of the Night.

The deities of the hours of the night are the same as those of the hours of the day, and their names follow each other in the order in which they occur as gods of the hours of the day.

[1] Var., An-ertā-nef-nebȧt, 

VII.—The Gods and Goddesses who watch before and behind Osiris-Serapis during the Twelve Hours of the Day and of the Night.

By Day	Before Osiris	Behind Osiris	By Night	Before Osiris	Behind Osiris
Hour 1.	Mātcheṭ	Ȧmseth	Hour 1.	Thoth and Ȧnep	Ȧmseth
„ 2.	Ȧmseth	Ḥāp	„ 2.	Ȧnep and Ȧp-uat	Ḥāp
„ 3.	Ḥāp	Ṭuamutef	„ 3.	Ḥeru and Thoth	Ṭuamutef
„ 4.	Ṭuamutef	Qebḥsennu-f	„ 4.	Ḥeru and Ȧst	Qebḥsennu-f
„ 5.	Qebḥsennu-f	Ḥeq	„ 5.	Ȧst and Nebt-ḥet	Ḥeq
„ 6.	Ḥeq	Ȧrmāiu	„ 6.	Shu and Seb	Ȧrmāiu
„ 7.	Ȧrmāiu	Maa-tef-f	„ 7.	Thoth and Ȧnep	Maa-tef-f
„ 8.	Maa-tef-f	Ȧri-ren-f-tchesef	„ 8.	Ḥeru and those in his train	Ȧr-ren-f tchesef
„ 9.	Ȧri-ren-f-tchesef	Ḥentch-ḥentch	„ 9.	. . . .	Ḥentch-ḥentch
„ 10.	Ḥentch-ḥentch	Qeṭ	„ 10.	Ḥeru and those in his train	Qeṭ
„ 11.	Qeṭ	Ȧn-ertā-nef-nebȧt	„ 11.	Neteru ent ḥa-ābt	Ȧn-erta-nef-nebȧt
„ 12.	Ȧn-ertā-nef-nebȧt		„ 12.	Ḥeru and Seb	Mātcheṭ

VIII.—The Gods of the Four Winds.

1. The North Wind was called Qebui, , or .

North Wind.

North Wind.

2. The South Wind was called SHEHBUI, , or .

South Wind.

West Wind.

3. The East Wind was called HENKHISESUI, , or .

4. The West Wind was called ḤUTCHAIUI, , or .

East Wind.

East Wind.

IX.—THE GODS OF THE SENSES.

1. SAA, , the god of the sense of Touch or Feeling and of knowledge and understanding, is depicted in the

ordinary form of a man-god, and he has upon his head the sign , which is the symbol of his name. One of the earliest mentions of this god occurs in the text of Unȧs (line 439), where it is said that the dead king has "taken possession of Ḥu and hath gained the mastery over Sȧa," . In the Theban Recension of the *Book of the Dead*, Saa, or Sȧa, appears in the Judgment Scene among the gods who watch the weighing of the heart of the deceased in the Great Balance, and he is mentioned in the xviith Chapter as one of the gods who came into being from the drops of blood which fell from Rā when he mutilated himself. From the same Chapter we learn that it was he who made the pun on the name of Rā, the Cat,

The gods of the Senses.

which he declared to be "Mȧu," , because it was "like" (*mȧu*,) that which he made. Saa with Thoth, and Sheta, and Tem formed the "souls of Khemennu" (Hermopolis),[1] and Saa had a place in the Boat of Rā (cxxxvi.B 12), with Ḥu and other gods. In Chapter clxix. (line 19), Saa is declared to protect the members of the deceased by his magical powers, , although what he was exactly supposed to do for him is unknown ; in this passage he is mentioned in connexion with the goddess Sesheta, the "lady of writing," and one of the female counterparts of Thoth. In Chapter clxxiv. (line 2), Saa is said to have been begotten by Seb, and to have been brought forth by

[1] See Chapter cxvii.

the company of the gods, and this statement supplies us with the reason why he is grouped among the gods of the cycle of Osiris. The texts make it clear that Saa was the personification of the intelligence, whether of a god or of a human being, and the deceased coveted the mastery over this god because he could give him the power to perceive, and to feel, and to understand. At the end of the clxxivth Chapter (lines 16, 17), a "Great Intelligence," , SAAU-UR, and an "Intelligence of the Åmenti of Rā," , Såa-Åmenti-Rā, are mentioned.

2. ḤU, , or , the god of the sense of TASTE is depicted in the ordinary form of a man-god, and he also has upon his head the sign , which is the symbol of his name. He is mentioned in the text of Unås with Saa, and he appears with him in the Judgment Scene, and he was present together with Åmen, Thoth, Nekhebet, Uatchet, and Saa, when Isis brought forth her son Horus in the papyrus swamps of the Delta. Like Saa, the god Ḥu came into existence from a drop of blood which fell from Rā when he mutilated himself. Ḥu was, however, not only the personification of the sense of taste in god and man, but also became the personification of the divine food upon which the gods and the beatified saints lived in heaven. Thus in the lxxxth Chapter of the *Book of the Dead* the deceased says, "I "have taken possession of Ḥu in my city, for I found him therein," and in Chapter clxix. (line 22) it is said to the deceased, "Ḥu is in thy mouth." In some passages it is difficult to decide whether the *ḥu* mentioned in the texts refers to the god of the sense of Taste, or to the divine food *ḥu*.

3. MAA, , the god of the sense of SIGHT, is depicted in the ordinary form of a man-god, who has upon his head an eye, , which is both the emblem of his chief attribute and the symbol of his name.

4. SETEM, , the god of the sense of HEARING, is depicted in the ordinary form of a man-god, who has upon his head an ear, , which is both the emblem of his chief attribute and the symbol

of his name. The gods of the Four Senses appear together in a relief which was made for Ptolemy IV. at Edfû. In this we have the Sun's disk on the horizon placed in a boat wherein are the gods Ḥeru-merti, Åp-uat, Shu, Hathor, Thoth, Neith, and Ḥeru-khent-khathet; the king stands in front of the boat and is offering Maāt, , to the god. Behind him are the gods of the senses of Taste and Touch, and behind the boat stand the gods of the senses of Sight and Hearing. An interesting variant form of the god Setem is reproduced by Signor Lanzone, from which we see that he sometimes had the head of a bull with the body of a man; the text which accompanies the figure describes the god as "the dweller in Pa-Shu" (i.e., Dendera), and calls him the "bull, lord of strength." [1]

X.—The Soul-God.

The mythological and religious texts contain indications that the Egyptians believed in what may be described as a "World-Soul," which they called Ba, ; its symbol was a bearded man-headed hawk, and it was identified with more than one god, for there was a Soul of Rā, a Soul of Shu,[2] a Soul of Seb, a Soul of Tefnut, a Soul of Osiris, and "the Soul of the Great Body which is in Saïs, [i.e.,] Neith." In the *Book of the Dead* (xvii. 109 ff.) we find that the Soul of Rā and the Soul of Osiris together form the double divine soul which inhabited the Tchafi, , who dwelt in Ṭeṭṭu. The existence of a World-Soul presupposed the existence of a World-Body, which is of course the material universe; and the type of this was, according to the priests of Heliopolis, the body of Osiris, and according to the priests of Saïs, the goddess Neith; in other cities the priests, no doubt, identified the World-Body with their local gods. Men and gods were supposed to contain the same component parts. Man possessed:—1. A physical body (, *khat*). 2. A

[1] *Dizionario*, pl. 384, No. 2.

[2] Brugsch, *Dict. Géog.*, p. 776.

soul (, or , *ba*). 3. A heart (, *åb*). 4. A double (, *ka*). 5. An intelligence (, *khu*). 6. Power (, *sekhem*). 7. A shadow (, *khaibit*). 8. A spiritual body (, *sāḥ*). 9. A name (, *ren*); and the gods possessed divine counterparts of all these. Thus Kheperå was "strong in his heart"[1] when he began to create the world, and according to one version of the Egyptian legend of Creation this god was united to his shadow. A god had only one heart and one shadow, etc., but he might possess several souls and "doubles," and we know that the souls of Rā were seven in number, and his doubles fourteen. The names of these last were:—1. ḤEQ, , "intelligence." 2. NEKHT, , "strength." 3. KHU, , "splendour." 4. USR, , "power." 5. UATCH, , "vigour." 6. TCHEFA, , "abundance." 7. SHEPS, , "wealth." 8. SENEM, , "interment." 9. SEPṬ, , "provision." 10. ṬEṬ, , "stability." 11. MAA, , "sight." 12. SETEM, , "hearing." 13. SA, , "intelligence." 14. ḤU, , "taste." Similarly the texts show that the Egyptians believed in the existence of a divine KHU, and of a divine SEKHEM, etc.

XI. GODDESSES AND GODS OF THE TWELVE HOURS OF THE NIGHT.

Goddesses.

Hour	I.	 . . .	NEBT-THEḤENT.
„	II.		SĀRSET.
„	III.	 . . .	SEḤER-ṬUT.
„	IV.	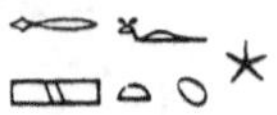	ĀA-SHEFT.

[1] 

Goddesses.

Hour	V.		NEB-ĀNKHET.
”	VI.	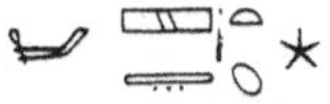	TCHESER-SHETAT.
”	VII.		ḤER-ṬEP-ĀḤA-ḤER-NEB-S.
”	VIII.		MERT.
”	IX.	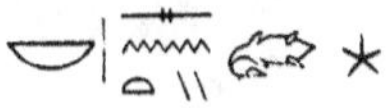	NEB-SENTI.
”	X.	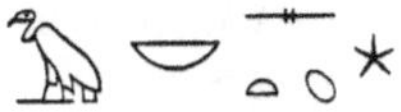	MUT-NEB-SET.
”	XI.		KHESEF-KHEMT.
”	XII.	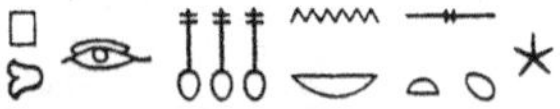	PAR-NEFERU-EN-NEB-SET.

Gods.

Hour	I.		KHEPERÀ.
”	II.	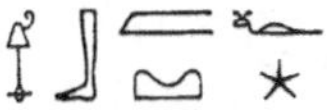	ĀB-EM-ṬU-F.
”	III.		NEB-NETERU.
”	IV.	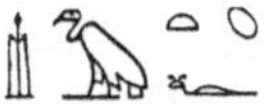	ÀN-MUT-F.
”	V.	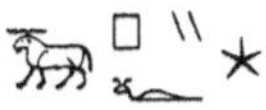	BAPI-F.
”	VI.		ḤERU-SBATI.
”	VII.	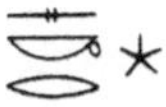	SEKER.
”	VIII.		ḤERU-ḤER-KHET.
”	IX.		MAĀ-ḤRÀ.
”	X.	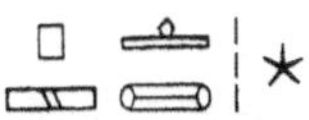	PESH-ḤETEP-F.
”	XI.	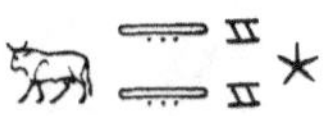	KA-TAUI.
”	XII.	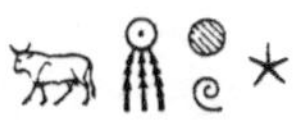	KA-KHU.

XII.—THE GODDESSES AND GODS OF THE TWELVE HOURS OF THE DAY.

Hour.	Goddesses.	Gods.
I.	. . . NUNUT.	. . . SHU.
II.	. . SEMT.	. . . ḤU.
III.	MĀK-NEBT-S.	. SAU.
IV.	. . SESHETAT.	. ÅSBET.
V.	. NESBET.	. . ÅḲERT.
VI.	. . . ĀḤĀBIT.	. . . TEḤUTI.
VII.	. NEKIU.	ḤERU-EM-ĀU-ÅB.
VIII.	. . KHEPERU.	. . KHENSU.
IX.	. TCHESER-SHETAT.	. . . ÅST.
X.	. SATI-ÅRUT.	. . ḤEQ-UR.
XI.	SENB-KHEPERU.	MAĀ-ENNU-ÅM-UÅA.
XII.	ḤAP-TCHESERTS.	ĀA-ÅM-KHEKH.

XIII.—THE PLANETS AND THEIR GODS.[1]

1. JUPITER, the "star of the South," , was called under the XIXth and XXth Dynasties ḤERU-ÅP-SHETA-TAUI, , and in the Graeco-Roman period Ḥeru-åp-sheta, , or Ḥeru-pe-sheta, . This planet was without a god.

2. SATURN, the "star of the West which traverseth heaven," , was called "ḤERU-KA-PET," , i.e.,

[1] See Brugsch, *Thesaurus*, p. 65 ff.; *Aegyptologie*, p. 336.

"Horus, Bull of heaven," under the XIXth and XXth Dynasties, and in the Graeco-Roman period ḤERU-P-KA and ḤERU-KA, , and . The god of this planet was Horus.

3. MARS, the "star of the East of heaven," , which is described as the "[star] which journeyeth backwards in travelling," , was called "ḤERU-KHUTI," , under the XIXth and XXth Dynasties, and in the Graeco-Roman period "ḤERU-ṬESHER," , i.e., "the Red Horus." The god of this planet was Rā, ☉.

Venus. Mercury. Mars. Saturn. Jupiter.

4. MERCURY was called SEBḲU, , under the XIXth and XXth Dynasties, and SEBEḲ, , or SEBEK, ,[1] in the Graeco-Roman period. The god of this planet was SET, .

5. VENUS was called the "star of the ship of the BENNU-ÁSÁR," , under the XIXth and XXth Dynasties, and "PI-NETER-ṬUAU," i.e., the "god of the morning," in the Graeco-Roman period. The god of this planet was Osiris. As an evening star Venus was called SBAT UĀTITHÁ, .

[1] Var., .

XIV.—The Dekans and their Gods.[1]

The Dekans. | Ptolemaïc Variants.[2]

1. Ṭepā-Kenmut . . 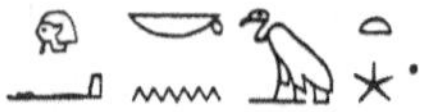 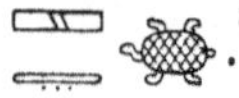[3]

1. Ṭepā-Kenmut.

2. Kenmut.

2. Kenmut . . . .  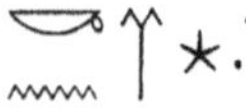[4]

3. Kher-khept-Kenmut 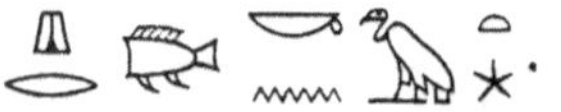 [5]

3. Kher-khept-Kenmut.

4. Ḥā-tchat.

4. Ḥā-tchat . . . 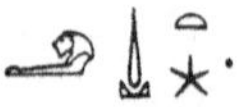 [6]

5. Peḥui-tchat . .  [7]

5. Peḥui-tchat.

6. Themat-ḥert.

6. Themat-ḥert . . 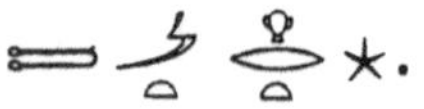 [8]

[1] See Lepsius, *Chronologie*, p. 69; Brugsch, *Thesaurus*, p. 137 ff.; *Aegyptologie*, p. 340.

[2] The Greek transcriptions are as follows:—

[3] CIT	[4] XNOYMIC	[5] XAPXNOYMIC
[6] HTHT	[7] ΦOYTHT	[8] TωM

The Dekans. | Ptolemaïc Variants.

7. THEMAT-KHERT . . 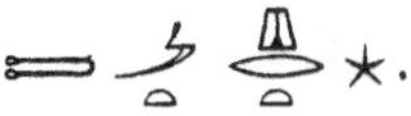 .  .[1]

7. Themat-khert.

8. Usthà.

8. USTHÀ. . . . .  . 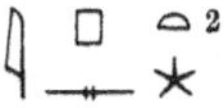 [2]

9. BEKATHÀ . . . . 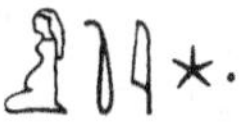 .  ,[3]

9. Bekatha.

10. Ṭepā-Khentet.

10. ṬEPĀ-KHENTET . .  .  .[4]

11. KHENTET-ḤERT . .  . 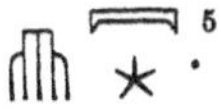 .[5]

11. Khentet-ḥert.

12. Khentet-khert.

12. KHENTET-KHERT .  .  .[6]

13. THEMES-EN-KHENTET  . 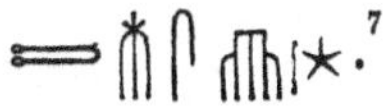 .[7]

13. Themes-en-khentet.

14. Sapt-khennu.

14. SAPT-KHENNU . .  . 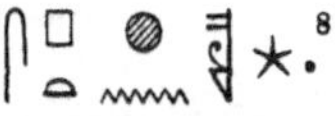 .[8]

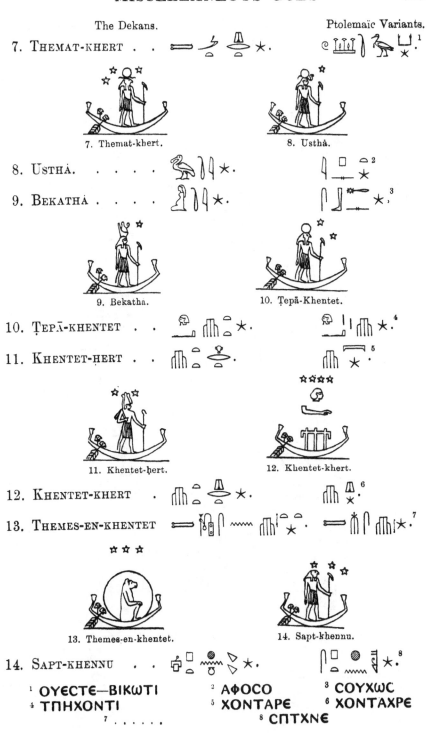

[1] ΟΥΕϹΤΕ—ΒΙΚΩΤΙ [2] ΑΦΟϹΟ [3] ϹΟΥΧΩϹ
[4] ΤΠΗΧΟΝΤΙ [5] ΧΟΝΤΑΡΕ [6] ΧΟΝΤΑΧΡΕ
[7] . . . . . . [8] ϹΠΤΧΝΕ

The Dekans. | Ptolemaïc Variants.

15. ḤER-AB-UȦA . . . 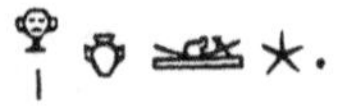 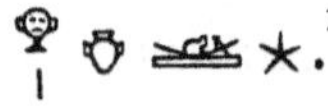 [1]

15. Ḥer-ȧb-uȧa.

16. Shesmu.

16. SHESMU . . . .   [2]

17. KENMU . . . .   [3]

17. Kenmu.

18. Semṭet.

18. SEMṬET . . . .  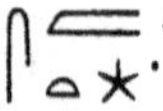 [4]

19. ṬEPĀ-SEMṬ . . .  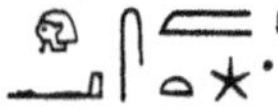 [5]

19. Ṭepā-semṭ.

20. Sert.

20. SERT . . . . .   [6]

21. SASA-SERT . . . 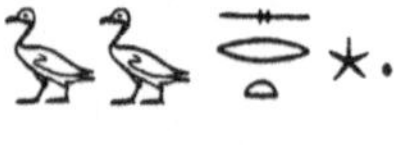 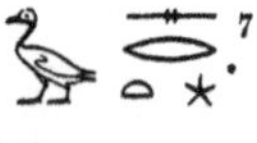 [7]

21. Sasa-Sert.

22. Kher-khept-sert.

22. KHER-KHEPT-SERT .  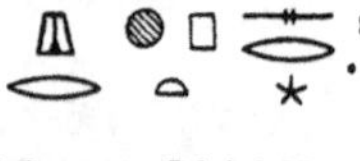 [8]

[1] ʽⲢⲎⲞⲨⲰ [2] ⲤⲈⲤⲘⲈ, ⲤⲒⲤⲈⲤⲘⲈ [3] ⲔⲞⲚⲒⲘⲈ [4] ⲤⲘⲀⲦ
[5] . . . . [6] ⲤⲢⲰ [7] ⲤⲒⲤⲢⲰ [8] . . . .

	The Dekans.	Ptolemaïc Variants.
23. Khukhu		 [1]

23. Khukhu.

24. Baba.

24. Baba		 [2]
25. Khent-ḥeru . . .		 [3]

25. Khent-ḥeru.

26. Ḥer-àb-khentu.

26. Ḥer-àb-khentu . .		 [4]
27. Khent-kheru . .		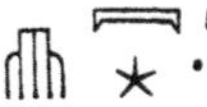 [5]

27. Khent-kheru.

28. Qeṭ.

28. Qeṭ	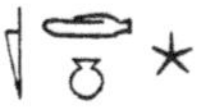	 [6]
29. Sasaqeṭ	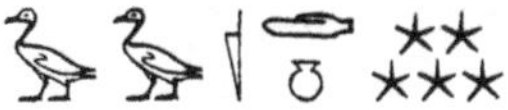	 [7]

29. Sasaqeṭ.

30. Āṛt.

30. Āṛt	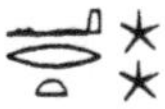	 [8]

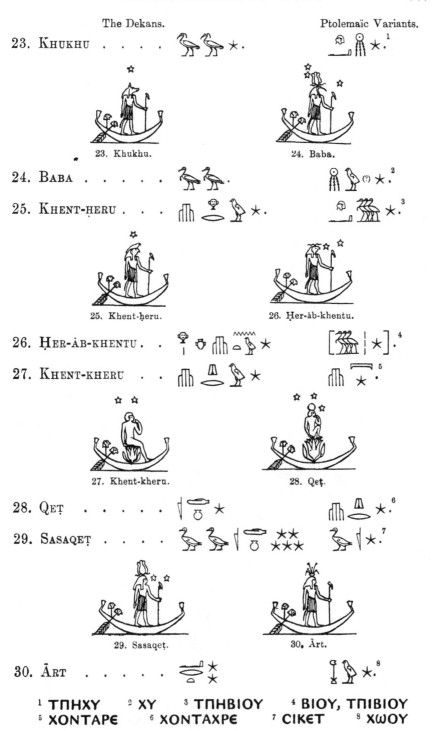

[1] ΤΠΗΧΥ [2] ΧΥ [3] ΤΠΗΒΙΟΥ [4] ΒΙΟΥ, ΤΠΙΒΙΟΥ
[5] ΧΟΝΤΑΡЄ [6] ΧΟΝΤΑΧΡЄ [7] ϹΙΚЄΤ [8] ΧωΟΥ

The Dekans.		Ptolemaïc Variants.
31. Khau		[1]

31. Khau.

32. Remen-ḥeru-an-Saḥ.

32. Remen-ḥeru-an-Saḥ		[2]
33. Mestcher-Saḥ . .		[3]

33. Mestcher-Saḥ.

34. Remen-kher-Saḥ.

34. Remen-kher-Saḥ .		[4]
35. A-Saḥ		

35. Ā-Saḥ.

36. Saḥ.

36. Saḥ . . . . . .

37. Septet . . . . [5]

37. Sepṭet.

[1] ⲈⲢⲰ, ⲀⲢⲞⲨ [2] ⲢⲈⲘⲈⲚⲀⲀⲢⲈ [3] ⲐⲞⲤⲞⲖⲔ
[4] ⲞⲨⲀⲢⲈ [5] ⲤⲰⲐⲒⲤ

The Gods of the Dekans.

1. SEB, [hieroglyphs] ★★, or ḤĀPI-ÀSMAT, [hieroglyphs], or Ḥāpi-Mesthá.

2. BA, [hieroglyphs] ★, or Isis.

3. KHENTET-KHAST, [hieroglyphs], or Isis, or the Children of Horus.

4. ÀST (Isis), [hieroglyphs], or Ṭuamutef, or the Children of Horus.

5. NEBT-ṬEP-ÀḤET, [hieroglyphs], or the Children of Horus.

6. MESTHÁ-ḤĀPI, [hieroglyphs], or Ṭuamutef.

7. QEBḤ-SENNUF, [hieroglyphs], or Ṭuamutef.

8. ṬUAMUTEF, ★ [hieroglyphs].

9. ṬUAMUTEF, QEBḤSENNUF, or Ḥāpi.

10. ṬUAMUTEF, ḤĀPI.

11. ḤERU, [hieroglyphs] ★★★.

12. SET, [hieroglyphs] ★★★.

13. ḤERU, [hieroglyphs] ★★★.

14. ÀST NEBT-ḤET, [hieroglyphs].

15. SET, [hieroglyphs], or Ur, [hieroglyphs].

16. ḤERU, [hieroglyphs], or Ur, [hieroglyphs].

17. MESTHĀ, ḤĀPI, ṬUAMUTEF, QEBḤSENNUF, [hieroglyphs] ★ [hieroglyphs] ★★★.

18. ḤERU, [hieroglyphs] ★.

19. ḤĀPI, [hieroglyphs] ([hieroglyphs] ★★★).

20. ÀST, [hieroglyphs].

21. ṬUAMUTEF, QEBḤSENNUF.

22. QEBḤSENNUF.

23. . . . .

24. Ṭuamutef, Qebḥsennuf.

25. Mesthȧ, Ḥāpi.

26. Ḥeru,

27. Ḥeru, or

28. Ḥeru,

29. . . . .[1]

30. Mesthȧ, Ḥāpi, Qebḥsennuf, Ṭuamutef, Qebḥsennuf, Ḥāpi.

31. Ḥāpi.

32. Mesthȧ.

33. Ṭuamutef, Qebḥsennuf.

34. Maat-Ḥeru, Ḥeru.

35. Maat-Ḥeru, Ḥeru.

36. Maat-Ḥeru.

37. Maat-Ḥeru Ȧst.

XV.—The Star-gods behind Sothis and Orion.

1. Shethu, or Shetu.
2. Nesru.
3. Shepet.
4. Ȧpsetch.
5. Sebshes.
6. Uash-neter.

[1] Variant for Nos. 29 and 30; variant of No. 29; variant of No. 30, Ḥāpi, Qebḥsennuf.

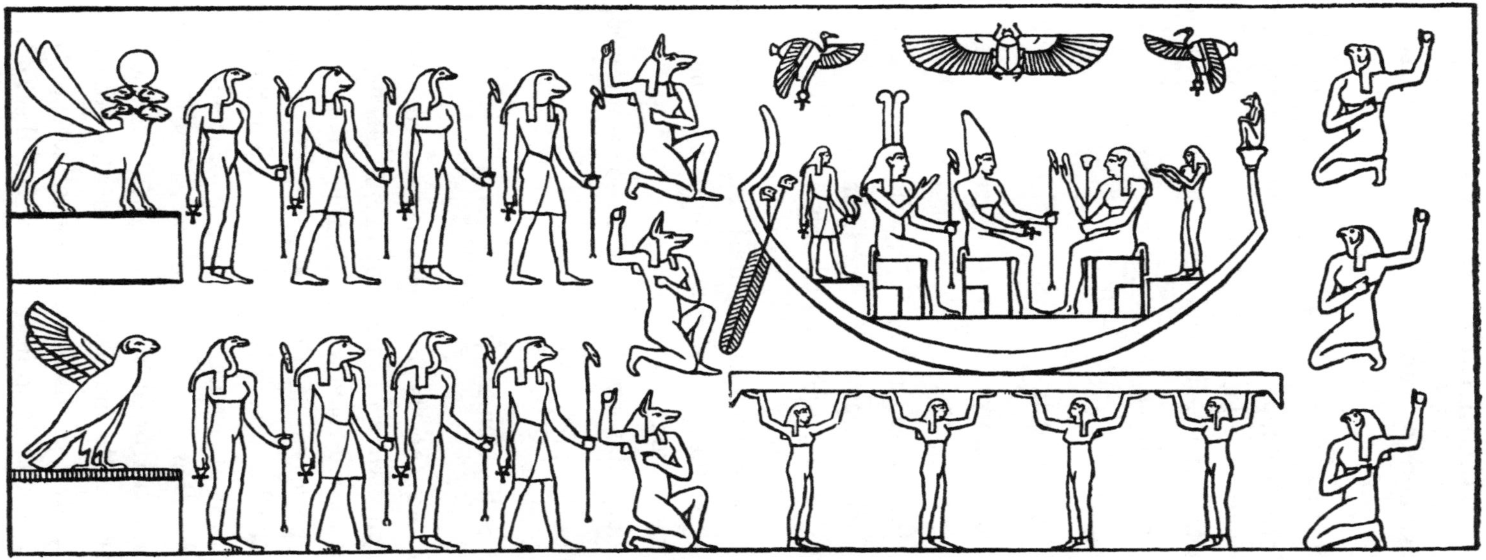

The bark of Osiris sailing over heaven, which is supported by four pillars, in the form of goddesses. On the right are three hawk-headed spirits, and on the left are:—1. Three jackal-headed spirits; 2. The eight primeval gods of Khemennu, frog-headed and snake-headed; 3. The four-headed ram of the North wind; and, 4. The Ram-headed hawk of the East wind.

XVI.—THE STAR-GODS OF THE SOUTHERN AND NORTHERN HEAVENS.

(*See p.* 313.)

1. The hippopotamus ḤESAMUT, , or RERET, , up the back of which climbs a crocodile without name; Dr. Brugsch identifies this representation with Draco. In a list of the hours the various parts of the body and members of the hippopotamus goddess are mentioned, e.g., 1. . 2. . 3. . 4. . 5. . 6. . 7. . 8. . 9. .

2. The bull MESKHETI, ; this was the Egyptian equivalent of our Great Bear.

3. Horus the Warrior ĀN, , who holds in his hand a weapon with which he is attacking the Great Bear.

4. A man standing upright and wearing a disk on his head; without name.

5. A man standing upright; he holds a spear which he is driving into a crocodile. This figure is without name.

6. A hawk; without name.

7. The goddess SERQET, , in the form of a woman.

8. The lion ȦM (?), , or , with eighteen stars.

9. The crocodile SERISA, .

XVII.—From the famous circular representation of the heavens, commonly known as the "Zodiac of Dendera," which was formerly in the second room of the Temple Roof at Dendera, but which is now preserved in the Bibliothèque Nationale at Paris, we learn that the Egyptians had a knowledge of the Twelve Signs of the Zodiac. It is wrong, however, to conclude from this, as some have done, that the Egyptians were the inventors of the Zodiac, for they borrowed their knowledge of the Signs of the Zodiac, together with much else, from the Greeks, who had derived a great deal of their astronomical lore from the Babylonians; this is certainly so in the matter of the Zodiac. It is at

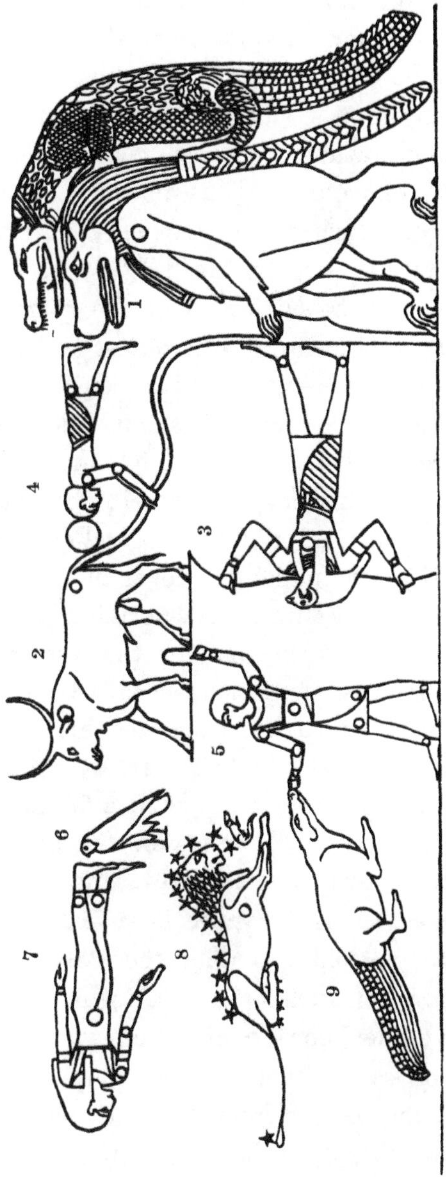

The Star-gods near the North Pole.

present a subject for conjecture at what period the Babylonians first divided the heavens into sections by means of the constellations of the Zodiac, but we are fully justified in assuming that the earliest forms of the Zodiac date from an exceedingly primitive time. The early dwellers in Babylonia who observed the heavens systematically wove stories about the constellations which they beheld, and even went so far as to introduce them into their national religious literature, for Babylonian astrology and theology are very closely connected. Thus in the Creation Legend the brood of monsters which were spawned by Tiamat and were intended by her to help her in the fight which she was about to wage against Marduk, the champion of the gods, possessed astrological as well as mythological attributes, and some of them at least are to be identified with Zodiacal constellations. This view has been long held by Assyriologists, but additional proof of its accuracy has recently been furnished by Mr. L. W. King in his "Seven Tablets of Creation,"[1] wherein he has published an interesting Babylonian text of an astrological character, from which it is clear that Tiamat, under the form of a constellation in the neighbourhood of the Ecliptic, is associated with a number of Zodiacal constellations in such a manner that they may be identified with members of her mythical monster brood. The tablet in the British Museum from which Mr. King has obtained this text is not older than the Persian period; but there is little doubt that the beliefs embodied in it were formulated at a far earlier time. That certain forms of the Creation Legends existed as early as B.C. 2300 there is satisfactory evidence to show, and the origins of the systematized Zodiac as used by the later Babylonians and by the Greeks are probably as old; whether the Babylonians were themselves the inventors of such origins, or whether they are to be attributed to the earlier, non-Semitic, Sumerian inhabitants of the country cannot be said. It is, however, quite certain that the Greeks borrowed the Zodiac from the Babylonians, and that they introduced it into Egypt, probably during the Ptolemaïc period. The following are the forms of the Signs of the Zodiac as given at Dendera.

[1] Vol. I., page 204.

1. Aries.

2. Taurus.

3. Gemini.

4. Cancer.

5. Leo.

6. Virgo.

7. Libra.

8. Scorpio.

9. Sagittarins.

10. Capricornns.

11. Aquarius.

12. Pisces.

Inasmuch as the idea of the Zodiac is Babylonian, it is well to give here a list of its Signs as they are found in late Babylonian, and their renderings in Assyrian.[1]

		BABYLONIAN	ASSYRIAN
1.	ARIES	[cuneiform] KU	[cuneiform] ILU EN-ME-SHAR-RA.
2.	TAURUS	[cuneiform] TE, or [cuneiform] TE TE	[cuneiform] KAKKABU GUD-AN-NA.
3.	GEMINI	[cuneiform] MĀSHU, or [cuneiform] MASH-MASHU	[cuneiform] ,, TUĀMU.
4.	CANCER	[cuneiform] NANGARU	[cuneiform] ,, AL-LUL.
5.	LEO	[cuneiform] A	[cuneiform] ,, UR-GU-LA.[2]
6.	VIRGO	[cuneiform], or [cuneiform] SHERU	[cuneiform] ,, AB-SIN.[3]
7.	LIBRA	[cuneiform] ṢAB, NURU(?)	[cuneiform] ,, ZI-BA-NI-TUM.
8.	SCORPIO	[cuneiform] GIR, or [cuneiform] GIR-TAB	[cuneiform] ,, GIR-TAB.
9.	SAGITTARIUS	[cuneiform] PA	[cuneiform] ,, PA-BIL-SAG.
10.	CAPRICORNUS	[cuneiform] BIR(?), LALŪ(?)	[cuneiform] ,, UZ, ENZU.
11.	AQUARIUS	[cuneiform] GU	[cuneiform] ,, GU-AN-NA.
12.	PISCES	[cuneiform] ZIB, or [cuneiform] NUNU	[cuneiform] ,, NUN-SHAME.

[1] See Strassmaier and Epping, *Astronomisches aus Babylon*, p. 7, at end; Jensen, *Kosmologie*, p. 57 ff.; R. C. Thompson, *Magicians and Astrologers*, p. xxiii. ff.

[2] Or [cuneiform] UR-MAH.

[3] Or [cuneiform] DIL-GAN.

XVIII.—In the Second Corridor of the Tomb of Seti I. are the following names of gods, with figures:[1]—1. Ṭemṭemtch, . 2. Khenti-qerer, . 3. Netch-baiu, . 4. Nef-em-baiu, . 5. Senki, . 6. Ba-Rā, . 7. Tem, . 8. Shu, . 9. Seb, . 10. Ȧst, . 11. Ḥeru, . 12. Remi, . 13. Āaṭiu, . 14. Entuti, . 15. Ȧment, . 16. Ȧakebi, . 17. Khenti-Ȧmenti, . 18. Mȧuti, . 19. Ṭebati, . 20. Shai, . 21. Ȧmen-khat, . 22. Ṭuati, . 23. Tchemtch-ḥāt, . 24. Āper (?) -ta, . 25. Thenti, . 26. Khepi, . 27. Sekheper-khati, . 28. Ȧmeni, . 29. Ȧāi, . 30. Mȧu-āa, . 31. Meṭu-khut-f, . 32. Ȧuai, . 33. Senk-ḥrȧ, . 34. Ȧntheti, . 35. Theta-enen, . 36 Besi-shemti, . 37. Semaāḥut, . 38. Kheperi, . 39. Rā-Ȧteni, . 40. Sekhem-ḥrȧ, . 41. Nȧkiu-Menȧt, . 42. Seḥetch-khatu, . 43. Kheperȧ, . 44. Nut, . 45. Tefnut, . 46. Nebt-ḥet, . 47. Nu, . 48. Ḥuaaiti, . 49. Nethert,

[1] See Lefébure, *Les Hypogées Royaux de Thèbes*, Paris, 1886, pt. i., pl. 15 ff.

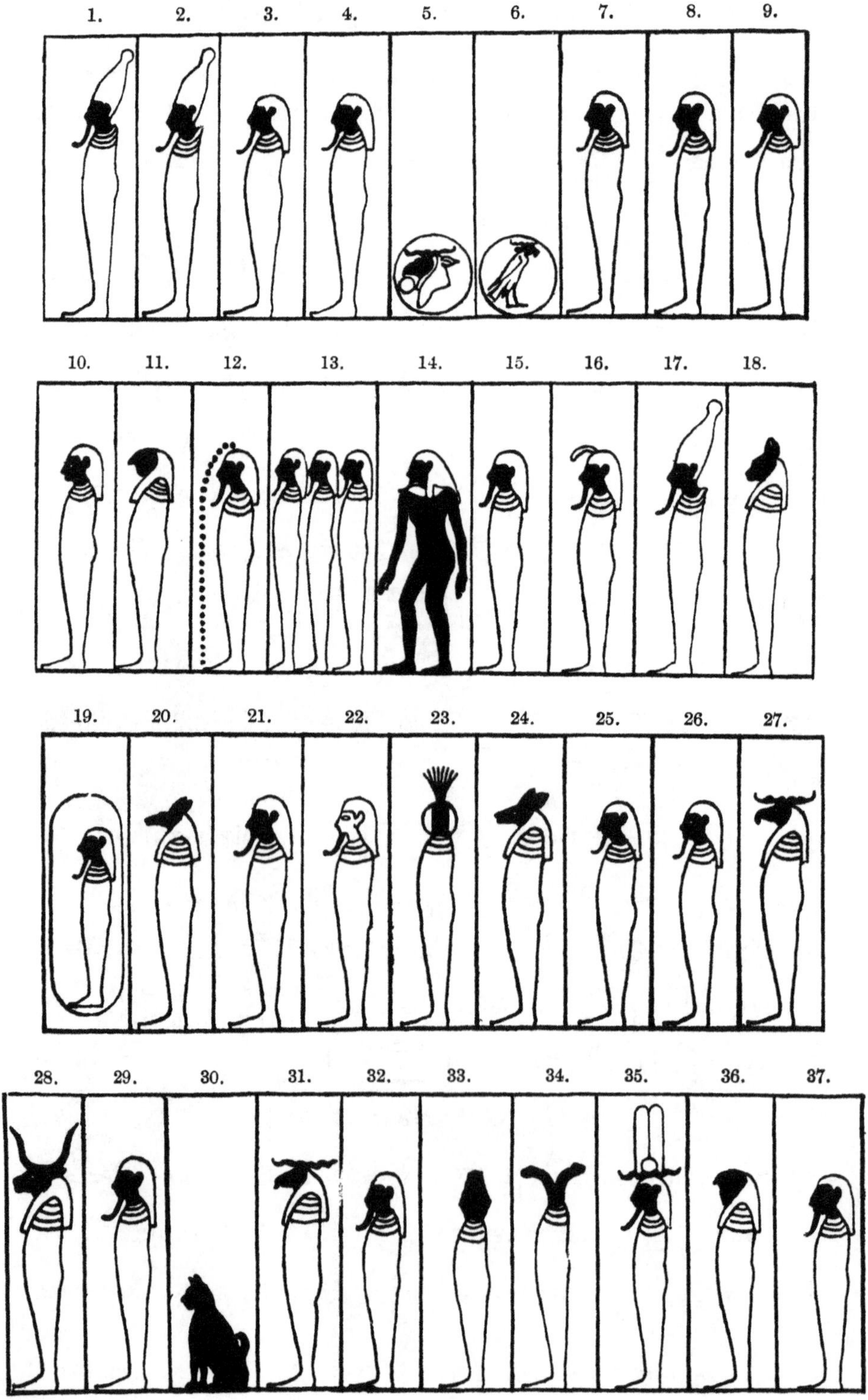
1. 2. 3. 4. 5. 6. 7. 8. 9.
10. 11. 12. 13. 14. 15. 16. 17. 18.
19. 20. 21. 22. 23. 24. 25. 26. 27.
28. 29. 30. 31. 32. 33. 34. 35. 36. 37.

46. 45. 44. 43. 42. 41. 40. 39. 38.

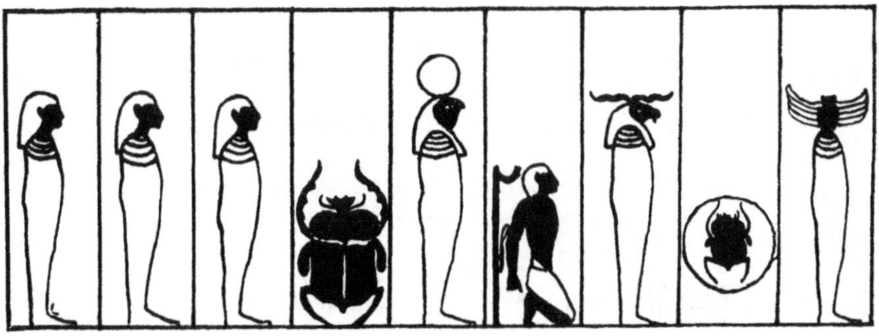

55. 54. 53. 52. 51. 50. 49. 48. 47.

65. 64. 63. 62. 61. 60. 59. 58. 57. 56.

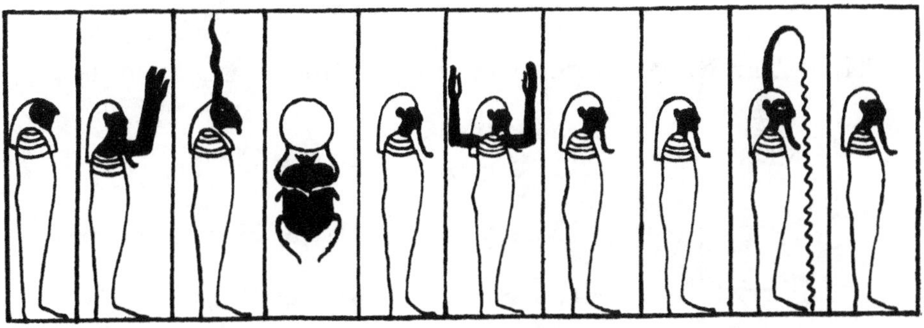

74. 73. 72. 71. 70. 69. 68. 67. 66.

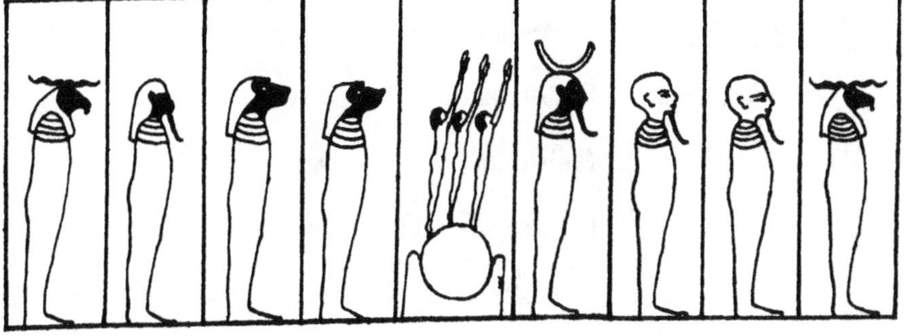

. 50. Serā̆a, . 51. Qererti, . 52. Åmen-ḥā, . 53. Khepreɾ, . 54. Āāai, . 55. Serqi, . 56. Sekhen-ba, . 57. Rekḥi, . 58. Shepi, . 59. Seshetai, . 60. Ḥāi, . 61. Maā-uat, . 62. Ḥetchuti, . 63. Uben, . 64. Then-åru, . 65. Ḥer-ba, . 66. Qa-ba, . 67. Netchesti, . 68. Amåm-ta, . 69. Ketuiti, . 70. Urshiu, . 71. Åānā-ṭuati, . 72. Neḥi, . 73. Neb-baiu, . 74. Neb-senku, .

XIX.—The Names of the Days of the Month and their Gods.

1.	Ḥeb-enti-paut, or	Day of Thoth.
2.	Ḥeb-åbet.	Day of Ḥeru-netch-tef-f.
3.	Ḥeb-mesper.	Day of Osiris.
4.	Ḥeb-per-setem.	Day of Åmset.
5.	Ḥeb-khet-ḥer-khau.	Day of Ḥāpi.
6.	Ḥeb-en-sås.	Day of Ṭuamutef.
7.	Ḥeb-tenå.	Day of Qebḥsennuf.
8.	Ḥeb-ṭep-[åbet]	Day of Maa-tef-f.
9.	Ḥeb-kep.	Day of Åri-tchet-f,

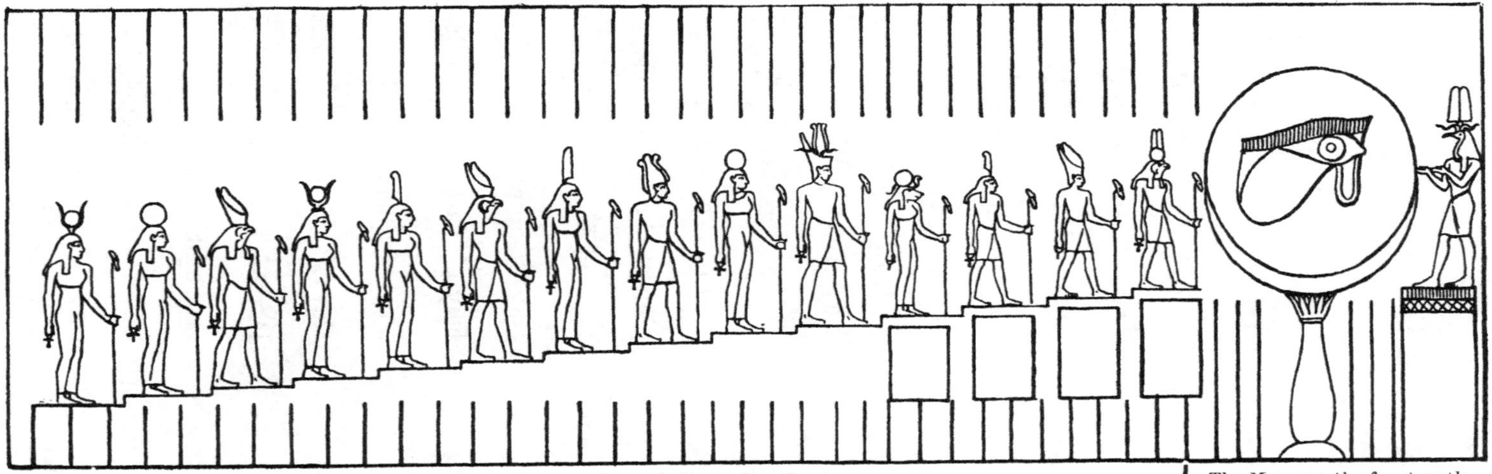

The Gods of the fourteen days of the waxing Moon.

The Moon on the fourteenth day.

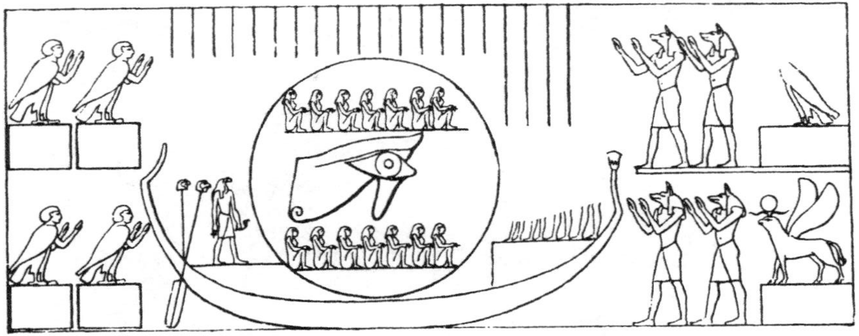

The Gods of the fourteen days of the waning Moon.

10.	Ḥeb-saf.	Day of Ȧri-ren-f-tchesef.
11.	Ḥeb-satu.	Day of Netchti-ur.
12.	Ḥeb-Ḥeru-en-......	Day of Netch-ān (?).
13.	Ḥeb-maa-set.	Day of Teken-en-Rā.
14.	Ḥeb-sa.	Day of Ḥen-en-ba.
15.	Ḥeb-ent-met-ṭua.	Day of Ȧrmāuai.
16.	Ḥeb-mesper-sen.	Day of Sheṭ-f-meṭ-f.
17.	Ḥeb-sa.	Day of Ḥeru-ḥer-uatch-f.
18.	Ḥeb-ȧāḥ.	Day of Ȧḥi.
19.	Ḥeb-setem-meṭu-f.	Day of Ȧn-mut-f.
20.	Ḥeb-ānep.	Day of Ȧp-uat.
21.	Ḥeb-āper	Day of Ȧnpu (Anubis).
22.	Ḥeb-peḥ-Sepṭ.	Day of Nāi.
23.	Ḥeb-tenȧt.	Day of Nā-ur.
24.	Ḥeb-qenḥ.	Day of Nā-ṭesher.
25.	Ḥeb-setu.	Day of Shem.
26.	Ḥeb-pert.	Day of Ma-tef-f.
27.	Ḥeb-usheb.	Day of Tun-ābui.
28.	Ḥeb-seṭ-ent-pet.	Day of Khnemu.
29.	Ḥeb-ȧri-sekhem (?)	Day of Utet-tef-f.
30.	Ḥeb-nu-pet.	Day of Ḥeru-netch-tef-f or Nehes.

XX. The gods and mythological beings who are mentioned in the Theban Recension of the *Book of the Dead.*[1]

Arethi-ka-sa-thika 

Aseb 

Ashu 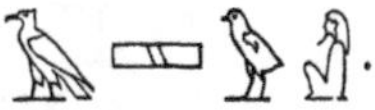

Ashbu 

Asher 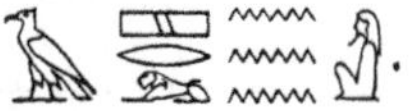

Akeru 

Atef-ur 

Aṭes-ḥrȧ-she 

Ȧaheṭ 

Ȧakhabit 

Ȧaqeṭqeṭ 

Ȧāḥ 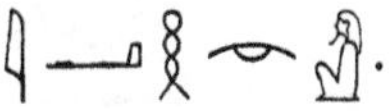

Ȧsȧr 

Ȧst 

Ȧuḳert 

Ȧuḳert-khentet-ȧst-s 

Ȧbu-ur 

Ȧp-uat 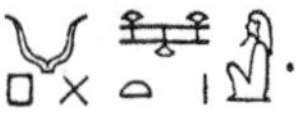

Ȧp-uat-meḥt-sekhem-pet 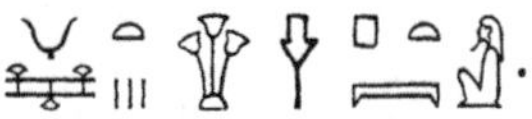

Ȧp-uat-resu-sekhem-taui 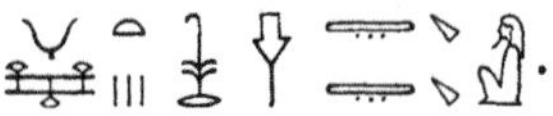

[1] The passages in which these names occur are given in the *Vocabulary* to my edition of the *Book of the Dead.* (*Chapters of Coming Forth by Day*, London, 1898.)

Åp-si . . . . .

Åp-shāṭ-taui . . .

Åm-beseku . . . .

Åm-snef . . . .

Åm-ḥauatu-ent-peḥui-f .

Åmen . . . . .

Åmen-Rā . . . .

Åmen-Rā-Ḥeru-khuti . .

Åmen-nathek-rethi-Åmen .

Åmen-na-ån-ka-entek-share .

Åmsu (*or*, Min) . . .

Åmsu-Ḥeru . . .

Åmseth . . . .

Ån-erṭā-nef-bes-f-khenti-heh-f

Ån-ḥeri-ertit-sa . . .

Åneniu . . . .

Ån . . . . .

Ån-ṭemt . . . .

Ån-åtef-f . . . .

Ån-ā-f . . . .

Ånpu . . . .

Ån-mut-f . . . .

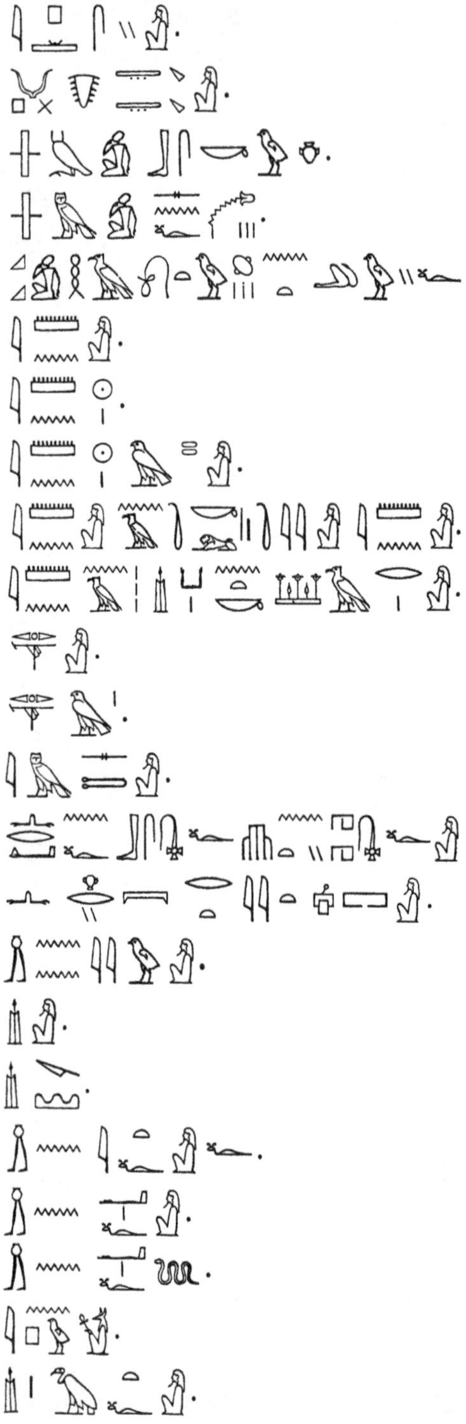

Ån-Ḥer 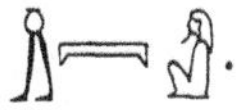

Ån-ḥrȧ 

Ån-ḥetep-f 

Ån-ṭebu 

Åri-Maāt 

Åri-em-ȧb-f 

Åri-en-ȧb-f 

Åri-ḥetch-f 

Åri-si 

Åḥ 

Åḥi 

Åḥiu 

Åḥibit 

Åḥeti 

Åkhsesef 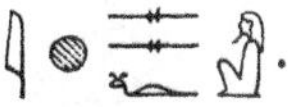

Åsṭennu 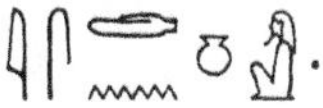

Åsṭes 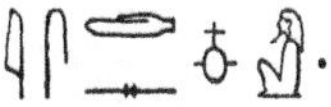

Åken-tau-k-ha-kheru 

Åkenti 

Åqen 

Åqeh 

Åḳau 

Åḳert-khent-ȧst-s 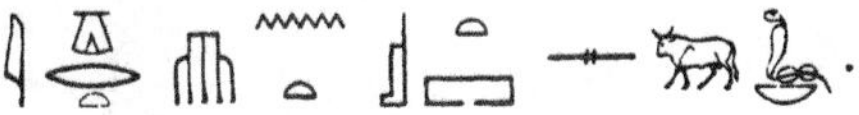

Åta-re-ȧm-tcher-qemtu-ren-par-sheta . . . . 

Åtem . . . . . 

Åten . . . . . 

Åtek-tau-kehaq-kheru . 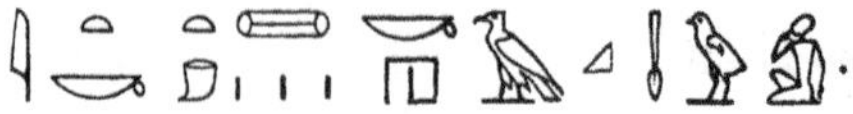

Āa-kheru . . . . 

Āu-ā . . . . . 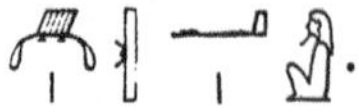

Āurȧu-ȧaqer-sa-ȧnq-re-bathi 

Āba-ta . . . . 

Āḥa-āāui . . . . 

Aḥau-ḥrȧu . . . . 

Ȧbt-ṭesi-ruṭ-en-neter . . 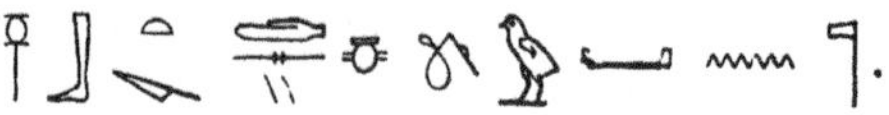

Āpep . . . . . 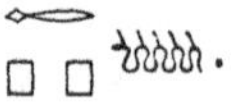

Āapef . . . . . 

Ām-āāu . . . . 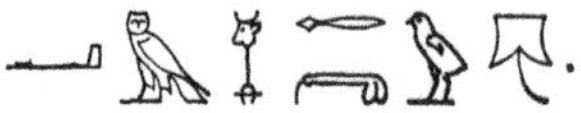

Āmam-maat . . . 

Ām-ḥeḥ . . . . 

Am-khebitu . . . 

Āmām . . . . 

Āmemet . . . . 

Ānkhi . . . . 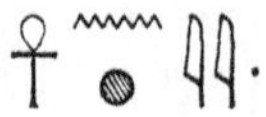

Ānkhti . . . . 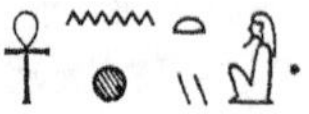

Ānkhet-pu-ent-Sebek-neb-Bakhau . . . . 

Ānkh-em-fentu . . . 

Ānṭi . . . . . 

Āḥā-ån-urṭ-nef . . . 

Ākhen-maati-f . . . 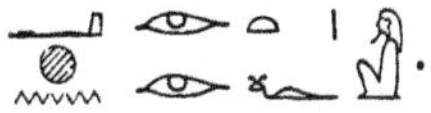

Ākhekhu . . . . 

Āq-ḥer-åmi-unnut-f . . 

Āqan . . . . . 

Āaṭi . . . . . 

Ātch-ur . . . . 

Ua . . . . . . 

Uaipu . . . . . 

Uamemti . . . . . 

Uart-neter-semsu . . 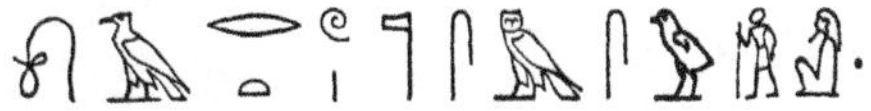

Uatch-Maati . . . 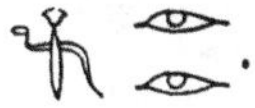

Uatch-Nesert . . . 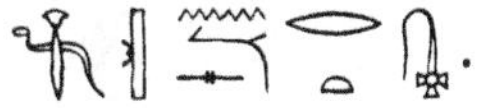

Uatchit . . . . . 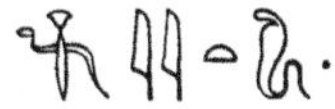

Uāau . . . . . 

Ui . . . . . . 

Ubes-ḥrå-per-em-khetkhet . 

Unpepet-ent-Ḥet-Ḥeru . 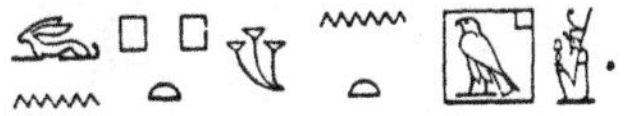

Unnut . . . . 

Unen-nefer 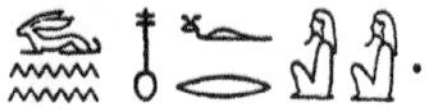

Un-ḥāt 

Unti 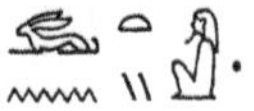

Ur-at 

Ur-peḥui-f 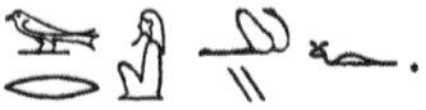

Ur-maat 

Ur-maat-s 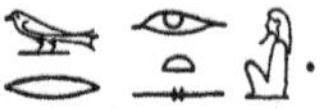

Ur-mertu-s-ṭeshert-sheni 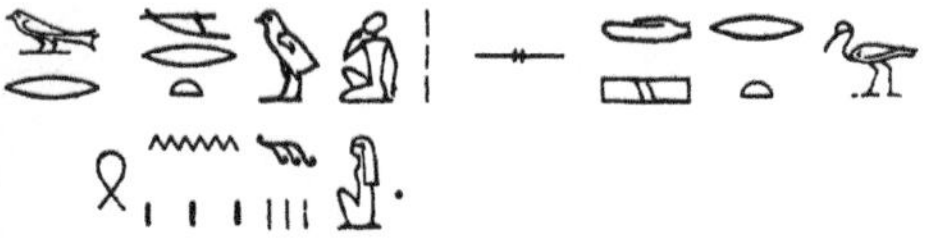

Ur-ḥekau 

User-åb 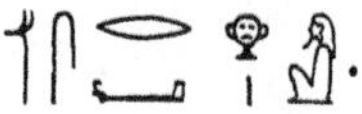

User-ba 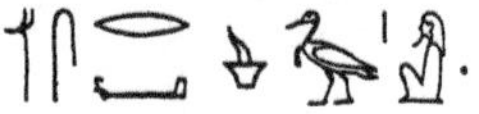

Usert 

Usekh-nemt 

Usekh-ḥrå 

Utu-rekhit 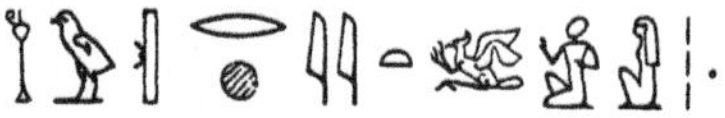

Utet-ḥeḥ 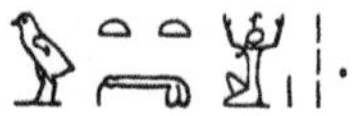

Utcha-re 

Ireqai 

Ba 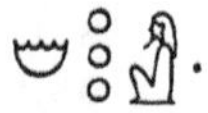

Bai 

Bati 

Bati-erpit 

Bau	
Bai	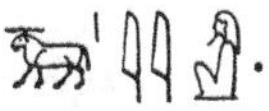
Baba	
Ba-neb-Ṭeṭṭeṭ	
Barekathȧtchaua	
Bast	
Basti	
Bȧbȧ	
Bāḥ	
Bebi	
Bennu	
Pa-rehaqa-kheperu	
Pa-shakasa	
Penti	
Peḥreri	
Pekhat	
Peskheti	
Pesek-re	
Pesṭu	
Peti	
Petrȧ	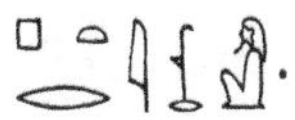
Ptaḥ	

Ptaḥ-âneb-res-f . . . 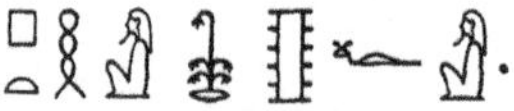

Ptaḥ-Seker . . . . 

Ptaḥ-Tanen . . . 

Fa-pet . . . . 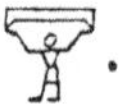

Maa-ânuf . . . . 

Maa-âtef-f-kheri-beq-f . . 

Maati-f-em-shet . . . 

Maati-f-em-ṭes . . . 

Maa-em-ḳerḥ-ȧn-nef-em-ḥru. 

Maa-ḥa-f . . . . . 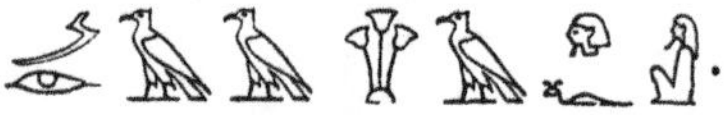

Maa-ḥeḥ-en-renpit . . 

Maatuf-ḥer-ā . . . 

Maaiu-su (?) . . . 

Maa-thet-f . . . . 

Maāt . . . . . 

Maāti . . . . . 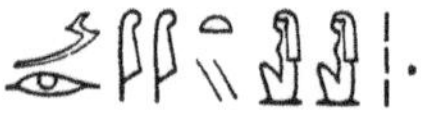

Māāu-taui . . . . 

Mārqathȧ . . . . 

Mi-sheps . . . . 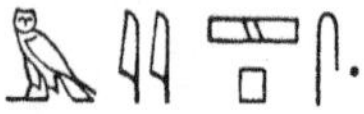

Ment . . . . . 

Menkh . . . . . 

Menqet	
Ment	
Menthu	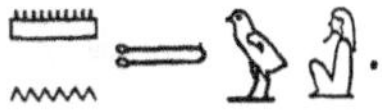
Mer	
Mert	
Merti	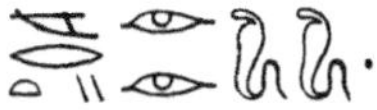
Mer-ur	
Meris	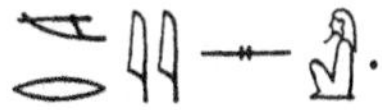
Mert	
Meḥ-urt	
Mehānuti-Rā	
Meḥi	
Meḥiu	
Meḥen	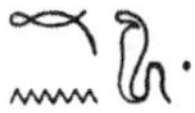
Meḥenit	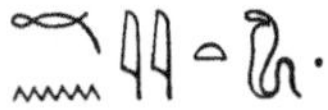
Meḥt	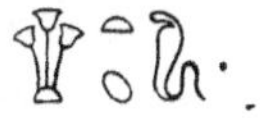
Meḥt-khebit-sāḥ-neter	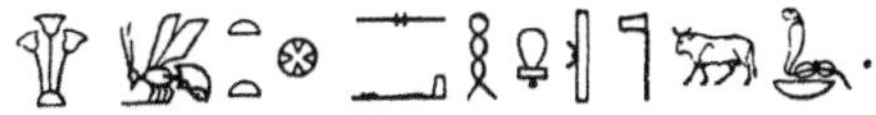
Mes-peḥ	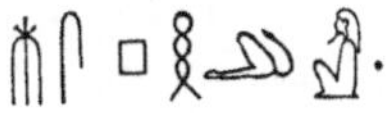
Mes-sepekh	
Mesthȧ	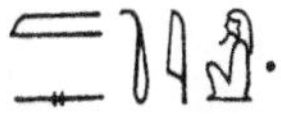
Meṭu-ta-f	
Meṭes-ḥrȧ-ȧri-she	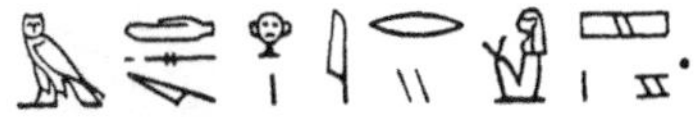
Meṭes-sen	

Naȧrik . . . . . 

Nasaqbubu . . . . 

Nak . . . . . . 

Nathkerthi . . . . 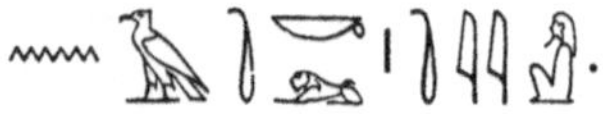

Nȧk . . . . . . 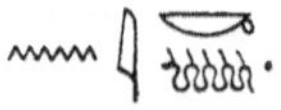

Nāȧu . . . . . . 

Nārt . . . . . . 

Nu . . . . . . 

Nubti . . . . . . 

Nut . . . . . . 

Neb-ābui . . . . . 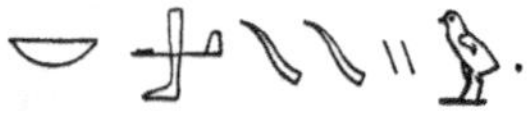

Nebt-unnut . . . . 

Neb-ḥrȧu . . . . . 

Neb-peḥtet-petpet-sebȧ . 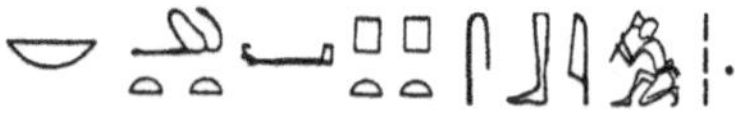

Neb-peḥti-thes-menment . 

Neb-maāt-ḥeri-ṭep-reṭui-f . 

Neb-er-tcher . . . . 

Nebt-ḥet . . . . . 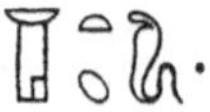

Neb-s . . . . . . 

Nebȧ . . . . . . 

Neperȧ . . . . . 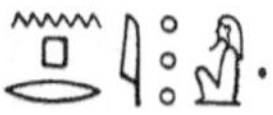

Nefert . . . . . 

Nefer-Temu . . . 

Nem-ḥrà	
Nem	
Nemu	
Nenutu-hru	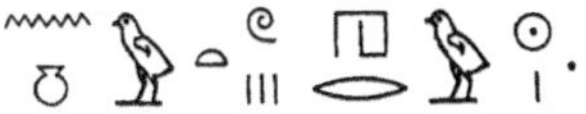
Nen-unser	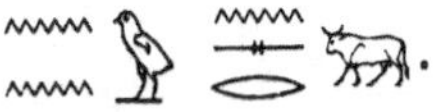
Nentchā	
Ner	
Neràu	
Neri	
Neràu-ta	
Nehesiu	
Neḥa-ḥrà	
Neḥa-ḥāu	
Neḥeb-nefert	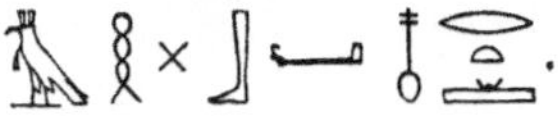
Neḥeb-ka	
Nekhebet	
Nekhen	
Nekà	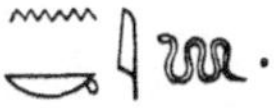
Nekàu	
Neḳau	
Neḳeḳ-ur	
Neti (?)	
Net (Neith)	

Neti-she-f . . . . . 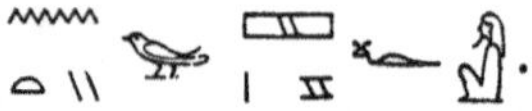

Neti-ḥrȧ-f-emmā-mast-f . 

Neteqa-ḥrȧ-khesef-aṭu . . 

Neṭit . . . . . 

Netcheb-ȧb-f . . . 

Netchefet . . . . 

Netchem . . . . 

Netcheḥ-netcheḥ . . . 

Netchesti . . . . 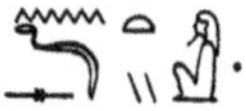

Netchses . . . . 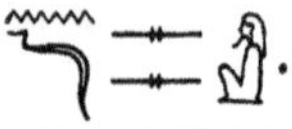

Re-Sekhait . . . . 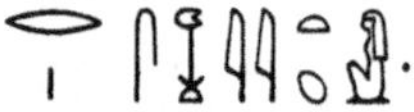

Re-iukasa . . . . 

Re-Rā . . . . 

Rā . . . . . 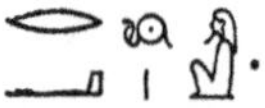

Rā-Ȧsȧr . . . . 

Rā-Ḥeru-khuti . . . 

Rā-Tem . . . . 

Rā-er-neḥeḥ . . . 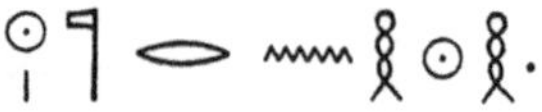

Ruṭ-en-Ȧst . . . . 

Ruṭu-nu-Tem . . . 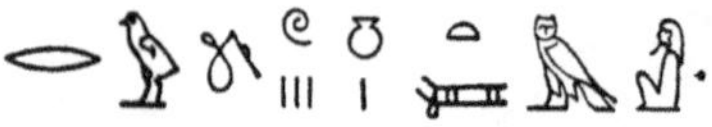

Ruṭu-neb-rekhit . . . 

Remi . . . . . 

Remrem . . . . 

Renenet . . . . 

Rennutet . . . . 

Rertu-nifu . . . . 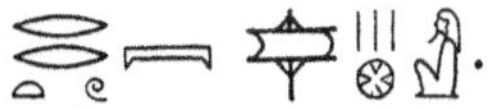

Rerek . . . . . 

Rerti . . . . . 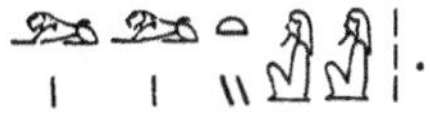

Reḥu . . . . . 

Reḥui . . . . . 

Reḥti . . . . . 

Re-ḥent . . . . 

Re-ḥenenet . . . . 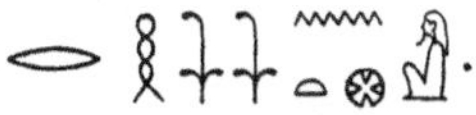

Rekhti-merti-neb-Maāti . 

Res-åb . . . . 

Res-ḥrå . . . . 

Rekes (?) . . . . 

Reqi . . . . . 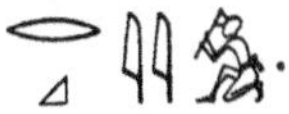

Retasashaka . . . 

Retā-nifu . . . . 

Reṭā-ḥen-er-reqau . . 

Reṭā-sebanqa . . . 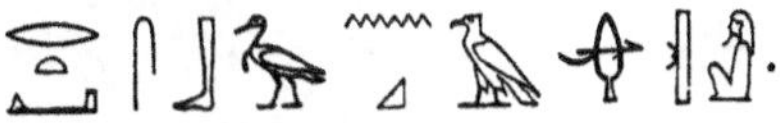

Hab-em-atu . . . 

Ha-ḥetep . . . . 

Ha-kheru . . . . 

Haker . . . . 

Haqa-haḳa-ua-ḥrȧ	
Hu-kheru	
Hemti	
Ḥai	
Ḥa-ḥrȧ	
Ḥapṭ-re	
Ḥarpuḳakashareshabaiu	
Ḥarethi	
Ḥāpi (Nile)	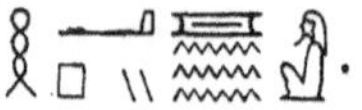
Ḥāpi	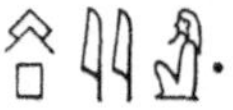
Ḥāpiu (Apis)	
Ḥu	
Ḥui	
Ḥu-tepa	
Ḥi-mu	
Ḥit	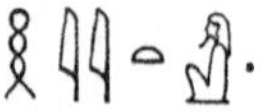
Ḥebṭ-re-f	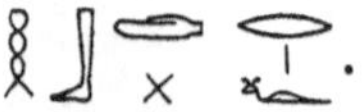
Ḥept-seshet	
Ḥemen	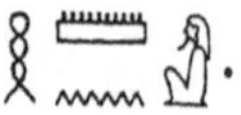
Ḥem-nu (?)	
Ḥenbi	
Ḥensek	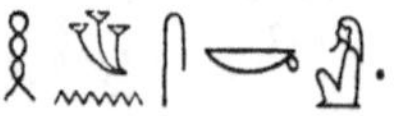

Ḥenti (Osiris)	
Ḥenti-requ	
Ḥent-she	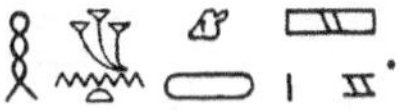
Ḥeri-akebȧ-f	
Ḥeri-uru	
Ḥertit-ān	
Ḥeri-sep-f	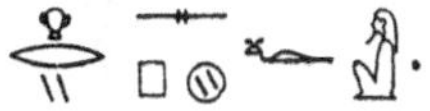
Ḥer-ta	
Ḥer-taui	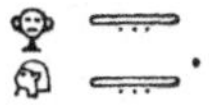
Ḥeru	
Ḥerui (Horus and Set)	
Ḥerui-senui (Horus and Set)	
Ḥeru-āi (?)	
Ḥeru-ur	
Ḥeru-em-khent-ȧn-maati	
Ḥeru-netch-ḥrȧ-ȧtef-f	
Ḥeru-khuti	
Ḥeru-sa-Ȧst	
Ḥrȧ-uā	
Ḥrȧ-nefer	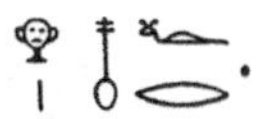
Ḥrȧ-f-ḥa-f	
Ḥeḥi	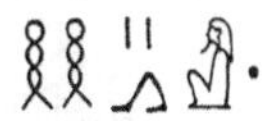
Ḥes-ḥrȧ	

Ḥes-tchefetch	
Ḥeqtit	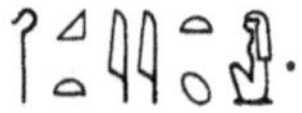
Ḥetep	
Ḥetep-sekhus	
Ḥetep-ka	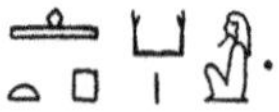
Ḥetep-taui	
Ḥetemet	
Ḥeṭeṭet	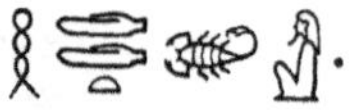
Ḥetch-re	
Ḥetch-re-pesṭ-ṭep	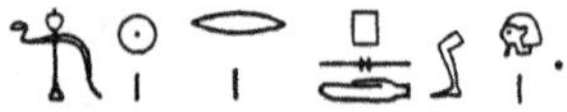
Ḥetch-ȧbeḥu	
Kharsathȧ	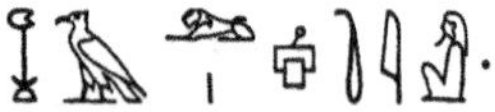
Khu-kheper-ur	
Khu-tchet-f	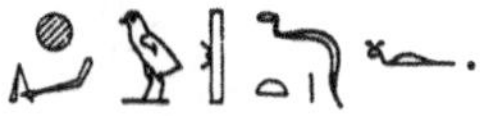
Khut	
Khebent	
Kheperȧ	
Khepesh	
Khemi	
Khemennu	
Khnemu	
Khnemet-em-ānkh-ȧnnuit	
Khenememti	

Khensu . . . . 

Khenti-Åmentet . . . 

Khenti-Khaṭṭhi . . . 

Kher . . . . . 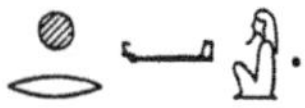

Kherȧ . . . . . 

Kherserȧu . . . . 

Khersek-Shu . . . 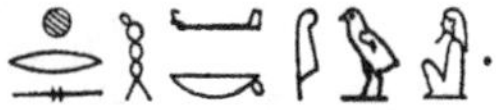

Khesef-aṭ . . . . 

Khesef-ḥrȧ-āsh-kheru . . 

Khesef-ḥrȧ-khemiu . . 

Khesef-khemiu . . . 

Sa-pa-nemmȧ . . . 

Sa-Åmenti-Rā . . . 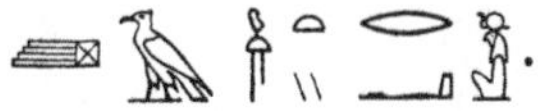

Saau-ur . . . . 

Sau . . . . . 

Sabes . . . . . 

Samait . . . . 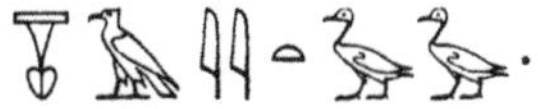

Saḥ (Orion) . . . 

Saḥ-en-mut-f . . . 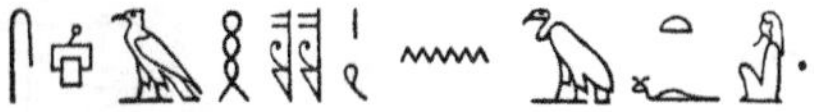

Saqenaqat . . . . 

Suḳaṭi . . . . 

Sut . . . . . 

Sebȧ . . . . . 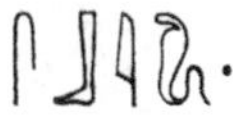

Sebȧu	
Sebek	
Sebeḳ	
Sepa	
Sepes	
Sepṭ	
Sepṭ-kheri-neḥait-ȧmi-beq .	
Sepṭ-mast-en-Rerti . . .	
Semu-taui	
Semu-ḥeḥ	
Smam	
Smamti	
Smetu	
Smetti	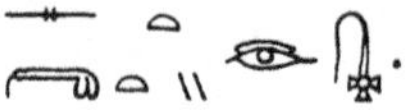
Ser-kheru	
Serȧt-beqet . . .	
Serekhi	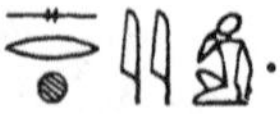
Seres-ḥrȧ	
Serqet	
Sekhiu	
Sekhem-ur	
Sekhem-em-ȧb-f . . .	

Sekhemet-ren-s-em-ābut-s . 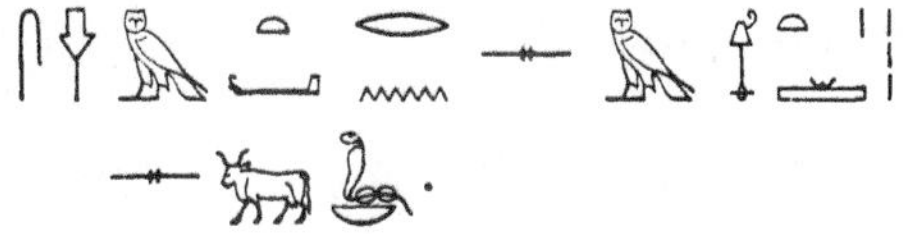

Sekhen-ur . . . . 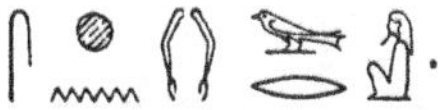

Sekher-āṭ . . . . 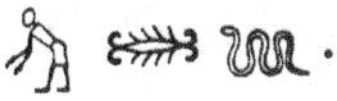

Sekher-remu . . . 

Sekhet . . . . 

Sekhti-ḥetep . . . 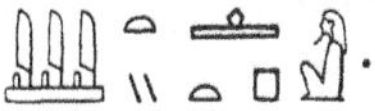

Sekheṭ-ḥrȧ-āsh-ȧru . . 

Seshet . . . . 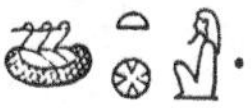

Sesheta . . . . 

Sesheṭ-kheru . . . 

Seker . . . . . 

Sek-ḥrȧ . . . . 

Seksek . . . . 

Seqebet . . . . 

Seqeṭ ḥrȧ . . . . 

Set . . . . . 

Seṭ-qesu . . . . 

Seṭeḳ . . . . . 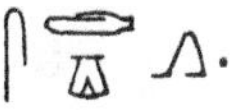

Shabu . . . . . 

Shapuneterȧrika . . . 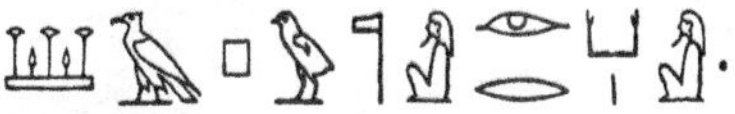

Sharesharesshapuneterȧrika . 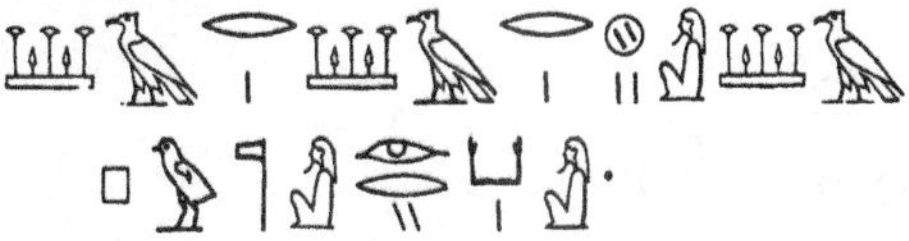

Sharesharekhet . . . 

Shareshathȧkathȧ . . 

Shakanasa . . . . . 

Shu . . . . . . 

Shefit . . . . . 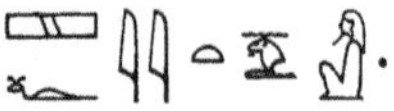

Shenȧt-pet-utheset-neter . 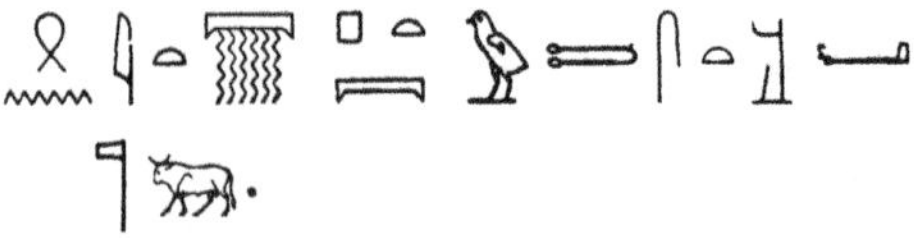

Shenthit . . . . . 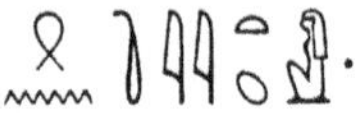

Sherem . . . . . 

Shes-khentet . . . 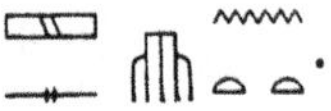

Sheta-ḥrȧ . . . . 

Ka-ḥetep . . . . 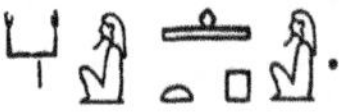

Kaa . . . . . . 

Kaȧrik . . . . . 

Kaharesapusaremkaḥerremt . 

Kasaika . . . . . 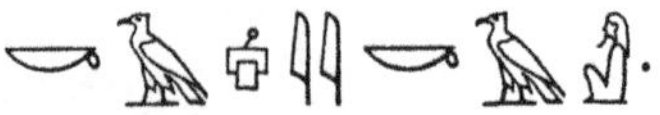

Kep-ḥrȧ . . . . . 

Kemkem . . . . . 

Kenemti . . . . . 

Ker . . . . . . 

Keḥkeḥet . . . . 

Qa-ha-ḥetep . . . 

Qa-ḥrȧ . . . . . 

Qaḥu . . . . . 

Qebḥ-sennuf . . . . 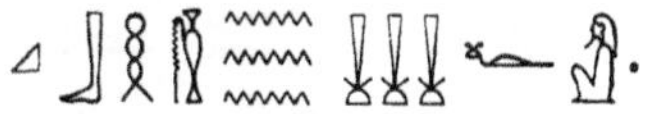

Qemamu . . . . . 

Qemḥusu . . . . . 

Qerti . . . . . 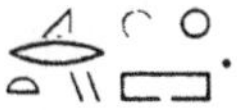

Qetetbu . . . . . 

Qeṭu . . . . . 

Ḳen-ur . . . . . 

Ta-reṭ . . . . . 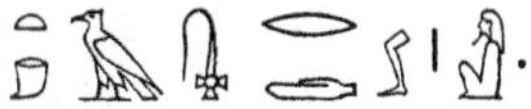

Taiti . . . . . 

Tait . . . . . 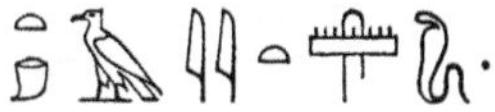

Tatunen . . . . . 

Tefnut . . . . . 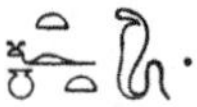

Temu . . . . . 

Tem-sep . . . . . 

Tenait . . . . . 

Tenemit . . . . . 

Teḥuti . . . . . 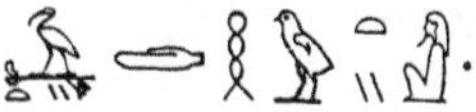

Teḥuti-Ḥāpi . . . . 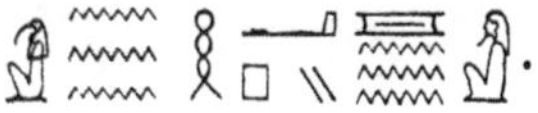

Teshtesh . . . . . 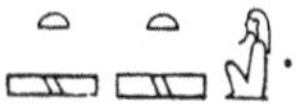

Tekem . . . . . 

Ṭuṭu-f . . . . . 

Ṭu-menkh-rerek . . . . 

Ṭuamutef . . . . . 

Ṭun-peḥti . . . . . 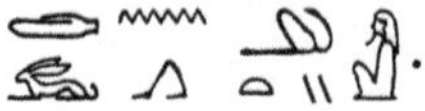

Ṭeb-ḥrȧ-keha-at . . . . 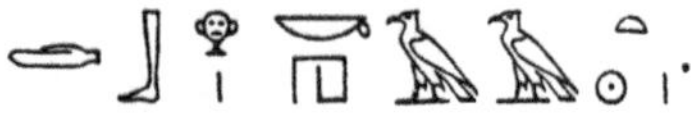

Ṭenȧ . . . . . . 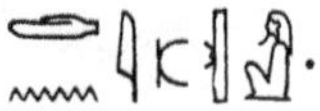

Ṭenpu . . . . . 

Ṭesher . . . . . 

Thȧnasa . . . . . 

Thenemi . . . . . 

Thest-ur . . . . . 

Tcheruu . . . . . 

Tcheḥes . . . . . 

Tchesert . . . . . 

Tcheser-ṭep . . . . 

CHAPTER XX

SACRED ANIMALS AND BIRDS, ETC.

THE Egyptian texts prove beyond all doubt that the Egyptians worshipped individual animals, and birds, and reptiles from the earliest to the latest times, and in spite of the statements to the contrary which are often made this custom must be regarded as a survival of one of the most popular forms of the religion of the predynastic peoples of the Nile Valley. At first animals were worshipped for their strength and power, and because man was afraid of them, but at a later period the Egyptians developed the idea that individual animals were the abodes of gods, and they believed that certain deities were incarnate in them. This idea is extremely ancient, and the Egyptian saw no absurdity in it, because at a very early period he had made up his mind that a god was always incarnate in the king of Egypt, and if this were so there was no reason why the gods should not become incarnate in animals. Animals which formed the abodes of gods, or were beloved by them, were treated with especial reverence and care, and apartments for their use were specially constructed in the temples throughout the country. When a sacred animal, i.e., the abode of a god, died, he was buried with great ceremony and honour, and, in dynastic times at least, his body was mummified with as much care as that of a human being. Immediately after the death of a sacred animal in a temple another beast was chosen and, having been led into the temple and duly installed there, the homage and worship of his predecessor were transferred to him. The new animal was a reincarnation of the god, i.e., a new manifestation and reappearance of the deity of the temple, and as such he was the visible symbol of a god. Of the manner in which sacred animals were thought to make known the will of the gods who were incarnate in them little can be said, but the priests of each animal must have formulated some system which would satisfy the devout, and they must have had some means of making the animals move in such a way that the beholder would be made to think that the will of the god incarnate was being revealed to him. We may assume, too, that when sacred animals became too old and infirm to perform their duties they were put to death either by the priests or at their command, and also that care was taken, so far as possible, to keep in reserve an animal which could take the place of that which was in the temple in the event of its sudden death. The monuments of the predynastic and archaic periods of Egyptian history which have been discovered during the last few years prove that Neith, Hathor, and Osiris were worshipped in the earliest times, and the traditions recorded by Greek and Roman writers supplement this first-hand evidence by a series of statements about the cult of animal gods in Egypt which is of the greatest importance for our purpose here.

One of the oldest animal cults in Egypt was that of Ḥāp, , whom the Greeks call Apis, and whose worship is coeval with Egyptian civilization. Apis was, however, one of many bulls which were worshipped by the Egyptians throughout the Nile Valley, and it is greatly to be regretted that the circumstances which led up to his occupation of such an exalted position among the animal gods of Egypt are unknown. According to Ælian,[1] Ḥāpi, or Apis, was held in the greatest honour in the time of Menȧ, the first historical king of Egypt, but Manetho[2] says that it was under Kaiekhôs, i.e., Ka-kau, 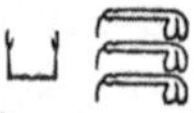, a king of the IInd Dynasty, that Apis was appointed to be a god. Herodotus (iii. 28) and Ælian call Apis Ἔπαφος, and the former describes him as the "calf of a cow which is incapable of conceiving another offspring; "and the Egyptians say that lightning descends upon the cow from

[1] Λέγει δέ τις τῶν προφητῶν λόγος οὐ πᾶσιν ἔκπυστος, ὅτι ἄρα [Μῆνις] ὁ τῶν Αἰγυπτίων βασιλεὺς ἐπενόησε ζῶον ὥστε σέβειν ἔμψυχον, εἶτα μέντοι προείλετο ταῦρον, ἁπάντων ὡραιότατον εἶναι αὐτὸν πεπιστευκώς. *De Nat. Animal.* xi. 10.

[2] See Cory's *Ancient Fragments.*

"heaven, and that from thence it brings forth Apis. This calf, "which is called Apis, has the following marks: it is black, and "has a square spot of white on the forehead; and on the back the "figure of an eagle; and in the tail double hairs; and on the "tongue a beetle." Pliny relates (viii. 72) that the Apis Bull was distinguished by a conspicuous white spot on the right side, in the form of a crescent, and he adds that when the animal had lived a certain number of years, it was destroyed by being drowned in the fountain of the priests. A general mourning ensued upon this, and the priests and others went with their heads shaven until they found a successor; this, however, Pliny says, did not take long, and we may therefore assume that an Apis was generally kept in reserve. As soon as the animal was found, he was brought to Memphis, where there were two Thalami set apart for him; to these bed-chambers the people were wont to resort to learn the auguries, and according as Apis entered the one or the other of these places, the augury was deemed favourable or unfavourable. He gave answers to its devotees by taking food from the hands of those who consulted him. Usually Apis was kept in seclusion, but whensoever he appeared in public he was attended by a crowd of boys who sang hymns to him. Once a year a cow was presented to him, but it is said that she was always killed the same day that they found her. The birthday of Apis was commemorated by an annual festival which lasted seven days, and during this period no man was ever attacked by a crocodile. In front of the sanctuary of Apis was a courtyard which contained another sanctuary for the dam of the god, and it was here that he was turned loose in order that he might be exhibited to his worshippers (Strabo, xvii. 31). Diodorus tells us (i. 85) that Apis, Mnevis, the Ram of Mendes, the crocodile of Lake Moeris, and the lion of Leontopolis were kept at very considerable cost, for their food consisted of cakes made of the finest wheat flour mixed with honey, boiled or roasted geese, and live birds of certain kinds.

The sacred animals were also washed in hot baths, and their bodies were anointed with precious unguents, and perfumed with the sweetest odours; rich beds were also provided for them to lie upon. When any of them died the Egyptians were as much concerned as if they had lost their own children, and they were wont to spend largely in burying them; when Apis died at Memphis of old age in the reign of Ptolemy Lagus his keeper not only spent everything he had in burying him, but also borrowed fifty talents of silver from the king because his own means were insufficient. Continuing his account of Apis Diodorus says, "After the splendid "funeral of Apis is over, those priests that have charge of the "business seek out another calf as like the former as possibly they "can find; and when they have found one, an end is put to all "further mourning and lamentation, and such priests as are "appointed for that purpose, lead the young ox through the city "of Nile, and feed him forty days. Then they put him into a "barge, wherein is a golden cabin, and so transport him as a god "to Memphis, and place him in Vulcan's grove. During the forty "days before mentioned, none but women are admitted to see him, "who being placed full in his view, pluck up their coats and "expose their persons. Afterwards they are forbidden to come "into the sight of this new god. For the adoration of this ox, "they give this reason. They say that the soul of Osiris passed "into an ox; and therefore, whenever the ox is dedicated, to this "very day, the spirit of Osiris is infused into one ox after another, "to posterity. But some say, that the members of Osiris (who "was killed by Typhon) were thrown by Isis into an ox made of "wood, covered with ox-hides, and from thence the city Busiris "was called."

In his account of Apis (xi. 10) Ælian states that Apis was recognized by twenty-nine distinct marks, which were known to the priests, and that when it was known that he had appeared they went to the place of his birth and built there a house towards the East, and the sacred animal was fed therein for four months. After this period, at the time of new moon, the priests made ready a barge and conveyed the new Apis to Memphis, where fine chambers were set apart for him, and spacious courts for him to walk about in, and where moreover, a number of carefully chosen cows were kept for him. At Memphis a special well of water was provided for Apis and he was not allowed to drink of the waters of the Nile because they were supposed to be too fattening.

Curiously enough the animals which were sacrificed to Apis were oxen, and according to Herodotus (ii. 38, 41) if a single black hair was found upon any one of them the beast was declared to be unclean. "And one of the priests appointed for this purpose "makes this examination, both when the animal is standing up "and lying down; and he draws out the tongue, to see if it is pure "as to the prescribed marks. . . . . He also looks at the hairs of "his tail, to see whether they grow naturally. If the beast is "found pure in all these respects, he marks it by rolling a piece of "byblus round the horns, and then having put on it some sealing "earth, he impresses it with his signet; and so they drive him "away. Anyone who sacrifices an unmarked animal is punished "with death." When an ox of this class was to be offered up to Apis it was led to the altar and was slain after a libation of wine had been poured out; its head was next cut off and its body was flayed. If the head was not sold it was thrown into the river and the following words were said over it:—"If any evil be about to "befal either those who now sacrifice, or Egypt in general, may "it be averted on this head." Plutarch (*De Iside*, § 56) and Ammianus Marcellinus (xxii. 14, 7) agree in stating that Apis was only allowed to live a certain number of years, which was probably twenty-five, and it seems that if he did not die before the end of this period he was killed and buried in a sacred well, the situation of which was known to a few privileged persons only.

The Egyptians connected Apis, both living and dead, with Osiris, and their beliefs concerning the two gods were very closely associated. The soul of Apis was thought to go to heaven after the death of the body in which it had been incarnate, and to join itself to Osiris, when it formed with him the dual god Åsår-Ḥāpi or Osiris-Apis. Early in the Ptolemaïc period the Greeks ascribed to Åsår-Ḥāpi the attributes of their god Hades, and Graecized the Egyptian name under the form "Serapis"; both Egyptians and Greeks accepted Serapis as the principal object of their worship, and after about B.C. 250 this god was commonly regarded as the male counterpart of Isis. It has already been said that the cult of Ḥāpi or Apis is very ancient, and there seems to be no doubt that in one place or another the bull was always worshipped in Egypt as the personification of strength and virility and of might in battle. Osiris, as a water god, poured the Nile over the land, and Ḥāpi provided the strength which enabled the Egyptians to plough it up; when theological systems began to be made in Egypt this ancient god was incorporated in them, and at Memphis we find that he was regarded as the "second life of Ptaḥ," , and also as the son of Osiris. From scenes on coffins, stelae, etc., we know that he possessed the attributes of Osiris the great god of the Underworld, especially after the XXVIth Dynasty, for he is often represented bearing a mummy upon his back, and "Bull of Amenti" is a common name of Osiris. Egyptian bronze figures of the Apis Bull represent the god as a very powerful beast, with massive limbs and body. A triangular piece of silver is fixed in the forehead, a disk and a uraeus are placed between the horns, above the fore and hind legs are cut in outline figures of vultures with outstretched wings, and on the back, also cut in outline, is a representation of a rectangular cloth with an ornamental diamond pattern. Herodotus (iii. 28) says that the patch of white on the forehead of Apis was square, λευκὸν τετράγωνον, and that the figure of an eagle was on the back, ἐπὶ δὲ τοῦ νώτου, αἰετὸν εἰκασμένον; of the beetle which he says was on the tongue of Apis and the double hairs in the tail the bronze figures naturally show no traces.

Of the tombs in which the Apis bulls were buried under the Early and Middle Empires nothing is known, but the discovery of the famous Serapeum at Ṣaḳḳâra, called by Strabo (xvii. 1, § 33) the "temple of Sarapis," which, he says, was "situated in a very "sandy spot, where the sand is accumulated in masses by the "wind," revealed the fact that so far back as the XVIIIth Dynasty the bodies of the Apis bulls were mummified with great care, and that each was buried in a rock-hewn tomb, above which was a small chapel. In the reign of Rameses II. a son of this king, called Khā-em-Uast, made a subterranean gallery in the rock at Ṣaḳḳâra, with a large number of chambers, and as each of these was occupied by the mummied Apis in his coffin its entrance was walled up, and the remains of the sacred animals were thus preserved for a very long period. Psammetichus I. hewed a similar gallery in the rock, and its side-chambers were prepared with great care and thought; the two galleries taken together are about 1200 feet long, 18 feet high, and 10 feet wide. Above these galleries stood the great Temple of the Serapeum, and close by was another temple which was dedicated to Apis by Nectanebus II., the last native king of Egypt. In the Serapeum of Khā-em-Uast and Psammetichus I. a number of Egyptian holy men lived a stern, ascetic life, and it appears that they were specially appointed to perform services in connexion with the commemorative festivals of the dead Apis bulls. Details of the rules of the order are wanting, but it is probable that the scheme of life which they lived there closely resembled that of the followers of Pythagoras, many of whom were celibates, and that they abstained from animal food, and had all things in common.[1] It is interesting to note the existence of the monks of the Serapeum, because they form a connecting link between the Egyptian priests and the Christian ascetics and monks who filled Egypt in the early centuries of our era. The worship of Apis continued in Egypt until the downfall of paganism, which resulted from the adoption of Christianity by Constantine the Great and from the edicts of the Emperor Theodosius.

As Apis was the sacred Bull of Memphis and symbolized the Moon, so MNEVIS was the sacred Bull of Heliopolis and typified the Sun, of which he was held to be the incarnation. The ancient Egyptians called the Bull of Heliopolis UR-MER, 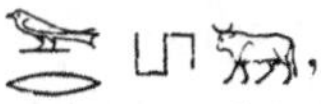, and described him as the "life of Rā"; he is usually depicted in the form of a bull with a disk and uraeus between his horns, but sometimes he appears as a man with the head of a bull. According to Manetho, the worship of Mnevis was established in the reign of Ka-kau, a king of the IInd Dynasty, together with that of Apis and the Ram of Mendes, but there is no doubt that it is coeval with Egyptian civilization, and that it was only a portion of the great system of adoration of the bull and cow as agricultural gods throughout Egypt. Strabo mentions (xvii. 1, § 22) that the people

[1] See Zeller, *History of Greek Philosophy*, London, 1881, vol. i., pp. 306-352; Ritter and Preller, *Historia Phil-Graece et Romanae*, 1878.

of Momemphis kept a sacred cow in their city just as Apis was maintained at Memphis, and Mnevis at Heliopolis, and adds, "these animals are regarded as gods, but there are other places, "and these are numerous, both in the Delta and beyond it, in "which a bull or a cow is maintained, which are not regarded as "gods, but only as sacred." Mnevis, like Apis, was consecrated to Osiris, and both Bulls were "reputed as gods generally by all the Egyptians;" Diodorus explains (i. 24, 9) this fact by pointing out that the bull was of all creatures the "most extraordinarily "serviceable to the first inventors of husbandry, both as to the "sowing of corn, and other advantages concerning tillage, of which "all reaped the benefit." The cult of Mnevis was neither so widespread nor so popular as that of Apis, and Ammianus Marcellinus says (xxii. 14, 6) that there is nothing remarkable related about him. A curious story is related by Ælian (*De Nat. Animal.* xii. 11) to the effect that king Bocchoris once brought in a wild bull to fight against Mnevis, and that the savage creature in attempting to gore the sacred animal miscalculated his distance, and having entangled his horns in the branches of a persea tree, fell an easy victim to Mnevis, and was slain by him. The Egyptians regarded this impious act with great disfavour, and probably hated him as they hated Cambyses for stabbing Apis.

Among the Egyptians another sacred bull was that of Hermonthis (Strabo, xvii. 1, 47) which, according to Macrobius (*Saturn.* i. 26) was called Bacchis (or Bacis, or Basis, or Pacis), and according to Ælian (xii. 11) Onuphis; the latter name is probably a corruption of some Egyptian name of Osiris Un-nefer. This bull was black in colour, and its hair turned a contrary way from that of all other animals, ἀντίαι δὲ αὐτῷ τρίχες ἤπερ οὖν τοῖς ἄλλοις εἰσίν; it was said to change its colour every hour of the day, and was regarded as an image of the sun shining on the other side of the world, i.e., the Underworld. The Egyptian equivalent of the name Bacis, or Bacchis, is Bakha, , and this bull is styled the "living soul of Rā," , and the "bull "of the Mountain of the Sunrise (Bakhau), and the lion of the "Mountain of the Sunset." He wears between his horns a disk, from which rise plumes, and a uraeus; over his hindquarters is the sacred symbol of a vulture with outspread wings.[1]

At several places in the Delta, e.g., Hermopolis, Lycopolis, and Mendes, the god Pan and a goat were worshipped; Strabo, quoting (xvii. 1, 19) Pindar, says that in these places goats had intercourse with women, and Herodotus (ii. 46) instances a case which was said to have taken place in the open day. The Mendesians, according to this last writer, paid reverence to all goats, and more to the males than to the females, and particularly to one he-goat, on the death of which public mourning is observed throughout the whole Mendesian district; they call both Pan and the goat Mendes, and both were worshipped as gods of generation and fecundity. Diodorus (i. 88) compares the cult of the goat of Mendes with that of Priapus, and groups the god with the Pans and the Satyrs. The goat referred to by all these writers is the famous Mendean Ram, or Ram of Mendes, the cult of which was, according to Manetho, established by Kakau, a king of the IInd Dynasty.

In the hieroglyphic texts he is called Ba-neb-Ṭeṭ,  , from which name the Greek Mendes is derived, and he is depicted in the form of a ram with flat, branching horns which are surmounted by a uraeus; pictures of the god of this kind are, of course, traditional, and since goats of the species of the Ram of Mendes are not found on Egyptian Monuments after the period of the Ancient Empire, we can only conclude that they were originally copied from representations of the Ram which were in use before about B.C. 3500. Ba-neb-Ṭeṭ, or Mendes, was declared to be the "soul of Rā," but allowance must be made for the possibility that the Egyptians did not really believe this statement, which may only have resulted from a play upon the words *ba* "ram," and *ba* "soul." The cult of the Ram of Mendes was of more than local importance, and his priesthood was a powerful body. The ram which was adored at Mendes was distinguished by certain marks, even as was Apis, and was sought for throughout the country with great diligence; when the animal was found he

[1] See Lanzone, *Dizionario*, pl. 70.

was led to the city of Mendes, and a procession of priests and of the notables of the city having been formed he was escorted to the temple and enthroned therein with great honour. From the Stele of Mendes[1] we learn that Ptolemy II., Philadelphus, rebuilt the temple of Mendes, and that he assisted at the enthronement of two Rams, and in a relief on the upper portion of it two Ptolemies and an Arsinoë are seen making offerings to the Ram, and to a ram-headed god, and his female counterpart Ḥātmeḥit. The cult of the Ram lasted at Mendes until the decay of the city, after which for a short period it was maintained at Thmuis, a neighbouring city, which increased in importance as Mendes decreased. In primitive times the Ram of Mendes was a merely local animal god, or perhaps only a sacred animal, but as the chief city of its cult increased in importance the god was identified, first, with the great indigenous god Osiris, secondly, with the Sun-god Rā, and thirdly, with the great Ram-god of the South and of Elephantine, i.e., Khnemu.

Among the animals which were worshipped devoutly as a result of abject fear must be mentioned the crocodile, which the Egyptians deified under the name of SEBEK, 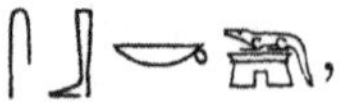, or SEBEQ, , and which was called SOUCHOS, Σοῦχος, by the Greeks. In primitive times when the canals dried up this destructive beast was able to wander about the fields at will, and to eat and kill whatsoever came into its way, and the Egyptians naturally regarded it as the personification of the powers of evil and of death, and the prince of all the powers of darkness, and the associate of Set, or Typhon. According to Herodotus (ii. 69), crocodiles were sacred in some parts of Egypt, but were diligently killed in others. At Thebes and near lake Moeris they were held to be sacred, and when tame the people put crystal and gold ear-rings into their ears, and bracelets on their fore paws, and they fed them regularly with good food; after death their bodies were embalmed and then buried in sacred vaults. Herodotus says they were called χάμψαι, a word which is, clearly, a transliteration of

[1] Mariette, *Monuments Divers*, pl. 42; *Aeg. Zeit.*, 1871, pp. 81-85; 1875, p. 33.

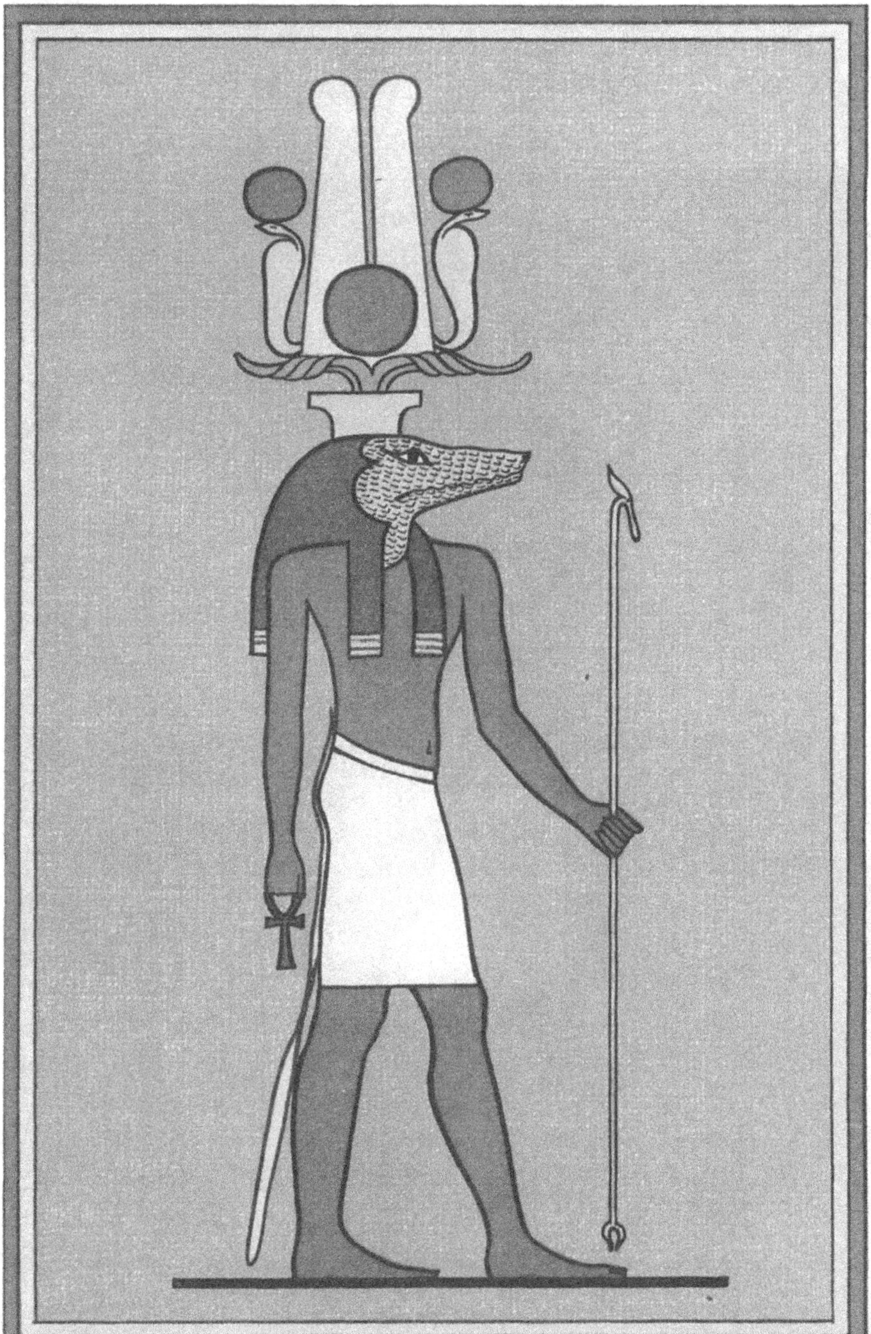

SEBEK-RĀ.

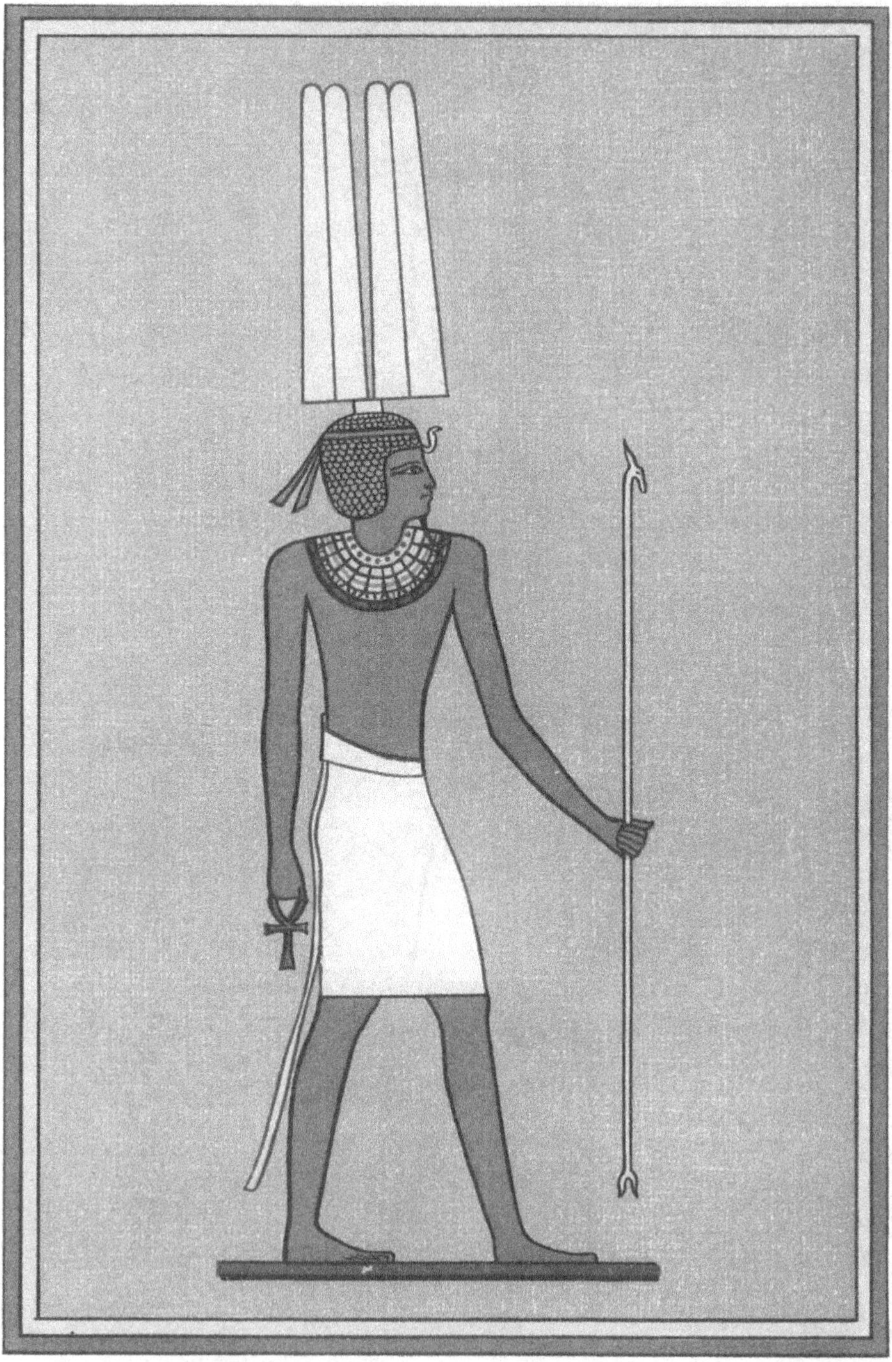

The God Ȧn-Ḥeru.

the Egyptian word 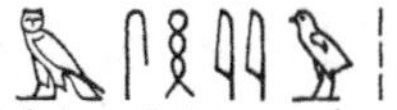, *emseḥiu.* Strabo gives an interesting account of his visit to the famous city of Crocodilopolis, which in his day was known by the name Arsinoë, and was the centre of crocodile worship; and tells us (xvii. 1, § 38), that the sacred crocodile there "was kept apart by himself in a lake; it is "tame, and gentle to the priests, and is called Σοῦχος. It is fed "with bread, flesh, and wine, which strangers who come to see "it always present. Our host, a distinguished person, who was "our guide in examining what was curious, accompanied us to the "lake, and brought from the supper table a small cake, dressed "meat, and a small vessel containing a mixture of honey and milk. "We found the animal lying on the edge of the lake. The priests "went up to it; some of them opened its mouth, another put the "cake into it, then the meat, and afterwards poured down the "honey and milk. The animal then leaped into the lake, and "crossed to the other side. When another stranger arrived with "his offering, the priests took it, and running round the lake, "caught the crocodile, and gave him what was brought in the "same manner as before."

In their pictures and reliefs the Egyptians represented the god Sebek in the form of a crocodile-headed man who wore either a solar disk encircled with a uraeus, or a pair of horns surmounted by a disk and a pair of plumes; sometimes a small pair of horns appears above the large ram's horns. Frequently the god is depicted simply in the form of the animal which was sacred to him, i.e., as a crocodile. What exactly were the attributes of Sebek in early dynastic times we have no means of knowing, but it is probable that they were those of an evil and destructive animal; before the end of the VIth Dynasty, however, he was identified with Rā, the Sun-god, and with the form of Rā who was the son of Neith, and with Set the opponent and murderer of Osiris. According to the late Dr. Brugsch, Sebek was a four-fold deity who represented the four elemental gods, Rā, Shu, Seb, and Osiris, and this view receives support from the fact that in the vignettes to the xxxist and xxxiind Chapters of the *Book of the Dead*, the deceased is seen repulsing four crocodiles. The same scholar thought that the name of the god was derived from a root which signifies "to collect, to bring together," and that he was called "Sebek" because he was believed to gather together that which had been separated by the evil power of Set, and to give a new constitution and life to the elements which had been severed by death.[1] This view may be correct, but it certainly cannot be very old, and it cannot represent the opinions which the predynastic Egyptians held concerning the god. That, however, Sebek was believed to be a god who was good to the dead is clear, and it was held that he would do for them that which he had done in primitive times for Horus.

From the cviiith Chapter of the *Book of the Dead*, we learn that Sebek, Temu, and Hathor were the Spirits of the West, and that Sebek dwelt in a temple which was built on the Mount of the Sunrise, and that he assisted Horus to be re-born daily. In the Pyramid Texts, Sebek is made to restore the eyes to the deceased, and to make firm his mouth, and to give him the use of his head, and to bring Isis and Nephthys to him, and to assist in the overthrow of Set, the enemy of every "Osiris." He opened the doors of heaven to the deceased, and led him along the bypaths and ways of heaven and, in short, assisted the dead to rise to the new life, even as he had helped the child Horus to take his seat upon the throne of his father Osiris. The centre of the cult of Sebek was Ombos, 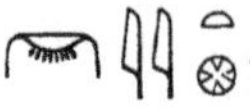, Nubit, where he was held to be the father of Ḥeru-ur, and was identified with Seb, and was called, "Father "of the gods, the mighty one among the gods and goddesses, the "great king, the prince of the Nine Bow Barbarians." As SEBEK-RĀ-TEMU he was the power of the sun which created the world, and he is styled, "the beautiful green disk which shineth ever, the "creator of whatsoever is and of whatsoever shall be, who proceeded "from Nu, and who possesses many colours and many forms."[2] Other important seats of the cult of Sebek were:—1. Silsila (Khennu, ), where he was adored with Tem, Nu, Ḥeru-ur, and Ḥeru-Beḥuṭet; 2. Pa-khent (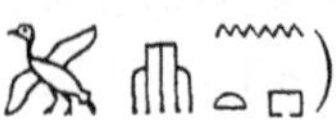), where he was worshipped with Ȧmen-Rā; 3. Latopolis, where he was identified

[1] *Religion und Mythologie*, p. 588.

[2] Brugsch, *Religion*, p. 591.

with Ḥeqa, the son of Shu-Khnemu-Rā and Tefnut-Nebuut-Sekhet-Neith; 4. Smen (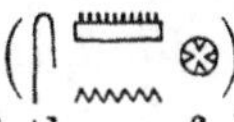), where he was merged in Rā and was held to be the father of Horus; 5. Pa-Sebek, near Hermonthis, where he formed the chief member of the triad of Sebek-Seb, Nut-Hathor, and Khensu; 6. Hermonthis, where he was merged in Menthu, and as Sebek-Seb became the counterpart of Menthu-Rā and Åmen-Ra, and the head of the company of the gods of Hermonthis and Thebes; at Tuphium, near Thebes, where he was worshipped under the form of a crocodile, with a sun-disk and the feathers of Åmen upon his head; 7. Krokodilonpolis-Arsinoë, the Sheṭet, , and Ta-Shetet, 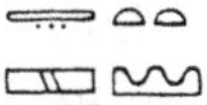, of the hieroglyphic texts, which was situated near Lake Moeris, and was called the "city of Sebek" *par excellence.* In the north of Egypt the chief sanctuaries of Sebek were Prosopis, Saïs, Metelis, Onuphis, and the city of Apis, which was situated in the Libyan nome;[1] in this last-named place Osiris was worshipped under the form of a crocodile, and Isis under the usual form of Isis.

From the statements made about the crocodile by classical writers, it is easy to see that several fantastic notions were current about the animal in the later period of dynastic history. Thus Ammianus Marcellinus, after describing the strength of the crocodile (xxii. 15) says, "savage as these monsters are at all "other times, yet as if they had concluded an armistice, they are "always quiet, laying aside all their ferocity, during the seven "days of festival on which the priests at Memphis celebrate the "birthday of Apis." Herodotus (ii. 68) and Diodorus (i. 35), like Aristotle, declare that the crocodile has no tongue, an error which was wide-spread in ancient times, and which was commonly believed even in the Middle Ages; it was also thought to eat no food during the coldest months of the year, and to be blind in the water. Many crocodiles were killed by an animal called the "hydrus" in the following manner. It is related that a little bird called the trochilus was in the habit of entering the mouth of the crocodile as it lay asleep with its jaws open "towards the west," and of picking out the leeches which clung to its teeth and

[1] For a list of Sebek shrines see Lanzone, *Dizionario*, pp. 1033-1036.

gums. The hydrus, or ichneumon, perceiving this, would also enter the crocodile's mouth, and crawl along through the throat into its stomach, and having devoured its entrails, would crawl back again; the hydrus also is declared to have been in the habit of searching for the eggs of the crocodile, which were always laid in the sand, and of breaking the shell of every one which it found. Notwithstanding the reverence in which the crocodiles were held in many parts of Egypt numbers of people made a living by catching them and killing them. According to Herodotus (ii. 70) and other writers, a hook baited with the chine of a pig was let down by the fishermen into the river, while a young pig was held on the bank and beaten until it squealed; the crocodile, hearing the noise, made its way towards the sound of the little pig's cries, and coming across the bait on the hook, straightway swallowed it. Then the men hauled in the line and the crocodile was soon landed, and its eyes having been plastered up, it was slain. Crocodiles at one time were regarded as the protectors of Egypt, and Diodorus held the view (i. 35) that but for them the robbers from Arabia and Africa would swim across the Nile and pillage the country in all directions.

The crocodile played a prominent part in Egyptian mythology, in which it appears both as the friend and foe of Osiris; one legend tells how the creature carried the dead body of Osiris upon its back safely to land, and another relates that Isis was obliged to make the little ark in which she placed her son Horus of papyrus plants, because only by this means could she protect her son from the attack of the crocodile god Sebek. The later Egyptian astrologers always considered the animal to be a symbol of the Sun, and it is probable that to its connexion with the Sun-god the statements of Ælian (x. 21) are due. This writer remarks that the female crocodile carried her eggs for sixty days before she laid them, that the number of the eggs was sixty, that they took sixty days to hatch, that a crocodile had sixty vertebrae in its spine, and sixty nerves, and sixty teeth in its mouth, that its life was sixty years, and that its annual period of fasting was sixty days. Among other curious but mistaken views about the crocodile, Plutarch (*De Iside*, § 75) mentions that the animal was looked upon as the image of God, and he explains the supposed absence of a tongue by saying that "divine reason needeth not speech." He credits the animal with great wisdom and foreknowledge, in proof of which he declares that in whatsoever part of the country the female lays her eggs, so far will be the extent of the inundation for that season. All the above mentioned views are interesting as showing how legends of the animal gods and their powers grew up in the later period of dynastic history, and how mythological ideas were modified in the course of the centuries which witnessed the decay of the old religion of Egypt.

Like the crocodile, the Hippopotamus was worshipped by the primitive Egyptians, and the hippopotamus goddess was called Rert, or Rertu, , and Ta-urt, , Àpet, , Sheput, , etc., and was, practically, identified as a form of every great goddess of Egypt, irrespective of the probability of her being so. In predynastic times the hippopotamus was probably common in the Delta, and the red and yellow breccia statue of the animal which was made in the archaic period, and is now preserved in the British Museum (No. 35,700), proves that its cult is coeval with Egyptian civilization. According to certain theological systems the hippopotamus goddess was the female counterpart of Set, and the mother of the Sun-god, or of Àn-ḥer, whom she brought into the world at Ombos; for this reason that city was called the "Meskhenet," , or "birth-house," of Àpet. On the whole, the hippopotamus goddess was a beneficent creature, and she appears in the last vignette of the Theban Recension of the *Book of the Dead* as a deity of the Underworld, and a kindly guardian of the dead. She holds in her right forepaw an object which has not yet been satisfactorily explained, and her left rests upon the emblem of "protective, magical power," ; on the other hand, the monster Ām-mit, which appears in the Judgment Scene, has the hindquarters of a hippopotamus, a fact which reminds us that the destructive power of the animal was not forgotten by the Egyptian theologians.

The cult of the Lion was also very ancient in Egypt, and it

seems to have been tolerably widespread in early dynastic times; the animal was worshipped on account of his great strength and courage, and was usually associated with the Sun-god, Horus or Rā, and with deities of a solar character. Under the New Empire the chief centre of the cult of the lion was the city of Leontopolis in the Northern Delta, but it is quite certain that sacred lions were kept in the temples at many places throughout Egypt. Ælian mentions (xii. 7) that lions were kept in the temple at Heliopolis, and goes on to say that in the Lion City (Leontopolis) the sacred lions were fed upon the bodies of slaughtered animals, and that from time to time a calf was introduced into the lion's den so that he might enjoy the pleasure of killing prey for himself; whilst he was devouring his food the priests, or men set apart for the purpose, sang songs to him. The original home of the lion in Egypt was the Delta, where he lived under conditions similar to those which existed in Southern Nubia and in the jungles of the rivers Atbara and Blue Nile; the deserts on each side of the Nile between Kharṭûm and the Mediterranean Sea of course also contained lions, but probably not in very large numbers. In Egyptian mythology the lion plays a comparatively prominent part, and one of the oldest known Lion-gods is Aker, , who was supposed to guard the gate of the dawn through which the Sun-god passed each morning; Aker is mentioned in the Pyramid Texts (e.g., Unȧs, lines 498, 614), and from the passages in which his name occurs it is clear that his position and attributes were even under the Early Empire well defined. In later days the Egyptian mythologists believed that during the night the sun passed through a kind of tunnel which existed in the earth, and that his disappearance therein caused the night, and his emerging therefrom caused the day; each end of this tunnel was guarded by a Lion-god, and the two gods were called Akeru (or Akerui) , or . In the Theban Recension of the *Book of the Dead* (Chapter xvii.) we find the Akeru gods represented by two lions which are seated back to back, and support between them the horizon with the sun's disk on it, ; in the later theology they are called Sef and

Ṭuau, i.e., "Yesterday" and "To-day" respectively. Because the Egyptians believed that the gates of morning and evening were guarded by Lion-gods, they placed statues of lions at the doors of their palaces and tombs to guard both the living and the dead, and to keep evil spirits and fleshly foes from entering into the gates to do harm to those who were inside them. To such lion guardians they sometimes gave the heads of men and women, and these are familiar to us under the name which was given to them by the Greeks, i.e., "Sphinxes."

The oldest and finest human-headed lion statue is the famous "Sphinx" at Gîzeh (in Egyptian Ḥu, ), which was regarded as the symbol of the Sun-god Rā-Temu-Kheperȧ-Ḥeru-khuti, and was made to keep away evil spirits from the tombs which were round about it. The age of this marvellous statue is unknown, but it existed in the time of Khephren, the builder of the Second Pyramid, and was, most probably, very old even at that early period. It may be noted in passing that the "Sphinx" at Gîzeh was intended to be a guardian and protector of the dead and of their tombs, and nothing else, and the idea of Plutarch and others that it typified the enigmatical wisdom of the Egyptians and strength and wisdom is purely fanciful. The men who made the Sphinx believed they were providing a colossal abode for the spirit of the Sun-god which they expected to dwell therein and to protect their dead; it faced the rising sun, of which it was a mighty symbol. The original idea of the man-headed lion statue has no connexion with the views which the Greeks held about their monstrous being the Sphinx, who is declared to have been a daughter of Orthus, or Typhon, and Chimaera, or of Typhon and Echidna; moreover, Greek sphinxes are winged, and their heads and breasts are always those of a woman, whilst Egyptian lion statues have sometimes the heads of men, and sometimes the heads of sheep or rams. The "Sphinx" at Gîzeh is probably the product of the beliefs of a school of theologians which existed when the cult of the lion was common in the Delta or Northern Egypt, but tradition perpetuated the idea of "protection" which was connected with it, and the architectural conservatism of the Egyptians caused reproductions of it to be made for all the great temples in the country in all periods of its history.

It is a moot point whether the lion was generally hunted in Egypt or not, but it is improbable; on the other hand we find that Ȧmen-ḥetep III. boasts of having shot with his own bow one hundred and two lions during the first ten years of his reign, but these were undoubtedly lions of Mitanni and not of Egypt. The bas-reliefs and texts prove that Rameses II. and Rameses III. each possessed a tame lion which not only accompanied them into battle, but also attacked the enemy; it is probable, however, that these kings valued their pet lions more as symbols of the Sun-god and of his protective power, than as effective combatants. In the Theban *Book of the Dead* the double lion-god who is so often mentioned under the name is, of course, Shu and Tefnut, or two gods who were identified with them. Other lion-gods bore the names Āri-ḥes-nefer, , Nefer-Tem, , Hebi, , Ḥeru-neb-Mesen, , Ma-ḥes, , etc.; lioness-goddesses were Pakheth, , Sekhet, , Menāt, , Renenet, , Sebqet, , Urt-ḥekau, , Āstherṭet, , and a form of Hathor, and another of Nekhebet. The destroying power of the Lion-god is alluded to in the figure of the monster Ām-mit, which was part crocodile, part lion, and part hippopotamus. The vignettes to the cxlvith and cxlviith Chapters of the *Book of th Dead* show that lion-headed deities guarded certain of the halls and pylons of the Underworld, and some connexion of the Lion-god with the dead is certainly indicated by the fact that the head of the bier is always made in the form of the head of a lion, and that the foot of it is frequently ornamented with a representation of a lion's tail. For an account of Bast, the great goddess of Bubastis, who was depicted with the head either of a lioness, or of a cat, the reader is referred to the section on the subject.

In connexion with the lion must be mentioned the Lynx

THE GODDESS URT-ḤEKAU.

and Cat, for each of these animals played an interesting part in Egyptian mythology. The lynx was called in Egyptian Mafṭet, , or ; the former spelling being that of the Pyramid Texts, and the latter that in use in the Theban Recension of the *Book of the Dead.* The animal is like a large cat and has a small patch of hair on the tip of each ear, and its disposition is, on the whole, benevolent. In the text of Unȧs (line 548) allusion is made to its attack upon the serpents Ȧn-ṭā-f, 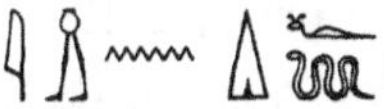, and Tcheser-ṭep, 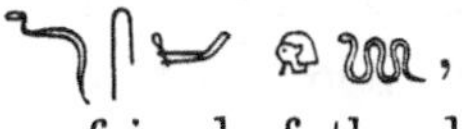, and it is evident from this that the Lynx-god was a friend of the dead. In the Theban Recension of the *Book of the Dead*, Mafṭet takes part with the gods, including Serqet and Maāt, in overthrowing the fiend Āpep (Chaps. xxxiv., xxxix., cxlix. § 7), and we must therefore assume that the lynx was a destroyer of serpents, and that the Lynx-god was supposed to ward off the attacks of serpents from the dead.

The Cat was sacred to Bast, the goddess of Bubastis, and was regarded as her incarnation; its cult is very ancient, and as a personification of the Sun-god the animal played a prominent part in Egyptian mythology. Thus in the xviith Chapter of the *Book of the Dead* mention is made of a Cat which took up its position by the Persea tree in Heliopolis on the night when the foes of Osiris were destroyed, and in the commentary which follows it is stated that this "male Cat" was Rā himself, and that he was called "Mȧu," , by the god Sa, and the vignette depicts the Cat in the act of cutting off the head of the serpent of darkness. In the cxxvth Chapter the deceased says (line 11) in the usually received text, "I have heard the mighty word which the Ass spake unto "the Cat in the House of Ḥapṭ-re," but what that word was is not stated. The Ass and the Cat are forms of the Sun-god, and it is probable that the deceased learned from them the words which would enable him, like them, to vanquish the powers of darkness. From a stele reproduced by Signor Lanzone,[1] we find that prayers were offered to *two* cats by the two women who dedicated it, but whether these represented two forms of the Cat-god, or two pet

[1] *Dizionario*, pl. 107.

animals only is not clear. The cat is here called Máit, 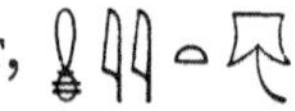, instead of "Mâu," as is usual. Another stele[1] contains reliefs in which worship is offered to a swallow and a cat, and the monuments and inscriptions contain abundant evidence that the greatest reverence was paid to the cat throughout Egypt, even as classical writers say. According to Diodorus (i. 83) the Egyptians fed their cats on bread and milk and slices of Nile fish, and they called the animals to their meals by special sounds. When a cat died its master had it placed in a linen sheet and taken to the embalmers, who treated the body with spices and drugs, and then laid it in a specially prepared case. Whosoever killed a cat, wittingly or unwittingly, was condemned to die, and an instance is cited by Diodorus in which a certain Roman who had killèd a cat was attacked in his house by the infuriated populace and was slain.

Herodotus narrates (ii. 68) that "When a conflagration "takes place a supernatural impulse seizes on the cats. For the "Egyptians, standing at a distance, take care of the cats, and "neglect to put out the fire; but the cats making their escape, "and leaping over the men, throw themselves into the fire; and "when this happens great lamentations are made among the "Egyptians. In whatsoever house a cat dies of a natural death, "all the family shave their eyebrows only; but if a dog die, they "shave the whole body and the head. All cats that die are "carried to certain sacred houses, where being first embalmed, "they are buried in the city of Bubastis."

Among the Egyptians several kinds of Apes were regarded as sacred animals, but the most revered of all was that which was the companion of Thoth, and which is commonly known as the Dog-headed Ape. This animal seems to have been brought in old, as in modern, times from the country far to the south of Nubia, but whether this be so or not it is certain that the Cynocephalus ape found its way into Egyptian mythology at a very early period. In the Judgment Scene he sits upon the standard of the Great Scales, and his duty was to report to his associate Thoth when the pointer marked the middle of the beam. Classical

[1] *Dizionario*, pl. 118.

writers rightly discuss this ape in connexion with the moon, and we know that sacred cynocephali were kept in many temples which were dedicated to lunar gods, e.g., of Khensu at Thebes; certain classes of apes were regarded as the spirits of the dawn which, having sung hymns of praise whilst the sun was rising, turned into apes as soon as he had risen. The cult of the ape is very ancient, and is probably pre-dynastic, in which period dead apes were embalmed with great care and buried.

In dynastic times the ELEPHANT could not have been a sacred animal in Egypt because he had long before withdrawn himself to the swamps and lands of the reaches of the White and Blue Niles. The Island opposite Syene was not called "Elephantine" because the elephant was worshipped there, but probably because it resembled the animal in shape, just as the city on the tongue of land at the junction of the White and Blue Niles was called "Kharṭûm," i.e., "elephant's trunk" on account of its resemblance in shape to that portion of an elephant's body. It is, however, quite certain that great reverence must have been paid to the elephant in predynastic times, because on the top of one of the standards painted on predynastic pottery [1] we find the figure of an elephant, a fact which indicates that it was the god either of some great family or district.

The existence of the BEAR in Egypt has not been satisfactorily proved, and it is unlikely that this animal was indigenous. In a passage in the Fourth Sallier Papyrus,[2] which was translated by Chabas, it is said that when Horus and Set fought together they did so first in the form of two men, and that they then changed themselves into two bears (ils se frappèrent l'un l'autre étant sur la plante de leurs pieds, sous la forme de deux hommes; ils se changèrent en deux ours, etc.). Now the word rendered "bears" by Chabas is *ṭebi*, , which he compared with the well-known Hebrew word, דּוֹב, "bear"; but he appears to have forgotten the Hebrew word זְאֵב, "wolf," with which *ṭebi* is most

[1] See J. de Morgan, *Recherches sur les Origines*, Paris, 1897, p. 93. A carnelian elephant amulet is preserved in the British Museum (4th Eg. Room, Table Case F, No. 626 [14,608]).

[2] Chabas, *Le Calendrier*, p. 28.

probably connected, and which provides a more reasonable suggestion for translating the Egyptian text correctly. That bears did exist in Egypt in the Predynastic and Archaic Periods is proved by the green slate or schist model of a bear which is preserved in the British Museum (3rd Eg. Room, Table-case L, No. 29,416). According to Herodotus (ii. 67) there were bears in Egypt, though he says they were few, *τὰς δὲ ἄρκτους, ἐούσας, σπανίας*, and as he mentions them with wolves it is probable that the animals to which he refers were not bears but a species of wolf.

The Dog, though a very favourite animal of the Egyptians, appears never to have been regarded as a god, although great respect was paid to the animal in the city of Cynopolis; on the other hand Herodotus tells us (ii. 66) that in "whatsoever house a "cat dies of a natural death, all the family shave their eyebrows "only; but if a dog die, they shave the whole body and head. . . . "All persons bury their dogs in sacred vaults within their own "city." If any wine, or corn, or any other necessary of life happened to be in a house when a dog died its use was prohibited; and when the body had been embalmed it was buried in a tomb amid the greatest manifestations of grief by those to whom it belonged. If we accept the statement of Diodorus (i. 85) that a dog was the guardian of the bodies of Osiris and Isis, and that dogs guided Isis in her search for the body of Osiris, and protected her from savage beasts, we should be obliged to admit that the dog played a part in Egyptian mythology; but there is no reason for doing so, because it is clear that Diodorus, like many modern writers, confounded the dog with the jackal. The dog, like the jackal, may have been sacred to Anubis, but the mythological and religious texts of all periods prove that it was the jackal-god who ministered to Osiris, and who acted as guide not only to him but to every other Osiris in the Underworld.

Like the dog, the Wolf enjoyed considerable respect in certain parts of Egypt, e.g., the Wolf-city, Lycopolis, but there is reason for thinking that ancient writers confounded the wolf with the jackal. Thus Herodotus tells us (ii. 122) of a festival which was celebrated in connexion with the descent of Rhampsinitus into the Underworld, and says that on a certain day "the priests "having woven a cloak, blind the eyes of one of their number "with a scarf and having conducted him with the cloak on him to "the way that leads to the temple of Ceres, they then return; "upon which, they say, this priest with his eyes bound is led by "two wolves to the temple of Ceres, twenty stades distant from "the city, and afterwards the wolves lead him back to the same "place." The two wolves here referred to can be nothing but representatives of the jackal-gods Ȧnpu and Ȧp-uat, who played very prominent parts in connexion with the dead. Another legend recorded by Diodorus (i. 88) declares that when Horus was making ready to do battle with Set, his father's murderer, Osiris returned from the Underworld in the form of a wolf to assist him in the fight. It is important to note here the statement of Macrobius, who says (*Saturn*, i. 19) that Apollo, i.e., Horus, and the wolf were worshipped at Lycopolis with equal reverence, for it connects the wolf with Horus and Set, and indicates that these gods fought each other in the forms of wolves and not of bears. Legends of this kind prove that the Egyptians did not carefully distinguish between the wolf, jackal, and dog.

At a very early period the JACKAL was associated with the dead and their tombs, because he lived in the mountains and deserts wherein the Egyptians loved to be buried. The principal jackal-gods were Ȧnpu (Anubis) and Ȧp-uat; for accounts of these the reader is referred to the sections which describe their history and attributes.

The Ass, like many animals, was regarded by the Egyptians both as a god and a devil. In a hymn to Rā as found in the Papyrus of Ani (sheet 1, line 14), the deceased says, "May I "journey forth upon earth, may I smite the Ass, may I crush the "serpent-fiend Sebȧu; may I destroy Āpep in his hour," a passage which proves that the animal was associated with Āpep, and Set, and the other gods of darkness and evil. On the other hand, the xlth Chapter of the *Book of the Dead* is entitled the "Chapter of driving back the Eater of the Ass," and its vignette shows us the deceased in the act of spearing a monster serpent which has fastened its jaws in the back of an ass. Here the ass is certainly a form of the Sun-god, and the serpent is Hai, a form of Āpep, and it is clear from this that the ass was at one period held to be a god. In the cxxvth Chapter we are told that the Ass held a conversation with the Cat, and the passage in which the statement occurs affords additional proof that the ass was a symbol of the Sun-god. The probable explanation of the existence of these two opposite views about the ass is that Egyptian opinion changed about the animal, and that the later form of it held the ass to be a devil and not a god as in the oldest times. Plutarch records a legend (*De Iside*, § 31) to the effect that Typhon, i.e., Set, escaped from out of the battle with Horus on the back of an ass, and that after he had got into a place of safety he begat two sons, Hierosolymus and Judaeus; but no reliance can be placed on a statement which is so absurd on the face of it.

The PIG possessed a reputation for evil in Egypt, as in many other countries of the East, and the Egyptians always associated the animal with Set or Typhon. The cxiith Chapter of the *Book of the Dead* supplies us with the reason why it was held in such abomination, and tells us that Rā said to Horus one day, "Let me "see what is coming to pass in thine eye," and having looked, he said to Horus, "Look at that black pig." Thereupon Horus looked, and he immediately felt that a great injury was done to his eye, and he said to Rā, "Verily, my eye seemeth as if it were "an eye upon which Suti had inflicted a blow." The text goes on to say that the black pig was no other than Suti, who had transformed himself into a black pig, and had aimed the blow which had damaged the eye of Horus. As the result of this the god Rā ordered his companion gods to regard the pig as an abominable animal in future. According to Herodotus (ii. 47), if an Egyptian had only his garment touched by a pig he would go straightway to the Nile and plunge into it to cleanse himself from pollution. The same writer tells us that swineherds were the only men who were not allowed to enter any of the temples, and that the Egyptians sacrificed the pig to the moon and Bacchus only. The poor, through want of means, used to make pigs of dough, and having baked them, they would offer them up as sacrifices, but the wealthy, having seen the tip of the tail of the animal and its spleen, and caul, and fat from the belly burnt in the fire, would eat the flesh at the period of full moon, but at no other time, Horapollo (ii. 37) says that the hog was the symbol of a filthy man, and Ælian, in his account of the pig (*De Natura Animalium*, x. 16), after stating that it eats human flesh, goes on to say that the Egyptians abominated it more than any other animal. On the other hand, they kept pigs and did not sacrifice them too abundantly, because they employed them to tread the grain into the ground with their feet. According to the Rubric to the cxxvth Chapter of the *Book of the Dead*, the vignette was to be drawn in colour upon "a new tile moulded from earth upon which "neither a pig nor any other animal hath trodden." Why, however, the pig should be especially mentioned is hard to say. From one point of view the pig was a sacrosanct animal, and it is clear that the idea of its being holy arose from its connexion with Osiris; the texts, unfortunately, do not explain its exact connexion with this god, and it is doubtful if the Egyptians of the dynastic period themselves possessed any definite information on the subject.

Though representations of the Bat, called in the texts *setcha-khemu*, , and *ṭaḳi* , have been found in Egyptian tombs, proof is wanting that it was worshipped by the Egyptians of the dynastic period; a green slate model of a bat was, however, found with other predynastic remains in Upper Egypt, and it seems that it must have been regarded at least as a sacred creature.

Among small animals the Shrew-mouse and the Hedgehog were considered to be sacred, but the texts afford no information about the parts which they played in Egyptian mythology; figures of both animals in porcelain and bronze have been found in the tombs. According to Herodotus (ii. 67) the shrew-mouse was sacred to the goddess Buto, i.e., Uatchit, and all mummies of the animal were buried in her city; one legend about it declared that Uatchit took the form of the shrew-mouse that she might be the better able to escape from Typhon, who was seeking to destroy Horus, the son of Osiris, after he had been committed to her charge. Curiously enough, the shrew-mouse was thought by the Egyptians to be a blind animal, and Plutarch declares

(*Symp.* iv. 5) that it was held to be the proper symbol of darkness; in connexion with this it is interesting to note that the inscriptions on the bronze figures of the animal identify it with Ḥeru-khent-ån-maa, i.e., the "Blind Horus," or, "Horus who dwelleth in darkness."

The Ichneumon, in Egyptian *khatru*, , in Coptic ϣⲁⲑⲟⲩⲗ, as a destroyer of snakes and the eggs of crocodiles, has formed the subject of many curious legends which have been preserved by classical writers.[1] Pliny says that "it plunges itself "repeatedly into the mud, and then dries itself in the sun: as soon "as, by these means, it has armed itself with a sufficient number "of coatings, it proceeds to the combat. Raising its tail, and "turning its back to the serpent, it receives its stings, which are "inflicted to no purpose, until at last, turning its head sideways, "and viewing its enemy, it seizes it by the throat." The ichneumon was said to destroy not only the eggs of the crocodile, but also the animal itself. According to Strabo, their habit was to lie in wait for the crocodiles, when the latter were basking in the sun with their mouths wide open; they then dropped into their jaws, and eating through their intestines and belly issued forth from the dead body. Diodorus declares that the ichneumon only breaks the eggs with the idea of rendering a service to man, and thinks that the creature derives no benefit itself from its act, and he goes on to say that but for the ichneumon the number of crocodiles would be so great that no one would be able to approach the Nile. Several figures of the ichneumon in bronze have been found in the tombs, but the texts supply no information about the beliefs which the Egyptians entertained about this remarkable animal. Modern naturalists have shown that there is no truth in the statement that it is immune from the effects of snake-bite, or that having been bitten it has recourse to the root of a certain plant as an antidote; the fact is that its great agility and quickness of eye enable it to avoid the fangs of the serpent, and to take the first opportunity of fixing its own teeth in the back of the reptile's

[1] Herodotus, ii. 67; Diodorus, i. 87; Strabo, xvii., i. 39; Plutarch, *De Iside*, § 74; Ælian, vi. 38; Aristotle, *Hist. Anim.*, ix. 6; Pliny, viii. 36.

neck. It is very fond of eggs, and for this reason seeks out those of the crocodile with great avidity, but it loves equally well the eggs of poultry, and in consequence it sometimes bears an evil reputation among the keepers of hens, turkeys, etc.

The HARE was worshipped as a deity, and in the vignette of the Elysian Fields we see a hare-headed god, and a snake-headed god, and a bull-headed god sitting side by side; a hare-headed god also guards one of the Seven Halls in the Underworld. The Hare-god was probably called Unnu.[1]

Among the birds which were worshipped by the Egyptians, or held to be sacred, the following were the most important:—

1. The BENNU, , a bird of the heron species which was identified with the PHOENIX. This bird is said to have created itself, and to have come into being from out of the fire which burned on the top of the sacred Persea Tree of Heliopolis; it was essentially a Sun-bird, and was a symbol both of the rising sun and of the dead Sun-god Osiris, from whom it sprang, and to whom it was sacred. The Bennu not only typified the new birth of the sun each morning, but in the earliest period of dynastic history it became the symbol of the resurrection of mankind, for a man's spiritual body was believed to spring from the dead physical body, just as the living sun of to-day had its origin in the dead sun of yesterday. The Bennu sprang from the heart of Osiris, and was, in consequence, a most holy bird; in a picture reproduced by Signor Lanzone,[2] it is represented sitting on the branches of a tree which grows by the side of a sepulchral chamber. In the lxxxiiird Chapter of the *Book of the Dead*, which provides the formula for enabling the deceased to take the form of the Bennu, this bird says, "I came into being from unformed "matter. I came into existence like the god Kheperà. I am the "germs of every god," 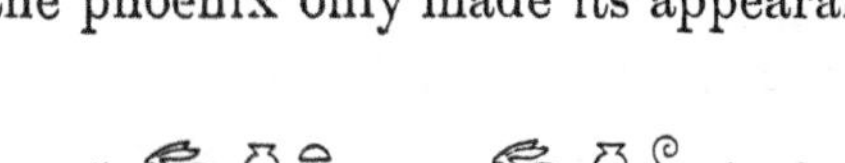. According to Herodotus (ii. 77), the phoenix only made its appearance once in

[1] "Unnut, lady of Unnut," , is the female form. See Lanzone, *Dizionario*, pl. 52.

[2] *Dizionario*, pl. 70.

five hundred years; his plumage was partly golden-coloured and partly red, and in size and form he resembled an eagle. He came from Arabia, and brought with him the body of his father, which he had enclosed in an egg of myrrh, to the temple of the sun, and buried him there. Pliny says (x. 3) that when the phoenix became old he built a nest of cassia and sprigs of incense, and that having filled it with perfumes he lay down and died. From his bones and marrow there sprang a small worm which in process of time changed into a little bird, which, having buried the remains of its predecessor, carried off the nest to the City of the Sun.

2. The VULTURE was the symbol of the goddesses Nekhebet, Mut, Neith, and others who were identified with Nekhebet; the cult of the vulture is extremely ancient in Egypt, and dates probably from predynastic times, for one of the oldest titles of the Pharaohs of Egypt is "Lord of the city of the Vulture (Nekhebet, or Eileithyiapolis), lord of the city of the Uraeus" (Uatchet, or Buto), and it is found engraved on monuments of the late predynastic and early archaic periods. Ælian, in describing the vultures (ii. 46), says that they hover about the dead and dying, and eat human flesh, and that they follow men to battle as if knowing that they would be slain. According to this writer, all vultures are females, and no male vulture was ever known; to obtain young they turn their backs to the south, or south-east wind, which fecundates them, and they bring forth young after three years.

3. The HAWK was sacred to Horus, Rā, Osiris, Seker, and to other cognate gods, and its worship was universal throughout Egypt in predynastic times; the centre of the cult of the Hawk-god was Hieraconpolis, or the "Hawk City." The hawk was not only a Sun-bird but, when represented with a human head, was symbolic of the human soul. According to Herodotus (ii. 65), death was the punishment of the man who killed a hawk or an ibis, and Diodorus records (i. 83) that the sacred hawks were maintained at the public expense, and that they would come to their keepers when called, and would catch the pieces of raw meat which they threw to them in full flight. The Egyptians venerated two species, i.e., the golden hawk, , and the

sacred hawk, ; from the lxxviith Chapter of the *Book of the Dead* it may be gathered that the former was supposed to be four cubits wide, and that it was identified with the Bennu, or Phoenix, is proved by the words in the texts which are put into the mouth of the deceased, "I have risen, and I have "gathered myself together like the beautiful hawk of gold, which "hath the head of a Bennu, and Rā entereth in day by day to "hearken unto my words." The divine hawk was, as we learn from the lxxviiith Chapter, the offspring of Tem, and the symbol of the One God, and of Horus as the successor of his father Osiris, to whom "millions of years minister, and whom millions of years "hold in fear; for him the gods labour, and for him the gods toil "millions of years."

4. The HERON, , was certainly a sacred bird, and that its body was regarded as a possible home for a human soul is proved by the lxxxivth Chapter of the *Book of the Dead*, which was composed with the view of helping a man to effect a transformation into a heron.

5. The SWALLOW also was a bird wherein the human soul might reincarnate itself, and the object of the lxxxvith Chapter of the *Book of the Dead* was to enable it to do so; the Rubric of the Chapter declares that if it be known by the deceased, "he shall "come forth by day, and he shall not be turned back at any gate "in the Underworld, and that he shall make his transformations "into a swallow regularly and continually." In the opening words the deceased is made to say, "I am a swallow, I am a "swallow, I am the Scorpion, the daughter of Rā," a fact which seems to show that the swallow was connected with the Scorpion-goddess Serqet. From a tablet at Turin, which is published by Signor Lanzone,[1] we see that offerings were made to the swallow; the bird is seen perched upon a pylon-shaped building, before which stands a table loaded with offerings, and above are a few short lines of text in which it is called the "beautiful swallow," 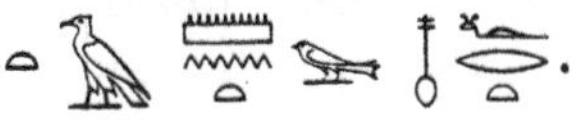. According to Plutarch, the goddess Isis

[1] *Dizionario*, pl. 118.

took upon herself the form of a swallow when she was lamenting the death of Osiris.

6. The Goose, or at least one species of it, was sacred to Åmen-Rā, a fact which is hard to explain. In a drawing given by Signor Lanzone[1] we have a vase of flowers resting upon the ends of two pylon-shaped buildings, and on each of these stands a goose with its shadow, , behind it, or by its side; the five lines of the text above read, "Åmen-Rā, the beautiful Goose," and "the beautiful Goose of Åmen-Rā." In another scene which is likewise reproduced[2] by Lanzone, is depicted a goose with its shadow standing on a building as before, and opposite to it is seated Åmen-Rā; before the god and the goose is a table of offerings. The words above the god read, "Åmen-Rā, the hearer of entreaty," and those over the goose are "the beautiful Goose, greatly beloved," . In the earliest time the goose, or rather gander, was associated with Seb the *erpāt*, 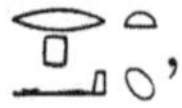, of the gods, who is called in the *Book of the Dead* "the Great Cackler" (Chapters liv., lv.). The goose was a favourite article of food in Egypt, and was greatly in request for offerings in the temples; according to Herodotus (ii. 37) a portion of the daily food of the priests consisted of goose flesh. The goose is said to have been sacred to Isis, and the centre of the great trade in the bird was Χηνοβοσκίον, or Χηνοβοσκια (Chenoboscium or Chenoboscia), i.e., the "Goose pen," a town in Upper Egypt, which was situated in the nome Diospolites, and was quite near to the marshes wherein large numbers of geese were fattened systematically. The Copts gave the name of "Shenesêt" to the town, and this has been identified with the Egyptian , "Ḥet-sa-Åst," by Brugsch;[3] on the other hand M. Amélineau thinks that the Greek name Chenoboskion is derived from the words 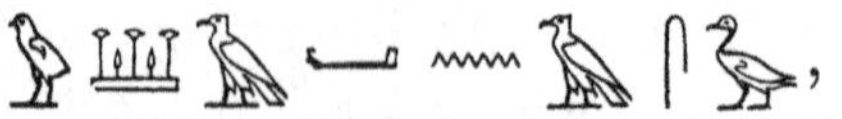, which, he says, are equivalent in meaning to "the place where the geese are fattened." The meaning of the goose as a hieroglyphic is "child"

[1] *Dizionario*, pl. 22. [2] *Ibid.*, pl. 361. [3] *Dict. Géog.*, p. 659.

or "son," and Horapollo goes so far as to say (i. 53) that it was chosen to denote a son from its love to its young, being always ready to give itself up to the hunter if only they might be preserved, and that owing to this trait in its character the Egyptians revered it.

7. The IBIS was universally venerated throughout Egypt, and the centre of its cult in very early times was the city of Ḳhemennu, or Hermopolis, where the bird was associated with the Moon and with Thoth, the scribe of the gods.[1] It seems to have been worshipped in the first instance because it killed snakes and reptiles in general in large numbers, and it was thought to destroy the winged serpents, which, it was declared, were brought over into Egypt from the deserts of Libya by the west wind. Herodotus tells us that he once went to a certain place in Arabia, almost exactly opposite the city of Buto, to make inquiries concerning the winged serpents. On his arrival he "saw the back-bones and "ribs of serpents in such numbers as it is impossible to describe; "of the ribs there were a multitude of heaps, some great, some "small, some middle-sized. The place where the bones lie is at "the entrance of a narrow gorge between steep mountains, which "there open upon a spacious plain communicating with the great "plain of Egypt. The story goes, that with the spring, the "winged snakes come flying from Arabia towards Egypt, but "are met in this gorge by the birds called ibises, who forbid their "entrance and destroy them all. The Arabians assert, and the "Egyptians also admit, that it is on account of the service thus "rendered that the Egyptians hold the ibis in so much reverence. "The ibis is a bird of a deep black colour, with legs like a crane; "its beak is strongly hooked, and its size is about that of the "landrail. This is a description of the black ibis which contends "with the serpents. The commoner sort, for there are two quite "distinct species, has the head and the whole throat bare of "feathers; its general plumage is white, but the head and neck "are jet black, as also are the tips of the wings and the extremity "of the tail; in its beak and legs it resembles the other species.

[1] See Ælian, *De Nat. Animal.*, x. 29; Horapollo, i. 10, 36; Herodotus ii., p. 75; Diodorus, i. 83; Plutarch, *De Iside*, § 75; etc.

"The winged serpent is shaped like the water-snake. Its wings "are not feathered, but resemble very closely those of the bat."[1]

Among the reptiles which were deified by the Egyptians, or were regarded as sacred creatures, may be mentioned the following:—1. The Tortoise or Turtle, which probably came from Nubia, and was worshipped or revered through fear. The Tortoise-god Āpesh, 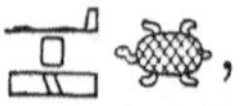, was associated with the powers of darkness, and night, and evil, and a place was assigned to him in the heavens with their representatives. In the clxist Chapter of the *Book of the Dead* mention is made of the Tortoise, or Turtle, in such a way as to suggest that he was an enemy of Rā, and the formula "Rā liveth, the Tortoise dieth," is given four times, once in connexion with each of the four winds of heaven. The tortoise Sheta, , is also mentioned in the lxxxiiird Chapter, wherein the deceased is made to declare that he has germinated like the things which germinate, and has clothed himself like the tortoise.

2. Of the Serpent and Snake many varieties were worshipped by the Egyptians for the sake of the good qualities which they possessed, and many were revered through fear only. In predynastic times Egypt was overrun with serpents and snakes of all kinds, and the Pyramid Texts prove that her inhabitants were terribly afraid of them; the formulae which are found in the pyramid of Unȧs against snakes are probably older than dynastic times, and their large numbers suggest that the serpent tribes were man's chief enemies. The cult of the uraeus, or asp, is extremely ancient, and its centre was the city of Per-Uatchet, or Buto, where a temple was built in honour of the Uraeus-goddess Uatchet, 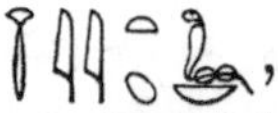, in early dynastic times. This city enjoyed with that of Nekhebet a position of peculiar importance among the Egyptians, and one of the oldest royal titles is "Lord of Nekhebet, lord of Uatchet," i.e., lord of the Vulture-city, lord of the Uraeus-city. The cities of Nekhebet and Uatchet were in fact the ecclesiastical centres of the Southern and Northern kingdoms of

[1] Rawlinson's *Herodotus*, vol. ii., pp. 124, 125.

Egypt, and they were first founded in primitive times when the vulture and the uraeus were especially worshipped. The great enemy of Horus, and Rā, and Osiris, and also of the deceased in the Underworld was the monster serpent Āpep, or Apophis, which directed the attacks on gods and men of numbers of serpent broods, and which was held to be the personification of all evil; on the other hand the uraeus was the symbol of divinity and royalty, for the walls of the abode of Osiris were surmounted by "living uraei," and the god Rā wore two uraei upon his forehead, and every king is represented with a uraeus upon his forehead. In primitive times, when man coveted the powers of various birds and reptiles, and when he appears to have wished to be able to assume their forms after death, the priests provided a number of formulae which would enable him to do this, and among them was one which gave the deceased the power of becoming the serpent SATA, , and which read, "I am the serpent Sata whose years are many. I die "and I am born again each day. I am the serpent Sata which "dwelleth in the uttermost parts of the earth. I die and I am "born again, and I renew myself, and I grow young each day."[1] In religious texts the uraeus is associated with Isis and Nephthys, but this is due to the fact that in comparatively late times these goddesses were identified with Uatchet, the uraeus-goddess, who was at one time or another absorbed into all the great goddesses, many of whom were regarded as benevolent and beneficent deities and the protectors of a man's house, and land and crops, and children.

3. The SCORPION was venerated in Egypt at a very early period, and the scorpion-goddess SERQET or SELQET was in some of her aspects associated with the powers of evil, and in others with the goddess Isis. In the xxxiind Chapter of the *Book of the Dead* she appears as a friend of the deceased, and in the xliind Chapter his teeth are identified with those of the goddess. From the legend of Isis which is told on the Metternich Stele we learn that this goddess was accompanied on her journey by Seven Scorpions, and that the child Horus was stung by a scorpion which

[1] *Book of the Dead*, Chapter lxxxvii.

made its way to him in spite of all the precautions which the goddess had taken. According to Ælian (x. 19), the scorpions of Coptos were of a most formidable character, and whosoever was bitten by one of them died of a certainty; in spite of this, however, they respected Isis so much that they never stung the women who went to the temple of the goddess to pray, even though they walked with their feet bare or prostrated themselves on the ground. This statement is useful as showing that the scorpion was sacred to Isis.

4. The xxxvith Chapter of the *Book of the Dead* mentions a kind of beetle called Āpshait, , which was supposed to gnaw the bodies of the dead. In one vignette of the Chapter the deceased is seen threatening it with a knife, and in the other the creature is represented in the form of an ordinary scarabaeus which is being speared by him. The Āpshait is probably the beetle which is often found crushed between the bandages of poorly made mummies, or even inside the body itself, where it has forced its way in search of food.

5. In the lxxvith and civth Chapters of the *Book of the Dead* an insect called Ābit, , or Bebait, , is mentioned which is said to lead the deceased into the "House of the King," and to bring him "to see the great gods who are in the Underworld"; this creature is probably to be identified with the praying Mantis (*mantis religiosa*) about which so many legends are current.

6. The Frog appears to have been worshipped in primitive times as the symbol of generation, birth, and fertility in general; the Frog-goddess Ḥeqet, , or Ḥeqtit, , was identified with Hathor, and was originally the female counterpart of Khnemu, by whom she became the mother of Ḥeru-ur. The great antiquity of the cult of the frog is proved by the fact that each of the four primeval gods Ḥeḥ, Kek, Nāu, and Ȧmen is depicted with the head of a frog, while his female counterpart has the head of a serpent. The cult of the frog is one of the oldest in Egypt, and the Frog-god and the Frog-goddess were believed to have played very prominent parts in the creation of the world.

THE GODDESS SERQET.

According to Horapollo (i. 25), the frog typified an imperfectly formed man, Ἄπλαστον δὲ ἄνθρωπον γράφοντες βάτραχον ζωγραφοῦσιν, because it was generated from the slime of the river, whence it occasionally happens that it is seen with one part of a frog, and the remainder formed of slime, so that should the river fall, the animal would be left imperfect; the half-formed creatures referred to by Diodorus (i. 10) seem to have been frogs. Ælian also declares (ii. 56) that in a shower which once fell upon him there were half-formed frogs, and that whilst their fore parts were provided with two feet their hind parts were shapeless!

7. With the GRASSHOPPER ideas of religious enjoyment seem to have been associated, for in the *Book of the Dead* (Chap. cxxv.) the deceased says, "I have rested in the Field of the Grasshoppers" (, SEKHET-SANEḤEMU), wherein was situated the "northern city;" it lay to the south of Sekhet-ḥetep. The grasshopper is mentioned as early as the VIth Dynasty, and in the text of Pepi II. (line 860) the king is said to "arrive in heaven like the grasshopper of Rā,"  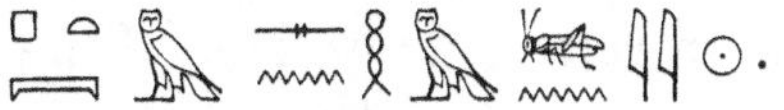.

8. Chief among insects in importance was the BEETLE, or SCARABAEUS, which was called by the Egyptians *kheprerȧ*, , and was the symbol of Kheperȧ, , the great god of creation and resurrection. The Beetle-god is represented at times with a beetle upon his head, and at others with a beetle for a head; as Kheperȧ's attributes have already been fully described we need only repeat here that he was the "father of the gods," and the creator of all things in heaven and earth, that he was self-begotten and self-born, and that he was identified with the rising sun, and new birth generally. The beetle or scarabaeus which was modelled by the Egyptians in such large numbers belongs to the family called *Scarabaeidae* (Coprophagi), of which the *Scarabaeus sacer* is the type. These insects compose a very numerous group of dung-feeding Lamellicorns, of which, however, the majority are inhabitants of tropical countries. A remarkable peculiarity exists in the structure and situation of the hind legs,

which are placed so near the extremity of the body, and so far from each other as to give the insect a most extraordinary appearance when walking.

This peculiar formation is, nevertheless, particularly serviceable to its possessors in rolling the balls of excrementitious matter in which they enclose their eggs; wherefore these insects were named by the first naturalists *Pilulariae.* These balls are at first irregular and soft, but, by degrees, and during the process of rolling along, become rounded and harder; they are propelled by means of the hind legs. Sometimes these balls are an inch and a half, or two inches in diameter, and in rolling them along the beetles stand almost upon their heads, with the heads turned from the balls. These manoeuvres have for their object the burying of the balls in holes, which the insects have previously dug for their reception; and it is upon the dung thus deposited that the larvae feed. It does not appear that these beetles have the instinct to distinguish their own balls, as they will seize upon those belonging to another, in case they have lost their own; and, indeed, it is said that several of them occasionally assist in rolling the same ball. The males as well as the females assist in rolling the pellets. They fly during the hottest part of the day.[1] From the above extract it is clear that the scarabaeus is in the habit of laying its eggs in dung, which is to serve as food for its larvae, and that the larvae are hatched by the heat of the sun's rays. The ball of matter containing potential life was compared to the sun's globe, which contained the germs of all life, and the beetle, with its ball of matter and eggs, was regarded as the symbol of the great god Kheperȧ who rolled the globe of the sun across the sky. Now, the god Kheperȧ also represented inert but living matter, which was about to begin a course of existence for the first time, or to enjoy a renewal of life, and he was thus not only the creator of life but also the restorer or renewer of life, and so at a very early period became associated by the Egyptians, first with the idea of the new birth of the sun daily, and secondly, with the resurrection of man. And since the scarabaeus was identified with him that insect became at

[1] J. O. Westwood, *An Introduction to the Modern Classification of Insects*, London, 1839, vol. i., p. 204 ff.

once the symbol of the god and of the Resurrection. Now the dead human body, from one aspect, contained the germ of life, that is to say, the germ of the spiritual body, which was called into being by means of the prayers that were recited and the ceremonies that were performed on the day of the funeral; from this point of view the egg-ball of the scarabaeus and the dead body were identical. Moreover, as the scarabaeus had given potential life to its eggs in the ball, so, it was thought, would a model of the scarab, itself the symbol of the god of new life and resurrection, also give potential life to the dead body upon which it was placed, and keep life in the living body, always provided that the proper words of power were first said over it or written upon it. The idea of "life" appears to have been associated with the scarab from time immemorial in Egypt and the Eastern Sûdân, for to this day the insect is dried, pounded, and mixed with water, and then drunk by women, who believe it to be an unfailing specific for the production of large families.

That the scarab was associated with the sun is clear from a passage in the text of Unȧs (line 477), where it is said, "This "Unȧs flieth like a bird, and alighteth like a beetle; he flieth like "a bird and he alighteth like a beetle upon the throne which is "empty in thy boat, O Rā,"   . In the text of Tetȧ (line 89) the king is said "to live [like] the scarab," , and Pepi I. is declared to be "the son of the scarab which is born "in Ḥetepet under the hair of Iusāas the Northern, and the issue "of the brow of Seb,"  . Among classical writers[1] the opinion prevailed that female scarabs did not exist, and Latreille thinks that this belief arose from the fact that the females are exceedingly like the males, and that both sexes appear

[1] Ælian, x. 15; Horapollo, i. x.; Porphyry, *De Abstinentia*, iv. 9.

to divide the care of their offspring equally between them. According to Horapollo, a scarabaeus denotes an "*only*-begotten, generation, father, world, and man." It represents an "only-begotten" because the scarabaeus is a creature self-produced, being unconceived by a female. The male, when desirous of procreating, takes some ox-dung, and shapes it into a spherical form like the world. He next rolls it from east to west, looking himself towards the east. Having dug a hole, he buries it in it for twenty-eight days; on the twenty-ninth day he opens the ball, and throws it into the water, and from it the scarabaei come forth. The idea of "generation" arises from its supposed acts. The scarabaeus denotes a "father" because it is engendered by a father only, and "world" because in its generation it is fashioned in the form of the world, and "man" because there is no female race among them. Every scarabaeus was also supposed to have thirty toes, corresponding with the thirty days' duration of the month. For accounts of the use of scarabs as amulets the reader is referred to other works.[1]

Concerning the cult of FISH among the Egyptians but little can be said, because the hieroglyphic texts afford us little information on the subject. According to Strabo (xvii. 2, 4), there were "in the Nile fish in great quantity and of different kinds, having "a peculiar and indigenous character. The best known are the "Oxyrhynchus, and the Lepidotus, the Latus, the Alabes, the "Coracinus, the Choerus, and the Phagrorius, called also the "Phagrus. Besides these are the Silurus, the Citharus, the "Thrissa, the Cestreus, the Lychnus, the Physa, the Bous, or ox, "and large shell-fish which emit a sound like that of wailing." Among these were chiefly worshipped the Oxyrhynchus, the Phagrus, the Latus, and the Lepidotus. The chief seat of the cult of the Oxyrhynchus Fish was the city of Oxyrhynchus, where it was held in the greatest reverence; this fish was supposed to have swallowed the phallus of Osiris[2] when Set was hacking the body of this god in pieces, and for this reason was sacred not only in the nome of the Oxyrhynchites and its metropolis, but all over Egypt.

[1] See my *Mummy*, p. 233 ff.; *Magic*, p. 35 ff.

[2] Plutarch, *De Iside*, § 18.

In certain places the Egyptians would not eat it. The Phagrus, or eel, was worshipped in Upper Egypt, and mummied eels have been found in small sepulchral boxes. Of the Lepidotus Fish no legends have been preserved; the Latus was worshipped at Esneh. The fish with the very wide and large mouth which is seen on the head of the goddess Ḥātmeḥit, , has not yet been identified. In the *Book of the Dead* two mythological fish are mentioned, the ÅBṬU, , and the ÅNT, ; these fish were supposed to swim, one on each side of the bows of the boat of the Sun-god, and to drive away from it every evil being or thing in the waters which had a mind to attack it. The identification of Nile fish is at present a difficult matter, but it is to be hoped that when the Egyptian Government issues the monograph on the fish of Egypt and the Delta, and of Nubia and the Sûdân it may be possible to name correctly the various bronze and wooden fish which exist in the many collections of Egyptian antiquities in Egypt and Europe.

INDEX

Ȧmsu (nome), **i. 97**
Ȧmsu, god of Panopolis, **i. 97**; **ii. 258**, 280, 291, 293, 324
Ȧmsu-Ȧmen, **ii.** 8
Ȧmsu-Ḥeru, **ii.** 324
Ȧmsu-Ḥeru-ka-nekht, **ii.** 139
Ȧmsu-Rā, **ii.** 36
Ȧmsu suten Ḥeru-nekht, **ii.** 183
Ȧmta **i.** 343
Ȧm-ta, **i.** 346
Ȧm-Ṭep, **i.** 90
Ȧm-ṭeṭ, **ii.** 129
Amu, **i.** 250
Āmu-āa, **i.** 211
Amulets in the Sûdân, **i.** 16
Ȧm-Unnu-Meḥt, **i** 90
Ȧm-Unnu-Resu, **i.** 90
Ȧm ut (Anubis), **ii.** 263
Ȧn, **ii.** 324
Ȧn, a form of Osiris, **i.** 446
Ān, a god, **ii.** 20
Ȧn, city of, **i.** 427
Ȧn (city), **ii.** 31, 32
Ȧn in Ȧnṭes, **ii.** 154
Ȧn, of millions of years, **ii.** 154
An, the warrior, **ii.** 312
Ȧnȧ, **i. 79**; **i.** 456
Ȧn-ȧarere-tef, **i. 495**
Ȧn-ā-f, **i.** 145, 419, 521; **ii.** 324
Ȧn-ȧret-f, **i.** 495
Ȧn-ȧtef-f, **ii.** 324
Ānāu gods, **i.** 202
Andrew, St., **i.** 280
Andrews, Dr. C. W., **i.** 11
Aneb, **i.** 514
Ȧneb-ȧbt, **i.** 514
Ȧneb-ȧthi, **i.** 514
Ȧneb-ḥetch (nome), **i.** 99, 512
Ȧneb-rest-f, **i.** 514
Ȧnebu, **i.** 513
Anémph, **i.** 281
Ȧneniu, **ii.** 324
Ȧnep, **i.** 437
Ȧn-erṭā-nef-bes-f-khenti-heh-f, **i.** 494; **ii.** 324
Ȧn-erṭā-nef-nebȧt, **ii.** 294
Anetch, **ii.** 176
Ȧn-f-em-hru-seksek, **ii.** 129
Angel of the two gods, **i. 83**
Angel of Death, **i.** 19
Angel of the Lord, **i.** 19
Angels, **i.** 6
Angels, functions of in Ḳur'ân, **i.** 5
Angels, mortal and immortal, **i.** 6
Angels of service, **i.** 21
Ȧngels of Thoth, **ii.** 119
Ȧnhai, Papyrus of, **i.** 507
Ȧn-ḥat, **i.** 482
Ȧn-ḥefta, **i.** 194
Ȧn-ḥer, **i. 172,** 173, 402; **ii.** 184, 325, 359
Ȧn-heri-ertit-sa, **ii.** 324
Ȧn-ḥetep-f, **ii.** 325
Ȧn-Ḥer, **i.** 97, 103, 115; **ii.** 118, 291
Ȧn-ḥer of Sebennytus, **i. 100**
Ȧnḥetep, **i.** 222
Ȧn-ḥetep-f, **i.** 419
Ȧn-ḥrȧ, **i.** 176; **ii.** 325
Ȧnhur, **i.** 103
Animals, sacred, **ii. 345** ff.
Ani, Papyrus of, **i.** 335, 360, 427
Ani (scribe), **ii.** 69
Ani, the scribe, **ii. 141-146**
Ȧni (city), **i.** 439
Ȧni (Esneh), **i.** 452
Ȧni, form of Sun-god, **ii.** 9, 10, 11
Animals, reason why adored, **i.** 22
Animals, the abodes of gods, **i.** 2
Ȧnit, **i.** 427, 431, 469; **ii.** 61, 65
Ānkh, **i. 79**
Ānkh-ȧapau, **i.** 222
Ankh-ȧru-tchefau, **i.** 234
Ānkh-em-fentu, **i.** 176; **ii.** 327
Ānkhet (Isis), **ii.** 216
Ānkhet-pu-ent-Sebek-neb-Bakhau, **ii.** 327
Ānkhet, scorpion goddess, **i.** 220
Ankhet-kheperu, **i.** 216
Ankh-f-en-Khensu, **i.** 460
Ānkh-ḥrȧ, **i.** 228
Ānkhi, **ii.** 326
Ānkhi (serpent), **i.** 200
Ānkhiu, **i.** 161
Ānkh=Osiris, **ii.** 139
Ānkh-s-en-Ȧten, **ii.** 83
Ānkh-s-en-pa-Ȧten, **ii.** 83
Ānkh-ta, **i.** 246
Ānkh-taui, **i.** 513
Ānkh-tauit, **i.** 433
Ānkhti, **ii.** 326
Ānkhtith, **i.** 234
Ānku, **i.** 234
Ȧn-mut-f, **i. 79**; **ii.** 183, 301, 322, 324
Ȧnnu, **i. 100**, 354, 471; **ii.** 4, 148
Ȧnnu, crops of, **ii.** 121
Ȧnnu Meht, **i.** 328
Ȧnnu, North, **ii.** 25
Ȧnnu, paut of gods of, **i. 88**

Ȧp-senui, ii. 142
Ȧpsetch, ii. 310
Apsh, ii. 25
Āpshait, ii. 378
Ȧp-shāṭ-taui, ii. 324
Ȧpsi, ii. 324
Apsit, ii. 92
Ȧpt, ii. 293
Ȧpt, city of, i. 427
Ȧpt (Thebes), ii. 3
Apt, goddess of the xith month, i. 444
Ȧpt, goddess of Thebes, ii. 3
Ȧpt-en-khet, i. 178
Ȧpt-en-qaḥu, i. 178
Ȧptet, ii. 25
Ȧpt-ḥent, ii. 293
Ȧpt-net, i. 178
Ȧpt-renpit, ii. 293
Ȧpts, the, ii. 6, 7, 9, 10
Ȧpt-taui, i. 254
Ȧpu, i. **97**, 470; ii. 188
Ȧpu, a god, i. 194
Apu (serpent), i. 230
Ȧp-uat, i. **79**, 102, 109, **206**, **210**, 454, **493**; ii. 26, 43, **119**, 156, **263**, 322, 323, 367
Ȧp-uat of Lycopolis, i. 98
Ap-uat meḥt sekhem pet, ii. 183, 323
Ȧp-uat rest sekhem taui, ii. 183
Ȧp-uat-resu-sekhem-pet, ii. 323
Apuleius, ii. 217, 218, 265, 266
Apzû, i. 291
Apzû-rishtu, i. 288, 289
Āqan, ii. 327
Aqebi, i. 182
Ȧqeh, ii. 325
Ȧqen, ii. 325
Aq-ḥer-ȧmmi-unnut-f, i. 494
Āq-her-ȧm-unnut-f, ii. 129
Āq-ḥer-ami-unnut-f, ii. 327
Arab angels, i. 6
Arabia, i. 353, 498
Arabian influence on Egyptian religion, i. 334
Arabian nome, i. 96
Arabs, i. 41, 119, 401
Ȧrānbfi, i. 241
Ȧr-ȧst-neter, i. 211
Archaic Period, gods of i. 78 ff.
Archangels, i. 5, 6
Archemachus, ii. 199
Ȧrenna, ii. 283
Arethi-kasathi-ka, ii. 20
Arethi-ka-sa-thika, ii. 323
Ȧr gods, ii. 249
Ȧr-hes-nefer, i. 464
Ȧri-ānkh, i. 511
Arians, i. 69
Ȧri-em-ȧb-f, i. 419; ii. 325
Ȧri-en-ab-f, ii. 325
Ȧri-ḥes, i. 446
Ȧri-ḥes-nefer, ii. 289, 362
Ȧri-Maāt, ii. 325
Ȧri-maat-f-tchesef, ii. 129
Ari-nef Nebȧt, ii. 294
Ȧri-ren-f-tchesef, ii. 322
Ȧri-si, ii. 325
Aristotle, ii. 357, 370; quoted, i. 62
Ārit, city, i. 433
Ȧrit (a pylon), i. 186
Ȧritatheth, i. 248
Ȧriti, i. 244
Ārits, the, i. 427
Arkharôkh, i. 266
Arkheôkh, i. 266
Ȧrmāua, ii. 291
Ȧrmāuai, ii. 322
Ȧrmāui, ii. 129
Arôêris, i. **467**
Arou, ii. 308
Aroueris, ii. 187
Ārq-ḥeḥ, ii. 128
Ȧr-ren-f-tchesef, ii. 129, 291
Arrows, i. 85
Arsaphes, ii. 58
Arsiêl, i. 275
Arsinoë, town of, ii. 355
Arsinoïtes, i. 96
Ārt, ii. 307
Ā-Saḥ, ii. 308
Ȧsȧr, ii. 323
Ȧsȧr Ȧa ȧm Ȧnnu, ii. 182
Asȧr Ȧḥeti, ii. 183
Ȧsȧr Ȧthi ḥer ȧb Ȧbṭu, ii. 183
Ȧsȧr Athi her ȧb Shetat, ii. 183
Ȧsȧr-ȧm-ȧb-neteru, i. 228
Ȧsȧr Ankhi, ii. 179
Ȧsȧr-Ānkhti, ii. 176
Ȧsȧr Ȧp-shat-taui, ii. 179
Ȧsȧr-Ȧsti i. 214
Ȧsȧr Athi, ii. 178
Ȧsȧr Ba ḥer-ȧb Qemt, ii. 183
Ȧsȧr baiu-tef-f, ii. 182
Ȧsȧr Ba sheps em Ṭaṭṭu, ii. 179
Ȧsȧr-Ba-Teṭṭeṭ, i. 371
Ȧsȧr-bati (?), i. 214
Asȧr Bati-er pit, ii. 176
Ȧsȧr em Ȧat-urt, ii. 181
Ȧsȧr em āḥāt-f em ta Meḥt, ii. 185
Ȧsȧr em aḥāt-f nebu, ii. 185
Ȧsȧr em Ȧkesh, ii. 182

231, **341**, **431**; ii. **29**, **85**, 108, **109**, **124**, **125**, **126**, **129**, 186, **187**, **202**
Isis and her Seven Scorpions, i. 487
Isis and Nephthys, Lamentations of, i. 293
Isis and the Virgin Mary, ii. 220, 221
Isis as enchantress, ii. 207
Isis, blood of, ii. 215
Isis Campensis, ii. 218
Isis, Festival Songs of, i. 294
Isis, forms of, ii. **213**
Isis and Rā, Legend of, i. **360** ff.
Isis, mysteries of, ii. 217; sorrows of, Egyptian text, ii. 222-240; wanderings and troubles of, ii. **206** ff.
Isis of Cabasus, i. **100**
Isis of Sȧpi-res, i. **99**
Isis of Tithorea, ii. 218-220
Isis-Athene, i. 459
Isis-Hathor, ii. 55
Isis-Nebuut, ii. 213
Isis-Net, i. 452
Isis-Sati, ii. 57
Isis-Sothis, ii. 55
Island of Ȧṭeḥ, ii. 209
Isokhobortha, i. 281
Israel, Children of, i. 19
Israelites, i. 136, 137
Israfel, i. 5
Israi, i. 280
It (city), i. 492
Ithyphallic god, ii. 17, 18
Iuȧa, ii. 69
Iubani, i. 326
Iubau, i. 326
Iukasa, ii. 20
Iusāas, i. **85**
Iusāās, ii. 289
Iusāas[et], city of, ii. 381
Iusāaset, i. 354, 432, 441, 446; ii. 29, **88**
Iusāaset-Nebtḥetep, i. 354

JACKAL, ii. 367
Jahannam, i. 273
James, Saint, i. 280
Jebel Barkal, i. 14, 15, 16
Jéquier, quoted, i. 178
Jerusalem, i. 273, 278
Jews, i. 19
Jinn, i. 14, 133
John, Saint, i. 144
Judaeus, ii. 254, 368
Judges, Book of, i. 19
Judgment Scene, ii. **142** ff.
Julius Africanus, i. 445
Juno, ii. 253
Jupiter, ii. 186, 253, 302, 303
Jupiter Ammon, ii. 22
Justinian, i. 289
Juvenal, i. 28, 36; quoted, i. 1, 2

KA, or "double," i. 34, 39
Ka of Osiris, i. 149
Ka, son of Meḥ-urt, i. 516
Ka, the god, i. 286
Kaa, ii. 342
Ka-Ȧment, i. 198
Ka-Ȧmentet, i. 240
Kaȧrik, ii. 342
Ka-ȧri-ka, ii. 20
Kadesh, ii. 27
Ka-en-Ānkh-neteru, i. 257
Kaharesapusaremkaḥer-remt, ii. 342
Ka-hemhem, i. 228
Ka-ḥer-ka-ḥeb, ii. 293
Ka-ḥeseb (nome), i. **100**
Ka-ḥetep, ii. 139, 156, 342
Ka-ḥetep (Osiris), ii. 61
Kahun, ii. 285
Ḳai, i. 230
Kaiekhôs, ii. 346
Kait, goddess, i. 286
Kakaȧ, i. 329
Ka-kau, ii. 346, 351, 353
Ka-khu, ii. 301
Kalâbsheh, ii. 288
Ka-qem, i. 492
Ka-q'em (nome), i. **100**
Kaqemna, i. 122, 138
Karȧu-Ȧnememti, i. 326
Karnak, ii. 22
Kasa, i. **98**
Kasaika, ii. 20, 342
Ka-set (nome), i. **99**
Ka-Shu, i. 206
Ḳasut, i. **83**
Ka-taui, ii. 301
Ḳaṭna, ii. 23
Kau of Rā, i. 34
Ḳeb, i. 369
Ḳeb-ur, i. 259
Kefi, i. 198
Keḥkeḥ, ii. 268
Keḥkeḥet, ii. 342
Kek, i. 371
Keket, ii. 2
Kekiu, i. 113
Kekiut, i. 113
Keku, i. 241
Kekui, i. **283**, **285**; ii. 2